National Income Accounts and Income Analysis

RICHARD RUGGLES
Professor of Economics, Yale University

NANCY D. RUGGLES
Associate Secretary, Econometric Society

SECOND EDITION

1956   McGraw-Hill Book Company, Inc.
New York   Toronto   London

VI

54248

National Income Accounts
and Income Analysis

Preface

This book was written primarily to avoid the task of giving detailed empirical and theoretical material in lecture form. In recent years there has been increasing recognition that economics should concern itself with observed facts, and the developments in national income accounting have been outstanding in this respect. By introducing the complete framework of national income accounting into economics, much of the vagueness of typical general economic theory can be overcome. This book attempts to build up the national income concepts from the basic accounts of individual firms, government units, and households; to a very large extent the purpose of this approach is to bridge the gap that exists between micro- and macro-economic theory, i.e., between value theory and general equilibrium theory. After the structural framework has been erected as a tool of analysis in Part One, it is applied in Part Two to income analysis. In so doing it is hoped that income analysis can be made more explicit and more realistic. This presentation contains little that is new; it merely brings together generally accepted material.

The material has been organized around the concepts of national income accounting and the theory of income analysis. Part One is devoted to the explanation of national income concepts and the creation of a general theoretical framework. The body of the chapters in Part One develops the central argument on an elementary level; they form a complete explanation of the theory of national income accounting. The appendixes to these chapters are of two types. Certain of them are simple but detailed elaborations of what was taken up in the chapters. Other appendixes will be useful only to those who are interested in a more detailed study of the subject of national income accounting. Part Two is an application of the framework developed in Chapters 1 through 5 to the specific problem of income analysis. By using national income accounts greater rigor can be introduced into this field of theory, and the mechanisms by which saving and investment affect economic flows can be more readily understood.

This book is a revision of an earlier one written in 1948. The same general plan has been retained, but substantial changes have been made within it. Part One presents a simple but comprehensive set of national

v

income accounts. The details of the specific national income accounting systems used by the United States and the United Nations are treated in an appendix. Two new chapters, on national income aggregates and their meaning (Chap. 6) and the use of national income aggregates for comparative analysis (Chap. 7), have also been added. The chapter taking up input-output data has been rewritten and expanded to include flow of funds accounting (Chap. 8). Part Two has been largely rewritten. The material on the mechanism of income analysis has been revised to include both the government and international trade in the analysis. A much closer relation between Part One and Part Two has been established.

We are indebted to a number of individuals for help in this revision. George Jaszi of the Department of Commerce was most helpful in the revision of Part One. Stanley Sigel of the Federal Reserve Board made a number of suggestions regarding the material on Related Systems of Economic Accounting. With respect to Part Two, we are especially indebted to James Tobin and Arthur Okun, both of Yale, for many very helpful suggestions.

Richard Ruggles
Nancy D. Ruggles

Contents

Part One

National Income Accounts

1. National Income Accounts and Their Relation to Economic Policy

The Growth of National Income Accounting Concepts

The development of the national income accounting concepts in recent years has proved to be very useful in understanding and explaining what takes place in the economy This development is not simply one of greater refinement in the collection of statistics about the economy but rather represents a marked change in the manner in which the measurements and their relation to each other have been envisaged. The pioneer work in this field has been concerned both with the theoretical implications of the subject and with the force of empirical reality.

On the one hand, the theoretical formulations have attempted to provide general methods of procedure and meaningful definitions of aggregates. Masses of unrelated statistics add little to the understanding of the economic system, and only by careful reasoning can the highly detailed data be combined in such a manner that the final set of statistics will present a related picture. Theorists must decide between relevant and irrelevant statistics; upon such decisions rests the usefulness of the structures that they erect. A systematic treatment of data is helpful only when the basis of the system is relevant and meaningful.

Actual data, on the other hand, have often brought to light internal inconsistencies in the theoretical objectives of the system or have confronted the theorist with unexpected problems when he has attempted to bring reality into his theoretical framework. Concepts in the minds of theorists seldom are refined to the point where they will fit all concrete situations. In the process of trying to fit actual data into the theoretical framework, the framework itself is forced to undergo change; with this change it acquires new implications and meaning.

3

The Income Accounts of the Economy

The income accounts for the economy provide a framework within which the current operations of the economy can be recorded, in much the same way that certain financial statements provide such a framework for recording the current operations of an individual enterprise. Essentially, the national income accounts can be looked upon as a system of classification that is necessary to provide a descriptive and factual account of what has happened in the economy. They are built up from and summarize the operations of individual enterprises. An understanding of the nature of the accounts of such individual enterprises is therefore essential to a comprehension of the basis of national income accounts and measurement.

Part One will consider the national income accounting framework. For this purpose the current accounts of productive units will be examined, and from these the national income accounts will be derived. The text of the chapters will carry through the development of the concepts in their broad outline, and the appendixes following each chapter will provide material that is either subsidiary or supplementary to the text. Readers wishing to understand only the general meaning and content of national income concepts will find it unnecessary to consult the appendixes. Those interested in obtaining a more detailed knowledge of national income accounts and measurements may find several of the appendixes helpful in going beyond the general principles stated in the text.

National Income Accounts as a Tool of Economic Analysis

In addition to providing a framework for statistical data, national income accounts are very useful in explaining how the economy operates. The erection of a classificatory framework that is descriptive of reality also provides a system that embraces important economic magnitudes and interrelationships. Many of the recent developments in economic theory have served to focus attention upon these magnitudes and relationships, so that in this sense national income accounts and measurements are a part of the theoretical structure of economics and provide well-defined schemata of the working of the system. An understanding of this function of national income accounting is essential to a comprehension both of the working of the system and of the underlying significance of national income itself.

Part Two of this book shows this interrelation between the national income accounting concepts and the theoretical structure of income analysis. The concepts and measurements that have been explained in Part One are related to the functioning of the economy, and the theory of income analysis is discussed in these national income accounting terms. Part Two has a dual purpose: the national income accounts and statistics are given more meaning by relating them to the functioning of the economy, and at the same time the theory of the operation of the economy is given reality by using the actual national income accounts.

THE DEVELOPMENT OF NATIONAL INCOME ACCOUNTING

National income accounting in recent years has passed the stage where it is of interest only to academicians, and has become an indispensable aid in the formulation of economic policy. The remainder of this chapter will discuss briefly why national income accounting is necessary in current formulations of economic policy, and how it pertains to the analysis of specific problems of economic policy.

A full appreciation of the usefulness of national income accounting as it is applied to economic policy requires first of all some idea of the coverage of the term "economic policy," both in past periods and in a modern industrial economy. The changing nature of economic policy has brought with it a need for a more comprehensive approach to economic analysis, an approach which is capable of presenting pertinent economic data in the perspective of the economy as a whole. It was because of this need that national income accounting has been developed, and the history of the development of national income accounting is in fact inseparable from the history of the economic problems posed by the depression of the thirties, by the industrial mobilization for World War II, and by the postwar economic readjustments among nations. A brief account of this history will make clear what must be the more important characteristics of a system of national income accounting designed to be useful for problems of economic policy.

Economic Development and the Increasing Necessity for Economic Policy

The rapid industrial development of the Western countries during the last 500 years has created a close mutual interdependence among the people of these countries, and it is from this interdependence that the problems of economic policy as we know them today have arisen. As long as small groups of individuals were relatively self-sufficient, the concept of private property and the feudal tradition together gave a determinate answer to the one major economic problem—who was to own or use the land. But as towns grew and some of the people ceased to be attached to the land, economic problems of a different nature arose. Since the manorial system permitted wages and most other payments to be made in kind, it had little need for money, but with the development of trade and specialization, some sort of specie payment became necessary. It was soon evident that the general public had an interest in the creation of a satisfactory money system, since inefficient or dishonest control of the money system led to periods of inflation or deflation. Laws regulating banking practices and the control of the issuance of money were made in the public interest. In similar manner, specific policies in the areas of international trade and public finance became necessary. Tariffs were imposed on certain commodities and subsidies were granted to certain industries, on the ground of the general public interest. Taxation and government expenditures became increasingly important, both in periods of war as munitions were needed and in periods of peace as the domestic need for such things as streets, highways, and general education increased.

It is important to realize that this increasing significance of economic policy results not from an increasing interest in, or movement toward, centralization and planning but rather from the increasing complexity of economic activity itself, and from the emergence of specific problems to which solutions must be found. For example, the very existence of railroads and other public utilities poses a problem of policy about which a decision, conscious or unconscious, must be made. The variety of decisions that can be made is very great, ranging from complete government ownership and operation at the one extreme to allowing free entry into the utility field and complete freedom to the producers to charge any rates they might wish at the other extreme. But following either of these courses, or indeed any other course, would require an economic policy decision. The existence of problems necessitating economic policy decisions is quite independent of any particular solution that may be adopted. The adoption of economic policies does not imply the introduction of "planning"; economic planning refers to one category of possible actions, but any other form of action or inaction taken to solve existing economic problems is fully as much an economic policy.

The Problem of Adequate Information

With the realization that there are economic problems to which some sort of solution must be found, it becomes obvious that, before any decisions are made, a careful consideration of all the relevant facts is of paramount importance. Facts by themselves rarely provide sufficient grounds for formulating a policy; in designing an adequate solution to any given problem, attention must be given to the over-all goals and aims of the society, and it is in this area that different individuals and different political parties will have widely divergent views. Nevertheless, irrespective of the particular aims and goals adopted, it will be found that basic information about the economy is necessary in order to design policies that are capable of achieving their purposes. The obvious fact that a great many of the economic policies that are put into effect do not achieve their purposes can frequently be traced to a lack of information or to a misunderstanding of the relationships involved. Unfortunately, the availability both of pertinent data and of adequate methods of analysis has lagged considerably behind the increase in the number and complexity of economic problems which must be faced. In the great majority of instances in which specific policies have in practice been found to be ineffective, unworkable, or definitely harmful, the technician has been at fault fully as much as the policy maker.

At first glance it may appear that the greatest contributing factor to the technical inadequacy of policy formulation is the lack of statistical information. Although this is often true, it is possible to overemphasize the importance of the lack of data with respect to the consideration of over-all economic policies. In problems which require the consideration of the economy as a whole, it is rather the plethora of unorganized economic data which either engulfs the investigator or enables him to obscure the issues. Data on the whole economy in its complete detail are meaningless, but unless all of the data are presented, the information will be one-sided. It is for this reason that it is often said that statistics will prove anything. By careful selection of certain data and omission or combination of the remainder, it is almost always possible to show only one facet of any situation. Different ways of combining, averaging, or aggregating data can give the individual investigator more than enough freedom to shape, consciously or unconsciously, almost any presentation into a form which supports his own views. It has therefore become imperative that some standard framework be erected which will enable the available economic information to be related objectively to the over-all economic problems which have to be solved.

The Historical Development of National Income Accounting

In its early stages national income accounting was not designed as a method of presenting information relevant to general economic problems. For the most part, the first investigations on the subject of national income accounting were carried on by academic economists and institutions. Their primary concern was the building up of a series of aggregates for successive time periods to show the total income of all individuals in a particular country. It was natural that these investigations should also concern themselves with production and with expenditures on goods and services since, when properly computed and adjusted, these measures could be used to estimate the total amount of income payments indirectly. At this stage in the development of national income, however, there was no explicit attempt to construct a framework of data for the economy as a whole.

Considerable impetus was given to the work on national income by the depression of the thirties. With the increase in unemployment, the lowering of wage rates, and the disappearance of profit, there was an obvious lowering of potential purchasing power, and for analytic purposes it was essential to be able to measure this change. The depression posed many economic problems which necessitated the formulation of specific economic policies. For example, with the fall in incomes, tax receipts fell, and the government was immediately faced with the choice of decreasing its expenditures accordingly, increasing the tax rates to try and raise more revenue, or borrowing to make up the difference between taxes and expenditures. In order to make intelligent decisions with respect to such problems, the government needed to know the type and magnitude of the effects which their tax collections and expenditures would have on the economy. In this connection information was required both on the total amount of income which was being received by individuals and on the total expenditures which were being made in the economy.

Recovery from the depression brought with it interest in such things as the relative amount of investment expenditures and the accumulation of inventories by businesses. The banking system realized that it was only in relation to information of this nature that credit control could usefully be employed with a view to keeping the economy on an even keel. The various individual components of national income and national expenditure, when placed within the framework of the other components, were gradually coming to be looked upon as useful information, important in and of themselves.

During World War II a great many economic problems arose which required a general understanding of the economy. Nations were forced to undertake war production. Although many of the countries probably had no carefully thought-out economic policy, in some countries there was a concerted effort to achieve as great a degree of efficiency as possible. First and foremost, such an effort required a knowledge of how much would be available in the way of economic resources. All armament production plans had to be considered together in order to make sure that the supply of manpower and basic materials in the economy was sufficient to carry them all out. The total quantity of resources which were available obviously had a limit, and total over-all production had to be designed to fit within this limit. To schedule a greater production would not only be unrealistic; it would cause serious bottlenecks in some areas and useless oversupply in others. To schedule less production than the available resources would permit, on the other hand, would be to operate at a level lower than full capacity. Accordingly, data on such things as the distribution of manpower among industries and the national income originating in the various industries became of extreme importance. For any realistic appreciation of the problem, furthermore, current consumption had to be taken into account. Not all production could be devoted to war purposes; the civilian population had to be supported if they were expected to turn out the war production. An examination of the minimum level of goods and services needed for consumption was therefore necessary, and national income accounting was again called upon to provide a framework showing the interrelationships among the end uses of production.

The task of deciding how the production plans were to be implemented, as well as the determination of the potential level of production, also required major economic policy decisions. The vast amount of war expenditure had to be financed, and the method of financing to be used was one of the most important questions which had to be faced. It was obvious that taxation should be increased. But how much could it be increased and how much additional tax revenue could be expected from the fact that the economy was working at a higher level of activity? And for that part of war expenditures which could not be financed out of taxation, how and from whom should the requisite funds be borrowed? What different repercussions on the economy would result from borrowing from banks as opposed to individuals, and what effect would such borrowing have upon the incomes of individuals and upon prices? In similar manner, how far could the price incentive be used to move resources such as labor from unessential to essential industries? Income payments would obviously be affected by any such use of the price incentive, and it was necessary to know the extent of the inflationary influence to be expected and whether means were available to offset it successfully. Finally, to what extent and by what means should civilian consumption be restricted to necessities? Relying on the price mechanism to provide the restriction again might result in a disastrous inflation, so that it was necessary to decide in what areas rationing and price control might be necessary. It is obvious that all these problems are highly interrelated, and that they can be solved satisfactorily only if they are considered within one framework of data. Under the wartime pressures national income accounting was developed to provide such a framework. With this framework it became possible to relate the amount of total available resources to the planned production for war and civilian consumption, and to examine the income payments and prices which would necessarily result from the adoption of any specific system of taxes, borrowing, incentive payments, price control, and rationing. By the end of the war national income accounting had thus emerged as an essential tool in the formulation of economic policy.

At the present time a large number of countries are using the national accounting approach to appraise their own current economic situations and to serve as a basis for designing realistic and consistent policies. The postwar period has brought with it a great many problems of readjustment. These readjustments, and the measures such as the Marshall Plan designed to assist in them, can have meaning only in terms of the relevant economic magnitudes in the different countries. A suitable adjustment within any country must be defined in terms of full utilization of capacity, workable trade patterns, and a reasonable and maintainable allocation of production between investments and consumption. The information provided by national income accounts is essential for achieving such a balance. If nations are to avoid the evils of inflation and deflation, they must carefully consider the repercussions of their tax policies, their debt management and other credit controls, and their general government expenditures; to disregard these repercussions is to invite disaster. National income accounting obviously does not ensure the success of these or any other policies, but it can place them on a more reasonable and enlightened basis.

National Income Accounting and the Formulation of Economic Policy

National income accounting is useful primarily because it constitutes a systematic record of basic information about economic activity, presented in such a manner that it is usable for carrying out meaningful economic analysis. This of course does not mean that there are specific formulas which can be applied to the national income accounts to yield an adequate solution to all economic problems. The situation is more nearly analogous to that of the typical business firm. Accounts are necessary for the intelligent operation of a business firm; unless a manager knows about the costs, sales, and financial condition of his firm, he is in no position to put well-designed policies into effect. But an adequate set of accounts does not by itself guarantee the success of the firm; there are no magic rules which the manager can apply to his accounts to solve all the problems he faces. For the policies of the firm to meet with success, they must be based on an intelligent appreciation of what has happened in the past, but they must also have behind them the creative ability and judgment of the policy makers. In similar manner, the analysis of national income accounts is necessary for the formulation of successful economic policies, but the accounts are not the only necessary ingredient. They do not and cannot provide a general panacea.

Although national income accounting is by itself in no sense a sufficient basis for formulating economic policy, it is of use in helping to answer certain questions about over-all economic policies. These questions are of three major types:

1. Is the policy which is being considered capable of being achieved in terms of the availability of resources?

2. How does the policy affect the operation of the economy in terms of prices, output, and employment?

3. What is the net effect of the policy in quantitative terms? Is it worth doing?

Each of these types of question will be examined briefly.

Economic Policy and the Availability of Resources. Perhaps the majority of economic policies are partial, in the sense that they deal with only one sector or one industry in the economy, and implicitly assume that the rest of the economy will automatically adjust or be adjusted to fit in. Any adequate evaluation of the usefulness of such a policy, however, requires some idea of the extent of the adjustment that will have to be made in the rest of the economy. For this reason one test of an economic policy which is partial in nature is the examination of how it fits into the framework of available resources. It might seem that almost any policy which advocates increased output somewhere in the economy is basically a good policy, since increased goods and services are a desirable goal. But when the problem is considered in the context of the potentially usable resources in the economy, it is apparent that advocating an increase in one particular industry is equivalent to declaring that it will be more beneficial to use additional resources in this industry than in any other industry. In other words, such an economic policy, either consciously or unconsciously, involves a decision about which use of resources among all possible uses is preferable. For a valid defense of the policy it would be necessary to show what additional resources would be needed to carry it out, from what part of the economy such resources could be obtained, and why this particular use would be more beneficial than alternative use of these same resources in other industries.

For all these questions the information available in the national income accounts is pertinent. The quantity of additional resources needed to carry out an economic policy cannot be computed without regard to interindustry relationships. Should, for example, an increase in naval construction be proposed? It is not enough to consider the increased manpower required for actual construction. The manpower and facilities involved in the components industry, in the steel industry, in coal mining, and even in industries as far removed as chemicals and electric power must also be considered. With a knowledge of the general requirements of the program, the national income accounts show the relative expansion in the output of these industries, or the contraction in the use of their products by other industries, which would be needed to carry the program forward. Alternatives to the proposed policy should also be considered in a similar manner—for instance, in this case it would be useful to study the cost, in terms of economic dislocation, of air fleets, relative to their possible substitutability for naval vessels. The usual comparison in money cost terms alone is not enough. Some parts of the economy cannot easily expand further, whereas other parts may actually be operating below capacity. To ensure the fullest possible utilization of resources, such factors as these should be taken into account, and the final economic policy which is recommended should be based on the explicit belief that it is superior to all possible alternatives.

A second major group of economic policies are those which refer to the economy as a whole and are quite general in their coverage. An economic policy of this type is meaningful only if it fits within the limits of the existing resources of the economy and if it is internally consistent. To try for output goals which far exceed the capabilities of the economy will result in an unbalanced economy, with serious shortages in some lines and supplies which cannot be used in others. Furthermore, the normal expansion of the economy is not brought about by an even over-all rate of growth in all industries. The production of food, for example, will not increase at the same rate as the production of steel or even textiles. The rate at which different industries grow is governed by the manner in which the consumer spends his income, the kinds of goods and services which are purchased by the government, and the nature and level of the capital goods industries. Further differences in rates of growth are introduced by technological factors; the ability to utilize mass production permits some industries to operate at decreasing cost, whereas the limitation of available resources prevents expansion in others. Inventions and changes in technology also complicate the situation for almost all industries.

Because of these complexities met in analyzing over-all economic growth, the governments of most countries in which national income accounts are available use these accounts to make projections of the effects they believe their economic policies will have. These projections are frequently referred to as "national budgets"; in effect, they show the change that is to be expected in each part of the economy. Since these projections of the national income accounts are usually presented in terms of constant prices, the separate accounts will balance and tie in with each other only if the net increase in output does not exceed the assumed change in available resources. The making of the projection therefore ensures that the projected changes will be within the expected potential limits of the resources. In this connection manpower budgets are usually also provided along with the national income budgets. A comparison of the projected changes in output shown in the national budget and the projected changes in employment shown in the manpower budget will reveal the expected changes in productivity for each industry.

Using the national income accounting system to integrate the effects of an over-all economic policy with the economy as it exists and as it is expected to change in the future, it becomes possible to see whether the proposed economic policy is consistent with itself and whether it can be expected to produce a result superior to those of alternative general economic policies. Without explicitly making up some sort of projection of national income accounts, it is almost impossible to draw up a general policy which is internally consistent and which is in accord with the expected future developments.

Economic Policy and the Operation of the Economy. The foregoing discussion has been concerned with the capabilities and consistency of economic policy in terms of resource allocation. There are many policies which would pass this type of examination, but which would still be harmful through their effects upon the operation of the economy. Badly designed economic policies can result in serious inflations or depressions, so that it is necessary to give careful consideration to the relation of any proposed policy to the actual functioning of the different sectors of the economy.

An example will demonstrate the use of national income accounts for this purpose. Consider a proposal to reduce the public debt. This at first glance may seem to be an entirely laudable economic policy. It might well be demonstrable, in accordance with the foregoing section, that such an undertaking would certainly be within the capabilities of the economic system. Suppose that the actual mechanism proposed is increased taxation of individual incomes in order to obtain a government surplus to be used for debt repayment. Further let us assume, for the sake of concreteness, that most of the debt repayments would be to banks holding government bonds, and that the economy is not in a period of inflation but has in fact excess bank reserves which could be loaned out for additional investment. The amount of personal taxes paid would increase, and individuals would be forced to curtail either their personal savings or their consumption expenditures. In practice it will be found that there is a tendency for both categories to absorb part of the decrease. In all probability, as a result of the decline in consumers' expenditures, producers will receive fewer orders, and they in turn will cut back production, causing some unemployment. Individuals will undoubtedly react to this decline in their incomes by cutting their expenditures again, and again producers will sell less and so be forced to dismiss more workers, increasing unemployment. In this manner a cumulative decline of output and employment in the economy can be started. Tracing through the effect of the debt repayment to the banks shows that it will not necessarily help the situation. There is no reason to believe that producers will borrow to expand their investment expenditures merely because the banks now have cash instead of bonds; the level of investment in the economy often depends on the current economic outlook—especially when it is unfavorable—more than upon the availability of bank credit. As a result, the more probable development is that with the initial declines in consumers' expenditures and in output and employment, producers will curtail their investment expenditures, so leading to an even sharper decline in output and employment. The use of national income accounting could provide the quantitative data necessary to help decide whether this economic policy designed in this particular way, on the surface apparently desirable, might actually have disastrous results.

Just as a badly designed economic policy can cause a depression, so it can also result in an inflation. Suppose, for example, that the government, although it desired to keep the budget balanced, decided to equalize incomes somewhat by removing some of the taxes from the lower income groups and placing equivalent taxes on the upper income groups. The immediate results of this action might be a rise in consumers' expenditures and a fall in personal saving. The lower income groups would be given larger incomes to dispose of by the tax reduction, and they would undoubtedly react by spending most of the additional money which became available to them. On the other hand, the people of the upper income groups who were now paying more taxes would have to reduce their savings in order to be able to meet the increased taxes and still maintain approximately the same standard of living. These reactions would amount to an increase in consumers' expenditures, and, if only a limited quantity of goods were available, the prices of consumers' goods would rise. Producers, because of the increase in consumers' expenditures, would have more money available to meet labor's wage demands and to distribute to the other factors of production. The income of individuals would therefore increase, and consumers' expenditures would again rise, starting the spiral all over again. Producers' reactions to the higher level of activity in the economy would reinforce the spiral; they would increase their expenditures on capital goods. Since only a limited amount of goods can be produced with existing resources, a point would be reached when all of the effect of increased expenditures would be felt in a rise in prices rather than in increased output. Here again, the use of national income accounting could provide the data necessary to help decide whether this particular policy would in fact be inflationary.

The design of an adequate economic policy therefore demands a careful investigation of the effect the policy will have upon the operation of the economy in terms of prices, output, and employment. If, in the examples considered above, it is decided that reducing the public debt and equalizing incomes are desirable ends in and of themselves, careful attention must be given to the design of the specific measures employed to accomplish these ends in order that they shall not lead to economic disruption. Problems of this nature can be analyzed adequately only within the framework of the national income accounts. Only a complete system of accounts is capable of making explicit the economic mechanisms involved.

Economic Policy and Its Quantitative Effect. The final question that must be considered is that of the actual results which an economic policy can be expected to achieve in terms of the goals of the society. National income accounting obviously can never give a complete answer to this question. The welfare of individuals cannot be measured in terms of a few summary statistics. There are many nonquantitative ingredients —such things as working conditions, freedom of opportunity, and the moral and political temper of a country. But national income accounting can and does shed some light on what is happening to the output of the economy. This information, even though it is by no means a complete basis for evaluating any policy, is very much needed.

A quantitative measurement of the net gain is necessary because a policy cannot be advocated solely on the grounds that its expected results would be beneficial. The expected benefits of the policy must be shown to be quantitatively great enough to make it worthwhile to undergo the risks involved. No action involving an estimate of the future is entirely without risk. Businessmen are constantly faced with the problem of choosing between those policies which have an excellent risk prospect of making a small gain and those policies involving greater risk but also a possibility of a correspondingly larger gain. Policies which have a large degree of risk attached to a small possible gain are naturally excluded from any reasonable consideration. In like manner, the expected results of an economic policy need to be estimated in quantitative terms in order that the possibility of gain may be weighed against the risks of failure. Many policies which in theory are beneficial may be found, when examined in quantitative terms, to make so little difference that they are not worth undertaking.

2. Production in a Modern Exchange Economy

The Nature of a Modern Exchange Economy

The exchange of goods and services through market transactions is an essential feature of a modern exchange economy. Such transactions are necessary for the functioning of the system, for only by this process can production occur and goods become available for consumption. The specialization of productive activity existing in an economy such as that of the United States demands that each individual devote the major part of his energies to one specific job. In return for this expenditure of effort the individual is customarily paid in money, which can be exchanged for whatever commodities and services he wants. The wage earner works for an employer who pays him wages for his labor; the farmer grows agricultural products for sale on the market in order to get income to buy other goods. Such examples as these need no further elaboration, since they are self-evident to everyone who lives in an exchange economy. But the mechanisms that permit such a system to operate successfully are very complex and are not self-evident.

In the early history of our economy exchange did not play the same role that it plays today. At that time individuals often provided directly for their own consumption instead of obtaining all they consumed from the market. A change in the production and consumption of an individual would not then necessarily have had repercussions on other individuals. If a man worked harder and built himself a better home or produced more products for himself, he might well have achieved a higher standard of living without affecting anyone else in the economy. In contrast, today almost every individual is linked to other individuals through the work he does and through the products he consumes. If an individual produces more, the amount of output that appears on the market will be changed. This will have repercussions upon other individuals in two ways. Those who are also producing this commodity for sale are in competition with the first individual; the price they can obtain for their output may be reduced by his increased output. Those buying the product, on the other hand, will find that more is available; this greater supply may make the product cheaper for the purchaser. Likewise, if an individual changes his consumption, the amount he removes from the market will be changed. This again will have repercussions both on those who produce and on those who consume.

This interrelation of individuals through transactions is partly obscured by the fact that action of one individual rarely appears to have a significant effect on either price or output in the economy. But when a sizable group of individuals react together, the effect upon others in the economy is often dramatically revealed. For instance, a new taxicab company in a small town will radically alter the earnings of those already employed in the taxi business, and it may also cause a change in taxi rates or improve the service given to consumers. A change in consumer tastes or fashions may also have repercussions on those who produce; changes in the popularity of lace, for instance, have caused violent fluctuations in the fortunes of those employed in lacemaking. The relationships of individuals to one another are thus both complementary and competitive. They are complementary because each individual is dependent upon the others for the commodities and services necessary for his existence, and the others in turn must utilize his production. On the other hand, individuals compete with one another both in offering services on the market and in purchasing goods and services from the market.

The modern exchange economy is thus essentially a mechanism that links production and consumption. The purpose of national income measurements is to provide a guide through the maze of complex interrelationships that develop in such a system. To the casual observer it may well seem that the economy in which we live is too complex for any useful generalizations to be made about it—there are billions of individual transactions each year, and almost all of them are in some way interdependent. One of the first tasks of the economist is to bring order into this apparent chaos, so that the various patterns which exist and the processes which take place can be analyzed. Before intelligent attempts can be made to improve the effectiveness of the economic system in meeting human needs, a thorough understanding of how the system operates is necessary.

Transactions and Economic Activity

In an exchange economy most economic activity is reflected in transactions. These transactions may be of very different types. The payment of taxes by a business, for example, is very different from the payment of wages or salaries to individuals. The expenditures of consumers and the outlays of producers for capital equipment represent still different types of transactions, all of which must be distinguished from each other if a useful analysis of what is taking place in the economy is to be made. National income makes use of these transactions to portray what has taken place in the economy over a past period of time. For this purpose it is necessary to establish a system of classification that is capable of revealing the patterns of economic activity.

Some economic activity does take place without transactions; and if only the actual transactions that have taken place were considered, national income statistics might well be an incomplete account of economic activity. For this reason it is sometimes necessary to impute certain transactions to various parts of the economy when actually no such transactions have taken place. No formal transaction, for instance, records the consumption by the farmer of food that he himself has produced. In cases such as this an imputed transaction is set up showing, on the one hand, the market value of the goods the farmer produces for home consumption and, on the other hand, the market value of the home-produced goods the farmer consumes. By this process national income can cover kinds of economic activity that never reach the market place.[1]

The Definition of Production in an Exchange Economy

Before going into the detailed techniques of classifying and combining transactions, it is necessary to obtain some idea about what is meant by production in the economy. To most people production calls to mind the activities of a manufacturing plant or perhaps a farm enterprise, but for economic purposes such a concept of production is too narrow. In broader terms any process that creates value or adds value to already existing goods is production. By shipping oranges from California to New York a dealer finds that he can obtain a higher price. This process of distribution is therefore production, since it has added value to the oranges. The narrower concept of production obviously fits within this definition too: manufacturing adds value to existing raw materials. By the use of labor and machinery, the raw materials are converted to a more highly fabricated form that has greater value.

The use of value as a criterion in defining production has other advantages. It permits the comparison of relative amounts produced by different types of activities. In comparing the production of an equal weight

---

[1] Certain economic activities, e.g., the services of the housewife, are not imputed even though they do not appear on the market, since the problem of measurement is too difficult to carry out in a statistically reliable manner.

of nails and screws, it is possible to say that the screws represent more production, since they have greater value. Similarly, the relative amounts of production carried out by such widely different enterprises as a textile spinning mill and a chemical plant producing sulphuric acid can be evaluated. Value is used as a common denominator; and by analyzing the value of the transactions that take place, measurements of production can be built up that will have meaning with reference to the various national income concepts.

The Factors of Production

The elements responsible for the creation of value or for the addition of value to existing products are called the "factors" of production. A farmer in producing his crops uses the natural resources of the soil, his labor, the services of agricultural equipment, and his own initiative to help create the goods. Economists frequently speak of these factors of production in more general terms as, respectively, land, labor, capital, and entrepreneurship. The last-named of these, "entrepreneurship," designates the element that binds all the other factors of production into a useful coherent purpose. The others are relatively self-explanatory. Any kind of productive activity can be analyzed in these terms. A manufacturing firm, for instance, uses the labor of wage earners, the services of capital equipment, and the services of the entrepreneur to aid in processing raw material; the value added by its activities is the result of these elements.

Payments to the factors of production may take many forms. Land and other scarce natural resources are often paid rent for their share in the productive process. Payments to labor may range from wages and salaries to fees and royalties. Capital may receive either interest or dividends. Finally, entrepreneurship often receives that portion of the total receipts which is left over after other costs are paid—this is called "profit." In actual practice the division between the factors of production is not always clear-cut, and the payments that are made, correspondingly, may cover several different types of contribution. The farmer, perhaps, represents the extreme—the amount of cash receipts that he has left over after cash outlays have been made may represent one lump payment to all the factors that have been used. In most businesses the accounting profit may well represent in part payment for the labor of the entrepreneur, quasi-rent, and even interest on the capital used in the business. The concept of the different factors of production is useful, but it should be kept in mind that in most instances it is not possible to show separately exactly what these factors are.

The Definition of a Productive Unit

The definitions of production and of the factors of production have laid the basis for defining a productive unit. Any individual, firm, or government agency that creates value by combining factors of production is considered to be a productive unit.

An individual who conducts his own activity to the degree that he produces a marketable commodity can be considered a productive unit by himself. There are many such individuals in our present-day economy. Doctors and lawyers who have private practices are individual productive units. Farmers, artists, or peddlers who are not paid for their labor by any one specific organization are also productive units. On the other hand, an individual who is an employee of a firm and as such receives a wage or salary cannot be considered an independent productive unit. He is part of a larger productive unit, which uses his services and those of other individuals in combination with other factors of production to create value. By definition, all productive activity in the economy is carried out by productive units, and every individual who is productive is either a productive unit in his own right or else a part of a larger productive unit.

The most familiar type of productive unit is the business enterprise. Business enterprises take the legal form of individual proprietorships, partnerships, cooperatives, or corporations. The majority of business firms in the United States are quite small (employing less than fifty people); but although such firms are very numerous, they carry out only a minor fraction of total production. Relatively few very large corporations are responsible for the major portion of manufacturing output in the United States.

A government agency may also be a productive unit. The Post Office Department, for instance, hires people and creates value by delivering the mails, and local water departments combine factors of production to provide water for a town. The police department provides protection. Even Congress provides highly important services in a nation so large that direct legislation by the citizens is not feasible.

Thus the economy is made up of productive units that combine the factors of production to create value. By analyzing the transactions of these productive units, national income accounts can be erected that will reveal the pattern of economic activity. The first step toward developing the necessary classifications of these transactions will involve a study of the accounts of productive units. From this it will be possible to develop further classifications and combinations of specific types of transactions into the national income accounts themselves.

3. The Function of Accounts in the Productive Unit

All but the smallest of productive units find it necessary to keep some record of the transactions into which the firm enters. A record of sales that are made to other firms on credit must be kept so that the amount owed to the firm will be known accurately. Similarly, purchases from other firms on credit must be recorded to keep track of how much the firm owes others. Cash transactions also are important, even though they do not change the debt position of the firm; an accurate accounting of costs and knowledge of the amount of cash and goods on hand will have important bearing on the policy of the firm. Every transaction will alter the position of the firm, and the accounts that the firm keeps to give it knowledge of its position must be altered when transactions take place so that a true picture will be given.

Many corporate productive units are extremely complicated. They may own buildings, machinery, and raw materials with which to carry out production. At the same time they may owe bills for goods they have bought, wages for work their employees have done, and money that has been borrowed from banks or other creditors. Funds will have been contributed to the enterprise by the stockholders when they purchase stock, usually in the expectation that they will get a return in the form of dividends or increased value of their stock. A portion of the profits that the productive unit has made may not have been paid out to the stockholders but instead may have remained in the business as an increase in its assets or may have been used to pay off prior indebtedness. To keep track of all these complicated interrelationships within the firm, two very natural sets of accounts have been developed. This chapter will explain the general purpose and nature of these sets of accounts and will show how they are related to the transactions made by the firm.

THE BALANCE SHEET AND THE INCOME STATEMENT

The Function of the Balance Sheet and the Income Statement

The first set of accounts is designed to show the economic position of a productive unit at any one time; it shows, for instance, the amount the firm owes to others as of a given date. This set of accounts is generally referred to as the balance sheet of the enterprise. The second set of accounts shows what has happened to the productive unit over a period of time; for instance, it shows what the total volume of sales over the past year has been. This set of accounts is referred to as the income statement or profit and loss account.

The Balance Sheet. There are basically three types of questions relating to the economic position of a productive unit at any one time: (1) What is the value of the assets owned by the productive unit? (2) What is the total of the bills and debts (liabilities) that are owed? (3) What is the residual share that the owners may claim after the total liabilities have been subtracted from the total value of the assets? The owners' share by definition is equal to the total value of the assets minus the total liabilities. For this reason the total value of the assets must exactly equal (or balance) the total amount of the liabilities plus the share that may be claimed by the owners. The balance sheet gives the answers to these three questions. It lists the total assets owned by the firm and shows the types of claims that are held against these assets.

The balance sheet gives a picture of the position of the firm at a given single instant. The assets and liabilities of a productive unit will always be changing, so that the picture presented in the balance sheet will ordinarily be true only for one specific time. Most companies draw up a balance sheet at least once a year; very often it shows the assets and the claims on these assets on December 31 of a specified year. By examining the balance sheets for a series of years, it is possible to see how the assets of a company have grown or declined and how the claims on these assets have changed.

The Income Statement. Individuals or companies usually attempt to operate a productive unit in the hope of gain or profit. Profit is residually determined: the profit realized on the sale of products can be computed by subtracting the total cost of producing these products from their sales value. A firm must keep account of its income and its cost, therefore, to be able to tell whether or not its operations are profitable. The income statement, or profit and loss account as it is sometimes called, is in general use by almost all except the smallest firms. Without such information, businessmen would not have an adequate guide for their policies or any reasonable basis for their decisions. Productive units that are at all complex must of necessity use such measurements if there is to be any intelligent management.

The income statement shows what has taken place over a given period of time, usually a year. It reports the sales of product that have been made during this period, together with figures showing the cost of the goods that were sold. The income statement contributes a great deal of information about what has happened to the firm during a particular year, whereas the balance sheet gives the economic position of the firm at the end of the year.

The Balance Sheet: A Simplified Example

In Table 1 a simplified sample balance sheet for a manufacturing corporation is given. The value of each major category of assets owned

Table 1. Simplified Sample Balance Sheet of a Manufacturing Corporation as of December 31, 19—

Assets			Liabilities and Proprietorship		
Cash		$ 122,048	Accounts payable	$	100,738
Accounts receivable		136,496	Bonds		191,197
Marketable securities		124,515	Capital stock		902,470
Inventories		306,745	Surplus		322,272
Plant and equipment:					
Cost	$2,568,247				
Less allowance for depreciation	1,741,374				
		826,873			
			Total liabilities and proprietorship		$1,516,677
Total assets		$1,516,677			

by the corporation is shown on the left part of this sheet. The total shown there for these assets is just over $1.5 million. The right-hand side of the balance sheet shows the liabilities and proprietorship of the corporation. The liabilities (accounts payable and bonds) total almost $300,000. Since the total assets of the corporation were about $1.5 million, the share remaining to the stockholders in the proprietorship accounts (capital stock and surplus) is about $1.2 million. For an explanation of the exact meaning of the various accounts and for an example of a more detailed and realistic balance sheet, see the appendix to this chapter.

The Income Statement: A Simplified Example

Table 2 gives an example of a simplified income statement for a manufacturing corporation. The right-hand side of the income state-

Table 2. Simplified Sample Income Statement for a Manufacturing Corporation for the Period January 1, 19—, to December 31, 19—

(*In thousands*)

Cost of goods sold:		Sales to Company A............... $	700
Goods and materials purchased		Sales to Company B...............	250
from other firms............... $	600	Sales to Company C...............	375
Depreciation of plant and equip-		Sales to Company D...............	80
ment.......................	70	Other sales......................	100
Taxes other than corporate profits		Interest received..................	5
taxes.......................	40	Dividends received................	3
Social insurance contributions.....	25	Subsidies received................	2
Wages and salaries..............	652		
Interest paid....................	15		
Provision for corporate profits taxes	37		
Dividends paid..................	50		
Undistributed profits............	26		
Total allocations of current re-			
ceipts...................... $1,515		Total current receipts............ $1,515	

ment shows the sources from which the receipts of the corporation were derived during the current period, in this case sales to various different purchasers, totaling over $1.5 million, and a small amount of other income. The left-hand side of the income statement shows how these receipts were allocated among the various costs incurred in producing the goods that were sold, how much was left over as profit, and how these profits were allocated among taxes, dividends paid to stockholders, and undistributed profits retained in the corporation. The various items of costs total just over $1.4 million; this leaves slightly over $100,000 as profits. An explanation of the various items of receipts and of costs and profits, together with a more detailed income statement, is given in the appendix to this chapter.

TRANSACTIONS: THEIR RELATION TO ACCOUNTS

Accounts as Records of Transactions

Transactions, to repeat, are the elements out of which the sets of accounts described in the previous section are built. The balance sheet is a picture of the position of the firm at any given moment; every transaction that takes place will alter that picture, and it cannot change except as the result of a transaction. Similarly, the income statement is a record of the sales and costs of the firm—its income-producing activities—over some period. These income-producing activities are nothing but a series of transactions. The summary accounts—the income statement and the balance sheet—are thus merely records of the effects of transactions upon the firm.

The Balance Sheet. Any transaction into which the firm enters will affect the balance sheet of the firm. This is true because the balance sheet will reflect any change in assets, in liabilities, in proprietorship, or in the composition of any of these, and all transactions will have an effect upon one or more of these items. This can be demonstrated by means of an example in which the effects of various types of transactions upon the balance sheet can be traced. Consider the extremely simplified balance sheet given below.

Assets		Liabilities and Proprietorship	
Cash	$ 1,000	Accounts payable	$ 2,000
Inventories	2,500	Capital stock and surplus	11,500
Plant and equipment	10,000		
		Total liabilities and	
Total assets	$13,500	proprietorship	$13,500

One of the commonest types of transaction that the firm can be expected to enter into is the sale of its product. Such a transaction—say, the sale of $500 worth of product for cash—would alter the balance sheet in two ways. (1) If the goods are sold for exactly what it cost to produce them, inventories will be reduced by $500, since the delivery of the product would mean that $500 worth less of finished products would be held in the stockrooms of the firm. (2) Cash would be increased by $500, to signify that payment of this amount had been made for the goods. The total amount of assets would remain unchanged, but its composition would be different. The altered account would appear as follows:

Assets		Liabilities and Proprietorship	
Cash	$ 1,500	Accounts payable	$ 2,000
Inventories	2,000	Capital stock and surplus	11,500
Plant and equipment	10,000		
		Total liabilities and	
Total assets	$13,500	proprietorship	$13,500

Alternatively, instead of paying cash, the purchaser might have bought the goods on credit. This would make necessary the addition of an accounts receivable item to the assets side of the balance sheet; accounts receivable would have increased by $500, and inventories would have decreased by $500.

Many kinds of transactions will alter the liabilities of the firm. For example, the purchase of raw materials that are not paid for immediately in cash will increase the accounts payable of the firm. If a firm buys $300 worth of raw materials for which it does not make immediate payment, accounts payable will increase by $300 and inventories will also increase by $300, since the quantity of raw materials on hand will have increased by that much. Total assets will increase by $300, and total liabilities will also increase by $300. The effect of this transaction upon the last balance sheet shown would be as follows:

Assets		Liabilities and Proprietorship	
Cash	$ 1,500	Accounts payable	$ 2,300
Inventories	2,300	Capital stock and surplus	11,500
Plant and equipment	10,000		
		Total liabilities and	
Total assets	$13,800	proprietorship	$13,800

The proprietorship of the firm will change whenever a transaction is made involving the capital stock or the surplus of the firm. Suppose the firm buys a plant for $1,000 and pays for the plant by giving the owner some shares of capital stock. Plant and equipment will increase by $1,000, since the firm now owns this much more plant, and capital stock will increase by $1,000, since this amount of additional stock has been issued to pay for the plant. The following balance sheet shows how this transaction would affect the last account shown.

Assets		Liabilities and Proprietorship	
Cash	$ 1,500	Accounts payable	$ 2,300
Inventories	2,300	Capital stock and surplus	12,500
Plant and equipment	11,000		
		Total liabilities and	
Total assets	$14,800	proprietorship	$14,800

The surplus account will change whenever a fixed asset is sold for an amount different from that at which it is listed on the balance sheet. If, for example, some machinery listed on the balance sheet as worth $200 is actually sold for $300, the plant and equipment account will be decreased by $200, cash will be increased by $300, and the difference between these two, $100, will appear as an increase in surplus. The actual cash received is $300, but the asset that has been sold was listed on the balance sheet at only $200. The total assets of the firm have therefore increased by the difference between the asset given up and the asset received in return, namely, $100. No liability account has increased, and the capital stock has not increased. This increase in total assets must therefore be balanced by an increase in surplus, since surplus is defined as the difference between total assets and the sum of the liabilities and the other proprietorship items. This $100 increase in surplus is called a capital gain; had it been a decrease, it would have been called a capital loss. Capital gains and losses can also arise when liabilities are paid off for amounts different from those at which they are listed on the balance sheet or when capital stock is issued or withdrawn for amounts different from those at which it is listed. The effect of the sale of machinery discussed above upon the last balance sheet is shown on the balance sheet which follows.

Assets		Liabilities and Proprietorship	
Cash	$ 1,800	Accounts payable	$ 2,300
Inventories	2,300	Capital stock and surplus	12,600
Plant and equipment	10,800		
		Total liabilities and	
Total assets	$14,900	proprietorship	$14,900

Capital gains and losses are not the only transactions that will alter the surplus account, however. All ordinary profits and losses will also show up in this account.[1] For instance, suppose the first transaction mentioned above, the sale of product for cash, had been made at a profit of $100, i.e., the cash received for the sale of the goods was $100 greater than their cost as listed in the inventory account. This $100 difference between the increase in cash and the decrease in inventory must appear as an increase in surplus, since no other account has changed. The change in the last balance sheet resulting from such a transaction, in which goods costing $500 are sold for $600 in cash, is shown below.

Assets		Liabilities and Proprietorship	
Cash	$ 2,400	Accounts payable	$ 2,300
Inventories	1,800	Capital stock and surplus	12,700
Plant and equipment	10,800		
		Total liabilities and	
Total assets	$15,000	proprietorship	$15,000

After these five transactions have taken place, the balance sheet has been considerably altered from its original appearance. Any transac-

---

[1] Balance sheets are ordinarily drawn up only once in a relatively long period— say a year—and surplus is increased only by the amount of those profits which are not distributed as dividends.

tion that takes place will similarly have an effect upon it. Every transaction will alter one or more of the categories of assets, liabilities, or proprietorship.

The Income Statement. Many of the transactions into which a firm enters will appear on its income statement as well as on its balance sheet. Transactions involving the sale of products or the costs and profits relating to products that are sold will alter the income statement.[2] For example, consider the simplified income statement shown below.

Allocations of Receipts from Sales			Sales	
Cost of goods sold		$ 9,500	Sales	$10,000
Materials	$3,000			
Wages	6,000			
Depreciation and other costs	500			
Profits		500		
Total allocations of receipts from sales		$10,000	Total receipts from sales	$10,000

The first transaction discussed above under the balance sheet—the sale of $500 worth of product for cash, at cost—will also appear on the income statement. Sales, obviously, will increase by $500. On the other side of the income statement cost of goods sold will increase by $500. The total amount of cost will be distributed among the various types of costs—wages, materials, and depreciation and other costs. Profits will not be increased, since in this transaction the goods were sold for exactly what it cost to produce them. This transaction will add to the income statement shown above as follows.

Allocations of Receipts from Sales			Sales	
Cost of goods sold		$10,000	Sales	$10,500
Materials	$3,200			
Wages	6,250			
Depreciation and other costs	550			
Profits		500		
Total allocations of receipts from sales		$10,500	Total receipts from sales	$10,500

[2] The more complicated case in which income is derived from sources other than sales, e.g., from interest or dividends, is discussed in the appendixes to this and the following chapter.

The second transaction discussed above—the purchase of materials on credit—will not appear on the income statement at all at the time the purchase is made. However, when the materials are used in the process of production and the output produced with them is sold, they will be entered on the income statement as an element in the costs relating to that sale. Thus some transactions will reach the income statement only after a delay. Items of costs are frequently incurred long before the goods to which these costs relate are sold, but the income statement deals only with actual sales. Transactions involving payments of costs, therefore, will ordinarily not show up on the income statement immediately but rather will appear some time after they occur, when the goods to which they relate are sold.

The third and fourth transactions discussed above—those involving the issuance of capital stock and the making of capital gains—will not appear on the income statement at all, either immediately or at any future time. They have no relation either to sales or to the costs and profits related to sales. They alter the total assets and proprietorship of the firm, but they do not affect its current income. The distinction between transactions such as these—capital transactions—and current transactions, which do appear on the income statement, will be discussed more fully in the last section of this chapter.

The fifth transaction in the series discussed above—the sale of output at a profit—will appear on the income statement immediately. Its effect will be similar to that shown above for a sale at cost, except that the excess of receipts from the sale over the cost of goods sold will appear as an addition to profits. The sale for $600 of goods that cost $500 to produce will alter the last income statement as follows.

Allocations of Receipts from Sales			Sales	
Cost of goods sold		$10,500	Sales	$11,100
Materials	$3,400			
Wages	6,500			
Depreciation and other costs	600			
Profits		600		
Total allocations of receipts from sales		$11,100	Total receipts from sales	$11,100

All transactions that involve the selling of output, on the one hand, or the incurrence of costs and the making of profits related to sales, on the other hand, will thus appear on the income statement as well as alter the balance sheet.

The Four Aspects of a Transaction

Every transaction necessarily involves both a buyer and a seller, and each of these must take account of two different aspects of the transaction. The buyer must record (1) that money (or some equivalent) has been given up and (2) that additional goods have been received. The seller, on the other hand, must record (1) that goods have left the firm and (2) that payment for them has been received. These entries on the part of the buyer and the seller represent four different aspects of the transaction. In the examples discussed above the firm was the seller when it sold finished goods, exchanging a part of its inventories for cash. On the other hand, when it bought raw materials on credit, it was the purchaser, exchanging a debt (a promise to pay cash in the future) for raw materials inventories. In either case, from the point of view of this one firm, each transaction had two different aspects. Both aspects of each transaction are equally important, and neither can be neglected. To consider the payment received when goods are sold without also considering the reduction in the amount of goods on hand, for instance, is to consider only half of the transaction.

Both aspects of each transaction will appear on the balance sheet; and if the transaction appears on the income statement at all, both aspects will appear there. The sale of goods, for instance, appeared on the balance sheet as an increase in cash *and* as a decrease in inventories. On the income statement this transaction appeared as an increase in sales *and* as an increase in cost of goods sold. The purchase of materials appeared on the balance sheet as an increase in inventories *and* as an increase in accounts payable. Each of the other transactions, similarly, will be found to appear in at least two places in each set of accounts in which it appears at all.

A transaction may appear in more than two places on the balance sheet or income statement. For instance, a sale that is made partly for cash and partly for credit will appear in three places on the balance sheet of the seller: inventories will decrease, cash will increase, and accounts receivable will increase. But the transaction still has essentially only two aspects for this firm: the increase in cash and the increase in accounts receivable together represent the payment received for the sale of the good. Their sum will equal the amount by which inventories have decreased, which is the other aspect of the transaction. The good or service bought or sold and the payment for it must always be equal. When goods are sold for exactly what it cost to produce them, this necessity for equality of the two aspects of the transaction raises no problem. When goods are sold for more than they cost to produce, the difference, as was shown above, will appear as surplus (or, on the income statement, profit). The equality of the two parts of the transaction is thus maintained: the value of the goods sold plus the profit on the sale is equal to the payment received. Whenever in any transaction the changes in all the other accounts do not balance, the surplus (or profit) account must be changed so that they will. This is true because changes in the surplus account represent changes in the net value of the proprietorship that can be claimed by the owners of the firm. When assets change without any offsetting change in liabilities, the net value of the proprietorship will have changed.

In summary, then, every transaction will have four complete aspects. In the first place, it will appear in the accounts of two different firms or individuals. In the second place, in the accounts of each of these firms or individuals it will appear twice, once to show the good or service exchanged and once to show the payment for it. All four of these aspects will be equal, and all four must be shown if the transaction is to be recorded completely.

The Relation between the Income Statement and the Balance Sheet

The transactions that appear on the income statement have been referred to above as current transactions, and those which appear *only* on the balance sheet have been referred to as capital transactions, but the difference between these two has not been made explicit. This section will define more exactly what is meant by the terms "current" and "capital" as applied to transactions.

Some of the transactions into which a firm enters relate only to the productive activity of the current period, whereas others may involve the productive activity of either past or future periods. For example, the payment of wages for work done during the current period on products that are sold during the current period relates only to the productive activity of this period, both from the point of view of the firm paying the wages and from the point of view of the laborer receiving them. Such a transaction is defined as current for both the firm and the laborer.

On the other hand, the purchase of a machine that is expected to last for, say, ten years is not a current transaction for the firm making the purchase. The machine will be used not only during the current period but during the next ten years as well. The expenditure that is made to purchase it, therefore, must be related to the productive activity of the next ten years as well as that of this year. This expenditure therefore cannot be considered a current transaction. It will appear on the balance sheet, since it will alter the assets of the firm—plant and equipment will increase, and cash will decrease by an equivalent amount. But the total amount of the expenditure obviously cannot appear on the income statement in the current period, since it does not represent in its entirety a cost related to the sales of the current period. Only a small portion—say one-tenth—of the cost of the machine can properly be charged against the sales of this period. This latter amount (called "depreciation") will appear on the income statement, since it is a current cost showing how much of the value of the machine has been used up in this period. A part of the remainder of the total expenditure on the machine will appear on the income statements of each of the next ten years, as the machine is gradually worn out over that period, and will contribute to the production that is sold over that period. From the point of view of the firm that *sells* the machine, however, the situation is entirely different. This firm manufactures machines for sale. For it, the sale of a machine is a current transaction, which relates entirely to the activity of the current period. It will appear on the income statement of this firm as an increase in sales on the one hand and an increase in cost of goods sold (and possibly profit) on the other hand. Thus it is possible for a transaction to be a capital transaction for the buyer and at the same time a current transaction for the seller.

The reverse of this situation is also possible. A transaction may well be a current transaction for the buyer and a capital transaction for the seller. An example would be the sale of an old machine for junk. For the buyer who deals in scrap iron the purchase is a current one; it represents the cost of acquiring the inventory from which current sales are made. For the seller, however, the sale of an old machine has nothing whatsoever to do with current productive activity. Current sales of product and the costs relating to these sales will not be altered in any respect by the sale of the old machine. The transaction is therefore a capital transaction. It will appear on the balance sheet as an alteration in the composition of the firm's assets, but it will not appear on the income statement.[3]

Finally, some transactions are capital transactions for both parties to them. The sale of an existing building by one firm to another firm that expects to continue to use the building for a long period is such a transaction. It will not appear on the income statement of either firm. For the seller it represents an alteration in the composition of assets, but it has no relation to current production. For the buyer the total expenditure on the building will be related to productive activity for

---

[3] As was pointed out above, if the machine is sold at an amount different from that at which it is listed on the balance sheet, the difference is called capital gain or loss. It is not profit. Profit can arise only from the current productive activity of the firm, i.e., from transactions that appear on the income statement.

a long period to come. Only a small fraction of the cost—current depreciation—can be related to the sales of the current period.

Summary

This chapter has shown how transactions will appear in the accounts of the productive unit. The balance sheet has been shown to reflect all transactions into which the firm enters, whereas the income statement shows only the current transactions. The development of the national income accounting concepts in the following chapters will be based upon these classifications of transactions in the accounts of the productive unit. The balance sheet and the income statement provide a framework within which the operations of the firm can be analyzed and from which a structure of the relationships among firms in the economy can be built up.

The national income accounting concepts and measurements are concerned with the *current* productive activity of the economy. For this reason they will be built up from the income statements of individual productive units rather than from their balance sheets. The transactions that will enter into the formulation of the national income accounts will be those which appear on the income statements of productive units, i.e., those which are, for at least one of the parties to them, current transactions. Some capital transactions will enter into the analysis, but these will include only those which are capital transactions for one party and current transactions for the other. Transactions that are capital transactions from the point of view of both the buyer and the seller bear no relation to the current productive activity of the economy and so will be excluded from further consideration.

APPENDIX TO CHAPTER 3. THE BALANCE SHEET AND INCOME STATEMENT

In Chap. 3 extremely simplified examples of a balance sheet and an income statement for a manufacturing corporation were presented. This appendix will present somewhat more complex and realistic versions of both sets of accounts and will explain in somewhat more detail the meaning of each item that appears in the accounts.

THE BALANCE SHEET

Table 3 gives an example of a balance sheet for a manufacturing corporation. This balance sheet includes a number of items that were not included in the balance sheet given in the text of Chap. 3. United States government securities, prepaid expenses, bad debts, and intangibles have been added to the assets side of the balance sheet; accrued taxes and long-term debt payable within one year have been added to liabilities; and the proprietorship accounts now include both preferred and common stock, as well as reserves for contingencies and surplus. The meaning of these additional categories, as well as of the categories that appeared on the simplified version, will be explained below.

The Asset Accounts

Cash. The item designated "cash" on the balance sheet includes not only the actual amounts of money in the safes and cash registers of the corporation itself but also the total amounts in its checking accounts in banks. In actual practice only a small portion of the funds listed as cash on the balance sheet is ordinarily held by the company in the form of currency. Since checking accounts represent money available on demand, and since companies make many of their payments by check, checking accounts are considered to be cash.

United States Government Securities. Corporations that have unused funds may invest them in securities, which will yield a return on their money, rather than hold them in the form of currency or bank deposits. United States government securities can be converted into cash very readily, and their value fluctuates very little. For this reason funds invested in them are practically equivalent to cash. United States government securities are ordinarily valued on the balance sheet at cost; since their value fluctuates so little, a valuation at current market price would be very little different.

Accounts Receivable. In almost every business, goods are sometimes sold on credit. Actual payment for these sales may be delayed as long as three to six months. At all times, therefore, there will be some uncollected amounts outstanding. The amounts that are owed to the firm are referred to as

Table 3. Sample Balance Sheet of a Manufacturing Corporation as of December 31, 19—

Assets

Cash		$ 222,048.65
United States government securities, at cost		479,319.43
Accounts receivable:		
Total	$137,875.67	
Less estimated bad debts	1,378.76	136,496.91
Inventories		306,745.97
Prepaid expenses		6,138.65
Marketable securities, at cost or market, whichever is lower		24,515.70
Plant and equipment:		
Cost	$2,568,247.54	
Less allowance for depreciation	1,741,374.19	826,873.35
Intangibles		1.00
Total assets		$2,002,139.66

Liabilities and Proprietorship

Accounts payable		$ 200,738.66
Accrued taxes		118,497.24
Long-term debt payable within one year		6,324.45
Bonds and mortgages		81,197.16
Total liabilities		$ 406,757.51
Preferred stock, 7% cumulative, par value $100 (3,603 shares)		360,300.00
Common stock, stated value $75 per share (8,703 shares)		652,725.00
Reserves for contingencies		142,171.03
Surplus		440,186.12
Total proprietorship		$1,595,382.15
Total liabilities plus total proprietorship		$2,002,139.66

35

accounts receivable. Accounts receivable cannot be shown on the balance sheet at their face value, since in all probability some of them will never be paid. Bad debts usually average a predictable small percentage of the total amount of accounts receivable. On the balance sheet shown above an allowance of 1 per cent of total accounts receivable has been made for probable bad debts, and this amount has been subtracted from the face value of accounts receivable to arrive at a valuation for the balance sheet.

Inventories. Inventories include a large number of different kinds of goods. (1) They include all types of raw materials and supplies that must be kept in stock if production is to flow smoothly. (2) The firm will ordinarily have a certain quantity of goods in a semifinished state; these will also be included in inventories, as work in process. (3) Inventories include the stocks of finished goods that are necessary so that orders from customers can be filled quickly out of current stock. The problem of estimating the value of these inventories is not simple. Many of the goods were bought or produced at some period in the past, and the present market price may be quite different from what the goods cost when they were purchased. One common method of valuation in such cases is to assign to the goods either the current market price or the original cost, whichever is lower. If the market price has fallen since the good was purchased, it is considered to have lost a part of the value that was paid for it, and this loss is recognized. On the other hand, if the price has gone up, the good is still valued at its original cost because the gain is not considered to have been realized. The major defense of this procedure is that it will never result in overvalued inventories. There are many other ways in which inventories may be valued, but these need not be taken up here.

Prepaid Expenses. Many of the assets used by a business in the process of production are services that must be purchased some time before they are used but are of such a nature that they are not included in inventories. For example, rent on buildings and machinery may be paid in advance. Similarly, an insurance premium may be paid to purchase protection during a future period. These services are quite similar to raw materials and supplies, in that they are assets which are available for future productive use.

Marketable Securities. Marketable securities of various types are purchased for much the same reason that United States government securities are purchased. The firm may find that in some periods it has funds available in excess of its current needs for cash. It may not wish to use these funds for expansion or to pay them out to the owners. Investing the funds in marketable securities will presumably bring some income to the firm. Unlike United States government securities, most other marketable securities are likely to fluctuate in value and for this reason entail more risk. On the other hand, many of them yield a higher rate of income. Marketable securities are frequently valued at cost or market, whichever is lower, for much the same reason that inventories are so valued.

Plant and Equipment. Almost all productive processes require that some plant and equipment be used by the productive unit, and the enterprise ordinarily owns at least part of the necessary plant and equipment. These holdings are referred to as the "fixed assets" of the firm. On the balance sheet these fixed assets are listed at their original cost less an allowance for depreciation. This depreciation allowance represents the amount by which the value of the asset is estimated to have declined since it was originally purchased. Fixed assets are ordinarily expected to last for a period of years and to contribute their services to production all through their life. The purchase of such an asset is thus equivalent to the purchase of a stream of services that will become available during a series of future years. In this respect such a purchase is quite similar in nature to prepaid expenses such as rent or insurance, except that the period covered is ordinarily longer. As the years pass and the asset is used for production, it is slowly worn out, and the quantity of future services that it is capable of yielding becomes smaller. The value of the asset to the firm therefore declines, and the allowance for depreciation measures this decline.

An example may help to clarify this concept. Suppose that a firm purchases a piece of machinery for $10,000 and that this machine is expected to last ten years and to give equal services in each of these years. At the moment of purchase this machine can be considered equal to $10,000 worth of prepaid services, which will be available for use in production at the rate of $1,000 worth each year for the next ten years. During the first year the first $1,000 worth of services will be used up in production, and at the end of the year $9,000 worth of prepaid services will still remain. The allowance for depreciation will therefore be shown on the balance sheet at $1,000, and the net value of the machine at $9,000. After four years have elapsed, $4,000 worth of services will have been used up and $6,000 worth will still remain. The allowance for depreciation would now be shown at $4,000, and the net value of the machine (the original cost less the allowance for depreciation) at $6,000.

Estimation of the allowance for depreciation necessarily involves a calculation of how long the asset will continue to yield services. An asset sometimes ceases to yield services because it is worn out. In other cases the asset may still be in working order but may cease to yield services because it is obsolete and therefore useless for production where competition of goods produced by more up-to-date equipment must be met. The latter is especially true of many machines, patterns, and dies; their useful life may be very much shorter than their physical life.

The balance sheet of the manufacturing corporation shown above indicates that the corporation owns fixed assets that originally cost almost $2.6 million. The corporation estimates that over $1.7 million worth of the total services of these assets has been used up. This leaves a little over $800,000 worth of services still available to be used.

Intangibles. Intangibles are listed on the balance sheet to remind the reader that there is a body of assets which are difficult to appraise but nonetheless are of real value to the enterprise. A typical example of this type of asset is the trade-mark of a product, which may be very valuable to the producer. It not only may assure the producer of a ready market for his product but may also permit him to obtain a higher price than he otherwise could. Cigarette manufacturers, tooth-paste concerns, and soap companies are all prominently in this position. In addition to trade-marks, a firm may have valuable patents or secret processes that are not included with any of the other assets. By valuing all these intangibles at the nominal amount of $1, the corporation is reminding the stockholders and the public that more assets exist than are listed.

Liabilities and Proprietorship

Accounts Payable. Almost every firm buys some goods and services on credit and has at all times some bills that it has not yet paid. On the assets side of the balance sheet accounts receivable showed the amount that various other firms owed to this corporation. In much the same way the accounts payable show the amount that this corporation owes to other firms.

Accrued Taxes. The liability for some taxes is incurred some time before payment of the taxes becomes due. Corporate profits taxes, for example, do not have to be paid until the year following that in which the taxed profit was earned. Such taxes, which have been incurred but are not yet payable, are called "accrued" taxes. Most firms will also have accrued wages, salaries, interest, and even rents, the liability for which has been incurred but which are not yet due. All these accrued items appear on the balance sheet as liabilities. An obligation does not have to be immediately payable to be classed as a liability.

Long-term Debt Due within One Year. This classification includes bonds and mortgages that will fall due within one year. Like accrued taxes, it represents liabilities that will soon have to be paid.

Bonds and Mortgages. Bonds and mortgages are the long-term debt of the corporation. The issuing of bonds, which will be repaid at a fixed future date, and the mortgaging of fixed assets are two of the methods that firms can employ to obtain funds. Funds can also be obtained by borrowing from banks on shorter terms (this would appear as an additional item of liabilities, notes payable) or by the issuance of capital stock. The latter will be discussed below.

Preferred Stock. The total proprietorship can be divided into a number of different accounts. Those shown on this balance sheet are among the simplest. Preferred stock may be of a number of different types; the particular one shown here is 7 per cent cumulative, with $100 par value. The fact that it is preferred means that dividends on it must be paid before any dividends can be paid to common stockholders. The fact that it is cumulative means that if the dividend is skipped in any year, the total cumulated amount of the unpaid dividends must be paid to the preferred stockholders before any dividend can be paid to the common stockholders. The amount of the yearly dividend per share is $7; this is 7 per cent of the $100 par value per share. The par value of the stock does not necessarily have any relation to its present market value; it may have had some such relation when the stock was issued, but many influences aside from the stated par value determine the market value of a stock, even when it is first issued.

Common Stock. In addition to its preferred stock, this corporation has issued common stock. The stated value of the common stock, like the par value of the preferred stock, bears no necessary relation to its market value. It may have done so when the stock was first issued; but as the years have passed, the corporation has grown and other factors have become important. The present market value of the common stock is affected by the expected future dividends and by the speculative elements of the stock market, among other things.

Reserves. The proprietorship accounts very often contain reserves for contingencies. Their function is to point out to the stockholder that certain unforeseen contingencies may arise which will use up some of the assets. For example, a warehouse that is not fully insured may be destroyed by fire, or an unbonded cashier may abscond with funds. If something of this nature takes place, the reserve for contingencies could be decreased and no other proprietorship account need be affected. Reserves for contingencies are essentially a part of surplus.

Surplus. The value of the surplus account is determined by subtracting the total of the other proprietorship accounts and the liabilities from the total assets. As was pointed out in the discussion of transactions in the text of Chap. 3, an increase in assets that is not balanced either by an increase in liabilities or by an increase in some other proprietorship account must be balanced by an increase in the surplus account. The surplus account is the balancing item on the balance sheet. Profit that is not distributed to the owners will increase the surplus account unless offset by an increase in some other proprietorship account.

Summary

The balance sheet is thus a valuation of the assets of the corporation, accompanied by a statement of the claims against these assets. The total value of the assets does not necessarily determine the value of the enterprise, however. There are many types of intangible assets that, although they are very valuable to the enterprise, are not added into the balance sheet. Furthermore, the basic value of a concern is largely dependent upon its ability to make profits in the future, and this is not shown on the balance sheet.

THE INCOME STATEMENT

Table 4 gives an income statement for a manufacturing corporation. This income statement, like the balance sheet shown in Table 3, is more complex and realistic than that given in the text of Chap. 3. In addition to the items shown there, it includes receipts from dividends, interest, and subsidies and allocations of receipts to bad debt expense and charitable contributions.

Total Current Receipts

Sales. The sales figure shown on the income statement in Table 4 represents the value of products sold at market prices. The term "market prices" is used here because this is the price to the purchasers on the market. This

Table 4. Sample Income Statement for a Manufacturing Corporation for the Period January 1, 19—, to December 31, 19— *

Total current receipts..	$1,496,889.69
Total sales of products less discounts and allowances...................	1,479,189.72
Dividends received from holdings of stock in other corporations.........	1,028.75
Interest received on notes receivable, bonds of other corporations, and government bonds...	12,940.80
Subsidies received from the government.............................	3,730.42
Allocated as follows...	$1,496,889.69
Cost of goods, materials, and services purchased from other producers....	580,939.21
Depreciation of plant and equipment................................	68,739.17
Taxes and licenses other than corporate profits taxes...................	37,070.77
Bad debt expense..	1,285.34
Contributions to charity...	4,376.55
Cost of social insurance contributions..............................	24,586.86
Cost of wages and salaries.......................................	648,474.33
Interest charges...	14,777.17
Provision for corporate profits taxes................................	42,000.00
Dividends paid out...	50,032.64
Undistributed profits...	24,607.65

* The particular form of this income statement is similar to that used by many large corporations in reports to their stockholders. The more general accounting forms of income statements were not used here, since the following text does not make use of the classification of income into operating and nonoperating.

is what is actually paid by those who buy the products. It is not necessarily equal to the list price of the goods sold; discounts are frequently given for large purchases or prompt payment, and other allowances are made for various reasons.

Interest Received. The firm may receive interest on notes receivable, bonds of other corporations, and government bonds. It is a common business practice to sell products on credit; but if such service were given without charge, the practice would be equivalent to supplying the purchasers with working capital. There would be no incentive for customers to pay cash or even to pay their notes as promptly as possible. For this reason the producer will charge interest on his notes receivable. This interest is part of the total current receipts of the corporation. The balance sheet showed that this corporation owned United States bonds, and some of the marketable securities that it owns may be the bonds of other corporations or of state and local or foreign governmental units. Interest will be received on all these types of bonds as well as on short-term obligations such as notes receivable.

Dividends Received. A part of the marketable securities shown on the balance sheet of the corporation may be in the form of stocks of other corporations, which will yield income in the form of dividends. This income must be included as part of the current receipts of the corporation. Current income is not affected, however, by the purchase or sale of securities during the year. For this corporation the purchase or sale of securities is a capital transaction similar to the purchase or sale of a fixed asset. Gains and losses from such transactions are, as was pointed out in the text of Chap. 3, capital gains and losses. They alter the balance sheet of the corporation but do not enter into the income statement.

Subsidies Received. This item would not appear on the income statements of most manufacturing corporations in the United States. For the most part, subsidies in the United States have been given only to agricultural producers, although after World War II some subsidies were given to building-materials producers. Subsidies are included as a part of the total current receipts of this corporation to show how they would be treated for use in the later development of the national income accounts. Since many other countries do pay subsidies to all types of producers, it is important to understand how they are treated.

Allocations of Total Current Receipts

Goods, Materials, and Services Purchased from Other Producers. Virtually all firms make purchases from other producers in carrying out production. Raw materials, power and fuel, contract work, office supplies, rents, advertising, and all similar payments are included in the classification "goods, materials, and services purchased from other producers." This category is not simply the total of all outlays made to other producers during the current period, however. (1) All the materials and services bought in the present period were not necessarily used up in the production of the goods which were sold in this period. Therefore they should not all be considered as part of the cost of production of these goods. (2) The goods produced in this period may have been the result of outlays or purchases made in a previous period, so that counting only outlays in this period would not include all costs. Most services are used immediately as they are purchased, but materials and some few prepaid services are not; instead they enter into inventories or prepaid expenses. In order to obtain the correct figure for this category, the cost of the goods, materials, and services that actually did enter into the production of the goods that were *sold* during the period must be calculated. This involves calculating (1) the quantity of such goods and services and (2) their value or cost.

A number of methods can be used to estimate the quantity of materials that has been used up in producing the goods sold. Some methods of cost accounting provide accounts that record exactly what materials have been used up in production. If the products sold are known, the producer can determine from his books what materials are recorded as entering into his production. He will thus know the exact amounts of each element used in the production of the goods sold. Another method of calculating the quantity of materials used in producing the goods sold may be termed the "inventory method." Inventories represent the quantities of materials, semifinished goods, and finished products that are owned by the firm. Both the purchase of raw materials and the sale of finished products will change the amount of inventories the firm holds. The quantity of materials that has been used up in making the products sold can be estimated if inventories at the beginning of the period, purchases during the period, and inventories at the end of the period are all known. When inventories of materials, semifinished goods, and finished products all remain exactly the same, it can be said that the quantity of materials purchased from other producers exactly equals the quantity of these materials used up in the production of goods sold. Whenever inventories change, the producer must rely on the accountant to adjust the quantity of materials purchased from other producers so that it will correspond to the actual quantity of these items used up in producing the goods that were sold.

After the quantity of goods, materials, and services used in the production of the goods sold has been determined, the problem of how to value them still remains. If the first goods purchased are assumed to be the first ones used up in the process of production, the value of the inventories will reflect the prices of goods most recently purchased (first-in, first-out method of inventory valuation). If the last goods purchased are assumed to be the first ones used up, inventories will reflect the prices of goods purchased at early periods (last-in, first-out method of inventory valuation). Some businesses use the original cost valuation, and other businesses use current market valuation. Both practices are recognized as quite legitimate if the facts as to the valuation are disclosed and if the practice does not give a false impression for the purpose served by the accounting statement.

Depreciation. One aspect of the nature of depreciation has been discussed above in the section on the balance sheet. There it was pointed out that the allowance for depreciation represents the amount by which the value of an asset has declined since it was originally bought. The amount of this decline in value that takes place in any one year represents the cost of using the machine for production during that year; it is termed "depreciation expense" and must be shown on the income statement as a part of the cost of producing the goods sold during the year. A machine when originally purchased does not represent a cost; it is merely a shift of assets from one form to another. But as the machine is used, its purchase price gradually enters into the costs of the stream of goods that is produced with it. When the machine is finally discarded, its total original cost will gradually have appeared as depreciation expense over the years the machine has been in use.

Taxes Other than Corporate Profits Taxes. Any allocation of total current receipts must take into account the taxes, licenses, and fees that have to be paid to the government. Local property taxes will have to be paid on land and buildings owned. Many products such as tobacco, liquor, fur coats, and in some states all retail purchases, have excise or sales taxes levied on them. Some businesses must pay for government licenses or are subject to government fees in their operations. These are all part of the costs of producing or selling goods, and a business must allocate the necessary amount from total current receipts before it can compute its profits. The corporate profits tax, however, is different in its nature. It is levied on the firm *after* profits have been computed. The corporate profits tax is not a cost of production but rather a tax on the profits of the corporation; therefore it should not be included along with these other taxes in the calculation of the costs of producing the goods that were sold.

Bad Debt Expense. Some of the accounts or notes owed to the firm turn out to be uncollectible, and the firm loses the amount of these bad debts. Looked at another way, the total current receipts shrink by an amount equal to the bad debts. Some of the total current receipts must therefore be allocated to cover this expected shrinkage if the profit figure is to represent a reliable net gain. Bad debt expense can thus be considered equivalent to a cost item, although in most accounting procedure it is treated as an adjustment of total receipts.

Charitable Contributions. The Federal corporate profits tax laws permit corporations to deduct a certain amount of charitable contributions from their total current receipts in calculating taxable profits. If such were not the case, charitable contributions would be shown as a part of profits in much the same way that dividends are a part of profits.

Social Insurance Contributions. Both the employers' and the employees' contributions for social insurance are included in this category. These contributions are of the same nature as taxes other than corporate profits taxes, but they have not been included with these other payments to the government because they are usually considered a part of the cost of using labor.

Wages and Salaries. The cost of wages and salaries, like the cost of goods, materials, and services purchased from other producers, must be determined in relation to the products that were sold during the current period. Wages may have been paid duing the period for work on products that had not yet been sold at the end of the period; and similarly, some products may have been sold during the period that were worked on in previous periods. The problems involved in determining the amount of wages and salaries that should be included as a cost of the goods sold are much the same as those which were pointed out with reference to the cost of goods and materials purchased from other producers. The quantity and type of labor used in the production of the goods sold must be determined, and these services must be valued. These problems must be solved, implicitly or explicitly, before the cost of wages and salaries can be computed.

Interest. The ordinary operation of the firm will require that it pay interest on its long-term debt, on its notes payable, and on any other money that it has borrowed. In most instances the full amount of interest charges is deducted from total current receipts in calculating profits.

Provision for Corporate Profits Tax, Dividends Paid, and Undistributed Profits. These three items add up to give the total profits of the corporation. Total profit is the difference between the costs and expenses discussed above and total current receipts; it represents what is left over after the correct amount has been allocated to pay back all the proper costs and expenses. Out of these total profits the corporation must pay the corporate profits tax. Another portion of the profits may be paid out to the stockholders in the form of dividends. The remainder, which will be left in the firm, is called "undistributed" profits.

SUMMARY: ACCOUNTS AS TOOLS OF ANALYSIS

Before leaving the accounts of the individual firm, it should be pointed out that the balance sheet and the income statement are frequently used as tools of analysis. As is true with most tools, their form will in large measure depend on the purpose for which they are designed. The income statement, for example, may serve many different purposes. The manager may wish to know the relative profitability of the different items that are produced; for this purpose, product classifications can be made with the cost items allocated as well as possible among these products. On the other hand, he may be interested in the relation between manufacturing, administrative, and selling cost, and classifications can be made along these lines. The stockholders might wish to know how much of the profit was obtained from direct operations and how much was nonoperating income such as interest on government bonds; the income and cost accounts could easily be separated to reveal this relationship. In inflationary periods some people may be interested in how much of the profit is due to the rising price level—a situation in which a firm sells products whose costs were incurred at lower price levels. This, too, can be shown if desired. The balance sheet, similarly, may be designed to reveal many different relationships. Interest may center about the relative liquidity of the firm; the asset and liability accounts can be drawn up to reveal this. Or the proportion of the assets used in producing various different products might be important, and this could be shown on the balance sheet. Stockholders frequently are interested in the proportion of the assets that has been acquired through the earnings of the firm and the proportion that has resulted from capital transactions. These questions and many more can be answered if the balance sheet is properly drawn up to show the answers.

In other words, there is no one necessarily correct form for either the balance sheet or the income statement, although there may be incorrect forms. A form is correct if it shows clearly and accurately what it is intended to show. A so-called general-purpose accounting statement may well be a compromise among many purposes and therefore inadequate for any of them. Presentation of complete detail may obscure relationships as well as add to the information that is given. Like all tools, accounting statements should be designed to fit the needs for which they are intended.

4. Production Statements for the Firm and for the Economy

The Difference between an Income Statement and a Production Statement

One of the major functions of the income statement discussed in Chap. 3 was to show the sales of goods and services by a firm and the costs and profits that were related to these sales. This statement is useful to the firm, since it gives a picture of the sources of income and the ways in which this income is allocated to the various elements of costs and profits in a given period. In many instances, however, there is also need for another, somewhat different type of statement. For some purposes the productive activity of a firm over a period, rather than its sales, is important. The economist, for example, is interested in the actual functioning of various parts of the economy and wishes to know such things as the amount of wages paid out over a given period and the quantity of product produced. The income statement cannot answer such questions, since it refers only to the goods *sold* during the period and the wages that can correctly be allocated to these goods.

The aim of the present chapter is to show how a production statement for the individual firm can be obtained from its income statement, and how in turn such production statements for firms can be consolidated and combined to yield a production statement for the whole economy. The usefulness of a production statement for the whole economy is obvious; it will show the total production that has occurred in all firms and productive units in the economy and at the same time the costs and other allocations accompanying such production. Such items as depreciation, business taxes, wages, salaries, interest, dividends, and undistributed profits will all be shown in their relation to each other and to production. The development of such a consolidated production statement is essential as a first step in describing the activity of the economy in terms of the interrelated transactions that take place.

The Relation between Sales and Production in the Firm

The amount of goods sold by a firm may be quite different from the amount of goods produced by that firm. Most firms have a stock or inventory of finished goods [1] from which sales are made. The process of production adds goods to these inventories, and sales remove goods from these inventories. It therefore follows that when finished goods inventories increase, production in the current period must have added more goods to inventories than current sales have removed. Current production is thus greater than current sales by the amount of the net increase in inventories. Similarly, it is obvious that when inventories are decreasing, current production is adding fewer goods to inventories than current sales are removing, so that current production is less than current sales by the amount of the net decrease in inventories. The net change in inventories, therefore, reflects the difference between sales and production in the firm; it is possible to calculate the actual value of goods produced from information on the value of goods sold and on the net change in inventory. The value of sales plus the net increase in inventories or minus the net decrease in inventories will equal the value of production.

Computing the value of the change in inventories presents some technical problems. In the appendix to Chap. 3 it was pointed out that inventory valuations can be made in a number of different ways. Over a period of time the prices of goods and materials in the economy change, and the same physical amount of inventories may thus be valued differently in different periods. For instance, a producer might have 1,000 units of a given good on hand at both the beginning and the end of the year; but if the price of the item went up during the year by $1 per unit, his end-of-year inventory might be valued $1,000 higher, according to the new level of prices. If the inventory change were calculated simply by taking the difference between the value of the inventory at the beginning of the year and at the end, it would appear that the inventory had increased and that the amount of this increase should be added to sales in deriving the value of production. Such a procedure, however, would not correctly represent the production that had taken place, and would result in including in profits the gain due to the new price. The physical amount of inventories in this example remained unchanged at 1,000 units in each time period, so that the physical change in inventories valued at its market price would in fact be zero, and it is this amount which should be added to sales to adjust the latter to production. The fact that the physical volume

[1] Stocks of goods and materials in process should also be included in inventories. This would complicate the analysis but would not invalidate the principle involved.

of inventories showed no change, in other words, points out that sales exactly matched production in this example, so that no inventory change should be shown.

Thus it is the *change in the physical volume of inventories valued at market prices* that is desired for the purpose of reconciling sales and production, rather than the *change in the valuation of the inventories* as listed in the accounts of the firm.

The Production Statement as Derived from the Income Statement

It follows from the above discussion that a production statement for the firm can be derived from the income statement by taking into account the change that has occurred in inventories and the costs and profits that would be related to such change. The change in inventories will appear on the side of the production statement showing sources of total current receipts. If there has been a net increase, it will be added to sales to obtain the value of production; if there has been a net decrease, it will be subtracted from sales to obtain the value of production. On the allocation side of the production statement the costs and profits will now refer to those goods which have been produced rather than to those which have been sold. The problem of determining the costs and profits is the same as it was for the income statement; the only difference is that a different bundle of goods is being examined. Table 5 shows how the income statement given in Table 2 of Chap. 3 might be revised to present a production statement for the firm.

Table 5. Production Statement for the Firm
(In thousands)

Allocations		Sources	
Goods and materials purchased from other producers..................	$ 640	Sales to Company A................	$ 700
		Sales to Company B................	250
Depreciation......................	70	Sales to Company C................	375
Taxes other than corporate profits taxes.........................	40	Sales to Company D................	80
		Other sales.......................	100
Social insurance contributions.......	27	Inventory increase.................	100
Wages and salaries................	695		
Net interest......................	10		
Provision for corporate profits taxes	49		
Net dividends paid................	47		
Undistributed profits..............	29		
Minus: Subsidies received..........	2		
Total allocations of value of production......................	$1,605	Total value of production........	$1,605

A comparison of this production statement with the income statement in Chap. 3 will show how the value of the inventory increase was distributed among the various cost and profit elements in the allocations. Depreciation, taxes, and interest are the same on both the income statement and the production statement. This is because most producers charge as an expense to sales all depreciation, taxes, and interest [2] incurred over the period; thus there would be no change in these items. Interest and dividends received have been subtracted from interest and dividends paid to obtain net interest and net dividends paid by this firm. The rationale of this procedure is that interest and dividends are payments for factors of production, and in calculating the value of production for this firm, only the net amount of this factor used by this firm should be considered. If a firm receives interest and dividends and turns around and pays the same amount out again as interest and dividends, it is merely passing such payments along to other groups rather than producing this amount of goods and services itself. By netting interest and dividends, only those payments of interest and dividends over and above receipts enter into the allocations of the total value of production. [3]

The change in each of the other items on the production statement shows the cost of the increased inventory. The difference between the total of these costs and the market value of the increased inventory is allocated to undistributed profits and the provision for corporate profits taxes. Subsidies, which appeared as a source of income in Table 2, do not constitute a sale of a product or service, and thus should not be included in the total market value of production. Excluding them from the sources side of the statement, however, requires an adjustment on the allocations side, since the allocations which a producer will make during the period will in fact exceed his value of production by the amount of the subsidies. With this adjustment, the two halves of the production statement will balance in the same way that the income statement does.

[2] Under some methods of cost accounting these items are allocated to each unit of production rather than charged entirely to sales during the period. If this procedure is followed, the amounts of these items on the production statement would, of course, differ from their amounts on the income statement.

[3] It would have been possible, of course, to treat interest and dividends received by a firm the same as receipts from any other sale, and at the same time to list any interest and dividends paid by the firm to other producers as a part of the total cost of goods and materials purchased from other producers. This alternative treatment would have the statistical disadvantage that it is hard to distinguish how much of the interest and dividend payments made by a firm goes to other producers and how much goes to individuals. Conceptually, also, this treatment would have the disadvantage that income arising from the productive activity of another firm would be reported as a part of the production of this firm.

The Production Statement for the Economy

The production statement for the firm shown in Table 5 forms the basis for developing a measure of the national output. Much as the production statement of a firm is drawn up around the value of its output, a production statement for the economy can be drawn up around the value of national output. The national output in terms of its market value, i.e., the total market value that has been created by the productive activity of the economy over the period of a year, will be referred to hereafter as the "gross national product." It is this measurement about which the production statement for the economy will be centered.

The Production Statement for the Economy as a Consolidated Statement

Such a production statement will show who purchased the national output and how the receipts from such production were allocated among the various elements of costs and profit in the economy. The economy will be treated as if it were a single producer, which produced goods and paid the various factors of production for helping in production. To accomplish this, all the production statements of individual producers in the economy will have to be consolidated and combined into one over-all production statement, which will add up to the value of the national output. A similar problem of consolidation often confronts a large corporation that owns many interrelated plants. Income statements are drawn up for each of the individual plants, but from these alone it is very difficult to determine the results of the activity of the whole corporation. A consolidated income statement is needed, and specific accounting procedures have been developed to present such an over-all view of the relation of all of this corporation's plants to the outside market. Such a consolidated statement will, by its very nature, omit certain internal transactions in order to bring out more clearly the relation of the corporation to the rest of the economy. Although these accounting procedures are in many cases complicated and involved, the principles upon which they are based are fairly simple. Before a measure of national output can be drawn up, these principles must be examined further.

Value Added by Producers Selling Their Products

Up to this point the term "value of production" has been used to refer to the total market value of the products turned out by a firm in a given period. But this total value of production is not, from the point of view of the economy as a whole, a satisfactory measure of the productive contribution of the firm. The individual firm does not create by its own activity and the activity of its employees all the market value of its products. Goods and materials pass through many different producers in the process of their manufacture, so that the total value of production for the economy cannot be obtained by adding up the value of production at each stage. This summation would yield the total volume of transactions that is related to the transfer of the goods produced rather than the total value of the output. A good that passed through the hands of a number of producers in the process of its manufacture would increase the value of production of each of these producers by an amount equal to its total value; adding up the value of production of all producers would therefore count this same good a great many times instead of just once. For this reason a measure is needed that will count for each producer only the value it *adds* to the goods it processes.

The value added by a firm, i.e., the value created by the activities of the firm and its employees alone, can be measured by the difference between the market value of the goods that have been turned out by the firm and the cost of those goods and materials purchased from other producers. This measure will exclude the contributions made by other producers to the total value of this firm's production, so that it is essentially equal to the market value created by this firm. The value added measure assesses the net contribution made by each firm to the total value of production; by adding up all of these contributions, therefore, it is possible to arrive at a total for the whole economy that will represent the market value of production.

An example may clarify this concept somewhat. Suppose that a producer buys parts to build radios and assembles these parts in his shop. The total value of the resulting products cannot be attributed to the productive activity of his shop alone. If he pays $50,000 for the necessary parts, and after assembling them into radios finds that he can sell them for $75,000, he has added $25,000 to the value of the products that other producers had already produced. His contribution to the value of production is therefore $25,000. This is the value he has added; it is a measure of the market value of the production that can be attributed to his activity.

The derivation of value added for a firm from its production statement is shown in Table 6. The sources side of the production statement is adjusted by subtracting from the total value of production the cost of goods and materials purchased from other producers. The remainder represents the value added by the activity of this firm. On the allocations side of the value added statement, the cost of goods and materials purchased from other producers is omitted. With this change, the remaining allocations absorb all the value that has been added.

Table 6. Statement of Value Added for the Firm
(In thousands)

Allocations		Sources	
Depreciation	$ 70	Sales to Company A	$ 700
Taxes other than corporate profits taxes	40	Sales to Company B	250
Social insurance contributions	27	Sales to Company C	375
Wages and salaries	695	Sales to Company D	80
Net interest	10	Other sales	100
Provision for corporate profits taxes	49	Inventory increase	100
Net dividends	47		
Undistributed profits	29	Total value of production	$1,605
Minus: Subsidies received	2	Minus: Goods and materials purchased from other producers	640
Total allocations of value added	$965	Total value added	$ 965

Value Added by Producers Not Selling Their Products

In addition to the producers who normally sell their products on the market, there are also producers who (1) directly consume their own output in their role as consumers, (2) receive income in kind instead of money for their services, or (3) give their services away. A farmer, for example, consumes some of the products he produces, so that they do not appear on the market. Similarly, an individual owning his own home obtains the rental services of his house without going through the market. In other cases such as that of domestic servants, a part of the income payment may be made by the employer in the form of the provision of food and lodging. Likewise, a bank, instead of making money interest payments to its depositors for the money they have placed in the bank, may provide checking services. Finally, certain nonprofit institutions such as research foundations, and general government, make their services available free of charge and thus they are not sold on the market. If the production for the economy as a whole is to include this nonmarket production, it will be necessary to impute a value of production and a value added to producers engaged in such activity. The methods of doing this for different kinds of producers are shown in some detail in the appendix to this chapter. However, it is not necessary to go into such detail in order to explain the general principles involved. Instead, the procedures for obtaining the value of government production and value added by the government will be outlined as an example, indicating the basic concepts involved for an important part of the economy, and at the same time developing the general form of the value added statement for producers who do not sell their products.

Like the individual business firm, a statement may be drawn up for the government showing total receipts on one side and total allocations on the other. Such a statement can be used as the basis for deriving the value added of government. This statement is given in summary form in Table 7. On the left-hand side of this account the sources of govern-

Table 7. Government Receipts and Outlay Statement *
(In billions)

Allocations		Sources	
Goods and materials purchased from other producers.........................	$50	Sales of goods and materials...........	$ 1
		Personal income tax..................	30
Wages and salaries of government employees............................	25	Social insurance contributions..........	9
		Corporate profits tax.................	20
Subsidies............................	1	Property taxes.......................	10
Transfers paid.......................	12	Excise taxes.........................	15
Interest on the public debt............	7	Licenses, fees, fines, and other taxes....	5
Surplus.............................	−1	Dividends and interest received........	2
		Current surplus of government enterprises	1
		Transfers received from abroad........	1
Total outlays......................	$94	Total receipts......................	$94

* Although the figures shown in this table are illustrative only, they show general magnitudes which approximate the data given for 1953 in later tables.

ment receipts are shown. For the most part, the receipts are obtained from various kinds of taxes. The item "sales of goods and materials" consists mainly of such things as war surplus stores. The sales of government enterprises that sell their products in the market are not included in this account; rather, these enterprises are considered individual firms similar to the one treated in the previous section of this chapter. Intergovernmental transfers such as Federal grants to local governments, or purchases of one government agency from another, are not shown as receipts for the government as a whole. The allocations side of the statement, similarly, shows the purchase of goods and services from producers other than the government.

The evaluation of government services based upon a Government Receipts and Outlay Statement as given above presents a dilemma. The government does not sell most of its output on the market, and thus strictly speaking there is no market valuation of it. Two alternative procedures are possible.

First, the fiction could be adopted that the tax payments made by various groups in the economy are equal to the amount at which government services are valued by these groups; that in a democratic economy the voters are willing to give up an amount in taxes equal to what they consider to be the value of government services. However, taxes may in fact be quite out of line with the level of government expenditures desired by individuals, as might be reflected in the existence of a large deficit in wartime or in the use of tax funds not for productive purposes but for redistribution among other individuals in the economy. Under such circumstances there could be a wide divergence between the value of government productive activity desired by individuals and the taxes which they pay.

As a second alternative for the valuation of government production, the government services which are rendered free to the economy can be counted at their cost. To make a calculation of this cost it is necessary to exclude from both the sources and the allocations sides of the Government Receipts and Outlay Statement all those categories which do not pertain to either the actual sale of government-produced goods and services or costs incurred in producing such goods and services.

On the sources side of the statement, all taxes, transfers (including current surplus of government enterprises), and by convention, licenses, fees, fines, dividends, and interest received are omitted, leaving only one item: sales of goods and materials. The logic of omitting licenses, fees, and fines is clear if one makes the decision that these are in fact compulsory payments similar in nature to taxes and so should be treated like taxes. The logic of omitting interest and dividends received from the sources side of the account follows from the definition of dividends and interest as factor income rather than the sale of a good or service.

On the allocations side, subsidies, transfer payments, surplus, and by convention, government interest paid, are not considered to be part of the cost of producing government goods and services, and thus are omitted, leaving only two items: goods and materials purchased from other producers, and wages and salaries. The logic of omitting government interest paid is somewhat complex and needs further explanation. It is argued by the Department of Commerce [4] that government interest payments should not be regarded as measuring value added to output by government because they are subject to fluctuations which in any common-sense notion cannot be regarded as representing corresponding changes in the value of current production. The exclusion of government interest paid stems, as a practical matter, from the fact that the bulk of the government debt was created to finance wars and current expenditures. Interest payments on such debt should therefore not be taken to represent currently produced goods and services or the current use of economic resources. For example, it seems sensible that a comparison of the prewar and postwar volumes of production should not be distorted

---

[4] National Income Supplement, 1951, *Survey of Current Business*, U. S. Department of Commerce, pp. 27, 48.

by the continuing interest on the national debt that arose during the war. For these reasons the Department of Commerce excludes the interest paid by the government.

The Government Receipts and Outlay Statement adjusted in this manner to reflect the cost of government-produced goods and services provides the basis for a production statement for government showing the total value of government production. Such a statement is given in Table 8. On the sources side of this production statement a balancing item has

Table 8. Production Statement for Government *

(In billions)

Allocations		Sources	
Goods and materials purchased from other producers........................	$50	Sales of goods and materials..........	$ 1
Wages and salaries of government employees...........................	25	Imputed value of goods and services not sold (net purchases of goods and services by government)................	74
Total value of government production	$75	Total value of government production	$75

* Although the figures shown in this table are illustrative only, they show general magnitudes which approximate the data given for 1953 in later tables.

been introduced equal to the total value of government production minus sales of goods and services by the government; this item is the imputed value of government goods and services not sold. This imputed value of government production not sold is in fact equal to the government's net expenditures on goods and services. This production statement balances in the same manner that the production statement for a firm shown in Table 5 balances. For general government, a net change in inventories is not calculated or included in the production statement.

As in the case of the individual firm, the production statement for the government can be converted into a value added statement by subtracting the purchases of goods and services from other producers. This has been done in Table 9. On the allocations side of the statement, the only item remaining is wages and salaries paid to government employees. The value added by government is thus equal to the compensation it pays its employees.

Value Added for the Economy

Value added for the economy as a whole can be obtained by adding up value added for producers who sell their output [5] and value added for

[5] Domestic servants and self-employed individuals such as doctors and lawyers are considered to be producers who sell their services, and their value added is computed in a manner similar to that shown for a firm in Table 6.

Table 9. Statement of Value Added for Government *
(In billions)

Allocations		Sources	
Wages and salaries of government employees......................	$25	Sales of goods and materials...........	$ 1
		Imputed value of goods and services not sold.............................	74
		Minus: Goods and materials purchased from other producers..............	50
Value added by government...........	$25	Value added by government..........	$25

* Although the figures shown in this table are illustrative only, they show general magnitudes which approximate the data given for 1953 in later tables.

Table 10. Value Added Statement for the Economy *
(In billions)

Allocations		Sources	
Depreciation........................	$ 25	Value of all goods and services produced for sale by producers..............	$865
Taxes other than corporate profits taxes	30	Minus: Purchases from other producers of goods, materials, and services used for market production............	550
Social insurance contributions........	9		
Wages and salaries..................	200		
Entrepreneurial income..............	50	Value added by market economy......	$315
Net interest.......................	15		
Corporate profits taxes..............	20	Value of all goods and services produced for direct consumption or not for sale by producers......................	$100
Net dividends.....................	9		
Undistributed profits...............	8		
Current surplus of government enterprises............................	1	Minus: Purchases from other producers of goods, materials, and services used for nonmarket production..........	55
Business transfer payments..........	1		
Minus: Subsidies...................	1		
Government interest.........	7		
Statistical discrepancy...............	0	Value added by nonmarket economy...	$ 45
Total value added................	$360	Total value added................	$360

* Although the figures shown in this table are illustrative only, they show general magnitudes which approximate the data given for 1953 in later tables.

producers who either consume their products directly or produce goods and services not for sale. This operation is carried out in Table 10. The sources side of the account simply shows the derivation of value added for the two kinds of output, and the summation of these two parts into a total value added for the economy. The value of all goods and services produced for sale by producers includes, as shown in Table 6, total sales by producers and the net change in producers' inventories.

The allocations side of the statement shown in Table 10 is very similar to the allocations side of the value added statement for the firm. Only five new categories have been added. "Entrepreneurial income" has been added to take into account the income received by noncorporate owners such as farmers, and by individuals who own their own homes (imputed rental income) or other rental property. "Current surplus of government enterprises" has been added to take into account the surplus or deficit earned by government enterprises. "Business transfer payments" has been included to take into account the gifts that businesses make to charitable organizations and the bad debts that producers cannot collect from individuals. "Government interest" is needed as an adjustment to allocations similar in nature to subsidies. It was pointed out in the discussion of government production above that the interest which the government pays to producers and individuals is not considered to be a part of its value added, and is therefore omitted from the valuation of government product on the sources side of the statement. Nevertheless, these interest payments do become a part of total allocations, just as subsidies paid by the government do. Therefore government interest must be subtracted from the allocations side, so that the allocations will not exceed the sources by this amount. Finally, the item "statistical discrepancy" arises because it is not possible empirically to make precisely accurate estimates of the magnitude of each item on the two sides of the statement. In any statistical presentation, therefore, the totals on the two sides of the statement will be found to be slightly different. The statistical discrepancy represents this difference; by including it as a residual, the two totals can be reconciled.

The sources side of the statement in the form shown in Table 10 contains a number of items that can be consolidated if they are classified into more comparable groups. For this purpose it will be useful to distinguish between transactions involving (1) consumers, (2) domestic producers on current account, (3) domestic producers on capital account, and (4) other countries (abroad). In addition, it will be useful to show the change in inventories, and the nonmarket production classified into that done by the government and that done by other producers. The sources side of Table 10 is reclassified in this manner in Table 11.

The major consolidation that is now possible is the subtraction of purchases by domestic producers from domestic producers from sales to domestic producers by domestic producers. These items are identical, since they comprise the same set of transactions seen from two points of view. Table 12 shows the sources side of the statement after this consoli-

Table 11. Reclassification of Value Added Statement for the Economy *
(*In billions*)

Allocations		Sources	
Depreciation	$ 25	Value of all goods and services produced for sale by domestic producers sold to:	
Taxes other than corporate profits taxes	30		
Social insurance contributions	9	*a.* Consumers	$200
Wages and salaries	200	*b.* Domestic producers on current account	590
Entrepreneurial income	50		
Net interest	15	*c.* Domestic producers on capital account	50
Corporate profits taxes	20		
Net dividends	9	*d.* Abroad	20
Undistributed profits	8	*e.* Net change in inventories	5
Current surplus of government enterprises	1	Value of all goods and services produced for direct consumption or not for sale by producers:	
Business transfer payments	1		
Minus: Subsidies	1	*a.* Net government expenditure on goods and services	75
Government interest	7	*b.* Other nongovernmental imputed goods and services	25
Statistical discrepancy	0	Minus: Total purchases of goods and services used for market and nonmarket production:	
		a. Domestic producers	590
		b. Abroad	15
Total value added	$360	Total value added	$360

* Although the figures in this table are illustrative only, they show general magnitudes which approximate the data given for 1953 in later tables.

dation. This table shows the actual figures for 1953, not merely illustrative ones as used in previous tables.

Consumers' expenditures in this table includes not only the sales made by producers to consumers in the market economy, but also the imputed value of nongovernmental goods and services directly consumed or not sold. The value of government goods and services not sold is shown on a net basis as "government expenditures on goods and services." "Gross expenditures on producers' durables" are the expenditures by producers on capital account. "Net change in inventories" is the same as that appearing on the unconsolidated statement shown in Table 11. "Exports and property income received" and "imports and property income paid" are more descriptive terms for the items "sales to abroad" and "purchases from abroad," since factor payments such as wages, interest, and dividends are included.

Table 12. Consolidated Production Statement for the Economy, 1953

(In billions) *

Allocations		Sources	
Depreciation	$ 27.2	Consumers' expenditures	$229.6
Taxes other than corporate profits taxes	30.1	Government expenditures on goods and services	77.2
Social insurance contributions	8.7	Gross expenditures on producers' durables	51.6
Wages and salaries	200.4	Net change in inventories	1.5
Entrepreneurial income	49.0	Exports and property income received	21.3
Interest paid to individuals and government	15.9	Minus: Imports and property income paid	16.4
Corporate profits taxes	21.1		
Dividends paid to individuals and government	9.4		
Undistributed profits	7.9		
Current surplus of government enterprises	0.8		
Business transfer payments	1.0		
Minus: Subsidies	0.2		
Government interest	7.4		
Statistical discrepancy	1.0		
Gross national income	$364.9	Gross national product	$364.9

* Detail may not add to totals because of rounding.

SOURCE: See Table 21.

The total value added for the economy as a whole has been entitled on the sources side of the account "gross national product." This title indicates that it is the sum of all products turned out in the economy, including gross rather than net expenditures on producers' durables. In other words, this aggregate includes the total addition to capital goods in this period, and does not take into account the diminution in capital that may have occurred due to the passage of time or to the consumption of capital in the productive process. Further discussion of this point is included in Chap. 6, where the national income accounting aggregates are discussed in greater detail. On the allocations side of the account, net interest and net dividends for all producers are retitled "interest paid to individuals and government" and "dividends paid to individuals and government." The interest and dividends paid to abroad have already been included as a part of imports and property income paid to abroad. The total on this side of the account is entitled "gross national income," to designate the income (gross of depreciation) that originates from productive activity in the economy. The breakdown given in Table 12 shows how the gross national product was used in the year 1953. Of a total of $364.9 billion produced, $229.6 billion, or 63 per cent of the total, represented the value of goods consumed by individuals. Another $77.2 billion, or 21 per cent, represented the cost of government goods and services. The value of capital goods produced was $51.6 billion, or 14 per cent of the total. Exports exceeded imports by $4.9 billion, indicating that net exports were 1 per cent of the total. Finally, the increase in inventories was $1.5 billion, indicating that total production in the economy exceeded total sales by $1.5 billion, or less than half of 1 per cent.

The consolidated production statement for the economy is thus based on a consolidation and combination of the production statements of individual productive units. It gives the total market value of the national output. The sources side of the consolidated production statement for the economy shows the relation between the total output produced and the output sold to the various purchasers in the economy. The allocations side of the consolidated production statement shows how the income arising from gross national product is split up among various kinds of payments. The current transactions that have taken place over a period of time are thus so consolidated and combined as to reveal the pattern of productive activity that has occurred in the economy.

APPENDIX TO CHAPTER 4. GROSS PRODUCT CALCULATIONS FOR SPECIFIC TYPES OF PRODUCTIVE UNITS

VALUE ADDED AND GROSS PRODUCT ORIGINATING

The explanation of the conversion of the income statement for firms and the receipts and outlay statements for the government and other productive units that do not sell their products into a production statement for the economy was carried out in this chapter in terms of the concept of value added. Value added by manufacture is a concept employed by the *Census of Manufactures* to show the production arising from manufacturing activity in firms. In the Census measure, nonmanufacturing costs and receipts are excluded from consideration. Gross product originating is substantively the same concept, except that it is applied to all kinds of productive activity. In this connection it will be useful to give specific consideration to gross product in financial institutions, unincorporated enterprises, and certain other productive units.

In calculating gross product it is found in most instances that it is somewhat simpler if the productive contribution of the firm is considered to be the total of the contributions of the factors of production and the other relevant allocations which the firm makes. This approach is the obverse of value added; what the value added approach obtains as a residual by deducting cost of goods and services purchased from other firms from the total value of production, gross product originating builds up element by element. For the simple case illustrated by the production statement shown in Table 5 both methods will result in the same figure.

GROSS PRODUCT IN FINANCIAL INSTITUTIONS

Problems arise in calculating gross product for financial institutions because of the treatment of interest and dividends. The interest and dividends received by such institutions often exceed the interest and dividends that they pay out. If the procedure outlined in the previous sections is followed, gross product for these institutions might then be negative. This result is a consequence of the omission of certain imputed transactions. The following section will discuss the addition of these imputations to the accounts, and show the derivation of gross product in these cases.

Imputed Interest as a Payment in the Form of Services

Financial institutions such as banks, insurance companies, and building and loan companies are quite different from other enterprises. They usually sell their services indirectly. For example, a commercial bank receives deposits that it may in turn lend out or use to buy securities yielding income. In return for the use of such deposits the commercial bank provides banking services.

60

A depositor may write checks on his account; and if his account is large, he may be permitted a large number of checks without having to pay any service charge. On the other hand, if his account is small, he may have to pay a service charge for every check he writes. Thus the bank pays its depositors for the use of their money by allowing them to draw checks on their accounts; it performs a service to the depositors in exchange for the use of their money. By paying the depositors interest on all the money deposited and at the same time charging each depositor a service charge according to the number of checks he has drawn, the bank could have made all the transactions that are going on *explicit* rather than *implicit*. The result of this procedure would be identical with the current practice, but it would make the function of the bank more explicit, so that it could readily be seen that the bank is selling a product—checking services for the individuals and firms who have accounts in the bank.

Table 13 presents an income statement for a commercial bank. This income statement does not explicitly show what has actually taken place, namely, that

Table 13. Income Statement for a Commercial Bank
(In thousands)

Allocations		Sources	
Goods and services purchased from other firms..............................	$ 40	Interest received on loans and securities $200	
Depreciation.......................	10	Dividends received on stocks held.....	50
Taxes other than corporate profits taxes	40	Payments of service charges by deposi-	
Bad debt expense..................	5	tors.............................	115
Contributions to charity............	5	Other income......................	35
Social insurance contributions........	10		
Cost of wages and salaries...........	195		
Interest paid......................	30		
Provision for corporate profits taxes...	25		
Dividends paid.....................	30		
Undistributed profits...............	10		
Total allocations of income........	$400	Total income....................	$400

the depositors have received payment for the use of their money in the form of banking services rather than cash. In order to develop a production statement that would make all the transactions explicit, it would be necessary to treat all interest and dividends which the bank receives as if they were paid to depositors and as if the depositors in turn repaid most of this money to the bank for rendering banking services. These two sets of transactions, although they do not actually take place, can be imputed to the bank and to the depositors. These imputed payments have been added to the two sides of the production statement shown in Table 14.

The amount of interest and dividends paid to depositors shown in Table 14 is actually $60,000. If all interest and dividends the bank received had been

Table 14. Production Statement for a Commercial Bank Showing Imputed Payments

(In thousands)

Allocations		Sources	
Goods and services purchased from other firms............................	$ 40	Interest received on loans and securities	$200
Depreciation........................	10	Dividends received on stock held......	50
Taxes other than corporate profits taxes	40	Payments of service charges by depositors............................	115
Bad debt expense..................	5	Other income......................	35
Contributions to charity.............	5		
Social insurance contributions........	10		
Wages and salaries.................	195		
Interest paid......................	30		
Provision for corporate profits taxes...	25		
Dividends paid....................	30		
Undistributed profits...............	10		
Imputed interest and dividends paid to depositors......................	190	Imputed payments of service charges by depositors......................	190
Total...........................	$590	Total...........................	$590

paid out, individuals would have received $250,000. An imputed interest payment of $190,000 ($250,000 − $60,000) must therefore be added to the allocations side of the account to represent the total payments (actual and imputed) made by the bank, and an equal amount of imputation must also be made on the sources side of the account to show the total receipts (actual and imputed) of the bank.

Once the adjusted production statement has been obtained, it is a simple matter to obtain a gross product account by following the procedure that has been set up for the general corporation. This is done in Table 15. Since the

Table 15. Gross Product Statement for a Commercial Bank

(In thousands)

Allocations		Sources	
Depreciation........................	$ 10	Payments of service charges by depositors............................	$115
Taxes other than corporate profits taxes	40	Other income......................	35
Bad debt expense..................	5	Imputed payments of service charges by depositors......................	190
Contributions to charity.............	5		
Social insurance contributions........	10		
Wages and salaries.................	195	Minus: Goods and services purchased from other firms..................	40
Provision for corporate profits taxes...	25		
Undistributed profits...............	10		
Total gross product...............	$300	Total gross product...............	$300

dividends and interest received by the bank exactly equal the actual dividends and interest paid plus the imputed interest, the netting of interest and dividends will result in zero interest and dividends on the allocations side of the account. The remaining adjustment to the allocations side, the omission of goods, materials, and services purchased from other firms, is the same as for the general corporation. On the sources side the subtraction of interest and dividends received by the bank leaves as the sources of gross product the actual payments of service charges by depositors, other income, and imputed payments by depositors, from which, as before, the goods and services purchased from other firms must be deducted.

Effect of Imputed Interest on the Gross Product of the Depositors

This treatment of imputed interest received by depositors and imputed service charges paid by depositors obviously affects the production statements of the depositors as well as that of the bank.

If the depositor is a business firm, the imputed interest received on deposits will appear on the sources side, and on the allocations side a corresponding increase in the services this firm is purchasing from other firms will appear. An alteration of Table 5 to show the effect of imputed interest and imputed service charges on the firm's production statement is given in Table 16.

Table 16. Production Statement for a General Corporation, Showing Imputed Interest Received and Imputed Charges Paid for Banking Services

(In thousands)

Allocations		Sources	
Goods, materials, and services purchased from other firms (including imputed payment for banking services of $1)......................	$ 641	Sales to Company A...............	$ 700
Depreciation.....................	70	Sales to Company B..............	250
Taxes other than corporate profits taxes........................	40	Sales to Company C..............	375
Social insurance contributions.......	27	Sales to Company D..............	80
Wages and salaries...............	695	Other sales.....................	100
Net interest......................	10	Change in inventories............	100
Provision for corporate profits taxes	49	Imputed interest received.........	1
Net dividends paid...............	47		
Undistributed profits.............	29		
Minus: Subsidies received.........	2		
Total........................	$1,696	Total........................	$1,606

The totals for both sources and allocations are larger than they were in Table 5 by the amount of the imputed interest and imputed service charges. Gross product, however, is smaller (see Table 17).

Table 17. Gross Product for a Corporation after Including Imputed Interest Received and Imputed Charges Paid for Banking Services

(In thousands)

Allocations		Sources	
Depreciation.........................	$ 70	Sales to Company A.................	$700
Taxes other than corporate profits taxes	40	Sales to Company B.................	250
Social insurance contributions.........	27	Sales to Company C.................	375
Wages and salaries..................	695	Sales to Company D.................	80
Net interest.......................	9	Other sales........................	100
Provision for corporate profits taxes...	49	Change in inventories...............	100
Net dividends paid..................	47	Minus: Goods, materials, and services	
Undistributed profits................	29	purchased from other firms........	641
Total...........................	$966		
Minus: Subsidies received...........	2		
Total gross product................	$964	Total gross product................	$964

Net interest is now smaller than it was before, since imputed interest received as well as actual interest received is subtracted from the interest paid to obtain net interest. The item "goods, materials, and services purchased from other firms" has increased, thus making the gross product contribution of this firm less than before.

A depositor who is a private individual would also have his accounts altered by the imputed interest and imputed service charges. The imputed interest would increase his personal income, and the imputed service charges would be an equal addition to his expenditures.

Imputed Interest as Withheld Interest Payment

Imputed interest payments of the type discussed above are not the only type of imputed interest of which account must be taken. Certain financial institutions such as life insurance companies, mutual banks, savings and loan associations, and credit unions may receive interest and dividends that accrue to the accounts of the participants but are not currently paid out by the financial intermediaries to individuals in the form of monetary interest payments. This income which is not paid out is treated as imputed interest accruing to the participants. Once this adjustment has been made, the gross product measurements may be carried through in much the same way as has been shown above.

The attention given to the problem of interest is out of proportion to its importance in the gross national product, but it is important to have some knowledge of the various imputations if the allocation of net interest in the economy and the place of financial institutions in the national income and product account are to be understood.

Gross Product in Unincorporated Business Enterprises

The ordinary unincorporated enterprise does not pose any special problems, except that the titles of some of the accounts on the allocations side of the income statement will be different from those shown for an incorporated enterprise, and certain items will never appear on the sources side. Since many unincorporated enterprises are owned by proprietors who contribute their own efforts to the organization, the net return realized by the firm may be a combination of wages, salary, interest, rent, and profit. Unlike the corporation, there will be no dividends, corporate profits taxes, or undistributed profits. After all other appropriate allocations have been made, the remaining amount will be termed "net income of proprietor." Personal taxes on this income are not considered to be an allocation by the business but rather an allocation by the proprietor as an income receiver. On the sources side, the unincorporated business enterprise will not receive either interest or dividends.[6] All such payments will be treated as part of the personal income of the proprietor rather than part of the gross product of the firm.

Aside from these minor problems of classification and definition, certain distinct problems do arise for special types of unincorporated enterprises. Two of these will be considered below to show the general principles of treatment involved.

Unincorporated Farm Enterprises

The farmer, operating a farm that he owns or rents, is an example of a common type of unincorporated enterprise. Calculating the gross product for a farm enterprise involves a consideration of more than just the monetary income statement for the farm. Some of the production of the farm is never sold but is consumed by the farmer and his family; if only the production that is sold and its related costs were considered, the actual value of production and its allocation would be understated. Furthermore, the farmer receives the productive services of the farmhouse he lives in and in turn must make allowance for the depreciation and other expenses of his house. Although these do not represent cash income, they are nevertheless output that would have a value on the market if sold, i.e., if the home-consumed products were sold or if the house were rented. They must therefore be included in the production statement. Adjustments for these elements as well as the usual adjustments for inventory changes have been made in the production statement shown in Table 18.

The imputed value of the farm products consumed is obtained by taking the value (at prices received by the farmer) of the estimated home consumption of farm products. The taxes shown on the allocations side do not include personal income taxes since, as was pointed out above, personal income taxes are considered to be an allocation of personal income rather than of the income of the unincorporated enterprise. The allocation to wages

---

[6] An exception is made for unincorporated financial institutions, which are treated in a manner parallel to the treatment of incorporated financial institutions.

Table 18. Production Statement for an Unincorporated Farm Enterprise

Allocations		Sources	
Goods, materials, and services purchased from other firms..........	$ 300	Sales of farm products.............	$2,750
Depreciation (farm equipment, buildings, and house)................	150	Change in farm inventories.........	50
		Imputed value of farm products consumed........................	850
Taxes...........................	100	Imputed gross rental value of farmhouse.........................	250
Wages..........................	1,000		
Interest........................	50		
Net income of proprietor..........	2,500		
Minus: Agricultural subsidies......	200		
Total.....................	$3,900	Total.........................	$3,900

includes those payments in money and in kind which the farmer makes for his hired labor. The calculation of gross product from this production statement can be carried out for the farm enterprise following the procedure outlined above for the general corporation.

Unincorporated Lessors of Real Property

All lessors of real property are considered business enterprises. Anyone who rents any building or property that he owns is treated as operating an enterprise that contributes to gross national product. The gross rental received for renting the building or property represents the sources side of the total value of production for the enterprise, and the expenses, depreciation, taxes, and net rental income represent the corresponding allocations.

Table 19. Production Statement for an Unincorporated Lessor of Real Property

Allocations		Sources	
Goods, materials, and services purchased from other firms for maintenance........................	$ 150	Gross rents received..............	$1,200
Depreciation....................	400		
Taxes...........................	450		
Interest........................	50		
Net rental income of owner........	150		
Total.....................	$1,200	Total.........................	$1,200

This is shown in Table 19. The derivation of gross product from this production statement again follows the usual procedure.

As a corollary to the treatment of unincorporated lessors of real property, it follows that owner-occupied houses also yield gross product, although the services of these houses do not appear on the market. The owner, instead of receiving net rental income from the house, receives imputed net rental income in the form of the services that the house provides for him. For this reason all owners of houses are treated as lessors of real property, having production accounts such as Table 19. The only difference from Table 19 would be that the gross rents received on the sources side would appear as "imputed gross rent" and the net rental income of the owner on the allocations side would also be imputed. In the personal accounts of the owner the imputed rental income would be added to personal income and the imputed gross rental paid would be added to expenditures.

Gross Product in Other Kinds of Productive Units

In addition to the types of productive unit described above, there are a number of others that do not pose any special problems but should be mentioned in order to indicate the general way they are treated.

Government Enterprises

The government contains some productive units the products of which are sold on the market. Post offices, local water departments, and publicly owned power stations all sell their products and services to the public. These productive units are classed as government enterprises. The derivation of the gross product account for such government enterprises raises no special problems. On the sources side products and services and the change in inventories are valued at their market prices. Any funds received by the enterprise from the government that are not in return for goods and services sold are not considered a part of gross product. On the allocations side most of the items found on the gross product statement for a business firm will appear. A few of the items, such as profits, are not applicable, and one new item, current surplus, will appear instead of profits.

General Government

The treatment of general government economic activity according to the value added approach has already been covered in the body of this chapter. A gross product measurement of general government's productive contribution would be identical with the value added measurement.

Nonprofit Institutions

The value of production for nonprofit institutions which are engaged in productive activity and do not sell their products or services (e.g., research foundations, religious and educational institutions) is imputed at cost. If the receipts of the nonprofit institution come from property income, the gross product calculation is carried out in a manner similar to that for financial institutions. The nonprofit institution is considered to be receiving the property income on behalf of individual consumers as a group, and the use of this income is also treated as a consumer outlay on the services of nonprofit institutions. Thus an amount equal to the property income received by the nonprofit institution is added to the allocations side of their account as imputed property income received by individuals as a group, and on the sources side an equal amount would be imputed as consumers' expenditures on services of nonprofit institutions. Gross product is then calculated in the usual way, with the actual property income received subtracted from the imputed property income paid. If the activities of the nonprofit institution are financed by gifts or depletion of capital funds, there would be no income to be included with individuals' incomes, but the services provided by the nonprofit institution would be valued at cost and would be included in consumers' expenditures on goods and services.

Household Employees

To take into account the productive activity of household employees, the household is considered to be a productive unit. On the allocations side of this statement will be the compensation of household employees (domestic servants), including not only cash payment but also payment in kind (food, shelter, etc.). On the sources side this will be balanced by an equal item called "consumers' expenditures for household services." Since there are no other items in this statement, the gross product would be equal to the compensation of the employees. It would be possible, of course, to consider the housewife an employee of the household and impute payment in kind to her, or to value her services at the market value of domestic service. Since she is also a member of the household, it would also be necessary to impute an equal amount of additional income to the household. The financial position of the household (i.e., total income minus total expenditures) would remain unchanged by this imputation. In view of the arbitrary nature of this particular imputation, however, it has never been made in the United States national accounts, and is not now made in the national accounts of any other country.

5. A System of National Income Accounts for the Economy

The Definition of Economic Sectors

One of the major purposes of developing national income accounts is to provide information about the structure and functioning of the economic system itself. For this purpose it is useful to split the economy up into various parts, so that internal relationships can be observed. The parts into which the economy is split will be referred to in this chapter as "sectors." The accounts for these sectors will always be so defined that taken together they reflect all the current economic activity that takes place.

Many different kinds of sector breakdown of the economy are possible. There is nothing inherent in the concept that limits the number of sectors that may be used. For some purposes it would be useful to split the economy into only two sectors; but for other purposes a much finer subdivision of economic activity would be needed, with literally hundreds of sectors, all related to each other by direct or indirect chains of transactions. For different economic problems, furthermore, different types of sector classification would be useful. Those interested in regional development might want a regional breakdown, showing the growth and change of one region relative to another, and the transactions taking place between the various regions. For the purpose of planning national defense, an industrial breakdown might be very useful, emphasizing the relationships between the heavy industries and other industries in the economy.

In this chapter a functional sector breakdown of economic activity is used. This type of sector breakdown is consistent with the conventional national income accounts used both in the United States and in other countries, and it yields a system of accounts that can be used to describe the determination of prices, output, and employment in the economy. Three sectors will be used: (1) the producing sector, (2) the consuming sector, and (3) the government sector. These sectors include the economic activity of the whole economy, in the sense that an exhaustive listing of all the possible transactors in the economy can be fitted into these three groups. The sectors are functional in that they classify the function of the transaction under consideration rather than the nature of the individual or agency involved in the transaction. For example, a farmer is considered to be in the producing sector whenever the farmer acts in his role as a producer, combining factors of production to produce output. This same farmer, however, is considered to be in the consuming sector with respect to all transactions concerning his consuming household. The exact manner in which this separation is made will become clear in the following sections dealing with each sector. Here it is important to emphasize that the classification system used is not one which separates *individuals* into various groups with respect to their total activity but rather one which separates *transactions* according to their function.

The functions contemplated in this sector classification are rather obvious from the titles of the sectors. It will readily be recognized that production and consumption differ in nature. Although it would perhaps be possible to divide government activity into production and consumption, there is excellent reason for considering government as a separate functional sector. To the extent that the government is in fact a producer, its activity will be recorded in the producing sector, but the rest of the activities of the government are less easily assigned. Thus the collection of taxes, the giving of transfer payments, and even government expenditures on goods and services do not readily fit into either of the categories of production or consumption. If "public consumption" is excluded from the consuming sector, furthermore, the latter becomes a more easily understandable concept.

The producing, consuming, and government sectors are composed of decision-making transactors. The producer makes decisions on the basis of the transactions that have occurred in the past and those that he expects to occur in the future. The consumer operates within a budget of income received, making outlays from this budget. The government makes conscious policy decisions with respect to its taxation and expenditure.

An account can be drawn up for each of these sectors that will reflect its current activity. The account for the producing sector will reflect the productive activity of the economy, together with the manner in which producers allocate the income they receive from production. The accounts for consumers and government will consist of the current income and outlay of these sectors.

Although it would be possible to construct a national income accounting system having just these three accounts, the system can be made more meaningful if the transactions of the economy with foreign countries and the capital transactions that affect current income are shown separately and explicitly. These two additional accounts could be shown for each of the three sectors. In the system of accounts chosen here, however, one combined account indicating the foreign trade and payments of all sectors taken together, and one combined account showing the gross saving and investment of all sectors, will be used instead.

The Producing Sector Account

In the preceding chapter the accounts that record the activity of producers in the economy were discussed in considerable detail, and a consolidated production statement embracing the productive activity of all producers in the economy was drawn up. This production statement is repeated in Table 20.

Table 20. Consolidated Production Statement for the United States Economy, 1953
(In billions) *

Allocations		Sources	
Depreciation	$ 27.2	Consumers' expenditures	$229.6
Taxes other than corporate profits taxes	30.1	Government expenditures on goods and services	77.2
Social insurance contributions	8.7	Gross expenditures on producers' durables	51.6
Wages and salaries	200.4		
Entrepreneurial income	49.0	Net change in inventories	1.5
Interest paid to individuals and government	15.9	Exports and property income received	21.3
Corporate profits taxes	21.1	Minus: Imports and property income paid	16.4
Dividends paid to individuals and government	9.4		
Undistributed profits	7.9		
Current surplus of government enterprises	0.8		
Business transfer payments	1.0		
Minus: Subsidies	0.2		
Government interest	7.4		
Statistical discrepancy	1.0		
Gross national income	$364.9	Gross national product	$364.9

* Detail may not add to totals because of rounding.
SOURCE: See Table 21.

To be useful in economic analysis, the presentation in Table 20 needs to be changed somewhat and different terminology introduced. Since the purpose of developing sector accounts is to relate the activity of the

Table 21. Gross National Income and Product Account for the United States, 1953

(In billions) *

1. Payments by producers to individuals..........................		$281.9
a. Compensation of employees......		209.1
(1) Enterprise employees......		177.7
(2) Government employees....		31.4
b. Interest and dividends........		22.8
c. Entrepreneurial income.......		49.0
(1) Farm income.............		12.2
(2) Rental income...........		10.6
(3) Professional income......		
(4) Other income of unincorporated enterprises......		26.2
(*a*) Book value...........		26.4
(*b*) Minus: Inventory valuation adjustment......		0.2
d. Business transfer payments....		1.0
2. Income retained by producers....		35.1
a. Depreciation allowances.......		27.2
(1) Private enterprises........		27.2
(2) Public enterprises........		0.0
b. Undistributed profits.........		7.9
(1) Book value..............		8.9
(2) Minus: Inventory valuation adjustment..............		1.0
3. Tax and income payments by producers to government...........		54.4
a. Corporate profits taxes.......		21.1
b. Property taxes...............		9.1
c. Commodity and transactions taxes.......................		16.9
d. Licenses, fees, and other business taxes..................		4.1
e. Interest and dividends received by government...............		2.4
f. Current surplus of government enterprises..................		0.8
4. Minus: Subsidies and government interest.......................		7.6
a. Subsidies....................		0.2
b. Government interest..........		7.4
5. Statistical discrepancy..........		1.0

6. Consumers' expenditures on goods and services...................		$229.6
a. Food......................		77.2
b. Clothing...................		24.6
c. Housing...................		27.7
d. Other.....................		100.1
7. Government expenditures on goods and services.............		77.2
a. Federal....................		53.7
(1) National security........		45.8
(2) Agriculture and agricultural resources..........		3.9
(3) Natural resources........		0.8
(4) Veterans' services........		0.9
(5) Social security, welfare, and health..............		0.4
(6) Education and general research...................		0.1
(7) General government.....		1.1
(8) Other †.................		1.1
(9) Minus: Government sales		0.4
b. State and local..............		23.5
(1) Natural resources........		0.7
(2) Highways..............		4.8
(3) Public welfare...........		0.5
(4) Health and hospitals.....		2.3
(5) Education..............		8.9
(6) Police, fire, and sanitation		2.4
(7) General control.........		1.3
(8) Other ‡.................		2.6
8. Gross expenditures on producers' durables......................		51.6
a. Private enterprises..........		49.9
(1) Construction............		25.5
(2) Equipment.............		24.4
b. Public enterprises...........		1.7
(1) Federal................		0.2
(2) State and local..........		1.5
9. Net change in enterprise inventories......................		1.5
10. Exports and property income received......................		21.3
a. Merchandise exports........		16.5
b. Shipping services and tourism receipts...................		2.9
c. Property income received from abroad...................		1.9
Subtotal......................		$381.2
11. Minus: Imports and property income paid....................		16.4
a. Merchandise imports........		11.0
b. Shipping services and tourism		5.0
c. Property income paid to abroad		0.5

Gross national income.............	$364.9
Gross national product.............	$364.9

Table footnotes on p. 73.

different sectors to one another, one of the more useful forms of setting out the account for any sector is to group flows to each specific other sector of the economy together, and to develop subclassifications that reveal clearly the composition of the grouped flows. Such a rearrangement is presented in Table 21. The name of the account has also been changed to reflect more explicitly the content of its two sides. This table does not employ any categories or concepts that have not already been used in the discussion of the production statement for the economy; it is merely rearranged. The various flows will be discussed in somewhat greater detail below, in order to clarify the nature of the classifications.

Item 1 embraces all payments that producers make to individuals. These are classified as (a) compensation of employees, (b) interest and dividends paid, (c) entrepreneurial income paid, and (d) business transfer payments. The breakdown of the compensation of employees shows the amount paid to employees of private enterprise and the amount paid to government employees. Entrepreneurial income is broken down into the income of farmers, rental income (including imputed income of owner-occupied houses), professional income (doctors, lawyers, etc.), and other income of unincorporated enterprises. Business transfer payments are the payments that producers make to individuals or nonprofit institutions in the form of gifts (e.g., charitable contributions) or the bad debts that business cannot collect from individuals.

The inventory valuation adjustment, shown as a subtraction from the income of unincorporated enterprises under item 1 (and also again under item 2 below) is necessary since the profits reported by many businesses are calculated by taking into account the change in the total value of inventories held, and thus including as a part of profit the gain or loss resulting from the fluctuations in the prices at which goods were purchased. As was pointed out in Chap. 4, what is needed for the production statement is a measure of the change in the physical volume of inventories valued at current market prices. On the sources side of the pro-

---

Footnotes for Table 21

* Detail may not add to totals because of rounding.

† Includes transportation and communication; finance, commerce, and industry; and labor and manpower.

‡ Includes housing and community development; nonhighway transportation; and other and unallocable.

SOURCE: The data in the above table and other related tables in this and the preceding chapter were obtained mainly from National Income Supplement, 1954, *Survey of Current Business*, U.S. Department of Commerce, Tables 1–30. In addition, data on imports and exports were obtained from the *Survey of Current Business*, July, 1954, Table 1, p. 14. For certain estimates, e.g., the separation of current surplus of government enterprises from subsidies, the gross unilateral transfers to and from abroad, and the functional breakdown of government expenditures, data were supplied directly by the National Income Division of the Department of Commerce. The classifications used for federal government expenditures correspond to Bureau of the Budget classifications. State and local government expenditures are based on census classifications of direct general expenditures.

duction statement the net change in inventories is in fact valued according to this concept, but on the allocations side profits are those reported by business firms, and so contain the inventory loss or gain due to changing prices. The inventory valuation adjustment is the difference in terms of dollar valuations between the *value of the change in inventories* computed for the economy, and the business community's reports on the *change in the value of inventories*. The inventory valuation adjustment thus gives the amount by which the allocations side of the account must be adjusted to make the profits figures reported by business consistent with the method of valuing the change in inventories used on the sources side of the account. The amount shown as an adjustment to the income of unincorporated enterprises relates, of course, only to their inventories; the remainder of the inventory valuation adjustment appears in item 2.

Item 2 includes all those income items that are retained by producers. These are either depreciation allowances[1] or undistributed profits. The depreciation allowances are further broken down into those for private enterprises and those for public enterprises. In the case of the United States no data are available for depreciation allowances of public enterprises. The fixed assets of government enterprises in the United States are included in the general government budget as a part of current government expenditures on goods and services. As such current expenditures, these fixed assets of government enterprises are considered consumed when purchased by the government. All countries, however, do not follow this practice; investments in public enterprises are sometimes depreciated over the years. In these cases there would be an entry for the depreciation allowances on these capital goods. Undistributed profits are shown as reported by corporations, with the applicable inventory valuation adjustment shown explicitly.

Item 3, tax and income payments by producers to government, includes all the payments that business (including government enterprises) makes to the government. It consists of six subgroups: (*a*) corporate profits taxes, (*b*) property taxes, (*c*) commodity and transactions taxes, (*d*) licenses, fees, fines, customs duties, and other business taxes, (*e*) interest and dividends received by the government, and (*f*) the current surplus of government enterprises.

The fourth major item on the allocations side of the account contains two flows which must be deducted in order to arrive at the desired total; their treatment has already been discussed in connection with the deriva-

---

[1] Besides the actual depreciation allowances charged by producers, the aggregate depreciation charges will also include those capital outlays which are charged to current expense. In the Department of Commerce definition, accidental damage to fixed capital is also taken into account, yielding the concept "capital consumption allowances."

tion of the consolidated production statement. These are subsidies and government interest. The last item is the statistical discrepancy, which has also been discussed above.

On the sources side of the account the rearrangement is not great, and there are only relatively minor changes in terminology, but considerable detail has been added in order to make the content of the various items more evident. Thus item 6, consumers' expenditures on goods and services, is broken down into expenditures on food, clothing, housing, and other, all of which are largely self-explanatory.

Item 7, government expenditures on goods and services (net), has been broken down into (a) Federal and (b) state and local expenditures. The classifications within these two categories are functional in nature, that is, the purposes for which the money has been spent rather than the actual kinds of expenditures are shown.

Item 8, gross expenditures on producers' durables, has been classified into expenditures by private enterprises and by public enterprises, and private enterprise expenditures have been further broken down into expenditure on construction and expenditure on equipment. Item 9, net change in enterprise inventories, is identical with the similar item, net change in inventory, shown on the consolidated production statement on page 71. Item 10, exports and property income received, is identical with exports as shown on the consolidated production statement. Merchandise exports, shipping and tourism receipts, wages and salaries paid from abroad, and property income received from abroad are shown as components of this total. Item 11, imports and property income paid, is the same as imports shown on the consolidated production statement; it contains the same sort of detail as is given for exports, and is an offset to the total of the preceding items, giving the gross national product as the final summation on the sources side of the account.

Thus the account for the producing sector shows the allocations that producers make to individuals and to government, and the amount they retain, on the one side, and the expenditures of consumers, of government, and of business on capital account, and the sales and purchases to and from abroad, on the other side. In this manner the consolidated production statement for the economy has been cast into the form of a sector account showing the relationship of the function of producing to other functional activities in the economy.

The Consuming Sector Account

The consuming sector is concerned with the activities of individual households and nonprofit institutions in their role as private consumers. The account for this sector shows the income received by these consuming units on the one hand, and their total outlays and saving on the other hand. The total income of this sector is called personal income, and the account itself is entitled the Personal Income and Outlay Account. It is shown in Table 22.

Table 22. Personal Income and Outlay Account for the United States, 1953

(In billions) *

1. Consumers' expenditures on goods and services	$229.6		5. Payments by producers to individuals	$281.9
a. Food	77.2		a. Compensation of employees	209.1
b. Clothing	24.6		(1) Enterprise employees	177.7
c. Housing	27.7		(2) Government employees	31.4
d. Other	100.1		b. Interest and dividends	22.8
2. Tax payments by individuals	44.6		c. Entrepreneurial income	49.0
a. Income taxes	32.5		(1) Farm income	12.2
b. Total social insurance contributions	8.7		(2) Rental income	10.6
			(3) Professional income	
c. Fees, fines, personal property and other taxes	3.4		(4) Other income of unincorporated enterprises	26.2
3. Transfer payments by individuals to abroad	0.5		(a) Book value	26.4
4. Personal saving	20.0		(b) Minus: Inventory valuation adjustment	0.2
			d. Business transfer payments	1.0
			6. Transfer payments by government to individuals	12.8
			7. Transfer payments from abroad to individuals	0.0
Personal outlay and saving	$294.7		Personal income	$294.7

* Detail may not add to totals because of rounding.
SOURCE: See Table 21.

The flows in Table 22 are again classified according to the sectors in the economy from which they are derived or to which they go. The major source of personal income is the payments made by producers to individuals for their services or for the services of their property. This flow and its detail are identical with the same item as it appeared on the Gross National Income and Product Account as an allocation by producers.

Individuals also receive transfer payments from the government. These transfer payments consist of such things as relief payments, veterans' bonuses, and social security payments. The characteristic which all of these transfer payments have in common is that they are payments made by the government to individuals for reasons other than the purchase of services from these individuals. The government's compensation of employees and the interest paid by the government to individuals is included above in payments by producers to individuals.

Individuals may also receive transfer payments from abroad. Gifts of money sent from abroad to individuals in this country augment the income of those individuals receiving them, and are thus a part of total personal income.

Individuals do make gifts of money to other individuals, and it would be possible to include these as a part of personal income also. They are omitted in the account above, however, since a gift by one individual to another reduces the first individual's income by the same amount that it increases the second individual's income, leaving personal income for all individuals as a group unchanged. In other words, the Personal Income and Outlay Account is a consolidated account insofar as interpersonal gifts are concerned.

The allocations side of the Personal Income and Outlay Account shows the expenditures for goods and services by consumers, the tax payments that individuals make to the government, and the transfer payments (gifts) that are made by individuals to abroad. The remaining item, personal saving, is a residual; it is defined as the excess of personal income over outlays for all individuals as a group. Although total personal saving will generally be a positive item, it is not necessarily positive for all individuals in the economy. Many groups (e.g., unemployed individuals, retired persons, students, and low income families) spend more in a single year than their incomes in that year. They may draw on past accumulations of saving, receive gifts from other individuals, or go into debt.

It should be noted that the personal saving item does not imply that individuals are accumulating this amount of cash. A purchase of a house by an individual, for example, is not considered a part of consumers' expenditures on current consumption; such outlays, and outlays such as the purchase of securities, are alternative forms of personal saving.

The Government Account

The Government Receipts and Outlay Account has already been discussed in the previous chapter in connection with the derivation of the value of government product and the value added by the government. All that needs to be done here is to regroup the flows so that they fit into the sector classifications set up in this chapter. Such a rearranged Government Receipts and Outlay Account is shown in Table 23.

The sources side of this account shows receipts from producers and individuals, and transfers received from abroad. The item "transfer payments to government from abroad" covers such things as foreign aid received by the country. In the case of the United States this is not a major item, but for some countries it was of considerable importance in the immediate postwar period.

Table 23. Government Receipts and Outlay Account for the United States, 1953

(In billions) *

1. Government expenditures on goods and services	$77.2	7. Tax and income payments by producers to government	$54.4
a. Federal	53.7	*a.* Corporate profits tax	21.1
(1) National security	45.8	*b.* Property taxes	9.1
(2) Agriculture and agricultural resources	3.9	*c.* Commodity and transactions taxes	16.9
(3) Natural resources	0.8	*d.* Licenses, fees, and other business taxes	4.1
(4) Veterans' services	0.9	*e.* Interest and dividends received by government	2.4
(5) Social security, welfare, and health	0.4	*f.* Current surplus of government enterprises	0.8
(6) Education and general research	0.1	8. Tax payments by individuals	44.6
(7) General government	1.1	*a.* Income taxes §	32.5
(8) Other †	1.1	*b.* Total social insurance contributions	8.7
(9) Minus: Government sales	0.4	*c.* Fees, fines, personal property, and other taxes	3.4
b. State and local	23.5	9. Transfer payments to government from abroad	0.1
(1) Natural resources	0.7		
(2) Highways	4.8		
(3) Public welfare	0.5		
(4) Health and hospitals	2.3		
(5) Education	8.9		
(6) Police, fire, and sanitation	2.4		
(7) General control	1.3		
(8) Other ‡	2.6		
2. Subsidies and government interest	7.6		
a. Subsidies	0.2		
b. Government interest	7.4		
3. Capital grants to government enterprises	1.7		
a. Federal	0.2		
b. State and local	1.5		
4. Transfer payments by government to individuals	12.8		
5. Transfer payments by government to abroad	6.3		
6. Government surplus	−6.6		
Government outlay and surplus	$99.1	Government receipts	$99.1

* Detail may not add to totals because of rounding.

† Includes transportation and communication; finance, commerce, and industry; and labor and manpower.

‡ Includes housing and community development; nonhighway transportation; and other and unallocable.

§ Net of tax refunds.

SOURCE: See Table 21.

On the allocations side of the Government Receipts and Outlay Account the government's expenditures on goods and services are shown in exactly the same detail as appeared on the sources side of the Gross National Income and Product Account. Subsidies and net government interest appeared previously as an adjustment to the allocations side of the Gross National Income and Product Account. The next item, capital grants to government enterprises, consists of those funds provided by the general government for capital formation in public enterprises; since these funds are not regarded as current income by the public enterprise producers receiving them, they will not enter the Gross National Income and Product Account. Government transfer payments to individuals are the same as those shown as receipts by individuals on the sources side of the Personal Income and Outlay Account. Transfers to abroad covers economic aid given by the government to other countries. When the government purchases goods and services (e.g., military goods) and gives them to other countries, however, these might not appear as transfers to abroad by the government, but instead could be classified as a part of government expenditures on goods and services. Considerable confusion exists regarding the line of demarcation between government expenditures on goods and services given to other countries and transfer payments to other countries. Unfortunately, this confusion cannot be dispelled by making an arbitrary rule since it is not always obvious, especially in the case of military aid, whether an item is a gift or is in fact a use of resources by the domestic government in its own self-interest. For this reason no attempt at separation is made by the Department of Commerce in drawing up the United States accounts; it treats all gifts by the government to abroad as a part of government expenditures on goods and services.

The residual in the government account is the item "government surplus." Whenever government outlays exceed government receipts, this item will be negative, indicating that the government has a deficit of this amount.

Foreign Trade and Payments Account

As has been pointed out above, the Foreign Trade and Payments Account is not a sector account like the other accounts discussed thus far. Rather, this account consolidates the transactions between the various domestic sectors of the economy on the one hand, and foreign countries on the other hand. The Foreign Trade and Payments Account is shown in Table 24.

The sources side of this account lists those items which provide receipts for the foreign countries, and the allocations side shows how these foreign countries allocate payments to the various domestic sectors. Im-

Table 24. Foreign Trade and Payments Account for the United States, 1953

(In billions) *

1. Exports and property income received..............................	$21.3		5. Imports and property income paid.	$16.4
a. Merchandise exports............	16.5		a. Merchandise imports..........	11.0
b. Shipping services and tourism...	2.9		b. Shipping services and tourism...	5.0
c. Property income received from abroad........................	1.9		c. Property income paid to abroad.	0.5
2. Transfer payments to individuals from abroad......................	0.0		6. Transfer payments from individuals to abroad........................	0.5
3. Transfer payments to government from abroad......................	0.1		7. Transfer payments from government to abroad....................	6.3
4. Net borrowing from abroad.......	1.9			
Receipts from abroad...............	$23.2		Payments to abroad...............	$23.2

* Detail may not add to totals because of rounding.
SOURCE: See Table 21.

ports into the domestic economy and property income paid to foreigners, together with the transfers given to them by individuals and government, total up to the receipts of foreigners. Exports made by the domestic economy and property income paid by foreigners, together with the transfer payments received from foreigners by individuals and government, give the total payments to the domestic sectors by foreigners.

The residual item in this account is net borrowing from abroad. If the payments made to foreigners exceed the receipts from foreigners, this deficit will have to be made up either from loans or through a decrease in the current holdings of foreign assets by the domestic economy, and vice versa.

The Gross Saving and Investment Account

The Gross Saving and Investment Account, like the Foreign Trade and Payments Account, does not refer to a single sector. It is used instead to record all those transactions or residual items that enter the preceding current accounts once but do not have a balancing entry in any of the other current accounts. Table 25 shows the Gross Saving and Investment Account.

The sources side of the Gross Saving and Investment Account contains, first, those items appearing on the allocations sides of the preceding accounts that indicate the surplus (or if negative, the deficit) of receipts in each account over outlays. Thus the first item, "personal saving,"

Table 25. Gross Saving and Investment Account for the United States, 1953

(In billions) *

1. Gross expenditures on producers' durables.............................	$51.6	3. Personal saving..................	$20.0
a. Private enterprises............	49.9	4. Income retained by producers.....	35.1
(1) Construction...............	25.5	a. Depreciation allowances........	27.2
(2) Equipment................	24.4	(1) Private enterprises.........	27.2
b. Public enterprises.............	1.7	(2) Public enterprises..........	0.0
(1) Federal...................	0.2	b. Undistributed profits..........	7.9
(2) State and local............	1.5	(1) Book value...............	8.9
2. Net change in enterprise inventories	1.5	(2) Minus: Inventory valuation adjustment...............	1.0
		5. Capital grants to government enterprises.........................	1.7
		6. Government surplus..............	−6.6
		7. Net borrowing from abroad.......	1.9
		8. Statistical discrepancy...........	1.0
Gross domestic investment..........	$53.1	Gross saving......................	$53.1

* Detail may not add to totals because of rounding.
SOURCE: See Table 21.

shows the difference between personal income received from other sectors by individuals and the outlays made to other sectors by individuals. Income retained by producers, government surplus, and net borrowing from abroad are all of this nature. The item "capital grants to government enterprises" is an allocation by government to another sector; since it is considered by those receiving it to be capital rather than current in nature, it does not enter the Gross National Income and Product Account, and so is shown here. The statistical discrepancy is a residual that arises because of the inaccuracy of the statistics, and like the other residuals, is recorded here.

The allocations side of the Gross Saving and Investment Account contains the expenditures of a capital nature that appear on the Gross National Income and Product Account only. They can be viewed as allocations by producers on capital, rather than current, account. None of the other sectors engage in capital transactions of this nature.

The total for the items on the sources side of the Gross Saving and Investment Account equals the total for the items on the allocations side without any new residual item being needed. Every item appears twice in the system of accounts, once as a source item and once as an allocation item or as an offset to sources or allocations. The Gross Saving and Investment Account contains on the sources side all the allocations in each account that are not passed on to other sectors. On the allocations side it contains the expenditures that are not sources for any other sector. Since the accounts of each of the other sectors balance, and this account contains only the second entry for those transactions that have not already appeared twice in the other accounts, this account must also balance arithmetically. The economic implications of the equality of gross investment and gross saving as defined by this account will be considered in Part Two of this book.

The Interrelation of the National Income Accounts

The interrelation among the various national income accounts will stand out more clearly if the system is presented in its simplest form without the detailed breakdowns. Table 26 shows the totals for each of

Table 26. A System of National Income Accounts for the United States, 1953

(In billions)

I. Gross National Income and Product Account

1.1. Payments by producers to individuals (2.5)................	$281.9	1.6. Consumers' expenditures (2.1)..	$229.6
1.2. Income retained by producers (5.4)......................	35.1	1.7. Government expenditures, net (3.1).........................	77.2
1.3. Tax payments by producers (3.7)	54.4	1.8. Gross expenditures on producers' durables (5.1)................	51.6
1.4. Minus: Subsidies and government interest (3.2)...........	7.6	1.9. Net change in inventories (5.2)..	1.5
1.5. Statistical discrepancy (5.8)....	1.0	1.10. Exports and property income received (4.1)..............	21.3
		Subtotal......................	$381.2
		1.11. Minus: Imports and property income paid (4.5)...........	16.4
Gross national income............	$364.9	Gross national product...........	$364.9

II. Personal Income and Outlay Account

2.1. Consumers' expenditures (1.6)..	$229.6	2.5. Payments by producers to individuals (1.1).................	$281.9
2.2. Tax payments by individuals (3.8).......................	44.6	2.6. Transfer payments by government (3.4)....................	12.8
2.3. Transfer payments to abroad (4.6)......................	0.5	2.7. Transfer payments from abroad (4.2).........................	0.0
2.4. Personal saving (5.3).........	20.0		
Personal outlay and saving........	$294.7	Personal income.................	$294.7

Table 26. A System of National Income Accounts for the United States, 1953 (Continued)

III. Government Receipts and Outlay Account

3.1. Government expenditures, net (1.7).........................	$77.2	3.7. Tax payments by producers (1.3)	$54.4
3.2. Subsidies and government interest (1.4).....................	7.6	3.8. Tax payments by individuals (2.2)...........................	44.6
3.3. Capital grants to government enterprises (5.5).................	1.7	3.9. Transfer payments from abroad (4.3)	0.1
3.4. Transfer payments to individuals (2.6).....................	12.8		
3.5. Transfer payments to abroad (4.7)..........................	6.3		
3.6. Surplus (5.6).................	−6.6		
Government outlay and surplus.....	$99.1	Government receipts...............	$99.1

IV. Foreign Trade and Payments Account

4.1. Exports and property income received (1.10)..................	$21.3	4.5. Imports and property income paid (1.11)...................	$16.4
4.2. Transfer payments to individuals (2.7).........................	0.0	4.6. Transfer payments from individuals (2.3).....................	0.5
4.3. Transfer payments to government (3.9)....................	0.1	4.7. Transfer payments from government (3.5)....................	6.3
4.4. Net borrowing from abroad (5.7)	1.9		
Receipts from abroad..............	$23.2	Payments to abroad...............	$23.2

V. Gross Saving and Investment Account

5.1. Gross expenditures on producers' durables (1.8).................	$51.6	5.3. Personal saving (2.4)..........	$20.0
5.2. Net change in inventories (1.9)	1.5	5.4. Income retained by producers (1.2)...........................	35.1
		5.5. Capital grants to government enterprises (3.3).................	1.7
		5.6. Government surplus (3.6)......	−6.6
		5.7. Net borrowing from abroad (4.4)	1.9
		5.8. Statistical discrepancy (1.5)....	1.0
Gross investment..................	$53.1	Gross saving.....................	$53.1

the intersector flows given in the various accounts.[2] The detailed breakdown of each flow is omitted, and in some cases the title of the flow itself has been shortened to make presentation simpler. The items themselves are numbered as they were in the preceding accounts, except that each is preceded by the number of the account.

Every item appears twice in this system; numbers have been added after each flow to show where the duplicate entry for each item will be found. Usually each item appears in one account on the sources side and in another account on the allocations side. In two instances items appear on the same side of the accounts; in these cases each item appears once as an adjustment item to be subtracted. The item "subsidies and govern-

[2] Only twenty-one different flows are required by the system of accounts shown in Table 26. It is also possible to arrange the data in a single table as follows (A=Allocations and S=Sources):

(*In billions of dollars*)

	Producing sector		Consuming sector		Government sector		Foreign account		Capital account	
	A	S	A	S	A	S	A	S	A	S
1. Payments by producers to individuals.	281.9			281.9						
2. Income retained by producers	35.1									35.1
3. Tax payments by producers.	54.4					54.4				
4. Subsidies and government interest.	−7.6				7.6					
5. Statistical discrepancy	1.0									1.0
6. Consumers' expenditures		229.6	229.6							
7. Government expenditures (net).		77.2			77.2					
8. Gross expenditures on producers' durables.		51.6							51.6	
9. Net change in inventories.		1.5							1.5	
10. Exports and property income received.		21.3					21.3			
11. Imports and property income paid.		−16.4						16.4		
12. Tax payments by individuals.			44.6			44.6				
13. Transfer payments to abroad.			0.5					0.5		
14. Personal saving.			20.0							20.0
15. Transfer payments by government.					12.8	12.8				
16. Transfer payments from abroad.					0.0			0.0		
17. Capital grants to enterprises.						1.7				1.7
18. Transfer payments to abroad.						6.3			6.3	
19. Surplus.						−6.6				−6.6
20. Transfer payments from abroad.						0.1	0.1			
21. Net borrowing from abroad.							1.9			1.9
Total.	364.9	364.9	294.7	294.7	99.1	99.1	23.2	23.2	53.1	53.1

ment interest" appears as an allocation in the Government Receipts and Outlay Account (item 3.2) and also as a subtraction from allocations in the Gross National Income and Product Account (item 1.4). Imports, which appears on the sources side of the Foreign Trade and Payments Account (item 4.5), appears also as an offset to the source items in the Gross National Income and Product Account (item 1.11).

APPENDIX TO CHAPTER 5. THE UNITED STATES AND UNITED NATIONS SYSTEMS OF NATIONAL INCOME ACCOUNTS

The rapid development of national income accounting since World War II has resulted in the concurrent use of many different systems of national income accounts. No two countries use exactly the same system with the same classifications. In fact, in some countries there has been considerable change in the form of national income accounts from year to year.

The purpose of this appendix is to discuss in terms of general characteristics the nature of three of these systems of national income accounts. These are (1) the system presented in Chap. 5 above, (2) the system used by the United States, and (3) the system proposed by the United Nations. In connection with the discussion of the United States and the United Nations national income accounting systems, the accounts will be presented in the form and terminology given in official publications. No attempt will be made to give detailed definitions for the various items shown. For the United States, some discussion of the nature of each category will be found in the appendix to Chap. 8, on the detailed sources and methods used in obtaining United States national income data.

Although, relatively speaking, the variations among the three systems covered by this appendix are not very great, the discussion will illustrate the types of variation that can occur in national income accounting systems. The schematic presentation that will be given is of general applicability and may be useful to students studying systems of national income accounting used by other countries.

CHARACTERISTICS OF VARIOUS SYSTEMS OF NATIONAL INCOME ACCOUNTS

National income accounting systems can be described, in general terms, by two major characteristics. First, transactions or transactors are classified into sectors in different ways. Thus some systems may specify producers and consumers as sectors; other systems may choose to differentiate between business enterprises and households instead. Second, the transactions occurring in these sectors are set forth in different kinds of accounts. Examples of various kinds of accounts have already been given in Chap. 5, where a production account, income and outlay accounts, a foreign trade and payments account, and a gross saving and investment account were shown. Besides these two major characteristics, the national income accounts may also vary considerably in (1) the degree of "netness"—i.e., consolidation—used in presenting transactions between sectors, and (2) the kinds of national income aggregates presented as part of the accounting system proper. Although these last features are not as important as the sector classification and the kinds of accounts, they are of sufficient importance for users of national income accounts to merit attention. It is in terms of these characteristics that the various systems of national income accounts will be examined in this appendix.

There are, of course, other differences in the national income accounting systems of different countries, for example, the definitions of investment and consumption expenditures, and the kinds and amounts of imputations introduced into the accounts. For students interested in the comparability of national accounts data between countries, or the use of national accounts data in economic models, such information is very important. However, for describing the general nature of the systems themselves, these additional properties are of a second order of importance and therefore will be excluded from consideration in this appendix.

The System of National Income Accounts Presented in Chap. 5

The system of national income accounts presented in Chap. 5 is a fairly simple one. Three sectors are distinguished: producers, consumers, and government; and four different kinds of account are presented: production, income and outlay, foreign trade and payments, and saving and investment. This structure is shown schematically in the diagram below.

In this diagram the rectangles indicate the general coverage of each account. The columns show the sectors covered, and the rows show the kinds of account. As was indicated in Chap. 5, the sectors are defined functionally, so that only the producers' sector can have a production account. This production account for the producers' sector is consolidated with the producers' income and outlay account in such a manner that one account contains information of both kinds. Account 1, the Gross National Income and Product Account, thus is shown as a rectangle under the producers' sector covering both the production and the income and outlay accounts. Separate income and outlay accounts are shown for consumers and the government, as Accounts 2 and 3 respectively. These are the Personal Income and Outlay Account and the Government Receipts and Outlay Account. Accounts 4 and 5, the Foreign Trade and Payments Account and the Gross Saving and Investment Account, are shown as rectangles extending across all sectors. These accounts record certain kinds of transactions (foreign and capital) in which producers, consumers, and government are all involved. It would be possible to show separate accounts of these kinds for each of the sectors, but in the relatively simple system presented in Chap. 5, a single combined account is shown for the foreign trade and payments of all sectors and a single combined account is shown for the saving and investment of all sectors.

An alternative schematic presentation of the sectors and accounts used in this system of national income accounts could be drawn up that would consider the Foreign Trade and Payments Account to represent a rest of the world sector, and the Gross Saving and Investment Account to represent a capital sector, thus removing two lines from the list of kinds of accounts and adding them as sectors in the columns of the diagram. If this were done, only income and outlay accounts would be shown for these new sectors. This treatment is somewhat unrealistic, however, since these accounts do not represent the income and outlay of decision-making sectors in the same manner as do the accounts of this kind for the other sectors.

The system presented in Chap. 5 uses relatively gross flows. In one instance a net concept is required so that the system will fit into the conventional definitions used in national income accounting. In this case both the gross total and the subtraction required to obtain the net concept are shown. Government expenditures on goods and services are usually defined on a net basis as total expenditures minus government sales of goods and services. In the detailed breakdown both gross expenditures and gross sales are shown explicitly.

In terms of the usual national income accounting aggregates, the system shown in Chap. 5 yields gross national product (and gross national income) and personal income as integral parts of the accounting system. In addition to these totals, the economic constructs of gross domestic investment expenditures by enterprises, total government receipts, and total payments to abroad all appear as totals in the various accounts. With the exception of the gross national product, no special attempt has been made to arrange the accounts so that they show specific national income aggregates. National income, for example, is not shown explicitly at all, although it can be obtained from the allocations side of the Gross National Income and Product Account by making the appropriate adjustments.[3]

The United States System of National Income Accounts

The system of national income accounts for the United States prepared by the Department of Commerce divides the economy into four sectors: business, households, government, and the rest of the world. Three kinds of accounts are used: production, income and outlay, and saving and investment. A foreign trade and payments account is not used, since the rest of the world is considered a sector. The interrelation between the sectors and their accounts is shown schematically below.

[3] See Chap. 6 for a discussion of national income and the specific adjustments required to obtain it.

Account 1, the National Income and Product Account, is identical in content with the Gross National Income and Product Account discussed in Chap. 5. It is shown here as a dotted line embracing the productive activity of all sectors together with the allocation of income by the business sector. The line is dotted because in this accounting system this account represents a summary of information given in the other accounts rather than a necessary part of the system of sector accounts; all the information given in it is repeated in the succeeding accounts, and the succeeding accounts form a complete system without it.

The Department of Commerce defines the sectors in its system in somewhat institutional terms, such that production can take place in any of the sectors; transac*tors* rather than transac*tions* are for the most part the basis of classification. Exceptions to this principle are the activities of households with respect to real estate; even home owning is considered to be productive activity in the business sector. However, the payment of wages and salaries to domestic servants, the wages and salaries paid by nonprofit institutions, and the payment of interest by households and nonprofit institutions are shown as production in the household sector. One account is used for each sector to cover both production and income and outlay. Accounts 2, 3, 4, and 5 refer to business, households, government, and the rest of the world respectively. The rectangles drawn for these accounts extend over both the production account and the income and outlay account to indicate this combination. Account 6, Gross Saving and Investment Account, reflects the transactions of all sectors with respect to capital, and is shown as a rectangle extending across all sectors.

The United States system of national income accounts contains a relatively large number of net flows. In the Rest of the World Account, for example, only net current payments to the United States are shown. Similarly, on the National Income and Product Account, net foreign investment is shown on the sources side rather than exports minus imports.

National income [4] ("income originating" in the sector accounts), gross national product, and personal income are shown explicitly in the United States system of accounts. A special arrangement of items on the allocations side of the accounts has had to be adopted, and special rather minor flows shown, in order that national income and income originating could be shown as a subtotal. The accounts are strongly oriented in the direction of presenting the aggregates within the accounting structure rather than showing in the accounts themselves the detailed composition of the intersectoral flows.

Table 27 presents the form of the six accounts of the United States system of national income accounts.

Account 1, the National Income and Product Account, as has already been indicated, is a supplementary summary account that represents a combined production account for the entire economy, together with an income and outlay account for the business sector. It corresponds quite closely in content with the Gross National Income and Product Account shown in Chap. 5, although it does not serve the same purpose in the accounting system. The differences are merely those of arrangement of items, changes in terminology, and in one or

---

[4] For a discussion of the definition and meaning of this concept see Chap. 6.

Table 27. The United States System of National Income Accounts, 1953

1. National Income and Product Account, 1953

(In millions)

Compensation of employees:			Personal consumption expenditures	$230,080
Wage and salaries.............	$197,980		Gross private domestic investment	51,408
Supplements..................	11,081		Net foreign investment..........	−1,866
Income of unincorporated enter-			Government purchases of goods and	
prises and inventory valuation			services......................	85,235
adjustment...................	38,444			
Rental income of persons........	10,596			
Corporate profits and inventory				
valuation adjustment:				
Corporate profits before tax:				
Corporate profits tax liability	21,144			
Corporate profits after tax:				
Dividends................	9,365			
Undistributed profits......	8,921			
Inventory valuation adjustment	−964			
Net interest...................	8,435			
National income................	*305,002*			
Indirect business tax and nontax				
liability......................	30,037			
Business transfer payments.......	1,016			
Statistical discrepancy..........	1,047			
Less: Subsidies minus current sur-				
plus of government enterprises..	−529			
Charges against net national prod-				
uct..........................	*337,631*			
Capital consumption allowances...	27,226			
Charges against gross national prod-				
uct...........................	$364,857		Gross national product..........	$364,857

two cases consolidation of items. On the sources side of the account, gross private domestic investment includes the net change in enterprise inventories but excludes the gross investment expenditures of public enterprises. These gross investment expenditures of public enterprises are included as a part of government purchases of goods and services. The item "net foreign investment" is a consolidation of exports and property income received with the negative item imports and property income paid. On the allocations side of the account the rearrangement of items is substantial. The only major change in terminology is that what was called "depreciation" in Chap. 5 is here called "capital consumption allowances." This item in the Department of Commerce concept includes accidental damage to fixed capital as well as the regular depreciation

Table 27. The United States System of National Income Accounts, 1953 (Continued)

2. Consolidated Business Income and Product Account, 1953

(*In millions*)

Compensation of employees:		
Wages and salaries:		
Disbursements.............	$160,117	
Excess of accruals over disbursements..............	0	
Supplements:		
Employer contributions for social insurance............	3,717	
Other labor income.........	5,890	
Income of unincorporated enterprises and inventory valuation adjustment...................	38,444	
Rental income of persons........	10,596	
Corporate profits and inventory valuation adjustment:		
Corporate profits before tax:		
Corporate profits tax liability	21,144	
Corporate profits after tax:		
Dividends...............	8,959	
Undistributed profits......	8,180	
Inventory valuation adjustment	−964	
Net interest...................	5,087	
Income originating.............	*261,170*	
Indirect business tax and nontax liability.....................	30,037	
Business transfer payments.......	1,016	
Statistical discrepancy..........	1,047	
Less: Subsidies minus current surplus of government enterprises..	−529	
Charges against net product.......	*293,799*	
Capital consumption allowances...	27,226	
Charges against business gross product........................	$321,025	

Consolidated net sales:	
To consumers.................	$217,075
To government...............	50,311
To business on capital account..	49,914
To abroad....................	2,231
Change in inventories...........	1,494
Business gross product..........	$321,025

charges and capital outlays charged to current expense made by producers. The rationale of this procedure is discussed in the appendix to Chap. 8. Net interest as shown in this account is a consolidation of the interest paid to individuals and government and the (subtracted) interest paid by government. Subsidies are consolidated with the current surplus of government enterprises. The items on the allocations side of the account have been arranged so that they yield national income as a subtotal after the item "net interest."

Table 27. The United States System of National Income Accounts, 1953 (Continued)

3. Personal Income and Expenditure Account, 1953
(In millions)

Personal consumption expenditures:		Wage and salary disbursements:	
Purchases of direct services:		Business....................	$160,117
Compensation of employees:		Government.................	30,174
Wages and salaries paid....	$ 7,745	Households and institutions....	7,745
Supplements paid:		Rest of the world............	20
Employer contributions		Other labor income:	
for social insurance....	64	Business....................	5,890
Other labor income......	71	Government.................	375
Interest paid...............	3,015	Households and institutions....	71
Income originating in and net		Income of unincorporated enter-	
and gross product of house-		prises and inventory valuation	
holds and institutions......	*10,895*	adjustment..................	38,444
		Rental income of persons........	10,596
Net purchases from business....	217,075	Dividends....................	9,365
Net purchases from abroad.....	2,110	Personal interest income........	13,475
Personal tax and nontax payments	35,967	Government transfer payments...	12,785
Personal saving.................	20,019	Business transfer payments.......	1,016
		Less: Personal contributions for so-	
		cial insurance................	4,007
Personal outlay and saving.......	$286,066	Personal income................	$286,066

4. Consolidated Government Receipts and Expenditures Account, 1953
(In millions)

Purchases of goods and services:		Personal tax and nontax receipts..	$ 35,967
Purchases of direct services:		Corporate profits tax accruals.....	21,144
Compensation of employees:		Indirect business tax and nontax	
Wages and salaries:		accruals.....................	30,037
Disbursements..........	$ 30,174	Contributions for social insurance:	
Excess of accruals over		Personal contributions........	4,007
disbursements.........	−76	Employer contributions:	
Supplements:		Business....................	3,717
Employer contributions		Government...............	964
for social insurance....	964	Households and institutions..	64
Other labor income......	375	Deficit (+) or surplus (−) on in-	
Income originating and		come and product transactions..	6,631
net and gross product..	*31,437*		
Net purchases from business....	50,311		
Net purchases from abroad.....	3,487		
Transfer payments..............	12,785		
Net interest paid................	5,040		
Subsidies minus current surplus of			
government enterprises.........	−529		
Government expenditures........	$102,531	Government receipts and deficit...	$102,531

Table 27. The United States System of National Income Accounts, 1953 (Continued)

5. Rest of the World Account, 1953

(In millions)

Net payments of factor income to the United States:		Net disinvestment in the United States......................	$−1,866
Wages and salaries............ $	20		
Interest.....................	333		
Dividends...................	406		
Branch profits...............	741		
Income originating and net and gross product................	*1,500*		
Net purchases from the United States:			
From business...............	2,231		
From government.............	−3,487		
From persons................	−2,110		
Net current payments to the United States...................... $	−1,866	Net disinvestment in the United States......................	$−1,866

6. Gross Saving and Investment Account, 1953

(In millions)

Business purchases on capital account......................	$49,914	Excess of wage accruals over disbursements (business).......... $	0
Change in business inventories....	1,494	Excess of wage accruals over disbursements (government)......	−76
Net disinvestment in the United States by rest of world........	−1,866	Undistributed corporate profits (domestic)......................	8,180
		Corporate inventory valuation adjustment....................	−964
		Capital consumption allowances by private business..............	27,226
		Government surplus (+) or deficit (−) on income and product transactions......................	−6,631
		Foreign branch profits (net)......	741
		Personal saving.................	20,019
		Statistical discrepancy..........	1,047
Gross investment...............	$49,542	Gross saving and statistical discrepancy......................	$49,542

SOURCE: National Income Supplement, 1954, *Survey of Current Business*, U.S. Department of Commerce, pp. 160–161.

Account 2, the Consolidated Business Income and Product Account, is the combined production account and income and outlay account for the business sector. The form of this account is almost identical with the form of Account 1, the National Income and Product Account. The difference lies in coverage: the National Income and Product Account refers to the economy as a whole, whereas the Consolidated Business Income and Product Account refers only to the activities of those productive units included in the definition of the business sector. The total of this account is called "business gross product." A subtotal on the allocations side of the account also shows the component of national income originating in this sector.

Account 3, the Personal Income and Expenditure Account, represents a combined production account and income and outlay account for the household sector. In content it corresponds quite closely with the Personal Income and Outlay Account discussed in Chap. 5, but here again a different classification scheme is adopted, and the account is set up on the allocations side to yield the income originating in, and the net and gross product of, households and nonprofit institutions. The only differences in content between the two accounts are that in the Department of Commerce account, transfers to and from abroad are included in consumers' expenditures, employer contributions to social insurance are omitted entirely, and personal contributions to social insurance are shown as a deduction from income on the sources side of the account. The sources side of the account in this system shows the income of each type received from each of the other sectors. The allocations side of the account shows the net purchases that households and institutions make from the other sectors, including the payments that households and institutions make to each other for productive purposes. In the Personal Income and Outlay Account shown in Chap. 5, it was not necessary to show either the payments for services or the purchases of goods and services broken down by sectors, since all productive activity by definition occurred in the productive sector. However, because the Department of Commerce uses a more institutional concept of sector, the purchases of goods and the payments for services must be classified on an individual sector basis within each account.

Account 4, the Consolidated Government Receipts and Expenditures Account, represents the combined production account and income and outlay account for the government sector. Again, it is quite similar in content to the Government Receipts and Outlay Account discussed in Chap. 5. As in the case of the Personal Income and Expenditure Account, however, transfers received from abroad and transfers paid to abroad are included in purchases of goods and services. The item "capital transfers to government enterprises" does not appear; any such transfers would be included in subsidies. The allocations side of the account, aside from these changes, is merely a reclassification of the items that appeared on the corresponding account in Chap. 5.

Account 5, the Rest of the World Account, represents the combined production account and income and outlay account for the rest of the world sector. It performs some of the same functions in the accounting system as the Foreign Trade and Payments Account in the system described in Chap. 5, but it is very different in appearance. The account is oriented toward deriving the income originating and the net and gross product of this sector. The production that takes place in the rest of the world sector is represented by the *net* payments of factor income that other countries make to the United States. The account is presented in terms of net rather than gross transactions. Transfers to and from abroad are included with goods and services on both sides of the account.

Account 6, the Gross Saving and Investment Account, is a combined saving and investment account for all sectors. In both content and function it is similar to the Gross Saving and Investment Account described in Chap. 5. However, the gross investment shown here excludes the investment of public enterprises. One major item has been shifted from the sources side of the account to the allocations side (with, of course, a corresponding change in sign); this is net borrowing from abroad, here termed "net disinvestment in the United States" by the rest of the world. In addition, on the sources side of the account two new items have been added: "excess of wage accruals over disbursements," and "foreign branch profits (net)." The excess of wage accruals over disbursements is needed here since wage accruals are recorded on the Consolidated Business Income and Product Account, but only those wages that are actually paid are recorded as received in the Personal Income and Expenditure Account. The difference between these two amounts must thus be charged to the Gross Saving and Investment Account. Similarly, foreign branch profits (net) are recorded as paid in the Rest of the World Account, but they are not recorded as received in the Consolidated Business Income and Product Account. They are therefore carried in the Gross Saving and Investment Account.

The United Nations System of National Income Accounts

In the discussion accompanying the system of accounts proposed by the United Nations, sectors are classified on an institutional basis, in terms of (1) enterprises, (2) households, and (3) general government. Four kinds of account are described: (1) production account, (2) appropriation account (same as income and outlay account), (3) capital reconciliation account (same as saving and investment account); and (4) external account. It would appear on the basis of these definitions that the schematic presentation of the national income accounting system would be as follows.

	Enterprises	Households	Government
Production	1a	2a	3a
Appropriation	1b	2b	3b
Capital Reconciliation	1c	2c	3c
External	1d	2d	3d

The form of the accounts as they are in fact shown, however, is very different from the textual discussion. Unlike the United States system, production is not shown as arising in separate sector accounts for enterprises, households, and the government. The external account, furthermore, is given a capital reconciliation account of its own, so that it functions as a sector, not as a kind of account. Schematically, the interrelation among the sectors and kinds of account that are actually used is shown below.

	Producers	Households	Government	Rest of the World
Production	1			
Income and Outlay	2	4a	5a	6a
Saving and Investment	3	4b	5b	6b

Account 1, Domestic Product, is similar to the Gross National Income and Product Account discussed in Chap. 5 in that it shows the total production of the economy. The allocations side of this account, however, does not show the disposition of receipts by producers; rather, this is done in Account 2, National Income. Thus there are separate accounts for the production and for the income and outlay of producers. Account 3, Domestic Capital Formation, also refers to the producers' sector, covering its saving and investment. For each of the other sectors in the economy, separate accounts are shown for current transactions (income and outlay) and for capital transactions (saving and investment). Account 4, Households and Private Nonprofit Institutions, Account 5, General Government, and Account 6, External Transactions, are each split into two parts, the first part representing an income and outlay account and the second part representing a saving and investment account.

The transactions in the United Nations national income accounts are generally shown on a grosser basis than in the United States system. However, in the capital reconciliation accounts (savings and investment accounts) of the various sectors, transfers are shown on a net basis. Factor payments to and from abroad are also shown only on a net basis.

The aggregate of national income appears explicitly in the system, due to the introduction of Account 2, National Income. By showing separate accounts for the production and the income and outlay of the productive sector, it is possible to show both gross domestic product and national income explicitly as totals.[5] The equivalent of personal income is available as the total of the current account of households and nonprofit institutions.

Table 28 presents the six accounts of the United Nations system of national income accounts.

Account 1, Domestic Product, is the production account for the producers' sector. It corresponds in part to the Gross National Income and Product Account discussed in Chap. 5. On the sources side of the account, the end uses of gross domestic product are given. Since the account refers to gross domestic product instead of gross national product, the property income received from abroad has been excluded from exports, and the property income paid to for-

[5] These concepts are defined in Chap. 6.

Table 28. The United Nations System of National Income Accounts

Account 1. Domestic product

1.1. Gross domestic product at factor cost (2.9)....................	1.4. Private consumption expenditure (4.1).........................
1.2. Indirect taxes (5.7)...........	1.5. General government consumption expenditure (5.1).........
1.3. Less subsidies − (5.2).........	1.6. Gross domestic fixed capital formation (3.1).................
	1.7. Increase in stocks (3.2)........
	1.8. Exports of goods and services (6.1).........................
	Expenditure on gross domestic product and imports..........
	1.9. Less imports of goods and services − (6.3)..................
Gross domestic product at market prices........................	Expenditure on gross domestic product...........................

Account 2. National income

2.1. Compensation of employees (4.5)	2.9. Gross domestic product at factor cost (1.1).....................
2.2. Income from farms, professions and other unincorporated enterprises (4.6)..................	2.10. Net factor income payments from the rest of the world (6.2)
2.3. Income from property (4.7).....	2.11. Less provisions for the consumption of fixed capital − (3.3)....
2.4. Saving of corporations (3.4)....	
2.5. Direct taxes on corporations (5.8)	
2.6. General government income from property and entrepreneurship (5.5).......................	
2.7. Less interest on the public debt (5.6).......................	
2.8. Less interest on consumers' debt (4.8)........................	
National income.................	Net national product at factor cost..

eigners has been excluded from imports. Gross domestic fixed capital formation as shown on this account includes not only the gross domestic investment expenditures of public and private enterprises, but also the general government expenditures on fixed assets; general government consumption expenditure excludes these expenditures on fixed assets, so that the total on the sources side of the account is not changed by this reclassification. The payment of interest by consumers is not included in private consumption expenditure in the United Nations system, so that the total output for the economy

Table 28. The United Nations System of National Income Accounts (Continued)

Account 3. Domestic capital formation

3.1. Gross domestic fixed capital formation (1.6).................	3.3. Provisions for the consumption of fixed capital − (2.11)........
3.2. Increase in stocks (1.7).......	3.4. Saving of corporations (2.4)....
	3.5. Net capital transfers from households and private nonprofit institutions (4.11).................
	3.6. Net capital transfers from general government (5.11).........
	3.7. Net international transfers received by corporations (6.6)....
	3.8. Net borrowing of corporations − (4.14 + 5.15 + 6.9)........
Gross domestic capital formation....	Finance of gross domestic capital formation........................

Account 4. Households and private nonprofit institutions

Current account

4.1. Consumption expenditure (1.4)	4.5. Compensation of employees (2.1)
4.2. Direct taxes (5.9)............	4.6. Income from farms, professions, and other unincorporated enterprises (2.2)...................
4.3. Other current transfers to general government (5.10).............	4.7. Income from property (2.3).....
4.4. Saving (4.12).................	4.8. Less interest on consumers' debt (2.8)........................
	4.9. Current transfers from general government (5.3)..............
Disposal of income...............	Income of households and private nonprofit institutions...........

Capital reconciliation account

4.10. Net capital transfers to general government (5.13)...........	4.12. Saving (4.4).................
4.11. Net capital transfers to domestic capital formation (3.5).....	4.13. Net international transfers received (6.7)..................
	4.14. Net borrowing − (3.8 + 5.15 + 6.9) ....
Disbursements...................	Receipts......................

Table 28. The United Nations System of National Income Accounts (Continued)

Account 5. General government

Current account

5.1. Consumption expenditure (1.5)	5.5. Income from property and entre-
5.2. Subsidies — (1.3).............	preneurship (2.6).............
5.3. Current transfers to households	5.6. Less interest on the public debt
(4.9)........................	(2.7)........................
5.4. Savings (5.12)...............	5.7. Indirect taxes (1.2)...........
	5.8. Direct taxes on corporations (2.5)
	5.9. Direct taxes on households (4.2)
	5.10. Other current transfers from
	households (4.3).............
Disposal of current revenue.........	Current revenue...................

Capital reconciliation account

5.11. Net capital transfers to domes-	5.12. Saving (5.4)................
tic capital formation (3.6).....	5.13. Net capital transfers from
	households (4.10)............
	5.14. Net international transfers re-
	ceived (6.8).................
	5.15. Net borrowing — (3.8 + 4.14
	+ 6.9).....................
Disbursements...................	Receipts.......................

is smaller by this amount. On the allocations side of the account, the allocations of gross domestic product are not given, but in their stead two items are shown: indirect taxes, and subsidies as an adjustment item, leaving as the residual the item "gross domestic product at factor cost." [6]

Account 2, National Income, is the income and outlay account for the producers' sector. It shows on the sources side the gross domestic product at factor cost derived from Account 1, with the net factor income payments from the rest of the world added and the provision for the consumption of fixed capital (depreciation) subtracted, leaving as the total net national product at factor cost. Provision is made for general government depreciation, as well as enterprise depreciation. The allocations side of this account shows the allocations of the income originating from productive activity, together with the adjustments relating to interest paid by consumers and government.

Account 3, Domestic Capital Formation, is the saving and investment account for the producers' sector. It shows on the allocations side the domestic

[6] The concept of factor cost is discussed in Chap. 6.

Table 28. The United Nations System of National Income Accounts (Continued)

Account 6. External transactions (rest of the world account)

Current account

6.1. Exports of goods and services (1.8)........................	6.3. Imports of goods and services $- (1.9)$......................
6.2. Net factor income payments to the nation (2.10)..............	6.4. Surplus of the nation on current account (6.5)................
	Disposal of current receipts from
Current receipts from abroad.......	abroad........................

Capital reconciliation account

6.5. Surplus of the nation on current account (6.4).................	6.9. Net lending to the rest of the world $- (3.8 + 4.14 + 5.15)$...
6.6. Net international transfers to corporations (3.7).............	
6.7. Net international transfers to households (4.13)..............	
6.8. Net international transfers to general government (5.14)......	
Receipts........................	Disbursements....................

SOURCE: *A System of National Accounts and Supporting Tables*, United Nations, 1953, pp. 18–19.

capital formation of producers and the increase in stocks (inventories). On the sources side it gives the sources of finance of domestic capital formation: the provisions for consumption of fixed capital, the saving of corporations, the net capital transfers received from households and general government, the net international transfers received by corporations, and the net borrowing of corporations. This account differs from both the Gross Saving and Investment Account shown in Chap. 5 and that used by the United States in that it refers to the producers' sector only, not to the entire economy. The saving and investment of the producers' sector is shown explicitly, in a form substantially similar to the system described previously. The saving occurring in the other sectors, however, is shown consolidated into a single net transfer item for each sector, and to obtain the detail behind these consolidated items it is necessary to refer to the saving and investment accounts for the other sectors.

Account 4, Households and Private Nonprofit Institutions, is divided into two subaccounts entitled "Current Account" and "Capital Reconciliation Account." These are respectively the income and outlay account and the saving and investment account for the consuming sector. In the Current Account transfers to and from abroad are excluded, and interest paid by consumers is shown as a deduction from income received on the sources side of the account rather than an outlay of income on the allocations side. The Capital Reconciliation Account lists only two items on the allocations side: net capital transfers to general government, which includes death duties, gift taxes, capital levies, confiscations, and similar payments, with such things as payments of war damages to individuals subtracted; and net capital transfers to domestic capital formation, which covers the value of all net capital formation (in fixed assets and in inventories) in all unincorporated enterprises, private nonprofit institutions, and owner-occupied houses, with the exception of capital formation financed out of general government grants. It also includes the net flow of capital grants between corporations on the one hand, and households and private nonprofit institutions on the other, such as grants from corporations to research foundations. The sources side of this Capital Reconciliation Account shows the saving derived from the Current Account, plus the net international transfers received. The residual in this account is net borrowing.

Account 5, General Government, is also divided into two subaccounts, the Current Account and the Capital Reconciliation Account. The allocations side of the Current Account shows only the current government expenditures for goods and services, which is called consumption expenditure. This account, like the Current Account for households and private nonprofit institutions, treats interest paid as a deduction from income. Both government expenditures on fixed assets and capital grants to enterprises are excluded from the Current Account. In the Capital Reconciliation Account for general government, a single item, "net capital transfers to domestic capital formation," appears on the allocations side. This item consists of government expenditures on fixed assets and capital grants to enterprises, minus all capital transfers from corporations (such as capital levies and confiscations). On the sources side of the Capital Reconciliation Account, the saving (surplus) of government and the net transfers it receives from individuals and from abroad are shown as receipts. Net borrowing is the residual in the account.

Account 6, External Transactions, again contains two subaccounts. The Current Account lists imports of goods and services on the sources side and exports of goods and services on the allocations side. Payments to the factors of production are not included in these import and export items; these payments appear consolidated as a net item on the allocations side of the account. The residual item in this account appears on the sources side, and is entitled "surplus of the nation on current account." On the Capital Reconciliation Account for this sector, this surplus of the nation on current account plus the net international transfers to corporations, households, and general government are shown as allocations. The single item shown on the sources side of the account is the residual.

COMPARISON OF THE UNITED STATES AND UNITED NATIONS SYSTEMS

In comparing the systems of national income accounts developed by the United States Department of Commerce and by the United Nations Statistical Office, it should be borne in mind that the origin of each system is quite different. The United States system represents an evolutionary development that has been in process since work on this subject was initiated in the Department of Commerce in 1932. The requirements of World War II for relevant economic information accelerated the development of the national income statistics, in particular the measurement of the gross national product. Such an aggregate was necessary if the goals that were set up were to be consistent with the total output capabilities of the nation, and the diversion of production that would be necessary for war purposes was to be calculated. The statistical series on gross national product was first published by the Department of Commerce shortly after Pearl Harbor. In July, 1947, the national income data were basically recast into the framework of a comprehensive national economic accounting system, designed to show the economic activity of the nation in terms of flows among various interrelated sectors. The national income accounts of the Department of Commerce thus developed from the analytic need for an over-all framework to make the masses of existing interrelated data comprehensible.

The system of national income accounts designed by the United Nations, in contrast, was drawn up as a complete system at a fairly recent date by a committee of experts who could take advantage of the experiences of a number of different countries with national income accounts over the last two decades. They were able to view the problem without the task of providing continuity in statistical series. On the other hand, they were also faced with the necessity for developing a system that could be used by a wide variety of nations with different institutions and different kinds of economy. The problem of whether it was practical for the large number of less developed countries to try to get certain kinds of statistics had to be considered in setting forth the kinds of transactions that were to be recorded in the accounts. A system developed for one country alone without taking the problems of international comparability into consideration might well be quite different from a system that attempted to meet these problems.

The differences between the two systems are in part a product of these differences in their origin. Furthermore, the formal differences in the accounting presentations do not always represent substantive differences in the kinds of information available. One system of national income accounts can often easily be recast into a different system merely by rearrangement of the various flows. Whether the national income data of an economy are adequate for economic analysis often depends less on the formal accounting presentation than it does on the adequacy of the detailed tables underlying the accounting flows. With respect to this point, the supplementary tables given by the United States and the proposed supplementary tables of the United Nations system are both extremely useful. Nevertheless, since this appendix is concerned with the form of the national income accounting systems, it is the formal presentation in the accounts themselves that will be compared.

The Use of Sectors by the United States and the United Nations

The sector classification used in the national income accounts of the United States differs from that of the United Nations primarily in that the former is designed to classify transactors, whereas the latter is concerned primarily with transactions.

In the United States classification the economy is viewed as composed of business enterprises, households and nonprofit institutions, government, and the rest of the world. Each of the groups of transactors is considered to enter into various kinds of economic activity, which are recorded in the various accounts for each sector. Thus all activities of nonprofit institutions, even if they relate to production, are placed in the household sector. The hiring of domestic servants and the pay of employees of nonprofit institutions are considered to be production in the household sector. The hiring of employees by the general government is included in the government sector, but the productive activity of government enterprises is of course included in the business sector. However, it is in part recognized that hard and fast institutional lines clearly differentiating these institutional groups cannot be drawn. An unincorporated enterprise such as a farmer combines in a single unit both a producing and a consuming aspect. The Department of Commerce in this case separates the unit functionally, placing its productive activity in the business sector and its consuming activity in the household sector. Similarly, the real-estate activities of the household are placed in the business rather than the household sector.

Dividing up productive activity according to these institutional sectors entails considerable detail in the accounts. Wages and salaries, for instance, have to be classified as disbursed by business, households and institutions, government, or the rest of the world. The activity of employees of hospitals or schools would be classified in the business sector if the hospital or school is a private profit-making institution, in the household sector if it is nonprofit, and in the government sector if it is a public institution. Such a breakdown might be useful for some purposes, but it seems a rather strange sort of detail to highlight as one of the more prominent features of the accounts.

The United Nations system of national income accounting, in contrast, has taken the more functional approach, dividing the economy into producers, consumers, government, and the rest of the world. Thus all productive activity arises in a single sector. This makes the detailed articulation of factor payments by sector and of intersector sales unnecessary, and the accounts are freed from the requirement of deriving an amount of production originating in each sector. If it were thought desirable to show the factor payments and purchases broken down by sector, the detailed breakdowns could of course still be shown in the accounts for the producers' sector. Generally, however, other detail would be more interesting. A product breakdown under consumer expenditures, for example, showing food, clothing, housing, etc., would probably be more useful than a breakdown of the amount of consumer expenditures paid to businesses, to households and nonprofit institutions, and to the rest of the world sector. For these reasons the United Nations approach to sectoring seems to offer considerable advantage over that used at the present time by the Department of Commerce.

The Use of Accounts in the United States and United Nations Systems

The use of a combined production account and income and outlay account for each sector by the United States has been discussed above. The sector classification adopted by the United Nations, in contrast, makes it impossible for any sector except the producing sector to have a production account. As was pointed out above, this simplifies the accounting procedure considerably, abolishing for the sectors other than the producing sector the problem of whether the production account and the income and outlay account should be presented in consolidated form. For sectors other than the producing sector only an income and outlay account and a saving and investment account are possible.

The United Nations system employs two accounts for the producing sector, whereas the United States system uses a single consolidated account, the National Income and Product Account, to show the same information. The reason for the United Nations choice of two accounts is primarily to simplify the presentation of both the concept of gross domestic output and the concept of national income within the accounting framework. The United States system accomplishes much the same thing by presenting national income as a subtotal on the allocations side of the National Income and Product Account. The method used in the United States system has the advantage of utilizing a single summary account, whereas that used in the United Nations system has the advantage of integrating the summary accounts into the accounting system proper rather than presenting them as additional extra tables.

The United States and United Nations systems also differ considerably in their treatment of the saving and investment accounts. The United States system has a single consolidated saving and investment account for all sectors, whereas the United Nations system employs a separate saving and investment account for each sector. The United Nations system has resorted to the separate Capital Reconciliation Accounts in order to keep the income and outlay account for each of the sectors on a strictly current basis. Since some capital outlays or receipts do occur for each sector, the separate capital accounts are necessary. In the United States system the income and outlay accounts include these items of a capital nature where they occur. The use of the separate accounts by the United Nations seems somewhat overelaborate, since the differentiation could be shown as detail within the accounts fully as well. The problems of classification could thus be simplified and many of the purely formal balancing items that appear, especially in the Capital Reconciliation Accounts for each sector, would drop out.

The Classification of Transactions

The choice of sectors and accounts in both the United States system and the United Nations system has had considerable effect on the classification of transactions within the accounts. In the United States system, as has already been noted, much of the detail within the accounts is designed to show the production occurring within the sector at the expense of other possible uses.

The classifications in the rest of the world sector, for example, appear only on a net basis, separating the net payments of factor income to the United States (which equals income originating in this sector) from other net purchases from the United States. Through the use of a different definition of sector, the United Nations system has managed to avoid much of this kind of detail, and in the current accounts the transactions are generally shown in somewhat more revealing classifications. However, in the Capital Reconciliation Accounts the United Nations system has been forced to highlight a large number of relatively uninformative transfers (usually on a net basis) because of its introduction of the individual saving and investment accounts for each sector.

The problems of the kinds of classification and the relative degree of grossness are not accounting problems but rather questions of economic analysis. Grossness is not necessarily desirable in and of itself; rather, netness is undesirable when it shows as a net total the difference between two or more major flows having different determinants. Any aggregation is a poor classification if there is little that is similar about the categories it aggregates. The basis of proper classification should be homogeneity in terms that are meaningful for economic analysis. Both systems overcome this defect in their detailed breakdowns in tables separate from the accounts proper. It is nevertheless true, however, that in neither system do the accounts themselves reflect the optimum in terms of classifications; they introduce many minor classifications, yet at the same time present aggregates that conceal rather than expose the structural relationships involved.

The Presentation of National Income Aggregates and Other Economic Constructs

Both the United States and the United Nations systems of national income accounts succeed in presenting within the framework of the accounts a number of different national income aggregates. In the United States system the items on the allocations side of the National Income and Product Account are specifically arranged in such a manner that national income can be derived as a subtotal. In the United Nations system a special income and outlay account for the producers' sector is introduced for this purpose.

As will be pointed out in Chap. 7, the national income aggregates are economic constructs that under certain assumptions have meaning in terms of the volume of output, the use of resources, or economic welfare. Because the assumptions necessary for the national income aggregates to have the meaning ascribed to them are often not fulfilled, these constructs may be very misleading. The flows shown in the accounts, however, are more generally interpreted merely as the volume of transactions of given types that have occurred, and thus their use as data for economic analysis is often more valid. Furthermore, it is the flows that are basic to the construction of the aggregates, not the reverse. The national income accounting aggregates may influence the kinds of transactions included in the system of accounts, but there is no reason why the aggregates themselves should not be derived separately from the accounts rather than included as an integral part of them. If the accounts are freed from the necessity of showing the aggregates, the form of the accounts can be simplified and the classification of the flows made to conform more closely with the needs of economic analysis.

In other words, the national income accounts should be viewed as a framework for classifying the transactions that take place in the economy rather than as a method of deriving specific economic aggregates. Certain economic constructs, such as consumers' expenditures or gross domestic investment, may emerge from the accounts, but they should emerge because they represent useful classifications of certain types of transactions. The effort made to present the concept of national income in the accounting framework by both the United States and the United Nations systems is probably prompted by the desire to see this traditional economic construct in a place of importance in the system. An alternative to this procedure that would accomplish the same purpose would be a table showing the derivation of all the major national income accounting aggregates and their relation to each other. Such a table is in fact also provided in the United States statistics. The advantage of this latter procedure would be that other equally significant concepts could be included, so that the user of national income aggregates would become somewhat more aware of the range of possible aggregates and their relation to each other.

6. National Income Aggregates and Their Meaning

As has already been indicated, the national income aggregates were developed before the accounts, and in fact were largely responsible for the present form of the accounts. With the development of the accounts, however, some of the national income aggregates previously in use were dropped, the definitions of others were changed, and new aggregates were introduced. This chapter will discuss those concepts that are in current use.

Each of the national income aggregates will be defined in terms of the component flows of which it is made up. The flows that have already been shown in the national income accounts are sufficient to derive all the aggregates that will be discussed. The formal presentation of the various aggregates in terms of the flows will serve not only to indicate the general nature of each aggregate, but will also specify the exact differences between various aggregates and will show the basic interrelationships among them.[1]

A useful evaluation of the national income aggregates cannot be made on such a formal basis, however; the meaning and significance of the various aggregates will become clear only with an examination of the functions of the different concepts and an evaluation of the degree to which they fulfill these functions. Only in such a context can the nature of the various aggregates and their defects be appraised. Chapter 7 will therefore consider the usefulness of the aggregates in various types of comparative analysis.

The specific national income aggregates that will be presented in this chapter are (1) gross national income and gross national product, (2) gross domestic income and product, (3) net national product at market prices, (4) net national product at factor cost and national income, (5) personal income and outlay, and (6) disposable income. A diagram-

[1] The national income aggregates discussed here are those given in the system of accounts in Chap. 5. In those instances where these do not correspond precisely with the United States definitions, the differences are noted in the text.

matic presentation of the relationships among these concepts will also be given.

Gross National Income and Gross National Product

The gross national income and gross national product have already been presented as the totals in the Gross National Income and Product Account in Chap. 5. Gross national product represents the market value of the gross output of the nation, and gross national income represents the allocation of the income originating from the production of this output. The output under consideration is "gross" because it does not take into account the capital goods that have been consumed in the process of production. The output is "national" because it represents the productive contribution of nationals of a given country, together with the contribution of any property owned by such nationals, whether this property is located at home or abroad.

The derivation of the gross national income and gross national product from the transactions that take place in the nation requires further consideration of certain specific problems. These problems are largely conceptual in nature. Discussion of them will help to indicate the dimensions of the definitions of gross national income and product. The problems that will be considered are (1) the definition of intermediate goods and services, (2) the treatment of nonmarket production, and (3) the omission of unilateral transfers.

The Definition of Intermediate Goods and Services. It was pointed out in Chap. 5 that in adding up the market value of goods produced in the nation to derive the gross national product, it is necessary to exclude the "intermediate" goods and services that enter into the production of other goods and services, that is, those transactions that represent purchases by productive units from other productive units on current account should be omitted from the total market value of national output. In practice, certain problems arise in determining what are intermediate and what are final goods. What appears as a current expense on the accounts of an individual firm may not, in economic terms, represent the use of goods and materials in current output or in increases in inventories. Both conceptual and statistical problems are involved.

The conceptual problem of separating current from capital expenditures is not simple. The Department of Commerce has arbitrarily chosen to define as capital all expenditures for items that have a useful life of greater than one year. Unfortunately, this definition does not solve the problem. It is still necessary to decide how long each item that is purchased will last. For example, is the painting of a building a capital expenditure? It may in fact last a number of years. Similarly, repairs made to a machine may last over quite a long period. The Department of Commerce, however, has chosen to exclude such repair and maintenance as this from their definition of capital expenditure. Some countries, in particular the Scandinavian countries, do use a much broader concept of capital than does the United States. They include all such repair and current maintenance of capital goods as a part of new gross capital formation rather than as a current expense of producers. From an economic point of view there is considerable merit in this approach. Maintenance of plant and machinery can vary considerably from period to period. When profits are low and producers are experiencing difficulties they may postpone full maintenance, and conversely, when profits are high they may catch up on their maintenance, since they can afford to do so and it is to their tax advantage. It is argued by those in favor of such a broad concept of capital that the omission of maintenance and repair from the gross national product understates the true fluctuation in economic activity from prosperity to depression. From a statistical point of view this difference in definition is not a minor point, since the repair and maintenance of capital equipment is usually equal, on the average, to almost half of the value of newly produced capital goods.

In addition to the basic conceptual problems of determining what expenditures by producers are capital and what are current, a further problem arises because there are a number of different kinds of outlay that firms can treat as current expense that are in reality capital formation. For convenience or in order to minimize its taxes, the firm will charge some such capital outlays to its current account. The Department of Commerce makes a correction for this accounting difficulty in calculating the gross national product, showing as a separate category under capital consumption allowances an item called "capital outlays charged to current expense."

A problem also arises with respect to the government in distinguishing between intermediate and final goods and services. Government services may be considered final products given to the economy, or they may, in part at least, represent intermediate products that are given to business. In either case, since these services are usually offered free of charge, it is debatable whether they should be added in at cost to the total output of the nation. Such things as roads, conservation, and information services provided by the government could be considered primarily as services consumed by producers in the process of their production. It could be argued that if business were called upon to pay for these services directly, the market price of the specific goods requiring such services would rise; according to this reasoning, these items should be included at their cost. On the other hand, it could be maintained that business does pay for these services through such payments as gasoline taxes and other excise and corporation taxes, or that these services are not really necessary, or that consumers would shift their choices to lower-priced goods if the cost of the government services were included in the price of the goods; according to this reasoning, the cost of these government services should not be counted as a part of the market value of total national output. The Department of Commerce, together with almost all other Western countries at the present time, has chosen the first alternative, that of including in the gross national product all government services valued at cost.

Almost all consumers' expenditures are customarily considered outlays for final products. This procedure is to some extent arbitrary. In a few instances, such as certain kinds of uniforms, exceptions are made and these outlays are considered purchases made for use in current production. With almost equal justification, however, such items as commuting expenses or even office clothes could be excluded from final output under certain conditions. In fact, there seems to be no logical stopping place. Even food and shelter could be considered one of the costs involved in making the labor of an individual available. Because there is no stopping place, the simple convention is usually adopted that, with certain very minor exceptions, individuals do not have expenses that can be classed as the purchase of intermediate goods and services.

The Treatment of Nonmarket Production. Not all of the output of the nation appears on the market. The farmer, for example, may consume directly a portion of what he produces. The homeowner gets the benefit of the shelter his house affords. A domestic servant may get free board and lodging. The Department of Commerce attempts to take these items into account in adding up the total output of the nation.

A fairly serious problem arises, however, in the valuation of these goods and services. Should the food consumed by the farmer be valued at what he could sell it for, or should it be valued at what he would have to pay for it in retail stores? From his own point of view, its value would probably be what it would bring if he sold it on the market. It can also be argued that the food at the store is not just food; it is packaged and includes distribution costs that are not necessary in the case of the farmer, so that the goods in stores are essentially different from those on the farm. From a welfare point of view, however, it is reasonable that goods of equal utility to the individuals consuming them should be valued equally. If eggs are enjoyed as much by farmers as by city dwellers, there is no reason why those consumed by farmers are less valuable as final output than those consumed by city dwellers. On this basis commodities that are similar would be valued the same. The Department of Commerce has in this instance chosen the first alternative, valuing food consumed by the farmer at what he can get for it, rather than at the price at which it sells to consumers. This problem of valuation has to be faced and some sort of arbitrary decision made for each good or service that is counted as a part of total national output but does not appear on the market.

In addition to the valuation of imputed goods and services, it is also necessary to decide just how much nonmarket production should be counted. For example, should home laundering be counted as production? If the housewife sends her laundry out to be done commercially, it enters into the gross national product as a consumer expenditure on laundry services. Should there not be, therefore, a similar imputation for laundry that is done in the home? Similarly, if the housewife makes her own clothes, or the householder engages in home remodeling, should these not be included? Some countries have at times attempted to impute the value of housework done by the wife, on the ground that hired domestic service is normally included in the gross national product. Carried to its logical extreme, however, this line of reasoning would mean that a man who dresses himself should have imputed the wages of a valet, and a man who drives his own car, the wages of a chauffeur— and a man who walks instead of using a car might have both the cost of the car and that of a chauffeur imputed. Because, here again, there is no logical stopping place, the final decision is essentially arbitrary.

The Omission of Unilateral Transfers. Certain of the current transactions that take place in the economy are omitted from consideration in the calculation of gross national income and product, and others have to be deducted from the total income and payments in the economy to make gross national income in fact equal to gross national product. These transactions are all unilateral transfers of one sort or another—essentially gifts. They include gifts from one individual to another, transfer payments by government, subsidy payments by government, and net interest payments by government.

Gifts from one individual to another do not refer to any production, and so are omitted from gross national product and income. Similarly, government transfer payments, such as veterans' bonuses, relief payments, and pensions, are redistribution of income rather than income arising from current productive contributions and are omitted.

Subsidies to business are omitted on the ground that they are not payments to producers for goods or services; rather, they are payments to enable the producer to meet costs higher than the market value of the product. Since the gross national product is concerned with the market value of production rather than its cost, it is conceptually correct to disregard such subsidy payments in computing gross national product and, for the purpose of calculating gross national income, to show them as a negative adjustment to the total income and payments arising from production.

The treatment of government interest has been mentioned in Chap. 4 and Chap. 5. The Department of Commerce omits government interest payments from the gross national product on the ground that, since the bulk of government debt was created to finance wars and current expenditures rather than capital expenditures, interest payments on such debt should not be taken to represent currently produced goods and services or the current use of economic resources. Since government interest is treated by the individuals who receive it as income, however, it again is necessary to show it, in obtaining gross national income, as a negative adjustment to the total income and payments made in the economy.

Conclusions Concerning the Definition of Gross National Income and Gross National Product. It is obvious from the above discussion that the definition of gross national income and gross national product is considerably more arbitrary than might at first appear. The definition of intermediate goods, the degree of imputation adopted, and the convention adopted with respect to government interest payments all have a significant effect both upon the conceptual content and the magnitude of the totals. In view of the nature of the concepts these arbitrary decisions are necessary, but the user should be fully aware of the nature of the rules and how they affect the totals, the components of the totals, and the validity of any comparisons over time and space. The discussion of the use of the national income aggregates in Chap. 7 will give some consideration to the effects that these relatively arbitrary procedures may be expected to have upon the analysis.

Gross Domestic Income and Product

In the definition of gross national product the term "national" was used to denote that the total output under consideration represented the productive contribution of individuals residing in a given country, together with the productive contribution of any property owned by such residents, whether this property was located at home or abroad. In other words, the boundary of the gross national product is defined in terms of the nationals of a country and their property rather than in terms of geography. It is equally possible, of course, to measure the total output within specified geographical boundaries; this concept is called domestic product. It takes for its frame of reference the production occurring within a given geographical area, irrespective of whether the productive resources in question are owned by the nationals of that area or not. It also omits from consideration any foreign property that is held by nationals of the country in question. Thus the focus of gross domestic product is the productive activity taking place within designated boundaries, whereas that of the gross national product is the productive activity of a specific group of individuals (nationals) and their property. Aside from this difference in coverage, the two concepts are the same. The same problems of defining intermediate goods, making imputations, and treating transfers arise for gross domestic product as for gross national product.

From a statistical point of view the shift in coverage from gross national product to gross domestic product will, on the sources side of the account, affect exports and property income received (1.10 in Table 26) and imports and property income paid (1.11). In measuring gross domestic product, property income received from and paid to abroad must be excluded from consideration, so that only exports and imports will appear on the sources side of what will now be the Gross Domestic Income and Product Account. On the allocations side of the account the income payments that are made to foreigners and those received from foreigners will be omitted, so that some of the items (e.g., dividends) will be different.

Gross domestic product may be either larger or smaller than gross national product. If nationals of a country have large foreign investments and own such property as mines, oil wells, and foreign branch plants, the country's net property income from abroad may be substantial, so that gross domestic product will be much smaller than gross national product. Conversely, if a country has rich oil wells or mines as one of its main sources of productive activity, but these resources are owned and operated by nationals of other countries, gross domestic product may be very much larger than gross national product.

Net National Product at Market Prices

Gross national product is termed "gross" because it does not take into account the capital goods that are consumed during the process of production. The concept of net national product at market prices is designed to make an adjustment for this consumption of capital, showing the net output of the nation left over after the capital that has been used up is deducted from the gross output.

The use of total depreciation allowances (actual and imputed) for all producers as a measure of the consumption of capital for the purpose of deriving net national product raises a number of questions. Depreciation as the total of the financial allowances made by producers and depreciation as the degeneration of the productive power of the physical assets of the country are two very different things. The idea behind the estimation of depreciation allowances for the individual producer is that the money value of capital should be maintained intact. For the economy as a whole, on the other hand, depreciation of capital goods for the purpose of determining net product in the nation should be based upon the concept of keeping intact the total physical productivity of capital goods. In a dynamic economy these two concepts of depreciation must quantitatively continually diverge. Technological progress frequently does destroy the earning power, and thus the money value, of already existing capital goods, and this type of obsolescence should and does enter into the depreciation allowances of businessmen. But technological progress causes no real loss to the economy as a whole. Machinery that is rendered obsolete by a technological advance that introduces more productive machinery suffers no loss in absolute physical productivity; the fact that a new invention exists that does the same job better does not mean that the amount of replacement of capital goods required to maintain the existing level of production in the economy is increased. Yet if the depreciation allowances charged by businessmen are used as a measure of capital degeneration, this is exactly what is implied. Rather, technological progress that promotes efficiency should have the effect of reducing, not increasing, the amount of capital consumption. The technological advance makes it easier to maintain output, and therefore less investment is needed to keep the productive capital of the system intact. Wherever appreciable technological advance does occur, therefore, reliance on the business concept of preserving the money value of capital intact as a measure of the decline in capital goods in the economy as a whole will result in an estimate of capital consumption that is too large.

In this connection the Department of Commerce points out that the net measure of income had been established long before the problem of valuing depreciation was met in particularly acute form in connection with fixed asset formation, and the continued use of net income and product measures reflects in part the accident of this historical sequence. The Department of Commerce recognizes that the depreciation charges used in the current statistics are inadequate as measures of true capital consumption, and that a meaningful measure of net income cannot be obtained given the present state of theoretical and statistical knowledge. The problem of what is meant by "keeping capital intact" is a most controversial one in economic theory, basically because in a dynamic economy, with changes in prices, tastes, and technology, the nature of capital itself changes, and the simple notion of replacing worn-out capital must inevitably become much more complex.

As a record of an allocation that is actually made by business, rather than as a measure of the consumption of capital in the economy, the concept of the depreciation allowance is both reasonable and justifiable; in this sense it represents what businessmen believe their depreciation allowances are, and therefore is a magnitude that enters into their decisions. But even in this limited sense the adoption of a single concept of depreciation is difficult. Inasmuch as the businessman plays the roles of taxpayer, manager, and/or owner, he may legitimately have not one idea of proper depreciation allowances, but three. And if the government is permitted to have a view for tax purposes, a fourth idea may appear. A choice must be made among these four sets of books—or perhaps all four should be used, giving four different concepts of depreciation. Furthermore, in deriving the estimate of depreciation for the economy as a whole, it is customary to impute depreciation allowances for those sectors of the economy where no data exist. As a record of actual flows, it is questionable whether such imputations should be made. When farmers do not depreciate their tools and homeowners do not depreciate their houses, imputing depreciation to them may in fact yield flows that are not compatible with the decision-making processes of these individuals.

Inasmuch as net national product is calculated in almost all countries by deducting the estimated depreciation allowances of businessmen from the gross national product, the meaning of this aggregate thus does not in fact correspond to its conceptual definition. Unfortunately, in view of the very considerable conceptual and statistical problems involved, it does not seem likely that a truly satisfactory measure can be developed within the foreseeable future.

Net National Product at Factor Cost and National Income

Gross national product is the national output valued in terms of market prices. Net national product, derived by adjusting the gross national product for capital consumption, is thus also in terms of market value. Up to this point in the discussion no alternative method of evaluating production has been described. It would be quite possible, however, to value either an individual producer's output or the total national output at what it *costs* in terms of the factors of production rather than at what it brings on the market.

An example may help to clarify this point. In 1947 the tobacco-manufacturing industry produced tobacco products that it was able to sell on the market for about $3.0 billion. The goods, materials, and services it bought from other producers to make these tobacco products cost about $1.0 billion. Therefore the manufacturers added about $2.0 billion of market value to the goods they purchased from other producers; this is the gross product of the industry valued at market prices. But these tobacco products did not cost $2.0 billion to produce in terms of the factors of production that went into them. Tobacco products are heavily taxed, and the manufacturers paid over $1.5 billion in Federal and state excise taxes alone. Of the amount remaining to the manufacturers (about $0.5 billion), a little less than $0.4 billion was available for allocation to the current factors of production, including profits. In other words, the contribution of the tobacco industry was valued at about $2.0 billion on the market, yet in terms of the cost of the current factors of production used, this contribution was worth less than $0.4 billion.

This difference arises because some of the allocations of market value do not go into payments to the factors of production. For instance, indirect taxes paid by business to the government, such as excise and sales taxes, are not costs incurred by the producer for employing a factor of production. Taxes on the factors of production, such as the corporate profits tax and social insurance contributions, in contrast, *are* a part of the factor cost to the producer. He must pay these taxes only if he hires the specific factor of production; therefore they are part of the cost of using that factor of production. Such direct levies are quite different from indirect taxes. The indirect taxes are distinguished by the characteristic that they do not fall on any specific factor of production, and so cannot be considered a part of the cost of hiring any specific factor. Business transfer payments and the current surplus of government enterprises, for the same reason, cannot be included in factor cost, since they are not payments to the factors. Subsidies, on the other hand, should not be deducted from total factor payments. This item was subtracted as an adjustment on the allocations side of the Gross National Income and Product Account in order to make the allocations of income arising from production equal to the actual market value of output. In measuring factor costs, as opposed to market value, the total factor payments are needed without adjustment. For the same reason, the statistical discrepancy is omitted. Net national product at factor cost thus is equal to net national product at market prices minus indirect taxes, business transfer payments, the current surplus of government enterprises, and the statistical discrepancy, and plus subsidies.

Viewed from the allocations side of the account, the total factor income of the nation is called national income. It is equal to net national product at factor cost in exactly the same manner that gross national income is equal to gross national product.

Net national product at factor cost and national income have all of the basic defects discussed under net national product at market prices. Since they purport to show a net product or net income for the nation, they are dependent upon some measure of capital consumption.

In addition, the concept of factor cost raises further problems. It would be considerably more appropriate to term this measure "factor return" rather than factor cost. In farming, for example, the return the farmer receives for his efforts depends on the market price of the crop, not upon the costs of production. A bumper crop may force prices down so that the return to the farmer is very low indeed, whereas in a short-crop year he may profit handsomely. In terms of the measure of factor costs, it would appear that more resources were used in the short-crop year than in the year with the bumper crop, although the reverse is probably true. Factor cost is thus not really an independent method of valuation showing the costs necessary to obtain the services of the factors, but rather is an adjustment of market value to show the portion thereof that the factors receive.

A further problem arises in connection with taxes. From the point of view of the economy as a whole, the distinction between direct and indirect taxes is not entirely clear-cut. In the above discussion direct and indirect taxes were defined without resort to the concept of incidence, but historically the distinction was in fact based upon a simplified theory of tax incidence: direct taxes are those that cannot be shifted, and indirect taxes are those that can be. It is still often argued that the relevance of the differentiation between direct and indirect taxes, and thus also the relevance of net national product at factor cost and national income, lies in some such difference in the incidence of the taxes. To the extent that these aggregates must rest on such arguments, their validity is open to serious question.

Personal Income and Outlay

National income is the income accruing to the factors of production, but it is not the income that individuals actually receive. On the one hand, part of national income is not paid out to individuals. Corporate profits taxes and undistributed profits are considered a part of the factor share of the owners, but they are not received by the owners as a part of their personal income.[2] On the other hand, individuals receive some income other than that from factor payments. Both government and business firms may make payments to individuals for reasons other than payments for services rendered. For example, the government makes relief payments and gives bonuses to veterans, and business makes charitable contributions and gives out prizes for advertising purposes. Individuals also receive gifts from abroad.[3] These are all payments that individuals receive for reasons other than current services rendered. They are, in other words, nonfactor payments received by individuals. They

[2] In the definition of personal income used by the Department of Commerce, social insurance contributions are also excluded from personal income, although they are in national income. In the national income accounting system used in Chap. 5, social insurance contributions were considered to be a part of personal income, on the ground that there was no more reason to exclude them from personal income than to exclude other employee income withheld by the employer for tax purposes.

[3] In the definition of personal income used by the Department of Commerce, transfer payments received by individuals from abroad are not included in personal income, because the transfers received and paid are shown only as a net balance which is included as a part of consumers' expenditures.

The Interrelation of Various Income and Product Concepts in U.S. National Income Accounts

Capital Consumption Allowances
Indirect Tax and Nontax Liability
Social Insurance Contributions

Wages and Salaries

Income of Unincorporated Enterprises

Interest
Dividends
Corporate Profit Taxes
Undistributed Profits
Current Surplus of Government Enterprises
Business Transfer Payments
Statistical Discrepancy
Government Transfer Payments

Minus:

Subsidies
Net Government Interest
Personal Taxes

Total

Gross National Income (Market Prices)

National Income (Market Prices)

National Income (Factor Cost)

Personal Income

Disposable Income

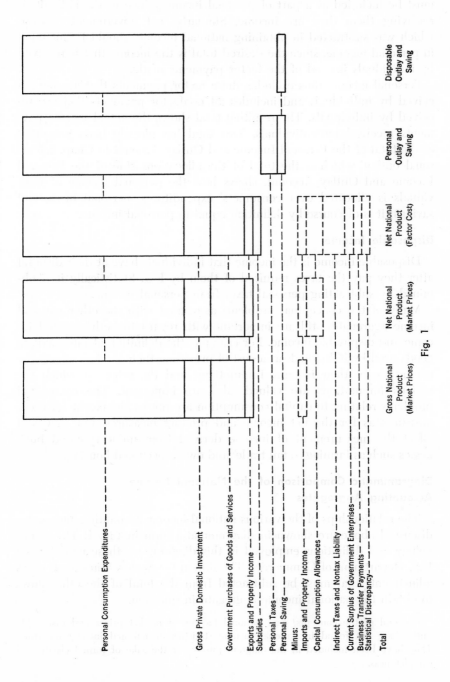

Fig. 1

Personal Consumption Expenditures				
Gross Private Domestic Investment				
Government Purchases of Goods and Services				
Exports and Property Income				
Subsidies				
Personal Taxes				
Personal Saving				
Minus:				
Imports and Property Income				
Capital Consumption Allowances				
Indirect Taxes and Nontax Liability				
Current Surplus of Government Enterprises				
Business Transfer Payments				
Statistical Discrepancy				
Total	Gross National Product (Market Prices)	Net National Product (Market Prices)	Net National Product (Factor Cost)	Personal Outlay and Saving	Disposable Outlay and Saving

must be included as a part of personal income, since to the individuals receiving them they are income. Similarly, net government interest, which was subtracted in obtaining national income, should be included in personal income, since the desired total is the income that is received by individuals instead of the factor payments made.

Personal income thus excludes those factor payments that are not received by individuals and includes all nonfactor payments that are received by individuals. The resulting total shows the actual income payments received by individuals. This total has already been presented as the total of the Personal Income and Outlay Account in Chap. 5. Personal outlay, which is the total of the allocations side of the Personal Income and Outlay Account, shows how the personal income of individuals is allocated over consumers' expenditures, personal taxes, and savings; it is of course by definition equal to personal income.

Disposable Income

Disposable income is the income that individuals have at their disposal after they pay the taxes required of them by law. Statistically it is obtained by subtracting personal taxes from personal income.

Many of the conceptual problems associated with the other national income aggregates still are important with regard to both personal income and disposable income. For example, the definition of intermediate goods used by individuals as a cost of providing their services affects the magnitude of their income. Imputations, and the prices at which the various imputations are valued, also are important. The conceptual problems relating to capital consumption are not as significant for these measures as for the net income and product measures, but they still affect the measurement of income derived from unincorporated businesses such as farming, retail trade, and owner-occupied housing.

Diagrammatic Comparison of the National Income Accounting Aggregates

The relationships of the various national income accounting aggregates discussed above are shown in diagrammatic form in Fig. 1. The terminology and definitions employed in this diagram are those used by the U.S. Department of Commerce.[4] The dotted boxes shown are in all cases adjustments that must be subtracted from the total of the other flows to obtain the national income aggregate in question.

[4] Several of the concepts, e.g., national income at market prices and disposable outlay, are not found in national income statistics or national income literature. They have been included in the diagram purely for the sake of formal clarity and completeness.

7. The Use of National Income Aggregates for Comparative Analysis

No national income aggregate is ever used as an isolated piece of information. Analysis implies comparison of some sort. For the purposes of the discussion in this chapter three different types of comparison involving national income aggregates will be distinguished: (1) structural comparisons, (2) comparisons over time, and (3) comparisons over space.

A national income aggregate may be used in structural comparisons as a total against which other flows are measured to get a comparison of magnitude or to give perspective to the component parts of the aggregate. In considering the industrial structure of an economy, for example, the relative output of various industries might be compared with some aggregate measure of total output. If on such examination agriculture were found to be 10 per cent of total output, and manufacturing 40 per cent, it could be concluded that manufacturing contributed about four times the output contributed by agriculture. Similarly, the relative composition of total output in terms of end products—consumer goods and services, producers' durable goods, and government services —might be examined. All these comparisons are essentially of a cross-sectional nature, showing the internal composition of the economy at a given moment of time. The aggregates provide totals against which the various components can be measured.

Comparisons over a period of time may involve only the national income aggregates themselves, as in the comparison of an aggregate with itself over a number of years to show the change in total output that has taken place in the economy as a whole. Or changes in the structure of an economy can be examined over time; in this case it is the change in the relation of an aggregate to a given flow or group of flows that is being studied.

Finally, comparisons of national income aggregates can also be made among various economic regions. Thus, for instance, the absolute level of output of the United States might be compared with that of the United Kingdom. Regional comparisons can also involve the comparison of the differences in structure, e.g., industrial composition of output; or the comparison of changes over time, e.g., changes in the rates of output among different countries.

The Use of National Income Aggregates for Structural Analysis

To be useful for structural analysis a national income aggregate must provide a meaningful total against which other flows can be measured to show relative magnitudes, or the breaking down of the aggregate into component parts must throw light upon the nature of the aggregate. It would be possible, in theory at least, to break the aggregates down into component parts in an infinite number of ways—personal income of individuals, for instance, might be shown classified according to the color of the recipient's hair. Generally speaking, however, the number of classifications that are considered sufficiently informative to warrant the considerable cost involved in deriving the statistics is quite limited. The breakdowns that are most common and that will be discussed in this chapter are (1) gross national product classified by type of expenditure, (2) gross national income and national income classified by distributive shares, (3) national income classified by the industrial sector in which it originates, and (4) personal income and disposable income classified according to the income size of the recipients. Each of these classifications will be discussed in turn.

Gross National Product by Type of Expenditure

The expenditure breakdown of gross national product has already been shown on the sources side of the Gross National Income and Product Account. This breakdown shows in fairly general terms the portion of gross output absorbed by consumers, the government, producers' durables, inventory change, and net foreign investment. Table 29 shows this breakdown in the form and terminology in which it is published by the Department of Commerce. This table is similar to that shown in Chap. 5, except that here exports and imports are shown only as a net balance, entitled "net foreign investment."

More detailed breakdowns are available in the Department of Commerce statistics for each of the major components shown in Table 29. For example, a more detailed classification of personal consumption expenditures is shown in Table 30. The total of this table equals personal consumption expenditures as shown in the expenditure breakdown in Table 29.

Considerably more detailed information than that shown in Table 30

Table 29. Gross National Product by Type of Expenditure, United States, 1953

	Billions of dollars	Per cent of gross national product
Gross national product..........................	$364.9	100.0
Personal consumption expenditures...........	230.1	63.1
Durable goods.............................	29.7	8.1
Nondurable goods........................	118.9	32.6
Services.................................	81.4	22.3
Gross private domestic investment............	51.4	14.1
New construction........................	25.5	7.0
Residential nonfarm....................	11.9	3.3
Other..............................	13.6	3.7
Producers' durable equipment..............	24.4	6.7
Change in business inventories.............	1.5	0.4
Nonfarm.............................	2.2	0.6
Farm................................	−0.7	−0.2
Net foreign investment......................	−1.9	−0.5
Government purchases of goods and services...	85.2	23.3
Federal.................................	60.1	16.5
National security......................	52.0	14.3
National defense.....................	50.0	13.7
Other national security...............	2.0	0.5
Other...............................	8.5	2.3
Less: Government sales.................	0.4	0.1
State and local..........................	25.1	6.9

SOURCE: National Income Supplement, 1954, *Survey of Current Business*, U.S. Department of Commerce, Table 2, pp. 162–163.

is also available in the statistics published by the Department of Commerce. For example, the item "household operation" shown in Table 30 is further broken down into an additional fourteen products and services. In all, personal consumption expenditures are classified into over eighty different subcategories. Similar, although less extensive, detail is available for the other major categories of gross national product by type of expenditure.

The significance of this information on the product composition of gross national product is readily apparent. It is useful to government, for instance, in analyzing the revenues that might be expected from different excise taxes. It is useful to business for what it shows about the magnitudes of total expenditures for different kinds of products by consumers,

Table 30. Personal Consumption Expenditures by Type of Product,
United States, 1953

	Billions of dollars	Per cent of total
1. Food and tobacco......................	$ 77.2	33.6
2. Clothing, accessories, and jewelry.........	24.6	10.7
3. Personal care.........................	2.6	1.1
4. Housing..............................	27.7	12.0
5. Household operation....................	30.1	13.1
6. Medical care and death expenses..........	11.2	4.9
7. Personal business......................	10.6	4.6
8. Transportation........................	26.8	11.6
9. Recreation...........................	11.9	5.2
10. Private education and research............	2.5	1.1
11. Religious and welfare activities...........	3.0	1.3
12. Foreign travel and remittances, net........	2.0	0.9
Total personal consumption expenditures	$230.1	100.0

SOURCE: National Income Supplement, 1954, *Survey of Current Business*, U.S. Department of Commerce, Table 30, pp. 206–208.

the government, and business. It is useful to economists in analyzing the significance of a change in government expenditures or a change in the rate of investment in the economy.

The various biases to which the gross national product estimates are subject will have a bearing upon the usefulness of these statistics because they may affect the magnitudes of the various components relative to each other and to the total. The broadness of the definition adopted for gross investment will affect the share of the total going into investment. In some countries a change in this definition has changed gross investment from 18 per cent of the total to as much as 30 per cent. Similarly, the method adopted for valuing government services will affect its magnitude. With respect to personal consumption expenditures, the extent of imputation of nonmarket productive activity, and the method of valuation used in this imputation, will affect the absolute and relative size of this share.

Gross National Product and National Income by Distributive Shares

The distributive share breakdown of the gross national product has already been shown on the allocations side of the Gross National Income and Product Account in Chap. 5. It is given in Table 31 in the terminology and form in which it is published by the Department of Commerce.

Table 31. Gross National Product and National Income by Distributive Shares, United States, 1953

	Billions of dollars	Per cent of gross national product
Compensation of employees....................................	$209.1	57.3
Wages and salaries...	198.0	54.3
Private..	164.5	45.1
Military..	10.2	2.8
Government civilian..	23.3	6.4
Supplements to wages and salaries............................	11.1	3.0
Employer contributions for social insurance...................	4.7	1.3
Other labor income..	6.3	1.7
Income of unincorporated enterprises and inventory valuation adjustment..	38.4	10.5
Business and professional...................................	26.2	7.2
Income of unincorporated enterprises........................	26.4	7.2
Inventory valuation adjustment.............................	−0.2	−0.1
Farm..	12.2	3.3
Rental income of persons......................................	10.6	2.9
Corporate profits and inventory valuation adjustment..............	38.5	10.6
Corporate profits before tax.................................	39.4	10.8
Corporate profits tax liability.............................	21.1	5.8
Corporate profits after tax.................................	18.3	5.0
Dividends..	9.4	2.6
Undistributed profits....................................	8.9	2.4
Inventory valuation adjustment.............................	−1.0	−0.3
Net interest...	8.4	2.3
National income...	$305.0	83.6
Indirect business tax and nontax liability........................	30.0	8.2
Business transfer payments...................................	1.0	0.3
Statistical discrepancy..	1.0	0.3
Less: Subsidies minus current surplus of government enterprises......	−0.5	−0.1
Capital consumption allowances...............................	27.2	7.5
Gross national product.......................................	$364.9	100.0

SOURCE: National Income Supplement, 1954, *Survey of Current Business*, U.S. Department of Commerce, Table 1, pp. 162–163; Table 4, pp. 164–165.

This table cannot be considered an accurate reflection of relative factor payments in terms of the theoretical factors of land, labor, capital, and entrepreneurship. The classifications must of statistical necessity be institutional rather than functional in nature. Entrepreneurial income, for example, as shown in this table, is a residual return to the proprietors of unincorporated enterprises such as farms, retail shops, and factories; it represents a payment for the labor of the proprietor (and sometimes his family), rent, and interest on capital, as well as profit or loss from the operation. It would be improper to consider the whole of this residual as a return to entrepreneurship, but it is of course not possible to separate it into its functional factor components. The defects of the capital consumption allowance estimates that were discussed above also will introduce a corresponding arbitrary element into both entrepreneurial income and the undistributed profits of corporations. Finally, as has been pointed out, the imputations that are made and their valuation will have serious effects upon the relative and absolute magnitude of such items as entrepreneurial income, rental income, and net interest.

In spite of the fact that this breakdown does not show a functional breakdown of factor payments, there are many purposes for which it is extremely useful. From a tax point of view, for example, the relative and absolute magnitudes of corporate profits and wages and salaries are needed to estimate yields of various kinds of taxes. Economists also are interested in the relative magnitude of the institutional flows that are generated by economic activity for analyzing the reactions that can be expected under various circumstances. This use will occupy the major portion of Part Two of this book.

National Income Originating

A classification of national income according to the industries in which it originates is published by the Department of Commerce in the form shown in Table 32. In some countries this type of industrial breakdown is also given for the gross national product.

The data given in Table 32 are a summary of the information published by the Department of Commerce; data on each of the industries are available in greater detail. Manufacturing, for example, is broken down into seventeen subgroups; these are shown in Table 33. The total in this table is equal to the entry for manufacturing in Table 32.

The Department of Commerce also presents breakdowns according to the same industrial classification for each of the distributive share components of national income shown in Table 31. Table 34 gives a summary of the industrial breakdown for the component of wages and salaries. The total in this table is again equal to the entry for compensation of employees in Table 31.

This information on the industrial breakdown of national income and its components provides the government, business, and economists with detailed knowledge of the industrial structure of the economy. Such information is essential to an analysis of the functioning of the economy

Table 32. National Income by Industrial Origin, United States, 1953

	Billions of dollars	Per cent of national income
Agriculture, forestry, and fisheries........	$ 16.8	5.5
Mining.............................	5.5	1.8
Contract construction..................	15.2	5.0
Manufacturing........................	97.3	31.9
Wholesale and retail trade..............	52.4	17.2
Finance, insurance, and real estate........	26.4	8.7
Transportation.......................	16.0	5.2
Communications and public utilities......	10.2	3.3
Services.............................	28.8	9.4
Government and government enterprises...	34.9	11.4
Rest of the world.....................	1.5	0.5
Total, all industries *.................	$305.0	100.0

* Detail may not add to totals because of rounding.
SOURCE: National Income Supplement, 1954, *Survey of Current Business*, U.S. Department of Commerce, Table 13, pp. 176–177.

with a view to understanding the impact of such factors as technological change, population growth, and social evolution. Again, however, it is important to keep in mind the limitations and possible biases in the data. The imputation of nonmarket transactions and the extreme unevenness of coverage of market and nonmarket activities will affect the relative importance of various industries. Furthermore, the data will reflect price changes as well as product changes; thus, for instance, agriculture will appear to be a much more important industry in a period of high agricultural prices than in a period of depressed agricultural prices.

Personal Income and Disposable Income by Size

In making a distribution of personal income or disposable income according to the income size of the individual recipient, the Department of Commerce introduces certain modifications into the concepts. First, personal income includes the income of nonprofit institutions, as well as that of families and individuals, and this institutional income is excluded. Second, the Department of Commerce has excluded the income of individuals in the Armed Forces and individuals who die during the year

Table 33. Income Originating in Manufacturing, United States, 1953

	Billions of dollars	Per cent of total manu- facturing
Food and kindred products......................	$ 8.1	8.3
Tobacco manufactures..........................	0.6	0.6
Textile-mill products...........................	4.4	4.5
Apparel and other finished fabric products.........	4.0	4.1
Lumber and furniture products...................	4.4	4.5
Lumber and wood products, except furniture.....	2.8	2.9
Furniture and fixtures........................	1.6	1.6
Paper and allied products.......................	3.3	3.4
Printing, publishing, and allied industries..........	4.4	4.5
Chemicals and allied products....................	6.5	6.7
Products of petroleum and coal..................	3.4	3.5
Rubber products...............................	1.7	1.7
Leather and leather products.....................	1.4	1.4
Stone, clay, and glass products..................	3.0	3.1
Metals, metal products, and miscellaneous.........	21.1	21.7
Primary metal industries......................	9.4	9.7
Fabricated metal products, including ordnance...	7.5	7.7
Instruments.................................	2.0	2.1
Miscellaneous manufacturing..................	2.3	2.4
Machinery except electrical.....................	10.6	10.9
Electrical machinery...........................	7.0	7.2
Transportation equipment except automobiles......	5.8	6.0
Automobiles and automobile equipment..........	7.7	7.9
Total manufacturing *........................	$97.3	100.0

* Detail may not add to totals because of rounding.
SOURCE: National Income Supplement, 1954, *Survey of Current Business*, U.S. Department of Commerce, Table 13, pp. 176–177.

in question, so that the resulting income size distribution will reflect family income. The specific adjustments that are made by the Department of Commerce to the personal income concept are shown in Table 35.

Using this adjusted concept, the distribution of family income by size for the United States in the year 1950 is shown in Table 36.

The same sort of information is available for family personal income after Federal income tax. Except for state income taxes and certain other minor personal taxes, this concept corresponds roughly to family disposable income. This distribution is given in Table 37.

Table 34. *Wages and Salaries by Industry, United States, 1953*

	Billions of dollars	Per cent of total wages and salaries
Agriculture, forestry, and fisheries.........	$ 3.5	1.7
Mining...............................	4.1	2.0
Contract construction....................	11.6	5.5
Manufacturing.........................	75.1	35.9
Wholesale and retail trade...............	35.1	16.8
Finance, insurance, and real estate........	8.0	3.8
Transportation.........................	13.0	6.2
Communications and public utilities.......	6.2	3.0
Services...............................	17.7	8.5
Government and government enterprises...	34.9	16.7
Rest of the world......................	*	*
All private industries †..................	174.2	83.3
All industries †........................	209.1	100.0

* Less than 0.05.
† Detail may not add to totals because of rounding.
source: National Income Supplement, 1954, *Survey of Current Business*, U.S. Department of Commerce, Table 14, pp. 178–179.

Table 35. *Reconciliation of Personal Income and Family Personal Income for the United States, 1946*

(*In billions*)

Personal income...	$177.7
Less:	
Civilian wages of persons who entered Armed Forces or died.................	0.8
Military money wages or salaries of Armed Forces personnel who had not returned to civilian life by end of year and military nonmoney wages or salaries	3.7
Property income received by nonprofit institutions or retained by fiduciaries...	0.6
Employer contributions to private pension and welfare funds.................	1.2
Business and government transfer payments to nonprofit institutions..........	0.6
Equals: Family personal income...	$170.7

source: Income Distribution Supplement, *Survey of Current Business*, 1953, Exhibit 16, p. 67.

Table 36. *Distribution of Consumer Units and Family Personal Income by Family Personal Income Level, United States, 1950*

Family personal income	Number of families and unattached individuals (In millions)	Aggregate family personal income (In billions)	Percentage distribution	
			Number	Income
Under $1,000	3.7	$ 1.9	7.6	0.9
$1,000–$1,999	7.3	11.2	15.1	5.1
2,000– 2,999	8.0	20.1	16.5	9.3
3,000– 3,999	8.5	29.6	17.4	13.6
4,000– 4,999	7.0	31.2	14.4	14.4
5,000– 7,499	8.5	51.2	17.5	23.6
7,500– 9,999	2.9	24.2	5.9	11.2
$10,000 and over	2.7	47.4	5.6	21.9
Total......................	48.6	$216.8	100.0	100.0

SOURCE: Income Distribution Supplement, *Survey of Current Business*, 1953, Table 19, p. 85.

Table 37. *Distribution of Consumer Units and Family Personal Income after Federal Individual Income Tax Liability by Level of After-tax Income, United States, 1950*

Family personal income after Federal individual income tax liability	Number of families and unattached individuals (In millions)	Aggregate after-tax family personal income (In billions)	Percentage distribution	
			Number	After-tax income
Under $1,000	3.7	$ 1.9	7.7	1.0
$1,000–$1,999	7.9	12.0	16.2	6.0
2,000– 2,999	8.7	21.9	17.9	11.1
3,000– 3,999	8.8	30.8	18.2	15.5
4,000– 4,999	7.0	31.2	14.4	15.7
5,000– 7,499	8.0	47.7	16.3	24.0
7,500– 9,999	2.3	19.7	4.8	9.9
$10,000 and over	2.2	33.4	4.5	16.8
Total......................	48.6	$198.6	100.0	100.0

SOURCE: Income Distribution Supplement, *Survey of Current Business*, 1953, Table 20, p. 85.

These distributions provide a great deal of information on the relative welfare of different groups in the economy and on the impact of the Federal tax system on different income groups. In considering these tables from a welfare point of view, however, a number of qualifications are necessary. First, the treatment of imputations and nonmarket production will have an important effect on the income distributions. If home-produced goods consumed by farmers are valued at what the farmer can sell them for rather than at what he would have to pay for them, farmers' income will appear to be much lower than that of comparably well-off persons in the city. Second, the treatment of intermediate products has a bearing. The clerk in the city must commute to work, pay high rent, and wear relatively expensive kinds of clothes to work, so that from a welfare point of view his income includes intermediate goods and services that are not recognized in the national income accounts. There are also other reasons why the income distribution may give a false impression of relative welfare differences. The low-income groups include older people who have retired or work only part time, but have other resources to live on. Others in the low-income groups are young single people starting their first jobs. Conversely, some families have multiple wage earners, giving them the appearance of high income, but when this income is divided among the larger number in the family, it may result in a relatively low income level per person. With these qualifications in mind, however, the statistics on income distribution do provide valuable information on how the income of the nation is divided among the families receiving it.

The Use of National Income Aggregates for Comparisons over Time

The national accounts data are available in the form of time series covering a number of years, both in terms of the prices that were in effect in these years and in terms of a constant price level. The interpretation of the constant price data is somewhat complex, so it will be discussed in a separate section. Attention will first be directed to the nature and use of the current price data.

Comparisons of National Income Accounting Data over Time: Current Prices

All the statistics referred to in the discussion in the preceding section of the use of national income aggregates for structural analysis are available for the United States in the form of a series of annual estimates covering a number of years, in most cases at least from 1929 to the present. Many of them are also available in the form of quarterly estimates. These statistics are in terms of "current prices"; that is, the estimates for each year reflect the actual flows of income and the actual transactions that took place in that year in terms of the prices in effect at the time. No attempt is made to adjust, correct, or compensate for any price changes that may have taken place subsequently. For instance, personal consumption expenditures for the year 1929 would record the actual dollar amount spent by consumers in that year.

The availability of the various national income aggregates and their components as series extending over a period of time makes possible the comparative analysis of structural change over time, as well as the examination of the structure at any given moment of time. In considering the gross national product by type of expenditure, for example, it is of considerable interest to determine how the relative importance of the expenditures on various types of products has changed over the years. The expenditure pattern in a depression year may be quite different from that in a prosperous year, and studying the differences will reveal how the expenditures for various commodities fluctuate. With respect to the breakdown of the distributive shares of national income over time, the series in current prices will show the relative fluctuation in profits, wages, farm income, etc., with changes in the level of economic activity, together with their changing importance in the total gross national income. The industrial origin of national income studied over time is of interest for much the same sort of reason. The changing importance of an industry will be reflected by its growth or decline as a percentage of the total output of the economy. The size distributions of income for different periods show how the distribution is shifting over time. For purposes of public policy it is of considerable importance to know whether the distribution of income is becoming more or less equal.

The data giving all these breakdowns of the national income aggregates for the United States for the years 1929 to 1954 are reprinted in the appendix to this chapter. They are published by the Department of Commerce in the *Survey of Current Business* and the National Income and Income Distribution supplements to the *Survey*. In general, considerably more detail is given in these sources.

In using the national income aggregates and their components for comparisons over time, it is particularly important that the user take into account the inherent qualifications and biases that have been pointed out above, since they become increasingly important in this use. For example, nonmarket activities that are omitted from consideration in one period may in a later period be replaced by substitute activities that do enter into the market and so are included. Thus twenty-five years ago some food preparation (e.g., canning and baking) that was done in the home would not have appeared in the data; now, however, the increasing employment of women outside the home means that a greater proportion of food preparation is done in commercial establishments and so does enter into the accounts. Likewise, the valuation of the imputations of nonmarket activities that are included is important. A shift from a largely farming to a largely urban population, for instance, would probably result in an overstated increase in output because of the valuation attributed to the output of the farming population.

With these qualifications, however, the national income data in time series form provide the careful user with a wealth of information upon which to base realistic public policy, business activity, or empirical economic research.

Comparisons of National Income Accounting Data over Time: Constant Prices

The national income accounting data in current prices have very considerable usefulness in making comparisons over time, but there are certain problems for which data in this form are not satisfactory. Certain of the national income aggregates purport to measure the *value,* in one sense or another, of the national output, but time series of these aggregates in current prices do not and cannot reflect the changes that occur in the *volume* of output during periods when significant price changes are taking place. The change in value is of course due to the combined effects of the changes in the volume of goods and services being produced and the changes in the valuation of these goods and services resulting from changing prices. For many purposes it is the change in volume that is needed. A doubling of the gross national product in current prices, for instance, might not mean any increase in the well-being of the nation if prices had also doubled and the physical volume of output had remained unchanged. In this kind of analysis the evaluation of the significance of changes in the aggregates and their components in terms of current prices must take into account what has happened to prices.

Unfortunately, with the myriad of price changes that are continually occurring and the extremely heterogeneous body of goods and services that go to make up the gross national product, the correction of an aggregate such as the gross national product for the effects of price changes is somewhat complex. The basic principles involved, however, are not very difficult. They can probably be explained most easily in terms of several extremely simplified examples.

The method of correcting a current value total to take into account the effect of price changes is readily apparent if it is assumed that the total output of an economy consists of a single commodity selling at a single price. By definition, the value of this commodity is the price of the commodity multiplied by the quantity or number of units produced. In conventional symbols this is p (price) $\times$ q (quantity). If the value of the commodity in the first year is known to be $100 billion ($p_1 \times q_1$) and the value in the second year is known to be $150 billion ($p_2 \times q_2$), the information available is comparable to a time series of gross national product in current prices, and without more information about prices, nothing can be said about whether the physical volume of production has changed. If the change in price between the two periods is known, however, the change in the volume of output can be derived by applying a correction to the current price figures for the price change. Suppose, for example, that the price in the first period was $1 per unit ($p_1$), and that it rose in the second period to $1.50 per unit ($p_2$). The correction for price change can be applied in either of two ways. The value of the product in the second year, $150 billion ($p_2 \times q_2$) can be "deflated" to remove the effect of rising prices, or the value of the product of the first year, $100 billion ($p_1 \times q_1$) can be "inflated" to bring it up to the level of prices in the second period.

The first method would involve calculating how much the price of the second year would have to be changed to be equal to the price of the first year, so that an equal adjustment can be made to the value of product of the second year to eliminate the effect of changing prices. Symbolically, the corrected value would be

$$(p_2 \times q_2) + \frac{p_1 - p_2}{p_2} \times (p_2 \times q_2)$$

In terms of the figures in this example, this would be $150 + ($1 - $1.50)/$1.50 \times $150, or $100 billion. The valuation of the output of the second year has been adjusted for the influence of the price rise, or in other words, it has been revalued in terms of the first-year price. Symbolically, this new valuation can be expressed as $p_1 \times q_2$. According to this calculation, there was no change in the volume of production, since the deflated figure of $100 billion obtained for the second year in terms of the first year's price is identical with the value of the first year's output.

The second method, that of inflating the value of production for the first year to bring it up to the level of prices in the second year, is in principle identical with that shown for the deflation process. It is first necessary to calculate the change in the first year's price that would be needed for it to equal the price of the second year. Symbolically, this would be $(p_2 - p_1)/p_1$. In terms of the figures in the example above, it would be ($1.50 - $1)/$1, or 50 per cent. An equal change would need to be made in the value of product of the first year to eliminate the influence of changing prices. Symbolically, the corrected value of product would be

$$p_1 q_1 + \frac{p_2 - p_1}{p_1} \times p_1 q_1$$

or in the above example, $\$100 + (\$1.50 - \$1)/\$1 \times \$100$, or $150 billion. This method is the converse of the first method outlined above. The valuation of output in the first year has been adjusted to take into account the price rise that occurred in the second year. In other words, the value of output of the first year has been revalued in terms of the second-year price. It is again found that there has been no change in the total volume of production. The first year's output expressed in the price level of the second year is $150 billion, and the second year's output expressed in the same price level is also $150 billion.

A comparison of the final results of the two methods outlined above is given below.

	First year	Second year
Value of output in prices of the first year....	$p_1 q_1 = \$100$	$p_1 q_2 = \$100$
Value of output in prices of the second year..	$p_2 q_1 = \$150$	$p_2 q_2 = \$150$

If the price instead of rising had fallen in the second year, say from $1 to 50 cents, while the value of output rose from $100 billion to $150 billion, using the first method above, output in terms of the prices of the first year would be $100 billion in the first year and $300 billion in the second year. Using the second method, in terms of the prices of the second year the corrected output of the first year would be $50 billion, compared with $150 billion in the second year. Both methods of adjustment again yield similar results, that output in the second year was three times that of the first year.

The difference between the two methods in this simplified example lies solely in the choice of period used as a basis for price valuation. Conceptually, both methods adjust the value of production in current prices to the price in effect at one single period of time; the only difference between the two methods is the choice of time period whose price will be used. Time series adjusted by using either price basis are referred to as constant price time series, and it is customary to designate the year that is used as the price basis for the adjustment of the other years as the base year.

When the assumption that only one commodity is produced in the economy is dropped, the problem becomes somewhat more complex.

For example, suppose that there are two commodities, and that the prices and values of these commodities change between two years in the manner shown below:

	Period 1		Period 2	
	Price	Value of output	Price	Value of output
Commodity A...........	$1	$300	$2.00	$100
Commodity B...........	1	200	0.50	400
Total value of output in current prices.......	....	$500		$500

The problem is the same as that posed by a single-product economy, namely, to compute the change in the volume of production by adjusting the current price data for the effects of the price changes that have occurred.

If the first method shown above is applied to each of the commodities, such that the value of product for the second year is adjusted to the price prevailing in the first period, the results would be as follows.

Value of Output Adjusted to Prices of Period 1

	Period 1	Period 2	Output of period 2 as per cent of output of period 1
Commodity A...........	$300	$ 50	17
Commodity B...........	200	800	400
Total value of output in constant prices.......	$500	$850	170

Thus, by this method the volume of output of commodity A is calculated to have declined in period 2 to 17 per cent of what it was in period 1, whereas that of commodity B increased in period 2 to 400 per cent of what it was in period 1. The volume of output for the economy as a whole in period 2 comes out to be 70 per cent greater than it was in period 1.

Using the second method shown above, that of adjusting the value of

output of each of the commodities in the first period to the prices prevailing in the second period, somewhat different results are obtained.

Value of Output Adjusted to Prices of Period 2

	Period 1	Period 2	Output of period 2 as per cent of output of period 1
Commodity A...........	$600	$100	17
Commodity B...........	100	400	400
Total value of output in constant prices.......	$700	$500	71

This second calculation gives exactly the same results for the relative
volume of each of the individual commodities in the two periods, but
very different results for the economy as a whole. According to this
method, the total volume of output of the second period is only 71 per
cent of that in the first period.

Thus it appears by the use of the first year's prices that production
rose by 70 per cent, whereas by the use of the second year's prices, the
conclusion is that the volume of production dropped by 29 per cent. The
answer to this apparent paradox lies in the fact that, in terms of the
volume of output, the two commodities behaved differently, and to obtain a single figure for what happened in the economy as a whole the
different relative movements have to be averaged in some manner or
other.

The problem of how to average the changes is called the index number problem. Merely adding up the percentage changes in the volume of
output and striking an average is no solution. This would weight
each commodity equally, so that very minor items would be considered
as important in the determination of the change in the economy's output
as major items. In index number theory the usual procedure is to weight
commodities by their relative importance. This is what was done in the
example above. Unfortunately, as was shown there, this criterion does not
lead to a single unambiguous answer. The difference in the relative
prices of the two commodities in the two periods results in different valuations of their importance in the two years. The method of calculation
employed implicitly weighted the changes by the relative prices of
period 1 in the first case and by the relative prices in period 2 in the
second case. In some price index formulas this conflict is resolved by
averaging the weights, either geometrically or arithmetically, but here

again there is no theoretical reason why such a scheme should be more valid than the choice of any other single period as a basis.

The choice of first-period prices as against second-period prices may introduce some bias into the measurement of production. With an unchanged schedule of wants in the economy, when the quantity of a commodity increases, its price will generally fall, since people will not want to purchase more except at a lower price; and conversely, if the output of a commodity is restricted, its price will be raised. For this reason the use of prices at the beginning of a period as a basis for computing volume changes overemphasizes the value of the additional output that occurs in lines where production is expanding, and undervalues the output of those lines where there is a contraction. For example, assume that the output of the economy is composed of two commodities and that in the beginning period the value of the output of each of these commodities is identical. If the physical volume of output of one commodity increases by 50 per cent, and that of the other is reduced by 50 per cent, a computation using the prices in the beginning year as a basis would indicate that the output for the economy as a whole was unchanged. But viewed in terms of the utility that individuals derive from the commodities, the increase of utility accompanying the increased output of the one commodity would be smaller than the decrease in utility accompanying the decreased output of the other commodity. Thus the utility of the output of the economy as a whole would in fact have been reduced.

It is beyond the scope of this discussion to go into the refinements of index number theory. The differences that result from using the prices of different periods as a basis for obtaining total volume of output measures have purposely been overdrawn to illustrate the principles involved. In practice it is often found that the results do not differ significantly.

There are, however, a number of other problems in deriving constant price series of national income accounting data. For example, obtaining representative and relevant price data for all the goods and services produced in the economy poses a technical problem of considerable importance. It is especially difficult in areas of the economy where only quoted prices are available. Discounts, rebates, and sales at reduced prices cause actual prices paid for commodities to diverge significantly from quoted prices. The quality of products may also change, thus in fact altering their relative value from period to period. Where such quality changes are very great, it in effect means that new products have entered the market and old ones have dropped out. In these cases, of course, no prices can exist for the new products in the earlier periods before they appeared. Even where quality changes are minor, it is still difficult or impossible to make appropriate price adjustments to take these quality changes into account. For many sectors of the economy, finally, a problem arises in deflating the services of employees that appear directly as a part of the final output of the economy. Should it be assumed that all changes in the rate of pay of schoolteachers, self-employed professionals, domestic servants, and government employees are in fact price changes, and that productivity never changes in these sectors of the economy? The manner in which these more technical problems are met in the deflation of the United States national income accounting data is explained in the following chapter on sources and methods and its appendix.

Statistics on gross national product by type of expenditure in constant prices are given in Table 38. These series are given in greater detail and for a greater span of years in the appendix to this chapter.

Table 38. Gross National Product by Type of Expenditure, in Constant Prices, United States, 1948–1953

(In billions of 1947 dollars)

	1948	1949	1950	1951	1952	1953
Personal consumption expenditures	$168.0	$172.3	$182.8	$183.6	$189.2	$196.7
Gross private domestic investment	38.8	28.1	45.3	45.2	39.9	39.3
Net foreign investment..........	2.1	0.8	−1.1	2.3	1.6	−0.3
Government purchases of goods and services......................	34.9	40.3	37.7	51.8	63.5	7.80
Gross national product..........	$243.9	$241.5	$264.7	$282.9	$294.2	$306.6

SOURCE: National Income Supplement, 1954, *Survey of Current Business*, U.S. Department of Commerce, Table 40, pp. 216–217.

A number of questions can be raised relating to the validity of using these constant price data for making comparisons over time. There is a problem of whether *all* productive activity in the economy is in fact comprehended in the measurement process. Specifically, leisure is nowhere included in the national income accounting data, so that a shift from work to leisure—a decrease in working hours, for instance—would be reflected in the constant price data as a decrease in real output. From the point of view of welfare, the significant shortening of hours in the United States over the years is very important, but it is not reflected in any of the constant price data; these data therefore understate the changes taking place in real output including leisure. There are also factors operating in a reverse manner. To the extent that more activities are carried on in the market sector instead of the nonmarket sector, the constant price data will reflect a greater increase in output than has actually occurred. Thus the greater employment of women in the labor force and the consequent increased reliance on laundries, restaurants, etc., may represent a shift in the nature of output rather than an absolute increase in output. Over the decades production has been shifting from nonmarket to market forms, so that the increase in output as expressed by constant price data may be somewhat overstated for this reason. Certain of the more technical aspects of constant price data may also lead to cumulative bias. The fact that quality changes are inadequately recorded, or ignored, will lead to a downward bias in the reporting of output changes. Similarly, by considering all changes in the rate of pay for services as *de facto* changes in the price of these services, the possibility of an increase in quality is denied.

There is a very real question how valid a time series of constant price data would be for the purpose of measuring welfare, even if it did not have the biases and defects mentioned above. Throughout the analysis thus far it has been implicitly assumed that the needs of society do not undergo any significant change over time. This assumption may not necessarily be so. A society may become geared to a way of life, so that what in one period was completely unnecessary and perhaps even unrelated to welfare becomes in a later period a vital part of the social fabric. Thus, for example, years ago life was constructed on the premise that transportation over long distances was extremely difficult or impossible. Today, however, when such transportation has been available, it might be a matter of major disutility if serious restrictions were imposed on it. Furthermore, many forms of social cost and benefit are not adequately taken into account by constant price national accounts data. The operation and upkeep of the modern city involves many costs that did not exist in earlier times, and that are recorded as productive services in the constant price data, although they may more properly be part of the cost of maintaining the particular form of society which now exists. Likewise, it is not possible to measure in monetary terms all the benefits of present-day society compared with previous periods. The increase in length of life, for example, does not enter into the constant price national accounts data in any observable form. On the other side of the ledger, of course, perhaps the increased pace of life and its strain represent positive disutility. The constant price data also make the assumption that the price of a product multiplied by the output of that product somehow or other represents the total value of the product in utility terms. Price at best actually represents only the marginal utility of the product, and two products that have identical marginal utilities may differ consideably in total utility. In fact, many commodities that are free provide a vast amount of utility. Air, for example, is most essential, yet it has no cost. Finally, an individual's welfare may depend less on the level of economic and other goods he enjoys than upon the expectations he has for the future. In such a case welfare might be more related to the rate of change shown by the constant price national income accounting data than to their absolute level.

The Use of National Income Aggregates for Comparisons over Space

Just as comparisons of national income aggregates are possible over time, so are they possible over space. Within a single economy the comparison can usually be made directly. Thus, for example, the national income originating in one region of the United States could be compared with that originating in another region. Such studies have been made by the Department of Commerce, and additional studies will probably be forthcoming as more work is done upon the development of the statistics for the various regions. In such comparisons a few qualifications again should be borne in mind.

First, the prices of commodities in two different regions may be very different. The prices in New York City may differ considerably from those of a rural community in the South. A careful comparison of regional income and product aggregates should take such differences in prices into account.

Second, and perhaps of equal importance, different regions differ considerably both in their resources and in their needs, and in the extent to which economic activity takes place in the market. Again, using the comparison of New York City and a rural community in the South, the needs of the two regions may be quite different. A large city requires a whole complex of intracity transportation, municipal services, and costs associated with the distribution of even the simplest goods in such a large area. How many of these are in fact intermediate goods required for the operation of the city is a matter of conjecture. Even the difference in climate means that the expense of heating in winter required in New York City may be unnecessary in the South. In such a regional comparison, therefore, it is necessary to decide what should be eliminated from the product of one area and what imputations should be made to the product of another. The problem of how farmers' output should be valued has already been discussed in a number of other places in this chapter, but should the Southern community have an imputation for its mild weather in the winter, since in economic terms this serves the function of the fuel consumed in New York City? For these reasons comparisons between different regions are difficult, and the presently available regional income and product aggregates may not be suitable for this purpose.

Comparisons of national income and product aggregates between different countries are of course even more complex than comparison between regions within one country. Besides all the complications of the regional comparisons, an additional problem arises in that the currencies of different countries are rarely the same. The problem of how to adjust the national income and product aggregates to a common monetary basis is in theoretical terms almost identical with the problem of removing the effect of price changes from current price data. From a theoretical point of view it would be possible to value the output of one country in terms of the prices of the other. The same problem would then face the analyst, in that he must choose the set of prices of one of the countries as the basis for calculating output. If the choice of price basis significantly affected the comparison, the dilemma of the index number problem would again be posed.

In actual practice it is never possible to choose a single set of prices and value the output of both countries in terms of it; commodities produced in different countries are too diverse. Thus it would not be possible to value housing in France by housing prices in the United States, because the products are too different. Because relevant prices do not exist, recourse is generally had either to the exchange rate between the countries in question or to some concept of purchasing power parity. The exchange rate at best reflects only those commodities that are capable of being traded across national borders, plus the influence of capital movements. Purchasing power parity would be a considerable improvement, but statistically this concept is also elusive since commodity-by-commodity comparisons of two different countries are difficult.

Estimates of gross national product on a total and per capita basis for different countries were prepared by the Statistical Office of the United Nations. This schedule has a very practical use in that it is used to calculate the relative contributions the various countries pay to support the cost of operating the United Nations. In viewing these per capita figures as real differences in economic welfare, however, it is important to bear in mind, in addition to all the qualifications that have been brought up concerning such regional comparisons in the preceding paragraphs, that the statistical reliability of data for many of these countries is not high. As will be seen in Chap. 8, on sources and methods, the task of obtaining reliable national income data is a formidable one, and many countries today have neither the experience nor the resources necessary to produce adequate statistics. In some instances, therefore, the United Nations figures represent informed guesses rather than accurate statistics.

Conclusion: The Function of National Income Aggregates

From the discussion of national income aggregates in this chapter it should be obvious that these measures should not be taken as thermometers or barometers for measuring the health of the economy or for comparison of different economies. The national income aggregates present a wealth of information that is pertinent to such analyses, but it needs to be considered in terms of the definitions that are set up and the assumptions that are made. The aggregates do little more than provide a classificatory framework for the analysis of economic problems, and for many purposes it will be found that these classifications and assumptions are unsatisfactory for the problem at hand. For this reason the form of the national income accounting aggregates, the assumptions upon which they are based, and the classification systems which are employed will undoubtedly be further developed and improved in time. In few instances, however, can it ever be expected that simple aggregate measures alone will yield meaningful answers to complex problems.

APPENDIX TO CHAPTER 7. NATIONAL INCOME ACCOUNTING STATISTICS, 1929 TO 1954

Table 39. Gross National Product
(In billions

	1929	1930	1931	1932	1933	1934	1935	1936	1937	1938
Gross national product.................	104.4	91.1	76.3	58.5	56.0	65.0	72.5	82.7	90.8	85.2
Personal consumption expenditure.......	79.0	71.0	61.3	49.3	46.4	51.9	56.3	62.6	67.3	64.6
Durable goods......................	9.2	7.2	5.5	3.6	3.5	4.2	5.1	6.3	6.9	5.7
Nondurable goods..................	37.7	34.0	28.9	22.8	22.3	26.7	29.3	32.8	35.2	34.0
Services..........................	32.1	29.8	26.9	22.9	20.7	21.0	21.9	23.5	25.1	25.0
Gross private domestic investment.......	16.2	10.3	5.5	0.9	1.4	2.9	6.3	8.4	11.7	6.7
New construction..................	8.7	6.2	4.0	1.9	1.4	1.7	2.3	3.3	4.4	4.0
Residential nonfarm...............	3.6	2.1	1.6	0.6	0.5	0.6	1.0	1.6	1.9	2.0
Other...........................	5.1	4.1	2.4	1.2	1.0	1.1	1.3	1.7	2.5	2.0
Producers' durable equipment........	5.8	4.5	2.8	1.6	1.6	2.3	3.1	4.2	5.1	3.6
Change in business inventories........	1.7	−0.4	−1.3	−2.6	−1.6	−1.1	0.9	1.0	2.2	−0.9
Nonfarm.......................	1.8	−0.1	−1.6	−2.6	−1.4	0.2	0.4	2.1	1.7	−1.0
Farm...........................	−0.2	−0.3	0.3	*	−0.3	−1.3	0.5	−1.1	0.5	0.1
Net foreign investment................	0.8	0.7	0.2	0.2	0.1	0.4	−0.1	−0.1	0.1	1.1
Government purchase of goods and services............................	8.5	9.2	9.2	8.1	8.0	9.8	10.0	11.8	11.7	12.8
Federal...........................	1.3	1.4	1.5	1.5	2.0	3.0	2.9	4.8	4.6	5.3
National security...............										
National defense...............	1.3	1.4	1.5	1.5	2.0	3.0	2.9	4.8	4.6	5.3
Other national security.........										
Other...........................										
Less: Government sales.............	*	*	*	*	*	*	*	*	*	•
State and local.....................	7.2	7.8	7.7	6.6	6.0	6.8	7.1	7.0	7.2	7.5

* Less than 0.05.

NOTE: Detail may not add to totals because of rounding.

SOURCE: *Survey of Current Business*, U.S. Department of Commerce, July, 1955, Table 2.

by Type of Expenditure, 1929–1954
of dollars)

1939	1940	1941	1942	1943	1944	1945	1946	1947	1948	1949	1950	1951	1952	1953	1954
91.1	100.6	125.8	159.1	192.5	211.4	213.6	209.2	232.2	257.3	257.3	285.1	328.2	345.2	364.5	360.5
67.6	71.9	81.9	89.7	100.5	109.8	121.7	146.6	165.0	177.6	180.6	194.0	208.3	218.3	230.6	236.5
6.7	7.8	9.7	7.0	6.6	6.8	8.1	15.9	20.6	22.2	23.6	28.6	27.1	26.6	29.8	29.3
35.1	37.2	43.2	51.3	59.3	65.4	73.2	84.5	93.1	98.7	96.9	100.4	111.1	116.0	118.9	120.9
25.8	26.9	29.0	31.5	34.7	37.7	40.4	46.2	51.3	56.7	60.1	65.0	70.1	75.7	81.8	86.4
9.3	13.2	18.1	9.9	5.6	7.1	10.4	27.1	29.7	41.2	32.5	51.2	56.9	49.6	51.4	47.2
4.8	5.5	6.6	3.7	2.3	2.7	3.8	10.3	14.0	17.9	17.5	22.7	23.3	23.7	25.8	27.8
2.7	3.0	3.5	1.7	0.9	0.8	1.1	4.0	6.3	8.6	8.3	12.6	11.0	11.1	11.9	13.5
2.1	2.5	3.1	2.0	1.4	1.9	2.7	6.3	7.7	9.3	9.2	10.1	12.4	12.6	13.8	14.3
4.2	5.5	6.9	4.3	4.0	5.4	7.7	10.7	16.7	19.1	17.8	21.1	23.2	23.1	24.4	22.3
0.4	2.2	4.5	1.8	−0.8	−1.0	−1.1	6.1	−1.0	4.2	−2.7	7.4	10.4	2.8	1.2	−2.9
0.3	1.9	4.0	0.7	−0.6	−0.6	−0.6	6.4	1.3	3.0	−1.9	6.4	9.0	2.1	1.9	−3.2
0.1	0.3	0.5	1.2	−0.2	−0.4	−0.5	−0.2	−2.3	1.1	−0.9	0.9	1.4	0.6	−0.7	0.4
0.9	1.5	1.1	−0.2	−2.2	−2.1	−1.4	4.6	8.9	2.0	0.5	−2.2	0.2	−0.2	−2.0	−0.3
13.3	14.1	24.8	59.7	88.6	96.5	82.9	30.9	28.6	36.6	43.6	42.0	62.8	77.5	84.5	77.0
5.2	6.2	16.9	52.0	81.2	89.0	74.8	20.9	15.8	21.0	25.4	22.1	41.0	54.3	59.5	49.2
1.3	2.2	13.8	49.6	80.4	88.6	75.9	21.2	13.3	16.0	19.3	18.5	37.3	48.8	51.4	43.2
—	—	—	—	—	—	—	—	12.3	11.6	13.6	14.3	33.9	46.4	49.4	41.4
—	—	—	—	—	—	—	—	1.1	4.4	5.7	4.3	3.4	2.4	2.0	1.8
3.9	4.0	3.2	2.7	1.5	1.6	1.0	2.5	3.8	5.6	6.6	3.9	4.2	5.8	8.5	6.3
*	*	*	0.2	0.6	1.2	2.2	2.7	1.3	0.5	0.4	0.3	0.4	0.4	0.4	0.4
8.2	7.9	7.8	7.7	7.4	7.5	8.1	10.0	12.8	15.6	18.2	19.9	21.8	23.2	25.0	27.8

Table 40. *Personal Consumption*

(*In billions*

	1929	1930	1931	1932	1933	1934	1935	1936	1937	1938
Food and tobacco......................	21.2	19.4	16.2	12.7	12.8	15.5	17.6	20.0	21.6	20.6
Clothing, accessories, and jewelry........	11.2	9.7	8.2	6.0	5.4	6.6	7.0	7.7	8.1	8.0
Personal care..........................	1.1	1.0	1.0	0.8	0.7	0.8	0.8	0.9	1.0	1.0
Housing..............................	11.4	11.0	10.3	9.0	7.9	7.6	7.6	7.9	8.4	8.8
Household operation....................	10.7	9.6	8.4	6.8	6.5	7.2	7.7	8.8	9.5	8.9
Medical care and health inspection.......	3.5	3.4	3.0	2.5	2.4	2.6	2.7	3.0	3.2	3.2
Personal business......................	5.1	4.0	3.5	3.0	2.9	2.9	3.1	3.4	3.7	3.5
Transportation........................	7.6	6.1	5.0	4.0	4.0	4.6	5.3	6.1	6.5	5.6
Recreation............................	4.3	4.0	3.3	2.4	2.2	2.4	2.6	3.0	3.4	3.2
Private education and research..........	0.7	0.7	0.7	0.6	0.5	0.5	0.5	0.5	0.6	0.6
Religious and welfare activities..........	1.2	1.2	1.1	1.0	0.9	0.9	0.9	0.9	0.9	0.9
Foreign travel and remittances—net.....	0.8	0.8	0.6	0.5	0.4	0.3	0.4	0.4	0.5	0.4
Total personal consumption expenditures........................	79.0	71.0	61.3	49.3	46.4	51.9	56.3	62.6	67.3	64.6
Durable commodities...............	9.2	7.2	5.5	3.6	3.5	4.2	5.1	6.3	6.9	5.7
Nondurable commodities...........	37.7	34.0	28.9	22.8	22.3	26.7	29.3	32.8	35.2	34.0
Services.........................	32.1	29.8	26.9	22.9	20.7	21.0	21.9	23.5	25.1	25.0

NOTE: Detail may not add to totals because of rounding.

SOURCE: National Income Supplement, 1954, *Survey of Current Business*, U.S. Department of Commerce, Table 30 (1929–1951); *Survey of Current Business*, July, 1955 (1952–1954).

Expenditure by Type of Product, 1929–1954
of dollars)

1939	1940	1941	1942	1943	1944	1945	1946	1947	1948	1949	1950	1951	1952	1953	1954
20.9	22.2	25.7	31.2	36.4	40.1	44.6	52.3	58.0	61.4	60.7	63.3	71.2	75.1	77.2	78.6
8.4	8.9	10.5	13.1	16.0	17.5	19.7	22.2	23.0	23.9	22.7	22.7	24.2	24.8	24.6	24.5
1.0	1.0	1.2	1.4	1.6	1.8	2.0	2.1	2.3	2.3	2.3	2.4	2.5	2.6	2.6	2.8
9.0	9.3	10.0	10.8	11.3	11.9	12.4	13.6	15.4	17.5	19.4	21.4	23.4	25.6	27.9	29.8
9.6	10.5	12.0	12.7	13.1	14.0	15.5	20.0	23.9	25.6	24.6	27.4	28.6	28.9	30.2	30.8
3.3	3.5	3.9	4.3	4.8	5.4	5.8	6.9	7.7	8.3	8.7	9.3	9.8	10.5	11.2	11.8
3.5	3.6	3.9	3.7	3.8	4.1	4.4	5.0	5.7	6.6	7.1	8.2	8.7	9.4	10.6	11.4
6.4	7.1	8.4	5.5	5.5	5.8	6.8	12.1	15.4	17.5	20.1	23.2	22.8	23.2	27.0	26.9
3.5	3.8	4.2	4.7	5.0	5.4	6.1	8.6	9.4	9.6	9.8	10.8	11.0	11.4	11.8	12.2
0.6	0.6	0.7	0.8	1.0	1.0	1.0	1.2	1.4	1.6	1.8	2.0	2.1	2.3	2.4	2.6
0.9	1.0	1.1	1.2	1.4	1.7	1.7	1.9	2.0	2.3	2.3	2.5	2.6	2.9	3.0	3.2
0.3	0.2	0.3	0.3	0.6	1.0	1.6	0.8	0.8	1.0	1.1	1.1	1.3	1.7	2.0	2.0
67.6	71.9	81.9	89.7	100.5	109.8	121.7	146.6	165.0	177.6	180.6	194.0	208.3	218.3	230.6	236.5
6.7	7.8	9.7	7.0	6.6	6.8	8.1	15.9	20.6	22.2	23.6	28.6	27.1	26.6	29.8	29.3
35.1	37.2	43.2	51.3	59.3	65.4	73.2	84.5	93.1	98.7	96.9	100.4	111.1	116.0	118.9	120.9
25.8	26.9	29.0	31.5	34.7	37.7	40.4	46.2	51.3	56.7	60.1	65.0	70.1	75.7	81.8	86.4

Table 41. Gross National Product

(In billions

	1929	1930	1931	1932	1933	1934	1935	1936	1937	1938
Compensation of employees............	51.1	46.8	39.7	31.1	29.5	34.3	37.3	42.9	47.9	45.0
Wages and salaries..................	50.4	46.2	39.1	30.5	29.0	33.7	36.7	41.9	46.1	43.0
Supplements to wages and salaries.....	0.7	0.7	0.6	0.6	0.5	0.6	0.6	1.0	1.8	2.0
Income of unincorporated enterprises and inventory valuation adjustment.....	14.8	11.5	8.7	5.3	5.6	7.0	10.4	10.5	12.7	11.1
Business and professional.............	8.8	7.4	5.6	3.4	3.2	4.6	5.4	6.5	7.1	6.8
Income of unincorporated enterprises	8.6	6.7	5.0	3.1	3.7	4.6	5.4	6.6	7.1	6.6
Inventory valuation adjustment.....	0.1	0.8	0.6	0.3	−0.5	−0.1	−0.1	−0.1	*	0.2
Farm..............................	6.0	4.1	3.2	1.9	2.4	2.4	5.0	4.0	5.6	4.3
Rental income of persons..............	5.4	4.8	3.8	2.7	2.0	1.7	1.7	1.8	2.1	2.6
Corporate profits and inventory valuation adjustment.......................	10.1	6.6	1.6	−2.0	−2.0	1.1	2.9	5.0	6.2	4.3
Corporate profits before tax..........	9.6	3.3	−0.8	−3.0	0.2	1.7	3.1	5.7	6.2	3.3
Corporate profits tax liability.......	1.4	0.8	0.5	0.4	0.5	0.7	1.0	1.4	1.5	1.0
Corporate profits after tax..........	8.3	2.5	−1.3	−3.4	−0.4	1.0	2.2	4.3	4.7	2.3
Dividends......................	5.8	5.5	4.1	2.6	2.1	2.6	2.9	4.5	4.7	3.2
Undistributed profits.............	2.4	−3.0	−5.4	−6.0	−2.4	−1.6	−0.7	−0.2	*	−0.9
Inventory valuation adjustment.......	0.5	3.3	2.4	1.0	−2.1	−0.6	−0.2	−0.7	−*	1.0
Net interest........................	6.4	6.0	5.8	5.4	5.0	4.9	4.8	4.7	4.7	4.6
National income.....................	87.8	75.7	59.7	42.5	40.2	49.0	57.1	64.9	73.6	67.6
Indirect business tax and nontax liability	7.0	7.2	6.9	6.8	7.1	7.8	8.2	8.7	9.2	9.2
Business transfer payments.............	0.6	0.5	0.6	0.7	0.7	0.6	0.6	0.6	0.6	0.4
Statistical discrepancy.................	0.3	−1.0	0.8	0.8	0.9	0.7	−0.2	1.1	−0.2	0.5
Less: Subsidies minus current surplus of government enterprises.............	−0.1	−0.1	−*	−*	*	0.3	0.4	*	0.1	0.2
Capital consumption allowances.........	8.6	8.5	8.2	7.6	7.2	7.1	7.2	7.5	7.7	7.8
Charges against gross national product...	101.4	91.1	76.3	58.5	56.0	65.0	72.5	82.7	90.8	85.2

* Less than 0.05.
NOTE: Detail may not add to totals because of rounding.
SOURCE: *Survey of Current Business*, U.S. Department of Commerce, July, 1955, Tables 1, 4.

by Distributive Shares, 1929–1954

of dollars)

1939	1940	1941	1942	1943	1944	1945	1946	1947	1948	1949	1950	1951	1952	1953	1954
48.1	52.1	64.8	85.3	109.6	121.3	123.2	117.7	128.8	140.9	140.9	154.3	180.4	195.3	209.2	207.9
45.9	49.8	62.1	82.1	105.8	116.8	117.6	111.8	122.9	135.2	134.3	146.5	170.9	185.1	198.5	196.2
2.2	2.3	2.7	3.2	3.8	4.5	5.6	5.9	5.9	5.8	6.5	7.8	9.5	10.2	10.8	11.7
11.6	13.0	17.4	23.9	28.2	29.6	30.8	35.3	34.4	38.4	34.1	36.1	40.8	40.0	38.2	37.9
7.3	8.4	10.9	13.9	16.8	18.0	19.0	21.3	19.9	21.6	21.4	22.9	24.8	25.7	25.9	25.9
7.5	8.5	11.5	14.3	17.0	18.1	19.1	23.0	21.4	22.1	21.0	24.0	25.1	25.5	26.1	26.0
−0.2	*	−0.6	−0.4	−0.2	−0.1	−0.1	−1.7	−1.5	−0.4	0.5	−1.1	−0.3	0.2	−0.2	−0.1
4.3	4.6	6.5	10.0	11.4	11.5	11.8	13.9	14.5	16.7	12.7	13.3	16.0	14.3	12.3	12.0
2.7	2.9	3.5	4.5	5.1	5.4	5.6	6.2	6.5	7.2	7.9	8.5	9.1	9.9	10.3	10.5
5.7	9.1	14.5	19.7	23.8	23.0	18.4	17.3	23.6	30.6	28.1	35.1	39.9	36.9	37.2	33.8
6.4	9.3	17.0	20.9	24.6	23.3	19.0	22.6	29.5	32.8	26.2	40.0	41.2	35.9	38.3	34.0
1.4	2.8	7.6	11.4	14.1	12.9	10.7	9.1	11.3	12.5	10.4	17.8	22.5	19.8	21.3	17.1
5.0	6.5	9.4	9.5	10.5	10.4	8.3	13.4	18.2	20.3	15.8	22.1	18.7	16.1	17.0	17.0
3.8	4.0	4.5	4.3	4.5	4.7	4.7	5.8	6.5	7.2	7.5	9.2	9.1	9.0	9.3	10.0
1.2	2.4	4.9	5.2	6.0	5.7	3.6	7.7	11.7	13.0	8.3	12.9	9.6	7.1	7.7	7.0
−0.7	−0.2	−2.5	−1.2	−0.8	−0.3	−0.6	−5.3	−5.9	−2.2	1.9	−4.9	−1.3	1.0	−1.1	−0.2
4.6	4.5	4.5	4.3	3.7	3.3	3 2	3.1	3.8	4.5	5.2	5.9	6.8	7.4	8.8	9.5
72.8	81.6	104.7	137.7	170.3	182.6	181.2	179.6	197.2	221.6	216.2	240.0	277.0	289.5	303.6	299.7
9.4	10.0	11.3	11.8	12.7	14.1	15.5	17.3	18.7	20.4	21.6	23.7	25.6	28.1	30.2	30.3
0.5	0.4	0.5	0.5	0.5	0.5	0.5	0.6	0.7	0.7	0.8	0.8	1.0	1.2	1.2	1.2
1.2	0.8	0.4	−0.8	−1.7	2.8	4.5	0.9	1.4	−2.1	0.1	0.2	1.3	0.7	1.3	−0.8
0.5	0.4	0.1	0.2	0.2	0.7	0.8	0.8	−0.2	−0.2	−0.2	0.2	0.2	−0.1	−0.4	−0.1
7.8	8.1	9.0	10.2	10.9	12.0	12.5	11.7	14.1	16.5	18.4	20.5	23.5	25.5	27.8	30.0
91.1	100.6	125.8	159.1	192.5	211.4	213.6	209.2	232.2	257.3	257.3	285.1	328.2	345.2	364.5	360.5

Table 42. National Income by
(In billions

	1929	1930	1931	1932	1933	1934	1935	1936	1937	1938
All industries, total....................	87.8	75.7	59.7	42.5	40.2	49.0	57.1	64.9	73.6	67.6
Agriculture, forestry, and fisheries.......	8.3	6.2	4.9	3.3	3.7	3.7	6.4	5.4	7.2	5.9
Mining..............................	2.0	1.6	1.0	0.7	0.6	1.2	1.2	1.5	1.9	1.5
Contract construction..................	3.8	3.2	2.2	1.1	0.8	1.1	1.3	2.0	2.1	2.0
Manufacturing........................	21.9	18.2	12.4	7.2	7.6	10.9	13.3	16.2	19.3	15.0
Wholesale and retail trade..............	13.4	12.2	9.7	6.4	5.5	8.1	9.2	10.6	12.2	11.9
Finance, insurance, and real estate.......	12.7	10.6	8.6	6.8	5.7	5.6	5.9	6.6	7.2	7.7
Transportation........................	6.6	5.6	4.4	3.2	3.0	3.4	3.7	4.3	4.6	4.1
Communications and public utilities.....	2.9	2.8	2.6	2.3	2.0	2.2	2.3	2.5	2.7	2.7
Services..............................	10.3	9.2	7.9	6.1	5.6	6.2	6.7	7.5	8.2	7.9
Government and government enterprises..	5.1	5.3	5.4	5.2	5.3	6.3	6.7	8.1	7.8	8.5
Rest of the world.....................	0.8	0.7	0.5	0.4	0.3	0.3	0.4	0.3	0.3	0.4

NOTE: Detail may not add to totals because of rounding.

SOURCE: National Income Supplement, 1954, *Survey of Current Business*, U.S. Department of Commerce, Table 13 (1929–1951); *Survey of Current Business*, July, 1955, Table 13 (1952–1954).

Industrial Origin, 1929–1954
of dollars)

1939	1940	1941	1942	1943	1944	1945	1946	1947	1948	1949	1950	1951	1952	1953	1954
72.8	81.6	104.7	137.7	170.3	182.6	181.2	179.6	197.2	221.6	216.2	240.0	277.0	289.5	303.6	299.7
5.9	6.2	8.5	12.4	14.1	14.5	14.9	17.3	18.2	20.8	16.6	17.2	20.3	18.7	16.8	16.6
1.6	1.9	2.3	2.6	2.7	2.9	2.7	3.0	4.2	5.2	4.4	5.0	5.6	5.4	5.6	5.2
2.3	2.6	4.2	6.5	5.5	4.1	4.3	6.5	8.4	10.3	10.4	11.5	13.6	14.6	15.3	15.7
17.9	22.3	33.0	45.3	58.1	60.1	52.0	48.5	58.7	66.6	62.8	74.2	87.7	89.3	96.7	89.9
12.5	14.3	17.3	20.3	23.8	25.7	28.0	34.4	37.3	41.5	40.5	43.4	47.9	50.1	51.8	52.0
7.9	8.2	9.2	10.6	11.6	12.2	12.8	14.5	15.3	17.4	18.9	20.7	22.4	24.4	26.3	27.9
4.6	5.0	6.3	8.6	10.8	11.2	10.5	10.2	11.5	12.6	12.0	13.3	14.9	15.4	15.8	14.6
2.9	3.1	3.3	3.7	3.9	4.1	4.2	4.8	5.1	5.9	6.6	7.2	8.3	9.1	10.1	10.8
8.3	8.9	9.8	11.0	12.3	13.6	14.6	17.2	18.9	20.5	21.2	22.8	24.8	26.6	28.7	29.8
8.5	8.8	10.5	16.3	27.0	33.7	36.8	22.6	18.6	19.7	21.9	23.4	30.2	34.4	35.1	35.3
0.3	0.4	0.4	0.4	0.4	0.4	0.4	0.6	0.9	1.1	1.1	1.3	1.5	1.5	1.4	1.8

Table 43. National Income Originating

(In billions

	1929	1930	1931	1932	1933	1934	1935	1936	1937	1938
Manufacturing.....................	21.9	18.2	12.4	7.2	7.6	10.9	13.3	16.2	19.3	15.0
Food and kindred products............	2.1	2.4	1.9	1.4	1.3	1.6	1.9	2.1	2.4	2.3
Tobacco manufactures................	0.3	0.3	0.3	0.3	0.1	0.1	0.2	0.1	0.2	0.2
Textile mill products.................	1.8	1.4	1.1	0.7	0.7	1.1	1.2	1.4	1.6	1.1
Apparel and other finished fabric products	1.3	1.0	0.8	0.5	0.5	0.8	0.9	1.0	1.0	0.9
Lumber and furniture products..........	1.5	1.1	0.7	0.3	0.3	0.5	0.7	0.9	1.1	0.9
Lumber and wood products, except furniture...........................	—	—	—	—	—	—	—	—	—	—
Furniture and fixtures................	—	—	—	—	—	—	—	—	—	—
Lumber and timber basic products.....	0.9	0.6	0.3	0.1	0.1	0.3	0.3	0.4	0.6	0.4
Furniture and finished lumber products	0.7	0.5	0.4	0.2	0.2	0.3	0.3	0.4	0.5	0.4
Paper and allied products..............	0.6	0.5	0.4	0.3	0.3	0.4	0.5	0.5	0.6	0.6
Printing, publishing, and allied industries	1.6	1.5	1.2	0.9	0.8	0.9	1.0	1.2	1.3	1.1
Chemicals and allied products...........	1.1	1.0	0.8	0.6	0.6	0.7	0.8	1.0	1.2	1.0
Products of petroleum and coal..........	0.9	0.8	0.3	0.1	0.1	0.1	0.2	0.3	0.5	0.5
Rubber products......................	0.4	0.3	0.2	0.1	0.1	0.1	0.2	0.2	0.3	0.2
Leather and leather products............	0.6	0.5	0.4	0.3	0.3	0.4	0.4	0.4	0.5	0.4
Stone, clay, and glass products..........	0.8	0.6	0.4	0.1	0.2	0.3	0.4	0.6	0.7	0.5
Metals, metal products, and miscellaneous	4.3	3.3	1.9	0.8	1.0	1.8	2.3	3.1	3.8	2.5
Primary metal industries.............	—	—	—	—	—	—	—	—	—	—
Fabricated metal products, including ordnance........................	—	—	—	—	—	—	—	—	—	—
Instruments........................	—	—	—	—	—	—	—	—	—	—
Miscellaneous manufacturing..........	—	—	—	—	—	—	—	—	—	—
Iron and steel and their products, including ordnance.................	3.0	2.2	1.1	0.4	0.7	1.1	1.5	2.1	2.6	1.6
Nonferrous metals and their products..	0.8	0.6	0.4	0.2	0.2	0.4	0.5	0.6	0.7	0.4
Miscellaneous manufacturing.,........	0.6	0.5	0.3	0.2	0.2	0.3	0.4	0.5	0.5	0.4
Machinery except electrical.............	1.9	1.5	0.8	0.3	0.4	0.7	1.0	1.4	1.8	1.2
Electrical machinery..................	1.0	0.8	0.5	0.2	0.3	0.4	0.5	0.7	0.9	0.7
Transportation equipment except automobiles...........................	0.3	0.3	0.1	0.1	0.1	0.1	0.1	0.2	0.3	0.3
Automobiles and automobile equipment..	1.4	0.8	0.6	0.2	0.4	0.6	0.9	1.2	1.3	0.7

NOTE: Detail may not add to totals because of rounding.

SOURCE: National Income Supplement, 1954, *Survey of Current Business*, U.S. Department of Commerce, Table 13 (1929–1951); *Survey of Current Business*, July, 1955, Table 13 (1952–1954).

in Manufacturing, 1929–1954

of dollars)

1939	1940	1941	1942	1943	1944	1945	1946	1947	1948	1949	1950	1951	1952	1953	1954
17.9	22.3	33.0	45.3	58.1	60.1	52.0	48.5	58.7	66.6	62.8	74.2	87.7	89.3	96.7	89.9
2.3	2.5	2.7	3.7	4.4	5.0	5.0	5.5	5.8	6.6	6.5	6.8	7.0	7.6	8.0	8.0
0.3	0.3	0.2	0.2	0.2	0.3	0.2	0.3	0.4	0.4	0.5	0.5	0.5	0.6	0.6	0.7
1.3	1.5	2.1	2.9	3.0	3.0	3.0	4.0	4.7	5.2	4.1	4.6	5.2	4.6	4.4	3.7
1.0	1.1	1.5	1.9	2.4	2.7	2.9	3.4	3.4	3.5	3.3	3.4	3.7	3.8	4.0	3.8
1.0	1.2	1.7	2.0	2.1	2.2	2.1	2.8	3.5	3.8	3.3	4.2	4.6	4.4	4.4	4.0
—	—	—	—	—	—	—	—	—	2.6	2.2	2.8	3.1	2.9	2.8	2.6
—	—	—	—	—	—	—	—	—	1.2	1.2	1.4	1.5	1.6	1.6	1.5
0.5	0.6	0.9	1.1	1.1	1.1	1.1	1.4	1.9	—	—	—	—	—	—	—
0.5	0.6	0.8	0.9	1.0	1.0	1.1	1.4	1.5	—	—	—	—	—	—	—
0.6	0.7	1.0	1.1	1.3	1.3	1.3	1.7	2.2	2.3	2.2	2.7	3.4	3.1	3.3	3.4
1.2	1.3	1.4	1.4	1.7	2.0	2.2	2.7	3.1	3.3	3.4	3.6	3.9	4.1	4.4	4.6
1.2	1.5	1.9	2.8	3.3	3.4	3.2	3.3	3.8	4.3	4.3	5.1	6.1	5.9	6.3	6.2
0.4	0.6	0.8	1.2	1.5	1.3	1.2	1.5	2.2	3.3	2.5	2.9	3.6	3.1	3.3	3.3
0.3	0.3	0.5	0.6	0.9	1.0	0.9	1.1	1.1	1.1	1.0	1.0	1.6	1.7	1.7	1.4
0.4	0.5	0.6	0.8	0.9	0.9	0.9	1.1	1.1	1.2	1.1	1.1	1.3	1.3	1.4	1.3
0.7	0.8	1.1	1.2	1.2	1.1	1.1	1.6	1.9	2.1	2.1	2.6	3.0	2.8	3.0	3.0
3.4	4.5	7.2	9.6	12.6	12.6	10.7	8.9	11.1	13.0	12.0	15.4	18.8	18.1	21.0	18.4
—	—	—	—	—	—	—	—	—	5.9	5.4	7.1	9.0	7.9	9.4	7.7
—	—	—	—	—	—	—	—	—	4.4	4.0	5.1	6.2	6.5	7.4	6.6
—	—	—	—	—	—	—	—	—	1.0	1.0	1.2	1.6	1.8	2.0	1.9
—	—	—	—	—	—	—	—	—	1.7	1.6	1.9	2.1	2.0	2.3	2.2
2.3	3.1	5.1	6.9	9.1	9.0	7.4	5.5	7.6	—	—	—	—	—	—	—
0.6	0.8	1.2	1.5	1.9	1.9	1.7	1.8	1.9	—	—	—	—	—	—	—
0.5	0.6	0.9	1.2	1.6	1.6	1.6	1.6	1.6	—	—	—	—	—	—	—
1.5	2.2	3.8	5.4	5.9	5.8	5.1	4.7	6.2	6.9	6.2	7.2	9.8	10.6	10.6	9.5
0.9	1.1	1.9	2.5	3.3	3.7	3.1	2.4	3.4	3.6	3.5	4.4	5.4	6.3	7.1	6.4
0.4	0.8	2.3	6.2	12.1	12.4	7.7	1.3	1.5	1.9	1.9	2.1	3.3	4.9	5.7	5.6
1.2	1.6	2.4	2.0	1.3	1.4	1.1	1.9	3.5	4.0	4.8	6.6	6.3	6.4	7.6	6.5

Table 44. Wages and Salaries,

(In billions

	1929	1930	1931	1932	1933	1934	1935	1936	1937	1938
All industries, total...................	50.4	46.2	39.1	30.5	29.0	33.7	36.7	41.9	46.1	43.0
Agriculture, forestry, and fisheries.......	1.4	1.3	1.0	0.7	0.7	0.7	0.9	0.9	1.1	1.1
Mining.............................	1.5	1.3	1.0	0.7	0.7	0.9	1.0	1.1	1.3	1.1
Contract construction.................	2.5	2.1	1.5	0.8	0.6	0.8	0.9	1.3	1.4	1.3
Manufacturing.......................	16.1	13.9	10.8	7.7	7.8	9.6	10.8	12.4	14.6	11.8
Wholesale and retail trade.............	9.3	8.7	7.6	5.9	5.3	6.1	6.6	7.2	8.2	8.0
Finance, insurance, and real estate.......	2.9	2.7	2.5	2.1	1.9	2.0	2.1	2.2	2.4	2.3
Transportation.......................	4.7	4.2	3.5	2.7	2.5	2.7	2.9	3.2	3.5	3.2
Communication and public utilities......	1.5	1.5	1.4	1.2	1.1	1.1	1.2	1.3	1.4	1.4
Services.............................	5.5	5.3	4.6	3.7	3.3	3.7	3.9	4.3	4.7	4.5
Government and government enterprises..	4.9	5.2	5.3	5.0	5.1	6.1	6.5	7.9	7.5	8.2
Rest of the world.....................	*	*	*	*	*	*	*	*	*	*
Addendum: All private industries........	45.5	41.0	33.9	25.5	23.9	27.6	30.2	34.1	38.6	34.8

* Less than 0.05.

NOTE: Detail may not add to totals because of rounding.

SOURCE: National Income Supplement, 1954, *Survey of Current Business*, U.S. Department of Commerce, Table 15 (1929–1951); *Survey of Current Business*, July, 1955, Table 15 (1952–1954).

Table 45. Distribution of Consumer Units and of Family Personal Income by Family Personal Income Level, 1944, 1946, 1947, and 1950

Family personal income (before income taxes)	Number of families and unattached individuals (in thousands)				Aggregate family personal income (in millions)			
	1944	1946	1947	1950	1944	1946	1947	1950
Under $1,000	4,352	3,826	3,748	3,704	$ 2,390	$ 2,017	$ 1,973	$ 1,854
$1,000–$1,999	8,108	7,606	7,370	7,328	12,338	11,570	11,231	11,170
2,000– 2,999	8,762	8,791	8,459	8,044	21,938	22,007	21,176	20,144
3,000– 3,999	7,723	8,590	8,628	8,463	26,960	29,906	30,045	29,569
4,000– 4,999	4,535	5,364	5,725	6,980	20,261	23,956	25,583	31,215
5,000– 7,499	4,774	5,612	6,625	8,484	28,681	33,558	39,769	51,200
7,500– 9,999	1,385	1,751	2,170	2,860	11,802	14,905	18,454	24,218
$10,000 and over	1,241	1,790	2,015	2,727	23,351	32,786	36,367	47,388
Total.................	40,880	43,330	44,740	48,590	$147,721	$170,705	$184,598	$216,758

Percentage distribution								
Under $1,000	10.7	8.8	8.4	7.6	1.6	1.2	1.1	0.9
$1,000–$1,999	19.8	17.6	16.5	15.1	8.4	6.8	6.1	5.1
2,000– 2,999	21.4	20.3	18.9	16.5	14.9	12.9	11.5	9.3
3,000– 3,999	18.9	19.8	19.3	17.4	18.3	17.5	16.3	13.6
4,000– 4,999	11.1	12.4	12.8	14.4	13.7	14.0	13.8	14.4
5,000– 7,499	11.7	13.0	14.8	17.5	19.4	19.7	21.5	23.6
7,500– 9,999	3.4	4.0	4.8	5.9	8.0	8.7	10.0	11.2
$10,000 and over	3.0	4.1	4.5	5.6	15.7	19.2	19.7	21.9
Total.................	100.0	100.0	100.0	100.0	100.0	100.0	100.0	100.0

SOURCE: Income Distribution Supplement, *Survey of Current Business*, U.S. Department of Commerce, 1953, Table 2, p. 81.

by Industry, 1929–1954
of dollars)

1939	1940	1941	1942	1943	1944	1945	1946	1947	1948	1949	1950	1951	1952	1953	1954
45.9	49.8	62.1	82.1	105.8	116.8	117.6	111.8	122.9	135.2	134.3	146.5	170.9	185.1	198.3	196.2
1.1	1.1	1.4	1.8	2.2	2.4	2.5	2.8	3.1	3.3	3.1	3.0	3.3	3.4	3.4	3.5
1.1	1.3	1.5	1.8	2.0	2.2	2.2	2.4	2.9	3.3	2.9	3.2	3.6	3.6	3.7	3.4
1.5	1.7	2.9	4.7	3.9	2.9	3.0	4.4	5.8	7.1	6.9	7.9	9.8	10.7	11.2	11.3
13.6	15.6	21.7	30.9	40.9	42.9	38.2	36.5	42.5	46.5	43.9	49.4	58.2	62.9	69.9	66.0
8.4	9.0	10.4	11.0	11.9	13.0	14.7	19.6	22.9	25.3	25.6	27.3	30.0	31.8	33.9	34.7
2.4	2.5	2.6	2.7	2.8	3.0	3.3	4.1	4.5	5.0	5.3	5.8	6.4	6.9	7.5	8.1
3.4	3.6	4.3	5.3	6.6	7.5	7.9	8.5	9.0	9.7	9.3	9.8	11.3	11.7	12.3	11.7
1.5	1.5	1.7	1.8	1.9	2.0	2.2	2.8	3.3	3.8	4.0	4.2	4.6	5.1	5.6	5.9
4.7	5.0	5.5	6.2	7.0	7.9	8.7	10.2	11.5	12.4	12.8	13.7	14.9	16.1	17.2	17.8
8.2	8.4	10.2	16.0	26.6	33.0	34.9	20.6	17.3	18.7	20.4	22.2	28.8	32.9	33.7	33.8
*	*	*	*	*	*	*	*	*	*	*	*	*	*	*	*
37.7	41.4	51.9	66.1	79.2	83.8	82.7	91.2	105.5	116.4	113.9	124.3	142.0	152.2	164.7	162.4

Table 46. *Gross National Product or*

(In billions

	1929	1930	1931	1932	1933	1934	1935	1936	1937	1938
Gross national product................	149.3	135.2	126.6	107.6	103.7	113.4	127.8	142.5	153.5	145.9
Personal consumption expenditures......	107.3	100.9	98.0	88.9	86.6	91.5	97.3	107.6	111.5	109.8
Durable goods......................	13.0	10.5	9.1	6.9	6.7	7.6	9.4	11.6	12.2	10.0
Nondurable goods..................	58.1	55.2	55.0	50.7	49.2	52.5	55.4	61.8	63.8	64.9
Services..........................	36.2	35.2	33.9	31.4	30.8	31.4	32.5	34.3	35.5	34.9
Gross private domestic investment.......	26.8	17.9	12.0	3.3	2.1	4.3	13.6	15.2	22.5	12.1
New construction..................	16.1	11.8	8.3	4.6	3.5	3.9	5.2	7.3	8.7	7.8
Residential nonfarm..............	6.9	4.0	3.4	1.7	1.3	1.5	2.5	3.6	3.9	4.0
Other..........................	9.3	7.8	5.0	2.9	2.3	2.4	2.7	3.7	4.8	3.8
Producers' durable equipment.........	8.5	6.8	4.6	2.7	2.9	3.9	5.2	7.1	8.1	5.6
Change in business inventories........	2.1	−0.7	−0.9	−4.1	−4.2	−3.5	3.2	0.9	5.7	−1.2
Nonfarm........................	2.6	−0.2	−3.0	−5.1	−3.0	0.3	0.7	3.7	3.0	−1.8
Farm...........................	−0.4	−0.6	2.1	1.1	−1.3	−3.9	2.6	−2.8	2.8	0.6
Net foreign investment................	1.6	1.2	0.6	0.3	0.1	0.5	−0.5	−0.7	−0.2	1.9
Government purchases of goods and services................................	13.6	15.1	15.9	15.1	14.9	17.2	17.4	20.3	19.7	22.1
Federal.........................	2.3	2.7	2.9	3.0	4.3	5.7	5.4	8.3	7.8	9.6
State and local....................	11.2	12.5	13.0	12.1	10.6	11.6	11.9	12.0	11.8	12.5
Gross government product..............	7.0	7.4	7.5	7.4	8.1	9.5	10.2	12.2	11.3	12.3
Other gross product..................	142.3	127.8	119.1	100.3	95.6	103.9	117.6	130.3	142.1	133.6

* Less than 0.05.
NOTE: Detail may not add to totals because of rounding.
SOURCE: U.S. Department of Commerce, *Survey of Current Business,* July, 1955, Table 40.

Expenditure in Constant Dollars, 1929–1954
of 1947 dollars)

1939	1940	1941	1942	1943	1944	1945	1946	1947	1948	1949	1950	1951	1952	1953	1954
157.5	171.6	198.2	223.6	248.9	268.2	263.1	233.8	232.2	243.9	241.5	264.7	282.9	293.3	306.5	300.5
116.3	122.5	130.9	128.1	131.4	135.9	145.2	162.4	165.0	168.0	172.3	182.8	183.6	189.2	197.4	200.7
11.8	13.5	15.6	10.1	8.7	7.9	8.9	17.2	20.6	21.3	22.4	27.2	24.2	23.9	26.7	26.9
68.5	71.6	76.4	78.0	80.8	84.3	90.6	95.4	93.1	93.3	94.7	97.2	99.0	102.3	105.3	106.5
36.0	37.4	38.9	40.1	42.0	43.7	45.6	49.8	51.3	53.5	55.2	58.4	60.4	63.0	65.4	67.4
16.8	22.8	28.9	14.7	7.4	9.2	13.0	32.4	29.7	38.8	28.1	45.3	45.2	39.1	39.6	36.7
9.4	10.6	11.8	6.0	3.4	3.6	5.0	12.3	14.0	16.1	15.8	20.0	19.0	18.8	19.8	21.3
5.4	5.8	6.2	2.9	1.4	1.1	1.4	4.8	6.3	7.7	7.6	11.1	9.0	8.9	9.4	10.6
4.0	4.8	5.6	3.2	2.0	2.5	3.6	7.5	7.7	8.4	8.2	8.9	10.0	10.0	10.5	10.6
6.5	8.4	9.8	5.7	5.2	6.9	9.7	12.3	16.7	17.7	15.7	18.3	18.4	18.3	19.1	17.4
0.8	3.9	7.3	3.0	−1.2	−1.3	−1.6	7.8	−1.0	5.1	−3.5	7.0	7.8	2.0	0.6	−1.9
0.5	3.1	6.0	0.6	−0.8	−0.8	−0.7	7.7	1.3	2.8	−1.7	6.0	7.1	1.6	1.5	−2.4
0.3	0.8	1.2	2.4	−0.3	−0.6	−0.9	*	−2.3	2.3	−1.8	1.0	0.6	0.4	−0.9	0.5
1.6	2.2	1.1	−1.1	−4.1	−4.0	−2.9	5.0	8.9	2.1	0.8	−1.1	2.3	1.6	−0.3	1.3
22.8	24.1	37.3	81.8	114.2	127.1	107.8	34.0	28.6	34.9	40.3	37.7	51.8	63.4	69.8	61.7
9.0	11.0	25.1	70.8	104.3	117.4	97.9	22.7	15.8	20.8	24.3	20.5	34.2	45.6	51.2	41.5
13.8	13.0	12.2	11.0	9.9	9.7	9.9	11.2	12.8	14.0	16.0	17.3	17.5	17.8	18.6	20.2
12.4	13.0	16.5	24.8	39.9	46.2	45.1	22.6	16.7	16.6	17.4	18.1	23.0	24.8	24.6	24.0
145.0	158.6	181.7	198.7	209.0	222.0	218.0	211.2	215.6	227.3	224.0	246.6	259.9	268.5	281.9	276.4

8. Sources and Methods of Computing United States National Income Accounting Statistics

National income accounting statistics cannot be obtained by a process of compiling individual income statements as reported by producers, consumers, and government. Nor can the total production taking place in the economy be compiled by adding together the value added by each productive unit in the economy. No single set of comprehensive reports specifically designed for national income accounting purposes is available from which such compilations could be made. Instead, there are large masses of information from a wide variety of different sources that yield useful data on specific parts of the economy or on certain kinds of transactions, and these different sources must be integrated into the national income accounting framework by building up the estimates piece by piece. The general approach to estimation, therefore, is not the direct derivation or compilation of broad totals, but rather the building up on an item-by-item basis of each of the major components which go to make up the various flows in the national income accounts.

Income Estimates

The allocations side of the National Income and Product Account includes a variety of income components such as the compensation of employees, the income of unincorporated enterprises, and rental income of persons. The information on these flows is derived largely as a by-product of the government's taxation and social insurance systems. For wages and salaries, employers are required by law to provide the government, for social insurance purposes, with tabulations of the amounts they have paid. Data filed with tax returns are useful in the estimation of such components as corporate profits and capital consumption allowances. Records of tax receipts provide information on the amounts of taxes of various types collected from producers. The estimates of farm income are built up by a different method; a separate computation is made of the gross receipts of farmers and the expenses of production incurred in farming to arrive at the net income from farming. Estimates of the gross receipts from farming are based on data on the crops and livestock produced and their market value. Expenses are also calculated on an item-by-item basis. Certain imputations such as the retail value of owner-occupied housing must be calculated separately. This is done by calculating the number of houses which are owner-occupied, together with their rental value, to arrive at a gross rental value for owner-occupied housing; from this gross total deductions for expenses are made.

Product Estimates

On the sources side of the National Income and Product Account the methods of estimation are for the most part quite different. This side of the account shows the goods and services purchased by various groups.

The major part of these are commodities rather than services. A considerable amount of information on the production of commodities is contained in the industrial censuses that are taken from time to time for the whole of the United States. The census material is comprehensive in scope. However, it reflects the value of the commodity at a stage in the manufacturing process rather than at the stage where it is purchased by consumers, by government, or by producers on capital account. For this reason it is necessary to study the flow of commodities through the system and add the increases in their market value due to transportation, taxation, and distributive services. This method of arriving at the total value of commodities purchased in the economy is called the "commodity flow approach."

Services purchased by consumers are estimated separately. A wide variety of different sources is used, including census material giving data on the occupations of individuals and trade association material. The purchases of government are also difficult to estimate directly; the estimate is arrived at by deducting from total government outlays those outlays that do not constitute expenditures for goods and services, thus arriving at the estimate for government expenditures on goods and services as a residual. Estimates of new construction are made on the basis of contract awards, building permits, and records of work done. Information on inventory changes is obtained by making appropriate adjustments in the inventory data contained in tax returns of business and adding to this the farm inventory data collected by the Department of Agriculture. Net foreign investment is based largely on data collected by the Department of Commerce.

General Methodology

In making estimates of various components it is always necessary to make many adjustments in the basic data so that the estimates that are derived will agree conceptually and statistically with the theoretical concepts. The large variety of different sources employed means that different classification systems will be used in the estimation of various flows. In the commodity flow procedure, for example, it is often necessary to adjust the various sources so that their classifications match, so that the correct transportation costs, taxes, and distributive margins can be added to the commodities. Some sources, furthermore, cover only a part of the economy, and the missing segments must be filled in with estimates from other sources. Thus in estimating wages and salaries, a number of occupational groups are not covered by the social security system. In order to obtain a total for all wages and salaries in the economy, the uncovered occupations must be estimated separately. In other cases, sources that purport to be comprehensive may, because of collection procedures or for other reasons, seriously understate the true values involved. Corporate profits as reported in tax returns, for example, require adjustment, since they understate the full amount of profits determined after audit of the returns.

Much of the information used in the estimation process is not available on a yearly basis but appears only at periodic intervals. Census data, for example, appear in some cases only at ten-year intervals. Methods of estimation must then be developed for periods that lack suitable comprehensive data. The procedure in such cases is to consider the years for which adequate information does exist as "bench marks," from which it is possible through the use of supplementary data to extrapolate estimates forward or backward. When it is possible to obtain data for two bench-mark years, the years between can be interpolated on the basis of both bench-mark years. The supplementary data which are required for extrapolation and interpolation need be far less comprehensive than the data used for bench-mark purposes, and they can even be of a completely different basic nature. Thus, for example, the bench marks for consumer expenditures are estimated by the commodity flow approach described above, but the year-to-year changes are estimated by data on the volume of retail sales, which are used to extrapolate or interpolate the bench-mark estimates.

THE RELIABILITY OF NATIONAL INCOME ACCOUNTING STATISTICS

The Meaning of Reliability

It has already been pointed out in the chapter relating to the uses of national income aggregates for comparative analysis that a single aggregate or flow cannot be used analytically in isolation. The reliability of a relationship observed among aggregates or flows does not depend as much on the reliability of each flow by itself as on their joint reliability. This aspect of reliability is very important in evaluating the national income statistics. A flow may be seriously understated or overstated, yet a year-to-year comparison of the estimates of the flow may give a very accurate appraisal of the year-to-year change that has actually occurred. If all the estimates for the various years are affected by the same kinds of bias, the accuracy of year-to-year comparisons may not be seriously impaired. Conversely, of course, a given component may have a high degree of accuracy with respect to general level, yet contain large errors in year-to-year change. Thus a change in an aggregate amounting to 1 or 2 per cent a year may not be reliable even if the aggregate itself is not more than 1 or 2 per cent off each year. The error in the aggregates for successive years could easily distort or obscure the true change involved.

The discussion so far has been carried on in terms of the level and change in level of a flow, so that it might appear at first glance that the only problem involved is to specify two types of reliability, the reliability of the level and the reliability of the change in level. However, although this might serve for a few very simple examples, it would not be adequate for the more general situation. In most instances it is not just a single homogeneous flow that is involved. Flows are added together to obtain more aggregative flows, or flows are related to one another. The measurement of reliability in such cases is quite complex; it is not possible just to add up the error terms that would result from the study of the variances of the individual estimates involved. The records that are used for one flow are often also used in part for other flows, so that, although the reliability of each flow alone may be low, the relationship among these flows may be given quite accurately. It is the intercorrelation of the possible errors in the flows that makes it difficult to speak categorically about reliability. The reliability of the data depends entirely on how they are used in the process of analysis. For this reason it is important for the analyst to know the nature of the data he is using, so that he can avoid uses in which the data would not yield reliable results.

Besides the conceptual problem, there is also a statistical problem in specifying error terms for the various flows. The wide variety of sources used in making the estimates and the nature of adjustments required to correct the basic data preclude any statistical estimation parallel to that used in sampling theory. Wider use of sampling procedures, furthermore, is not feasible in view of the extremely heterogeneous nature of many of the flows. Many of the errors in the statistics are the result of misstatements by the informants, poor reporting, and similar problems with which sampling would also have to contend.

Statistical Discrepancy and Bench-Mark Tests

Indications on the statistical variability of the over-all estimates are provided by two types of comparisons that are available. These are (1) comparison of the results obtained for total gross national income and product by the income method with the results obtained for the same totals by the product method, and (2) comparisons of preliminary estimates with the final estimates made later on the basis of more complete bench-mark information.

The statistical discrepancy between the totals obtained by the calculation of the income components and the product components of gross national product has generally been quite small (see Table 41 in the appendix to Chap. 7). Although the income and product calculations are not entirely independent, they are based generally on quite different sources and entirely different methods of adjustment. A large statistical discrepancy would indicate that at least one of the estimates was in serious error. A small statistical discrepancy is not positive indication that the two estimates are accurate, since they may both err in the same direction and by about the same amount, but nevertheless to the extent that the errors remain small year after year, it seems reasonable that the estimates fairly well approximate the true values.

The comparison of preliminary estimates for a given year with the bench-mark estimates which are subsequently made for the same year as the basic statistical materials become available provides an excellent check on the reliability of the extrapolation processes used. Evidence at hand indicates quite a high degree of correspondence between such preliminary estimates and the later corresponding bench-mark estimates. This sort of analysis, besides its usefulness as an indicator of the reliability of the preliminary estimates, enables the analysts responsible for the extrapolation of bench-mark estimates to develop methods which will improve the quality and reliability of the preliminary estimates. Thus, a "survival of the fittest" test is imposed on estimating methods.

Strengths and Weaknesses of the Data

The data for the various flows in the national income accounts come from a wide variety of sources and require the use of many different methods in their integration into the final estimates. Not all the flows, of course, are equal in reliability. Some, such as wages and salaries, tend to be very reliable because they are based on quite comprehensive tabulations of the actual amounts paid out by large segments of the economy. Others, such as the income of unincorporated enterprises or the change in inventories, are based on much less adequate information and are therefore probably much less reliable. The appraisal of reliability cannot be done simply and easily. It requires a knowledge of the sources used and how the estimates are constructed, and also speculation on the kinds of biases in sources of given types and the relative adequacy of different adjustment procedures. In this sense, therefore, the judgment of reliability becomes an analytic problem, not simply a statistical one.

APPENDIX TO CHAPTER 8. SOURCES AND METHODS OF COMPUTING SPECIFIC FLOWS IN THE UNITED STATES NATIONAL INCOME ACCOUNTING STATISTICS

Detailed information on the sources and methods used in obtaining individual flows in the United States national income accounting statistics is published in the 1954 edition of the National Income Supplement to the *Survey of Current Business*. This document was written by the National Income Division of the Department of Commerce, and is the basic source of information on United States national income accounting statistics. The student or research worker wishing to employ national income accounting data in economic analysis should use this work as a basic reference. A careful study of each of the individual flows is necessary to understand the nature of the sources used, the methods of estimation, and the possible types of biases, underestimations, or variabilities that will affect the data. As pointed out in the body of this chapter, it is only in such a context that reliability can be judged. Inasmuch as the use of national income data in economic analysis involves interrelating various flows, estimating the reliability of the relationships that emerge is an analytic rather than a purely statistical problem.

The following discussion of the individual flows does not attempt to cover the sources and methods of estimation fully. Such a lengthy exposition is beyond the scope of this book, and is of course available in the volume mentioned above. The purpose of the presentation here is to give the reader a general idea of the nature of the flows, the kinds of sources from which they are estimated, and the types of estimation procedure involved. In a great many cases summarization of methods and sources has been necessary. The flows will be discussed in the following order: (1) allocations of gross national income, (2) expenditures for gross national product, (3) other accounting flows, and (4) gross national product in constant dollars.

Allocations of Gross National Income

Compensation of Employees

The compensation of employees comprises the direct cost of hiring labor as viewed by the employer rather than the amount received by employees as their take-home pay. Thus employer and employee social insurance contributions and employer payments to private pension plans for employees are included as a part of the compensation of employees.

Wages and Salaries. Wages and salaries are the largest component in the compensation of employees, and they amounted to 51 per cent of the total gross national income for the year 1950. Since the year 1938 the major source for wage and salary data is the comprehensive reporting system on wages and salaries developed under the Social Security and Railroad Retirement Acts. The only major component of wages and salaries not covered by this source has been the wages and salaries paid by Federal, state, and local governments, amounting to about 15 per cent of total wages and salaries in the year 1950. Certain smaller components, such as farm wages, wages of domestic servants, wages paid by certain nonprofit institutions, and payments of tips, are also omitted from the social security data, but total wages and salaries for this part of the economy do not amount to more than 5 per cent of the total wages and salaries for the private sector as a whole.

For government employees, data on the wages and salaries paid by the Federal government are obtained from payroll data provided by various government agencies to the Civil Service Commission and to the Department of Labor, and from the Department of Defense. Wage and salary figures for state and local governments are based on either complete enumeration or monthly or quarterly sample surveys of state and local expenditures for both public education payrolls and nonschool payrolls made by the Census Bureau.

Data on wages of farm workers (including income in kind) are estimated from *Census of Agriculture* data, supplemented by monthly and quarterly samples of employment and wage rates. Wages of domestic servants are obtained as the product of employment and average earnings. Employment data for domestic services are based on the monthly sample survey given in the Census Bureau's *Current Population Survey*. Average earnings of domestic servants are based on *Census of Population* data and the domestic servant component of the Consumer Price Index of the Bureau of Labor Statistics. Basic information on earnings and employment of other employees not included in the above categories is obtained from a variety of sources such as the Census of Population and other special censuses (e.g., religious bodies, education), publications of a private nature (e.g., *Official Catholic Directory* and the Institute of Life Insurance's *Fact Book*), and special surveys made by the National Income Division itself.

Because the major components of the wage and salary estimate (over 90 per cent) are taken directly from accounting records, the annual estimates are extremely reliable. Since the data which are reported by business for social security purposes list each individual separately, the possibility of omissions, undercoverage, or accounting errors is quite small.

In the period before 1938, when social security data were not available on as large a scale, the most important sources were the periodic censuses of business and industry, which were interpolated or extrapolated for noncensus years by the sample data on payrolls and employment collected by the Bureau of Labor Statistics.

Contributions for Social Insurance and Other Labor Income. Employer and employee contributions for social insurance are obtained directly from the agencies administering the programs. These figures are derived from the actual accounting records and are highly reliable. The estimates for other labor income, however, are obtained from a variety of different sources and do not possess the same level of reliability. Benefits paid to workers insured under state and Federal laws on either a compulsory or a voluntary basis are estimated from data for private insurance companies contained in the *Insurance Yearbook*, from information furnished by state accident commissions, and from reports of the United States Employees Compensation Commission. Employer contributions under private pension and related plans are estimated from data in the Internal Revenue Service's *Statistics of Income*, supplemented by additional information from such sources as the Teachers' Insurance and Annuity Association, *Church Pension Conference Report*, and the *Statistics of Railways*. Estimates of directors' fees are made by applying a ratio figure to the compensation of corporate officers as reported in *Statistics of Income*.

Income of Unincorporated Enterprises

This flow contains the monetary earnings and the income in kind of sole proprietors, partnerships, and self-employed individuals, other than supplementary income derived from renting property. Estimation of the various components of this flow requires the piecing together of many different kinds of information, many of which are connected only indirectly with the income of unincorporated enterprises. Over a period of years the quality of these estimates has steadily improved because of experience, the development of additional sources, the improvement of existing sources, and the undertaking of major surveys in this area by the National Income Division. The flow may be viewed as composed of three major components: (1) net income of professional practitioners, (2) income of unincorporated business enterprises, and (3) net income of farm proprietors.

Net Income of Professional Practitioners. Estimates of the net income of professional practitioners are obtained by estimating the number of persons engaged in independent practice in each profession and multiplying this by their estimated average income. The number of persons in each profession is obtained from Census of Population data and from the records of professional associations. The scarcity of adequate data on the average income of the different professions led the National Income Division to undertake data collection on this subject. Surveys were made as early as 1933. In the postwar period surveys have been undertaken of lawyers, dentists, and physicians. Estimates on engineers, accountants, and other professional services n.e.c. are less satisfactory, relying on a combination of numerous trade sources and tax return data.

Income of Unincorporated Business Enterprises. Information available for estimating the income of unincorporated business enterprises has generally been fragmentary. The most comprehensive data are available for the years 1945 and 1947, for which the Internal Revenue Service has provided tabulations of the sole proprietors and partnerships filing tax returns. Because of the low tax exemptions and the high level of business activity in these years, the percentage of the total number of firms filing was very high. The general approach in making the estimates is to establish the magnitude of the universe, either in terms of gross receipts or the number of active proprietors in each industry. In those instances where gross receipts are used, these are multiplied by a profit ratio (net income to receipts) to obtain a measure of net income accruing to the proprietors of the industry. Where the number of active proprietors is used, this is multiplied by an estimate of average net income.

For most of the larger industries data on receipts of unincorporated business were available in industrial censuses of 1939 and 1947 or 1948, and this information, corrected for undercoverage, was used to supplement that of the Internal Revenue Service for 1945 and 1947. An intensive audit study by the Internal Revenue Service carried out in 1949 for the first time provided a suitable basis for estimating the amount of understatement in the tabulations of the unaudited returns which had been used for estimation purposes.

In instances where the number of active proprietors is used, the data have generally been obtained either from the industrial censuses or the Census of Population. For intercensal years the number of active proprietors was obtained by interpolations and extrapolations, utilizing for the more recent period mainly the business population series of the Office of Business Economics. Information on the average income of proprietors in various industries is obtained by making numerous adjustments to the data from tax returns of sole proprietors furnished by the Internal Revenue Service.

Net Income of Farm Proprietors. The net income of farm proprietors is derived by estimating gross income of farmers in detail by type of product, and deducting from this estimates of the expenses of production. This production statement for farming as a whole is developed by the Agricultural Economics Division of the Agricultural Marketing Service. The basic information behind these estimates comes partly from the quinquennial Census of Agriculture and partly from the current Crop and Livestock Reporting System, which is designed to have at least one reporter in every farming township in the United States.

Gross farm income contains estimates for the cash receipts of farmers from the marketing of crops and livestock, the value of food and fuel produced and consumed on the farm, and the gross rental value of farm dwellings on both owner-occupied and rented farms. The change in farm inventories is obtained by sample surveys. It is measured in physical terms: the difference in the quantity of crops and livestock held at the beginning and at the end of the year multiplied by prices of these commodities at the end of the year. Because of this method of measurement of inventory changes and the methods used in arriving at gross farm income, no inventory valuation adjustment is required for farm income or inventory change.

Production expenses of farmers are built up for some forty categories of production costs. Depreciation, purchased feed, hired labor, purchases of livestock, cost of operating motor vehicles, net rents to nonfarm landlords, and taxes accounted for about 80 per cent of the total production expenses in 1949. Farm depreciation is estimated in terms of replacement cost rather than original cost. Percentage rates of depreciation derived from a 1934 study and other data on length of useful life are applied to current value estimates of seven types of farm property and equipment. In some cases the increase in the stock of equipment is computed by adding the known increment of production and adjusting for price changes. Other categories of production expenses are based on Census of Agriculture data and additional surveys to provide a basis for extrapolation and interpolation.

The imputed net rent of owner-occupied farm dwellings is included as a part of the net income of farm proprietors. It is calculated by estimating the total value of such farm dwellings and multiplying this by the average rate of interest on farm mortgages.

Rental Income of Persons

The rental income of persons can be broken down into three major categories: (1) rent obtained from nonfarm property, (2) imputed rent of owner-occupied nonfarm dwellings, and (3) rent obtained from farm realty. The basic information on rental income is very inadequate. The large number of landlords who receive rent do not in general keep systematic accounts, and it is almost impossible to make adequate adjustments to tax return data. The estimates on rental income are among the least satisfactory of the national income accounting estimates. The main sources of information for the estimates are tax returns, census materials, and sample surveys.

Rent Obtained from Nonfarm Property. This consists of the net rent received by individuals from dwellings and from business and industrial property, and net royalties received by individuals. In order to obtain figures for the net rent received by individuals from dwellings, it was necessary to make estimates of the number of rental units and of the average rental charges and expenses, including depreciation. With respect to the charges and expenses, use was made of the data contained in the Consumers' Price Index. The net rent of business and industrial property received by individuals was computed on a residual basis. The net rents received by individuals from dwellings are subtracted from total net rents as given in the 1941 tax returns. This net residual is then blown up to a gross basis and extrapolated to other years. Expenses are obtained by subtracting the net from the gross and this also is extrapolated. Net royalty receipts are computed annually on the basis of Federal income tax returns, assuming that the ratio of royalty receipts to nonfarm residential rental receipts is the same for individuals as it is for corporations, and that the expenses connected with royalties are the same percentage of gross royalties for individuals as they are for corporations.

Imputed Rent of Owner-occupied Nonfarm Dwellings. The imputed rent of owner-occupied nonfarm dwellings is defined by the National Income Division as "the gross return which the owner-occupants of nonfarm dwellings could theoretically have realized had they offered their houses for rent, less their expenses." The 1940 Census of Population and Housing served as a basis for the estimates. The number of owner-occupied houses in the country was ascertained and enumerators were instructed to base the estimates on rents actually being charged for similar dwellings in the neighborhood. The methods used for extrapolating the estimate to other years were the same as that used for nonowner-occupied dwellings, namely, estimation of the number of units on a yearly basis through sample surveys, and of average rental charges and rent expenses from census data and the Consumers' Price Index.

Rent Obtained from Farm Realty. This component is estimated by the Department of Agriculture in connection with the computation of farm income. It should be noted that the imputed net rent of owner-occupied farm homes is considered to be part of the net income of farm proprietors. The gross rent payable to different landlord groups is based on surveys taken in 1936 and 1945. Expenses of the rented property are allocated among different landlord groups according to the use of acreage or property value ratios.

Corporate Profits

Corporate profits are defined as the total profits originating in corporate production before corporate profits taxes or dividend payments. The estimate of corporate profits is a consolidated figure in that dividends paid by corporations to corporations are excluded from the total. The basic data from which the estimates are derived are the annual tabulations of corporate income tax returns prepared by the Internal Revenue Service. These data are adjusted for such things as the inclusion of an allowance for additional profits disclosed by audit, the exclusion of foreign income taxes, the inclusion of depletion charged by corporations (since this is not included in capital consumption in the national income accounts), the exclusion of capital gains and losses, the inclusion of the profits of the Federal Reserve System, the exclusion of profits of mutual nonlife insurance companies, and a few additional minor items. The division of corporate profits into corporate profits taxes, dividends, and undistributed profits is obtained from the same source.

The reliability of the corporate profits series is quite high because of the mandatory filing of returns and the realization of corporations that the returns are likely to be audited. With respect to the breakdown of corporate profits among industries, the estimates for the period from 1929 to 1947 are not strictly comparable with the data after that period because of changes in the industrial classification system used by the Internal Revenue Service.

Interest

The definition of the interest component of national income is quite complex in that it involves the concept of net interest, imputations for financial intermediaries, and the assumption that government interest is to be excluded from the gross national product. The statistical measurement of the various elements in the interest flow is generally based on data which are reliable, but the validity of the various assumptions is more debatable.

The general procedure used in obtaining the net interest component involves estimating the monetary interest paid, adding to it the estimate for imputed interest paid, and subtracting the estimates of monetary interest received and imputed interest received. The sources of data for these estimates are tax returns as tabulated in *Statistics of Income;* reports of the Securities Exchange Commission and the Federal Deposit Insurance Corporation; census reports on agriculture, government finances, and government debt; and many other kinds of reports which provide basic information or are useful in extrapolating and interpolating well-established series.

Indirect Business Tax and Nontax Accruals

This flow consists of Federal excise taxes, customs duties, refunds of indirect taxes (as a subtraction), state sales taxes, other state taxes and nontax payments, local property taxes, and other local indirect taxes. For the Federal government, complete and reliable coverage of this flow is given by the Treasury accounts. For state governments, the census reports on state finances provide the basic data for all periods except that from 1933 to 1936. This period has been filled in from *Tax Yields,* compiled by the Tax Institute of the University of Pennsylvania from mail questionnaires sent to state tax officials. The data for local governments is quite scattered for the period prior to 1942, depending in large measure on data compiled by the National Industrial Conference Board; the estimates for this period are therefore generally less reliable. Since 1945 the Census Bureau coverage of local governments has been much more comprehensive.

Capital Consumption Allowances

Capital consumption allowances in U.S. national income accounting consist of (1) depreciation charges (including obsolescence) of business enterprises, farms, real estate, and institutions, (2) capital outlays charged to current expense by business, and (3) accidental damage to fixed capital. For all sectors except the farm sector the concept of depreciation used is the writing off of original cost on the basis of the length of life of the asset as embodied in the tax regulations. Farm depreciation, however, as pointed out in the section describing the derivation of the income of farm proprietors, is calculated by the Agricultural Economics Division of the Department of Agriculture in terms of replacement cost rather than original cost.

Depreciation Charges. Corporate depreciation charges are obtained from tax return data. Information on the noncorporate sector is not as satisfactory. In most cases the estimates are built up industry by industry on the basis of the Internal Revenue Service tabulation of sole proprietors and partnerships for the year 1945. The figures in this study were increased to include the depreciation charges of those firms which did not file returns. Estimates for other years were computed by applying on an industry-by-industry basis a depreciation-gross receipts ratio to the gross receipts of noncorporate business. The depreciation-gross receipts ratios were obtained by extrapolating the 1945 ratios by the ratios for partnerships available from tax returns for 1939 and 1947 and by the ratios of corporations for other years. The depreciation of farms and of noncorporate nonfarm real estate held by individuals has already been discussed in the sections on the income of farm proprietors and on the rental income of persons.

Capital Outlays Charged to Current Expense. Producers purchase some types of capital goods that are not considered capital equipment for tax purposes. Since these capital goods are charged off to current expense by producers, yet are counted as a part of capital equipment on the product side of the National Income and Product Account, a discrepancy between the two sides of the account would appear unless an adjustment is made. For this reason the item "capital outlay charged to current expense" is introduced under capital consumption allowances. These outlays are estimated in two parts: (1) the outlays incurred in drilling and development of oil and gas wells, which are included as new construction in the gross national product but are charged off as current expense by producers, and (2) items of producers' durable equipment (primarily tools), which it is believed are charged off as current expense. The estimates of the drilling and development costs of oil and gas wells will be covered later in connection with the discussion of new construction. The estimates for producers' durable equipment charged to current expense are derived from the estimates for the detailed commodity groups which, according to accepted accounting practice, are likely to be charged to current expense. These commodities are estimated by the methods discussed in the section on producers' durable equipment.

Accidental Damage to Fixed Capital. From the point of view of the economy as a whole, accidental damage to fixed capital is a form of capital consumption which can be expected to take place every year and which is not covered in the conventional depreciation charges of individual firms. Such things as fires which destroy buildings, forest fires, ship sinkings, damage caused by tornadoes, windstorms, and floods, accidents involving railways, aircraft, or business vehicles are all included in accidental damage to fixed capital. The property of private individuals (e.g., automobiles) which is lost or damaged is not included in this estimate, since such items are not part of producers' plant or equipment. Furthermore, since the repair of producers' goods is also excluded from gross domestic investment expenditures, it is necessary to exclude reparable damage that occurs to producers' plant and equipment. The sources of information on accidental damage to fixed capital are rather scattered. The estimates on loss by fire come mainly from insurance companies. Forest fire damage estimates are obtained from the reports of the United States Forest Service. Business vehicle accidents are estimated mainly from the state and city police reports compiled by the National Safety Bureau. Other sources are the reports of the Weather Bureau and the Interstate Commerce Commission.

Other Income Allocations and Adjustments

The remaining allocations and adjustments of gross national income are (1) business transfer payments, (2) subsidies minus current surplus of government enterprises, (3) inventory valuation adjustment, and (4) statistical discrepancy.

Business Transfer Payments. Business transfer payments consist of gifts to nonprofit institutions, consumer bad debts, personal injury payments by business other than to employees, unrecovered thefts of cash or goods from business, and cash prizes. Estimates on corporate gifts to nonprofit institutions and on consumer bad debts are based on data contained in tax returns. Estimates of personal injury payments are obtained by allocating the total losses paid on automobile policies derived from insurance records between business and individuals, and adding to this the railroad personal injury payments. Unrecovered thefts from business are estimated from the reports of the Federal Bureau of

Investigation. Figures on cash prizes are covered by a token estimate of $25 million annually.

Subsidies Minus Current Surplus of Government Enterprises. This flow consists of subsidies paid by the general Federal government, plus the operating deficit or minus the operating surplus of both Federal and state and local government enterprises. The data for the Federal government come from Treasury accounts, and those for state and local government come from the census reports on government finances.

Inventory Valuation Adjustment. This adjustment is necessary since the change in inventories recorded in the gross national product represents the value of the change in the physical volume of inventories, whereas the bookkeeping records which are used to calculate the income of corporate and noncorporate nonfarm business compute the change in the value of the inventories that are held. Because of this difference in the method of inventory valuation, the two sides of the gross national income and product account will fail to balance unless an inventory valuation adjustment is introduced. The methods of obtaining this adjustment are discussed in the section dealing with the measurement of the net change in inventories.

Statistical Discrepancy. The statistical discrepancy is residually determined. It represents the difference between the aggregate of the estimates of the allocation flows and the aggregate of the estimates of the expenditure flows. Although these are theoretically equal, the process of estimating separately each of the components on each side of the account will inevitably lead to some discrepancy in the two totals. In general this item is quite small.

EXPENDITURES FOR GROSS NATIONAL PRODUCT

By far the greater part of the expenditures for gross national product are made on commodities, as opposed to services. The flow of these commodities through the economic system from producers to wholesalers to retailers to final purchasers can be traced,[1] and by this means the total expenditures for that part of the gross national product which is composed of commodities can be estimated. The remaining expenditures for gross national product can then be estimated separately. In this section the theory of the commodity flow analysis will be discussed and the general sources from which the estimates are obtained will be outlined. The sources for the remaining components of gross national product expenditure will then be taken up separately.

The Theory of Commodity Flow

The commodity flow analysis is essentially a process of tracing the flow of commodities through the economic system, adding at each step the additional costs and expenses involved, so that finally an estimate is obtained of sales to consumers and to business on capital account or, in other words, of the commodity expenditures by these sectors on gross national product.

[1] The commodity flow going to government is not estimated by the "commodity flow method." For the actual procedure see p. 174.

The first step in this analysis involves the classification of several thousand categories of commodities as finished durable consumption goods, finished semidurable consumption goods, finished perishable consumption goods, finished durable producers' goods, and unfinished commodities destined to enter further into the productive process. Classification of a commodity as finished does not depend solely upon the degree of processing; it is also based on the use to which a commodity is put. Flour, for example, is classified as finished if consumed in households, institutions, or government agencies, but it is classified as unfinished if consumed by a factory making bread or other products using flour as a raw material. The commodities classified as unfinished are dropped from the analysis. By considering only finished goods, all raw materials purchased by producers from other enterprises are automatically excluded, and this element of double counting is eliminated. This is essentially the same as obtaining the value added by the producing sector of the economy as a whole. After the classifications are made, estimates are obtained for the output of each class of finished commodities.

At this point the commodity estimates are valued in the producers' prices, f.o.b. factory, farm, or mine. To pass from output at producers' prices to the final cost to ultimate users, all commodities except those produced and consumed on farms have to be followed through the distributive system. The first step in this process involves adjustments for changes in producers' inventories. Sales are equal to production plus inventory increases or minus inventory decreases. If both production and the change in inventories are known, the production data for all commodities can be adjusted by the inventory change so that the amount of commodities sold by the producer can be estimated.

The next step in tracing the commodity flow involves adding transportation charges to the f.o.b. sales estimates in order to obtain the delivered value of sales. After this it is necessary to estimate how much of the producers' sales were to wholesalers, how much to retailers, and how much direct to consumers. This must be known before the commodities can be followed further through the channels of distribution. The goods that are sold to wholesalers must be adjusted for changes in wholesalers' inventories in order to give an estimate of the cost of goods sold by wholesalers. The sales of wholesalers are partly to retailers and partly to consumers, and the proportion of each of these must next be determined. Wholesalers' markups on sales to each of these groups are then estimated on the basis of operating expenses of wholesalers to obtain the total value of wholesale sales. At the retail level similar adjustments are made. Goods purchased by retailers are adjusted for inventory changes to obtain the cost of goods sold by retailers, and a markup based on operating expenses is added to obtain the retail value of goods sold.

Thus when the direct sales made by producers and wholesalers to ultimate users and the total value of goods sold by retailers are added, the total market value of commodities sold can be obtained. As was pointed out above, this accounts for a large part of the total value of goods and services in the economy. This somewhat roundabout method of tracing the commodity flow in the economy was chosen because of the availability of very detailed data at the production level and the relative scarcity of detail at the wholesale and retail levels. The general sources of these data will be outlined in the following section.

The Commodity Flow: Sources of Data

The basic source for data on manufactured commodities is the *Census of Manufactures,* published by the Bureau of the Census for the odd years up to 1939 and for 1947. Generally speaking, the data for most Census periods were similar enough so that the same general methodology could be employed for all periods. The major exception is the year 1947. Where the methods used in this year were radically different from those used in other years, this will be noted.

The *Census of Manufactures* provides detailed output data for specific commodities, and the National Income Division of the Department of Commerce has classified these commodities into several thousand commodity groups. For Census years output totals at the producing level can be obtained directly by adding up the figures for the commodities classed as finished. For intercensal years the estimates are based on as many different interpolating series for each minor commodity group as are available. These series were checked against the Census totals for Census years, and reasonably good intercensal interpolations have been obtained for every commodity group.

Nonmanufactured commodities relevant to the study are found in the products of farms, fisheries, and mines. Of all these products only nonmanufactured foods and fuels can be classified as finished. Data on nonmanufactured foods are obtained from the annual statistics of the Department of Agriculture and from compilations made by the Bureau of Fisheries. Special tabulations of the Department of Agriculture and data in the *Census of Manufactures* give information on the amount of materials consumed in manufacturing. Data on nonmanufactured finished fuels were obtained from the Bureau of Mines for coal and from the Department of Agriculture for firewood.

The change in manufacturing inventories for the years 1937, 1938, and 1939 was obtained chiefly from detailed inventory data reported in the *Census of Manufactures.* The relation between sales and production was computed for these years, and the value of the change in inventories derived from this relation. The analysis was extended to earlier years by computing similar relationships for related corporate industry groups as reported in *Statistics of Income,* which is published annually by the Bureau of Internal Revenue. Since the original values obtained for nonmanufactured foods were in terms of sales, no inventory adjustment had to be applied to this group. For 1947, shipments rather than production was generally reported, so that inventory information was not necessary.

Freight revenues of Class I steam railways as percentages of commodity values at point of origin were compiled for 1928, 1930, 1933, 1936, 1939, and 1947 by the Interstate Commerce Commission. Similar percentages were obtained for the intervening years by using the annual freight commodity statistics of the commission, supplemented by price data from various sources, principally the Bureau of Labor Statistics. For those groups which used other forms of transportation such as trucking or pipelines, the data were checked and, where necessary, supplemented by whatever sales figures could be obtained on these forms of transportation.

The distribution of sales by type of purchaser was required at both the producing and the wholesale levels. The basic source used in distributing the sales of producers among wholesalers, retailers, and consumers was the Cenus data for 1929, 1935, and 1939, reported in the Census Bureau publication *Distribution of Sales of Manufacturing Plants*. For the intercensal years, the derived census year percentages, which did not change appreciably, were interpolated along a straight line.

The 1947 *Census of Manufactures* did not include information on sales distributions, so the approach was altered somewhat. The exact procedure used for 1947 will be discussed below.

For the periods other than 1947 the sales of wholesalers were distributed between retailers and consumers on the basis of data in the 1935 and 1939 *Wholesale Census*. Between 1935 and 1939 the percentages were interpolated along a straight line. Prior to 1935 the 1935 percentages were used. The goods purchased and sold by wholesalers were also corrected for the imports and exports made by wholesalers. The source for this correction was the annual data in *Foreign Commerce and Navigation,* published by the Department of Commerce.

The inventory changes for wholesale and retail trade were obtained for the years 1929, 1933, 1935, and 1939 from the *Wholesale Census* and the *Retail Census* data of these years. For other years they were interpolated from *Statistics of Income* data in much the same way that the inventory data were obtained for manufacturers.

The markup estimates for both wholesalers and retailers were based on a large variety of sources. Operating expenses as a percentage of net sales for comparable kinds of business were derived for 1929, 1933, 1935, and 1939 from the *Wholesale Census* and the *Retail Census* of these years. Expense ratios derived from noncensus data were used to interpolate for intercensal years whenever possible. Profit and loss allowances required to translate the operating expense ratios into the desired markup estimates were derived from noncensus data. These were checked and substantiated by relevant data in *Statistics of Income* for 1929 to 1939. Special studies such as *Distribution Costs,* by the Harvard Business School, were used in some instances.

For the year 1947 a different procedure was adopted, since, as noted above, data on the distribution of manufacturers' sales were not available. Wholesale margins for 1947 were broken down on a commodity basis, and between consumer and nonconsumer uses, utilizing the detailed estimates of wholesaling in 1947 developed by the Interindustry Economics Division of the Bureau of Labor Statistics. The 1948 *Wholesale Census* provided much of the basic information for these estimates. With this information and the sources previously utilized, the procedure for obtaining the 1947 commodity flow estimates was as follows: After obtaining the total value of producers' sales of finished commodities on a commodity-by-commodity basis, Federal excise taxes, transportation charges, and imports were added, and the change in inventories in the hands of wholesalers was deducted. The wholesalers' markup and state excise taxes were added, and exports were subtracted, yielding the value of finished goods sold to producers, retailers, and consumers. Deductions were then made for producers' durable equipment, producers' sales directly to consumers, wholesalers' sales directly to consumers, and changes in retailers' inventories, to adjust the total to the cost of goods sold by retailers. At this point the retailers' markup, Federal retail excise taxes, and general retail sales taxes were added to adjust the final valuation to the expenditure for the commodities by consumers.

The commodity flow method is complex and highly detailed, but it appears to yield accurate and reliable results. The data obtained are not only internally consistent, but they check extremely well with other sources of information available for various parts of the universe and with new information that becomes available after the estimates have been made. Not all components in the expenditures side of the gross national product are covered by the commodity flow analysis. The methods used for the other components and for extrapolation and interpolation of the bench-mark years will be taken up for the individual flows below.

Personal Consumption Expenditures

From the point of view of the methods of estimation used, personal consumption expenditures consist of two major components: (1) personal consumption expenditures for commodities, and (2) personal consumption expenditures for services.

Personal Consumption Expenditures for Commodities. The personal consumption expenditures for commodities are derived in the bench-mark years for the most part by the commodity flow method described above. In 1947 over 80 per cent of the consumption expenditures for commodities were derived by this method. For another 13 per cent of commodities, such as tobacco products, new automobiles, gasoline and oil and other fuel, the "retail valuation method" was utilized. This method involves multiplying an estimate of the quantity of commodities purchased by consumers by an appropriate retail price. The imputations for food and fuel produced and consumed on farms have been discussed above in connection with the derivation of the income of farm proprietors. The only other imputation that is made is for the standard clothing issued to military personnel.

The interpolation and extrapolation of the bench-mark estimates for consumers' expenditures on commodities are based largely on the relative movements of retail sales. The main sources for this information are (1) the retail sales series by type of store which was prepared through 1951 by the Office of Business Economics of the Department of Commerce, and since then by the Bureau of the Census, and (2) department store sales by type of department, compiled by the Board of Governors of the Federal Reserve System. Use is also made of state sales tax data, Federal excise tax data, sales data from trade associations, and other kinds of price and quantity data. The processing of the Census data for 1947 for national income accounting purposes provided an excellent check on the reliability of the methods used to extrapolate previous bench-mark data to that date. The projection of the 1939 commodity flow bench-mark information to 1947 by the use of retail sales shows a difference from the new 1947 bench-mark estimate of only 3 per cent. Although the error for some commodity groups was larger than this, the error for most of them was less than 7 per cent. This high degree of correspondence between the earlier extrapolation and the new bench-mark information is especially remarkable in view of the considerable economic dislocations which had been occasioned by World War II and by the substantial rise in prices that followed.

Personal Consumption Expenditures for Services. This component of personal consumption expenditures cannot be estimated by the commodity flow method, and has had to be built up from a wide variety of very different sources. Broadly speaking, these sources may be classified into four major groups: (1) comprehensive annual reports, (2) periodic comprehensive sources, (3) sample information, and (4) other miscellaneous sources. The estimation of the imputed services provided by financial intermediaries has already been discussed in the section on interest income; data for computing this item are available from the reports of the Federal Deposit Insurance Corporation, the Board of Governors of the Federal Reserve System, and the Internal Revenue Service. Various government agencies also report annually on telephone services; railway, bus, and airline transportation; and a few other services. Private sources provide annual data for the expenses of handling life insurance and accident and health insurance; the services of private hospitals and sanatoriums; and public utilities such as electricity, gas, and local transportation. Information of a comprehensive nature is available on a periodic basis from such sources as the *Census of Population and Housing,* the *Census of Business,* the *Census of Agriculture,* the *Census of Religious Bodies,* and the *Biennial Survey of Education.* The *Census of Population and Housing* and the *Census of Agriculture* are used to obtain the rental value of homes (nonfarm and farm) in the manner already described in the sections on the income of farm proprietors and the rental income of persons. The Census of Business provides a wide variety of information on laundries, barbershops, theaters, hotels, repair shops of all kinds, photo studios, etc. Periodic sample information has been used by the National Income Division to obtain data on professional services furnished to individuals. These samples have already been mentioned in the discussion of the net income of professional practitioners. Sample information such as that contained in the 1935–1936 Consumer Purchases Study helps to provide bench-mark data for some kinds of services. In the category of miscellaneous sources are special studies made by private research organizations and correspondence with trade associations.

Gross Private Domestic Investment

In the definition of the National Income Division this flow includes (1) private new construction, (2) producers' durable equipment, and (3) change in business inventories. Each of these flows has different sources.

Private New Construction. The estimates of private new construction are prepared jointly by the Bureau of Labor Statistics and the Building Materials and Construction Division of the Department of Commerce. There is considerable difficulty in obtaining adequate information on construction activity. Much of the work in the industry is done by producers who are in the business only irregularly or on a part-time basis. The construction projects are by their very nature nonrepeating activities, and are not standardized either with respect to the location of the activity or the size of the project. Four major types of source may be identified for information on the construction industry: (1) direct reports of work done or paid for, (2) contract awards, (3) building permits, and (4) other miscellaneous sources.

Direct reports of work done are available mainly for public-utility construction work, where a formal reporting system is in force. New electric-light and power construction thus is reported by the Federal Power Commission. The American Gas Association, American Telephone and Telegraph, and Western Union Telegraph Company cover new construction activity in their areas. Petroleum pipeline construction is covered by the Interstate Commerce Commission, which, together with the Association of American Railroads, also covers railroad construction. Local transit construction is covered by the American Transit Association. Construction reported by these groups accounted for about 15 per cent of total private construction in 1950.

Data obtained from contract awards, covering construction activity for business purposes (including apartment houses), accounted for another 18 per cent of private construction activity in the year 1950. The F. W. Dodge Corporation is the main source for information on contract awards. Local correspondents keep track of contract awards in their area. These data are adjusted for understatement in accord with information derived from the 1939 *Census of Construction.* Since most construction work takes a considerable period of time to complete, the contract award information must be allocated over an appropriate time span. On the basis of surveys of thousands of actual projects, the Building Materials and Construction Division of the Department of Commerce has established typical activity patterns for various types and sizes of construction projects, yielding the percentage of the total contract values which were put in place in successive months. This information is used to convert the value of starts data into estimates of construction activity.

Building permit information accounts for about another 45 per cent of the construction estimates, and is used to estimate new nonfarm private residential dwellings and alterations and additions to nonfarm dwellings done under permit. Coverage of permit-issuing localities is fairly comprehensive, and adjustment is made to raise the estimate to full coverage and to allow for lapsed permits and understatement of the estimates in building permits. Periodic field studies are made by the Bureau of Labor Statistics to determine the amount of such adjustments. As in the case of the contract awards data, it is again necessary to allocate the value of the construction over an appropriate time span. The general kinds of estimating procedures applied are the same. With respect to additions and alterations, studies of family expenditures such as the Consumer Purchases Study of 1935–1936 are used to provide the basis for adjustments of understatement and undercoverage.

Other sources account for the remaining 20 per cent of construction. This covers private nonfarm residential dwellings in nonpermit areas, farm construction, and oil and gas drilling. The first of these categories is covered on a sampling basis by the Bureau of Labor Statistics. Farm construction is obtained from the Department of Agriculture, based mainly on sample surveys of construction expenditures by farm operators for the years 1934 to 1937, 1939, 1946, and 1949. These are interpolated and extrapolated on the basis of other indicators such as price changes, sales of building materials in rural areas, etc. Oil- and gas-drilling estimates are derived from the 1939 *Census of Mineral Industry* and compilations in trade publications. The estimates have been projected from 1939 on the basis of number of wells completed multiplied by the average cost per well.

Producers' Durable Equipment. For the most part, producers' durable equipment is estimated by the commodity flow method described above. In 1939 the commodity flow method covered 66 per cent of the total, and in 1947 this increased to 88 per cent.

The application of the commodity flow method to producers' durables raises the problem of eliminating producers' durables purchased by the government. A variety of sources were used for this purpose, including the tabulations made by the Bureau of Labor Statistics of orders under the Walsh-Healy Act and of detailed expenditures by various government agencies. The commodity flow bench mark for 1947 is probably an improvement over the 1939 bench mark, since greater detail was available; over 6,000 different products were available in the 1947 census, in contrast with 4,000 in the 1939 census.

For years other than the primary census years the methods differed from those employed for consumer expenditures. For many of the years secondary bench marks were in effect set up, utilizing the same commodity flow approach. For the years 1942 to 1945, for example, War Production Board reports on commodity sales for most producers' durable groups made the continuation of the commodity flow approach possible. The number of individual commodity items which could be derived was substantially fewer, and the allocations had to be based on the relationship developed for 1947. Government purchases of producers' durables were deducted on the basis of War Assets Administration and Census-Civilian Production Administration reports, together with Bureau of Labor Statistics data on purchases by government agencies and data contained in the census reports on state and local government expenditures. For the years 1948 to 1952 the Census Bureau's annual *Survey of Manufactures* (1950–1952) was used, in conjunction with the manufacturers' sales series (1948–1949) of the Office of Business Economics, to provide estimates of commodity sales. Because the 1948 and 1949 data were less complete, these estimates represent an interpolation between the 1947 and the 1950 primary and secondary bench marks. Government purchases of producers' durables were estimated and deducted from the total for producers' durables by developing a bench mark for the second half of 1951 and 1952, and interpolating for the intervening period. The bench mark was established through the use of data reported by the National Production Authority and by the Bureau of Labor Statistics and census sources mentioned for previous periods.

The major producers' durable not estimated by the commodity flow approach since 1947 is passenger vehicles. The number of vehicles produced was multiplied by their price, and the total was allocated between business and individuals on the basis of information for the period 1934 to 1937. Prior to 1947, other business vehicles were also estimated directly on the basis of trade publication data and *Census of Manufactures* information.

Change in Business Inventories

For national income accounting purposes the value of the change in the physical volume of inventories in the economy is needed. Such a measurement of inventory change is not the one which is customarily used by business in the calculation of its income. The usual methods, such as first-in first-out (FIFO), last-in first-out (LIFO), or some combination of methods, take into account changes in the prices of the commodities in the inventories as well as the change in the physical volume.

The basic source of information on business inventories is the tax return information contained in *Statistics of Income*, prepared by the Internal Revenue Service. The coverage of this source is quite high, and it is possible to adjust it to full coverage on the basis of census bench-mark data. The major problems arise in the adjustment of the inventory data to the concept desired for national income accounting.

Not all businesses keep books on the same basis, so that a single process of adjustment of inventory data is not possible. It is first necessary to allocate inventory data by industry and separate out that portion of each industry's inventory data that is reported on a LIFO basis. The estimates of the proportion of LIFO inventories are based on surveys by the Office of Business Economics, private research studies, and Moody's *Manual of Industrial Securities*. After the value of non-LIFO inventories in each industry is determined, these are reduced to constant prices by using the revelant price data contained in the indexes of wholesale prices of the Bureau of Labor Statistics. The change in the physical volume of inventories is then found by subtracting the beginning year inventories expressed in constant dollars from the end of the year inventories expressed in constant dollars. This value of the change in the volume of inventories expressed in constant dollars is then reconverted to current dollars to obtain the current value of the change in the volume of inventories. Inventories reported on a LIFO basis are adjusted in a different manner. If LIFO inventories increase, they reflect the current value of the change in the volume of inventories without any adjustment. If there is a decline in LIFO inventories, however, a conversion to current prices is necessary. Thus far the price adjustments for declines in LIFO inventories have been negligible, and since LIFO inventories represent less than one-tenth of total nonfarm inventories, the accuracy of this adjustment is not crucial. The change in farm inventories is added to that in business inventories to get the total change in inventories for the economy. Farm inventories do not need adjustment in the manner described above, since farm inventories are calculated by the Department of Agriculture in terms of the physical volume of specific kinds of farm products held.

The inventory valuation adjustment is obtained by subtracting the adjusted estimate of the current value of the change in the physical volume of inventories from the change in the total book value of inventories as reported by business firms.

Net Foreign Investment

Net foreign investment as defined by the National Income Division is subject to somewhat larger errors of estimation than might be expected on the basis of the nature of the sources involved, because it is residually determined as the difference between the gross outflows and the gross inflows. Even small errors in the gross flows can result in considerable relative error in the difference between them.

This flow is made up of net payments of factor income to the United States, net interest received, net dividends received, net branch profits received, net merchandise receipts, net transportation receipts, and other net receipts for travel services, transfers, royalties, etc. The basic source is the balance of payments published by the Office of Business Economics. Net foreign investment is also estimated by the change in assets and liabilities, and the difference between this method and the alternative one is considered to be errors and omissions. Many of the individual flows are difficult to adjust to the desired concept. For example, data on the net wages and salaries of "border workers" cannot be obtained. Interest received from abroad is in part estimated on the basis of the bench marks established by the Treasury's 1942 *Census of American-owned Assets in Foreign Countries* and the Commerce Department's 1950 *Census of American Direct Investments Abroad*. Interest paid to abroad is estimated in two categories: interest subject to withholding paid to abroad as reported to the Internal Revenue Service, and foreign holdings of United States government long- and short-term issues multiplied by their average yield. Merchandise imports and exports are obtained chiefly from the declaration forms filed with the Collectors of Customs and tabulated by the Foreign Trade Division of the Census Bureau, together with the foreign trade transactions of different agencies of the Federal government. The major problem with the merchandise import and export data relates to whether the valuations placed on goods are in fact accurate. Estimates of ocean freight transport services are based on Census Bureau or Maritime Administration data, and estimates of ocean passenger traffic are derived from the records of arrivals and departures of passengers. In addition to the items mentioned above, there are also a large number of other transactions that are calculated on the basis of records of government agencies (e.g., port charges, air travel, rail travel, etc.) and sample questionnaires (e.g., tourist expenditures, motion-picture rentals, etc.).

Government Purchases of Goods and Services

The general procedure used in obtaining an estimate of government purchases of goods and services is to start from the major fiscal reports of the government, giving general totals for all outlays, and then subtract from such totals those outlays which are not for purchase of goods and services. Thus the estimate is essentially residual; the government records are not kept in such a manner that the list of goods and services purchased can be built up on an item-by-item basis.

The three major basic sources for the Federal government are the annual Budget of the United States Government, the Treasury's Combined Statement of Receipts, Expenditures, and Balances, and the Daily Statement of the United States Treasury. The differences among these three documents are mainly differences in the type and arrangement of details reported and slightly different closing dates. The Daily Statement of the United States Treasury is adopted as the basic source for the total of government outlays because it is the only one of the three documents that is not on a fiscal year basis. Starting with this total, the following deductions are made: transfers to trust funds, tax refunds, general government loans, investments, and capital transfers, purchases of land and existing capital assets, budgetary transfer payments, grants-in-aid to state and local governments, interest and subsidy payments other than those paid by government enterprises, overpayments established by renegotiation of war contracts, and budgetary expenditures relating to government enterprises. A number of additions are also made as follows: capital formation of government enterprises, government contributions to social insurance, changes in net payables to private business, and other miscellaneous adjustments. These adjustments yield as the residual gross Federal government purchases of goods and services. Sales by government are then deducted to arrive at the final estimate of net Federal government purchases of goods and services. In 1950 the initial budgetary expenditures were about $38 billion and were reduced by the above process of adjustment to a net Federal government expenditure on goods and services of about $22 billion. There were only four individual adjustments that exceeded $1 billion; these were budgetary transfer payments of $4.6 billion, grants-in-aid to state and local governments of $2.3 billion, interest payments of $5.7 billion, and budgetary expenditures relating to government enterprises of $1.5 billion.

State and local government purchases of goods and services were obtained by the same process of adjusting total outlay figures. The major source of information in this case is the summary statistics on state and local finances collected by the Governments Division of the Bureau of the Census.

Government expenditures on goods and services as shown in national income accounts are classified into compensation of employees, expenditures on construction, and other expenditures on goods and services. The derivation of the wages and salaries paid to government employees has already been discussed in the section on the compensation of employees. The construction expenditures of the Federal government are based on data from the Bureau of Public Roads (highways), the Department of Defense (military facilities), and other Federal agencies (Federal or Federally aided housing construction and other construction). For state and local government construction the Bureau of Public Roads provides highway construction data, and other construction information is provided by the F. W. Dodge Corporation data on contract awards discussed in the section on private new construction.

The other expenditures of the government on goods and services are derived as a residual. To the extent that some of the government construction is force construction, it may be included both in the compensation of employees and in construction expenditures, thus causing a corresponding understatement in the other expenditures on goods and services.

OTHER ACCOUNTING FLOWS

Personal Tax and Nontax Payments

This flow is primarily the Federal individual income tax. Monthly reports of the Internal Revenue Service are used as the direct source for these data. Since January, 1951, the Internal Revenue data have combined collections of the individual income taxes with employment taxes, and it has been necessary to subtract the latter on the basis of the sources discussed in the section on the compensation of employees.

Other Federal taxes such as estate and gift taxes are also obtained from the Internal Revenue reports. Personal nontax payments to the Federal government, including fines, penalties, forfeitures, etc., are obtained from the annual Budget of the United States Government. Personal tax refunds are based mainly on the Daily Statement of the United States Treasury. State and local personal tax and nontax receipts are dependent on detailed analysis of the census data on state and local government finances.

Personal Saving

Personal saving is obtained residually by subtracting consumer expenditures and personal tax and nontax payments from total personal income. Since it is the difference between much larger totals, even small errors of estimation in one or both of the totals (unless directly correlated) will lead to large relative errors in the residual saving figures. Reconciliation of the national income accounting personal saving figures with the Securities and Exchange Commission data on saving, however, indicates a close correspondence between the two series.

Government Transfer Payments to Individuals

Federal government transfer payments are obtained from Treasury data. State and local government transfer payments are somewhat more difficult to obtain; they are based on estimates of pension payments prepared by the

Department of Health, Education, and Welfare, and upon census reports of the financial statistics of state and local governments.

Government Surplus or Deficit

Government surplus or deficit is also a residual figure, arising in this case as the difference between government receipts and government outlays. It should be noted that this government surplus or deficit applies to all governmental units on a consolidated basis. It also differs conceptually from the budgetary surplus and deficit usually shown for the Federal government, because of a difference in timing and also because of a difference in the content of government outlays. Thus, for example, all the transfer payments to individuals are recorded in the national income account as Federal government outlays, whereas certain of these payments in the Federal government accounting practice are recorded as payments out of extrabudgetary trust funds.

GROSS NATIONAL PRODUCT IN CONSTANT DOLLARS

Gross national product in constant dollars is obtained by price adjustment of gross national product in current dollars. Therefore the basic statistical sources and methods used in deriving estimates of gross national product in current dollars apply equally to data on gross national product in constant dollars.

The general procedure used in making the price adjustment to obtain constant dollar estimates is to divide the current dollar estimates into as fine a product breakdown as possible and apply to each group relevant price indexes (in this instance based on 1947), to eliminate the price changes that have taken place since the base period.

Inasmuch as information available on price changes in the economy is obtained from quoted prices, the amount of price change which actually occurs will generally be understated, especially in a period of falling prices. In a period when it is difficult to sell goods, businessmen resort to special sales, or give discounts and extra services such as free delivery, and the quality of the goods offered for sale at a given price may improve. For the most part, such changes as these are not adequately reflected in the price series, so that the amount of price drop tends to be understated. Similarly, in a seller's market the services offered by a producer may be curtailed, there will be fewer sales and discounts, and the quality of goods offered may decline, so that in fact the rise in prices is understated. Since prices tend to fall in periods of falling output and to rise in a period of rising activity, the understatement of price fluctuation will cause in the deflation process an overstatement of the amount by which output has fluctuated. For example, in a period of falling output and prices, the failure to record the full amount of the price fall will result in too small a price correction, so that more of the decline will be attributed to the fall in output than has actually been the case.

The price data are frequently available in greater product detail than are the current dollar estimates. For example, personal consumption expenditures for shoes and other footwear cannot be broken down into any greater detail for all years in the current dollar estimates. Price indexes, however, exist for a large number of individual shoe and footwear items. In these cases the detailed price indexes are utilized by combining them into a composite index for the category, i.e., shoes and footwear as a group, and using the composite index to adjust the corresponding current dollar estimates. In making up such composite price indexes, the weights used to combine the individual price indexes are derived from the 1939 census data for the period from 1929 to 1939 and from the 1947 census for 1947 and later years. Weights for the years between 1939 and 1947 were obtained by a straight-line interpolation between the 1939 and 1947 weights.

For personal consumption expenditures the price series used were those in the Consumers' Price Index of the Bureau of Labor Statistics, and in the series on prices paid by farmers of the Agricultural Marketing Service. The Consumers' Price Index is based on prices paid by moderate income families living in large cities. Prices paid by individuals living in small cities and towns, or individuals with low and high incomes, were not included. It should be pointed out in this connection, however, that insofar as the cost of living of two income groups differs because they purchase different groups of goods, the process of deflation of the individual goods will not be affected. For the period 1942 to 1947 adjustments were made to the published price indexes to take into account their understatement of the price rise that occurred during and immediately after World War II. The basic study on which procedures relating to such adjustments are based is contained in the *Report of the Technical Committee Appointed by the Chairman of the President's Committee on the Cost of Living, June 15, 1944.*

Private new construction was deflated by a detailed list of construction cost indexes prepared by private and government agencies. These indexes pertain for the most part to construction materials and labor, and were applied on an item-by-item basis to the components of the private new construction estimates in current dollars. Producers' purchases of durables were adjusted mainly by using the Bureau of Labor Statistics wholesale price indexes and the Interstate Commerce Commission price indexes. As in the case of consumer expenditures, the detail on prices exceeded the detail on current dollar estimates; composite indexes were derived in much the same manner as described for the consumer expenditures composite price indexes. The deflated series on nonfarm inventories was obtained directly from the procedure used to obtain the value of the change in the physical volume of inventories from the change in the book value, as described in the section on change in inventories. The net change in farm inventories in constant prices was derived from the quantity data supplied by the Agricultural Marketing Service.

Net foreign investment was deflated by adjusting each component insofar as possible for the effect of price changes. Merchandise imports and merchandise exports were deflated by indexes of unit value prepared by the Bureau of Foreign Commerce of the Department of Commerce. With respect to the other components of the net foreign investment, theoretical problems as well as lack of statistical information made accurate deflation infeasible.

The deflation of government purchases of goods and services was difficult because of the lack of adequate price indexes. The construction component is deflated by the same general procedure as that discussed above for private new construction. The compensation of employees in constant dollars represents an extrapolation of man-hours wherever possible. Munitions expenditures were deflated for the war years by a special index of munitions prices compiled by the Defense Department. The remaining types of government purchases from business were deflated by using those components of the Bureau of Labor Statistics wholesale price index which seemed to be most applicable.

9. Related Systems of Economic Accounting

National income accounting represents but one of the various kinds of economic accounting systems that could be set up. As has been seen, it focuses attention on the total output of the economy in terms of the final goods that are produced and the incomes and other payments generated by such production. The role of functional sectors—producers, consumers, and the government—as receivers of income and as purchasers is shown related to the total activity of the economy. It is equally possible, however, to draw up different systems of economic accounting that focus on different aspects of the economy and use different systems of sectoring and different classifications of transactions to achieve their purposes. This chapter will discuss two such systems: input-output accounting and flow-of-funds accounting. These two systems are introduced not so much to explain the systems themselves, since this cannot be done adequately in the very brief treatment that follows, but rather to place the discussion of national income accounting in proper perspective. By describing other valid and useful forms of economic accounting, some idea of the limitations of national income accounting can be established and its general area of usefulness can be indicated more clearly.

The Input-Output Matrix as a Form of Economic Accounting

The Rationale of Input-Output Accounting Procedures

For an individual firm the meaning of the terms "input" and "output" is fairly clear. The firm purchases raw materials, labor, fuel, and power, which it uses in conjunction with its plant and equipment to produce goods and services for the market. What is used up in the process of production is input. Strictly speaking, certain of the taxes that the firm pays and part of its profit may not represent actual inputs of goods and services; nevertheless, from the point of view of the economy as a whole, these payments are necessary for this production to take place and so are considered a part of the inputs required to obtain the output of this firm. It is in this light that the input requirements of the economy are viewed in the input-output accounts: the market value of production is divided up among the purchases of goods, materials, and services from other firms, the payments to the factors of production, and the other elements having a legal claim for payment. The output pattern, similarly, shows how the output of a given firm, industry, or sector is purchased by other firms, industries, or sectors. The focus of input-output accounting is on the interindustry relationships in the economy, and therefore the classification of inputs and outputs is primarily in terms of the industries involved in the supplying of inputs and the purchasing of outputs.

An example of the input-output classification system for an individual firm is given in Table 47.

Table 47. Input-Output Schedule for an Individual Firm

Inputs		Outputs	
Purchases from other industries.....	$ 665	Sales to other industries............	$1,403
Agriculture....................	85	Agriculture....................	5
Mining........................	10	Mining........................	10
Contract construction............	20	Contract construction...........	15
Manufacturing.................	400	Manufacturing.................	1,325
Wholesale and retail trade.......	105	Wholesale and retail trade.......	20
Finance, insurance, and real estate	15	Finance, insurance, and real estate	8
Transportation and public utilities	15	Transportation and public utilities	5
Services......................	5	Services......................	5
Foreign countries...............	10	Foreign countries...............	10
Payments to government..........	116	Sales to and payments from government.........................	52
Payments to households...........	735	Sales to households...............	50
Capital allocations................	99	Sales to producers on capital account	10
		Inventory change................	100
Total inputs...................	$1,615	Total outputs..................	$1,615

This account will be recognized as a reclassification of the items in the production statement for an individual firm previously shown as Table 5 in Chap. 4. The reclassification involves the expansion of detail relating to the purchases of goods and materials from other firms and the sales to other firms, to show the industrial composition of purchases and sales. Other items shown in detail in the production statement are here combined into summary lines. Thus on the input side of the account all taxes paid to the government are combined as a single item, and on the output side sales to government and subsidies received are combined. Since the functional aspects of transactions are not considered in the classification system, a single system of classifying industries and sectors can be

Table 48. Input-Output Table for the United States, 1947

																																														FINAL DEMAND					
	1 AGRICULTURE & FISHERIES	2 FOOD & KINDRED PRODUCTS	3 TOBACCO MANUFACTURES	4 TEXTILE MILL PRODUCTS	5 APPAREL	6 LUMBER & WOOD PRODUCTS	7 FURNITURE & FIXTURES	8 PAPER & ALLIED PRODUCTS	9 PRINTING & PUBLISHING	10 CHEMICALS	11 PRODUCTS OF PETROLEUM & COAL	12 RUBBER PRODUCTS	13 LEATHER & LEATHER PRODUCTS	14 STONE, CLAY & GLASS PRODUCTS	15 IRON & STEEL	16 NONFERROUS METALS	17 PLUMBING & HEATING SUPPLIES	18 FABRICATED STRUCTURAL METAL PRODUCTS	19 OTHER FABRICATED METAL PRODUCTS	20 AGRIC'L, MINING & CONST. MACHINERY	21 METALWORKING MACHINERY	22 OTHER MACHINERY (except electric)	23 MOTORS & GENERATORS	24 RADIOS	25 OTHER ELECTRICAL MACHINERY	26 MOTOR VEHICLES	27 OTHER TRANSPORTATION EQUIPMENT	28 PROFESSIONAL & SCIENTIFIC EQUIPMENT	29 MISCELLANEOUS MANUFACTURING	30 COAL, GAS & ELECTRIC POWER	31 RAILROAD TRANSPORTATION	32 OCEAN TRANSPORTATION	33 OTHER TRANSPORTATION	34 TRADE	35 COMMUNICATIONS	36 FINANCE & INSURANCE	37 RENTAL	38 BUSINESS SERVICES	39 PERSONAL & REPAIR SERVICES	40 MEDICAL, EDUC. & NONPROFIT ORG'S.	41 AMUSEMENTS	42 SCRAP & MISCELLANEOUS INDUSTRIES	43 UNDISTRIBUTED	44 EATING & DRINKING PLACES	45 NEW CONSTRUCTION & MAINTENANCE	46 INVENTORY CHANGE (additions)	47 FOREIGN COUNTRIES (exports to)	48 GOVERNMENT	49 GROSS PRIVATE CAPITAL FORMATION	50 HOUSEHOLDS	TOTAL GROSS OUTPUT
1 AGRICULTURE & FISHERIES	10,856	15,048	783	2,079	19	192	–	9	–	1,211	–	–	49	*	–	11	–	–	–	–	–	–	–	–	–	–	–	4	4	–	5	1	8	–	2	–	–	–	–	116	–	–	250	865	92	1,008	1,276	569	21	9,785	44,263
2 FOOD & KINDRED PRODUCTS	2,378	4,910	15	60	9	*	*	30	*	685	*	–	444	2	3	*	–	–	*	–	–	*	–	–	*	–	–	5	21	1	81	6	34	71	9	–	–	–	2	251	*	9	134	3,469	2	608	1,528	728	–	22,141	37,636
3 TOBACCO MANUFACTURES	–	–	828	–	–	–	–	–	–	1	–	–	–	–	–	–	–	–	–	–	–	–	–	–	–	–	–	–	–	*	–	–	*	–	–	–	–	–	–	–	–	7	45	–	–	77	217	3	–	1,485	2,663
4 TEXTILE MILL PRODUCTS	64	2	–	1,303	3,882	3	285	43	25	13	2	444	88	33	–	–	*	*	8	2	1	18	2	9	36	147	9	47	76	8	–	8	7	27	*	–	–	*	29	4	–	15	580	–	47	61	919	101	21	1,469	9,838
5 APPAREL	44	204	–	–	1,963	–	5	20	–	30	–	–	2	3	–	–	*	–	1	*	–	2	–	*	*	100	10	2	*	*	*	*	3	15	1	–	–	–	20	16	*	12	150	21	1	214	301	193	1	9,987	13,321
6 LUMBER & WOOD PRODUCTS	148	81	18	18	2	1,094	385	267	1	45	6	–	17	17	36	28	23	5	34	15	4	67	3	10	41	46	33	5	65	60	–	5	1	28	*	–	135	1	*	1	–	17	444	5	2,330	174	170	14	36	67	6,002
7 FURNITURE & FIXTURES	–	–	–	12	–	–	7	5	–	–	–	–	–	–	–	–	*	–	–	–	–	5	–	102	1	26	20	1	–	*	–	–	*	–	*	41	78	–	–	4	–	–	199	–	198	78	35	52	569	1,459	2,892
8 PAPER & ALLIED PRODUCTS	2	453	65	78	25	5	15	2,597	1,081	331	112	20	54	179	*	*	9	5	79	2	2	39	4	17	48	33	20	75	69	4	2	–	4	568	2	1	–	2	62	26	–	145	836	57	170	44	154	59	–	344	7,899
9 PRINTING & PUBLISHING	–	39	–	2	–	–	–	–	767	16	–	–	–	–	–	–	1	–	11	2	1	5	–	1	5	–	–	2	–	*	36	4	20	98	33	213	–	2,234	27	173	13	321	585	30	–	*	72	156	89	1,491	6,447
10 CHEMICALS	830	1,451	25	800	142	26	63	183	97	2,655	213	604	126	116	99	85	21	18	88	17	5	62	10	9	178	111	22	55	167	55	32	5	20	73	3	*	–	7	198	222	2	30	1,181	42	635	305	812	186	–	1,964	14,050
11 PRODUCTS OF PETROLEUM & COAL	457	58	*	30	5	74	1	63	3	325	4,829	12	2	50	846	49	7	3	12	9	4	24	1	2	18	31	11	2	8	471	270	87	448	200	2	15	780	*	57	56	1	8	357	15	617	56	680	177	*	2,437	13,670
12 RUBBER PRODUCTS	122	9	–	13	18	9	6	9	3	1	1	41	50	8	*	*	2	2	5	75	2	53	2	2	31	496	12	5	37	1	1	–	130	63	1	7	*	–	71	4	–	5	468	4	56	94	168	21	8	709	2,825
13 LEATHER & LEATHER PRODUCTS	–	–	–	2	53	4	7	–	4	–	–	–	1,037	–	–	–	*	*	1	3	11	7	*	*	1	13	3	8	10	*	–	–	2	2	–	–	–	–	34	6	–	14	283	–	1	108	84	30	17	2,065	3,810
14 STONE, CLAY & GLASS PRODUCTS	65	253	1	1	*	14	34	28	–	258	46	7	5	430	180	33	9	6	52	7	10	57	23	7	92	192	6	26	59	17	12	1	2	37	*	–	–	–	25	6	–	3	363	59	1,741	99	205	17	15	341	4,844
15 IRON & STEEL	6	2	–	–	1	10	97	–	–	5	6	14	1	23	3,982	33	172	553	1,374	532	143	930	118	13	196	1,102	370	16	35	44	153	–	6	–	1	–	–	–	–	–	–	130	719	–	876	57	605	13	–	–	12,338
16 NONFERROUS METALS	–	–	–	–	–	2	16	–	14	189	1	*	*	13	324	2,599	94	63	272	24	23	366	40	26	654	176	62	55	170	6	45	–	2	–	*	–	–	–	–	*	–	21	524	2	315	98	167	5	–	19	6,387
17 PLUMBING & HEATING SUPPLIES	–	–	–	–	–	–	–	–	–	–	–	–	–	–	15	–	39	41	7	–	–	35	1	–	32	8	6	–	–	*	–	–	–	–	–	–	–	–	–	–	–	7	106	–	878	64	42	7	60	397	1,745
18 FABRICATED STRUCTURAL METAL PRODUCTS	–	–	–	–	–	–	5	–	–	–	–	–	–	–	7	–	19	42	18	33	1	67	*	–	9	10	31	1	–	*	7	–	1	–	–	–	–	–	–	–	–	9	248	–	1,564	15	67	4	145	13	2,316
19 OTHER FABRICATED METAL PRODUCTS	83	543	15	*	6	35	132	17	1	130	78	12	16	4	24	4	72	90	213	93	67	326	28	63	211	956	62	68	38	5	26	5	7	59	1	–	–	1	32	6	–	46	1,138	24	652	127	280	38	74	537	6,445
20 AGRIC'L, MINING & CONST. MACHINERY	59	–	–	–	–	–	–	–	–	–	–	–	–	5	15	7	–	83	–	115	20	96	–	–	–	3	14	–	–	28	3	–	*	–	–	–	–	–	57	*	–	11	261	–	116	105	566	82	1,640	66	3,292
21 METALWORKING MACHINERY	–	–	–	–	–	–	–	–	–	–	–	–	–	–	8	7	6	9	53	51	57	90	7	6	19	223	12	8	*	–	8	–	1	–	–	–	–	–	–	–	–	6	264	–	–	17	205	11	734	31	1,833
22 OTHER MACHINERY (except electric)	–	13	–	35	21	14	11	14	35	1	5	–	–	2	27	4	110	43	41	307	68	565	50	2	82	402	195	26	3	6	47	–	12	8	–	16	–	–	146	1	–	53	1,717	–	338	288	990	84	3,450	1,080	10,312
23 MOTORS & GENERATORS	–	–	–	–	–	–	–	–	–	–	–	–	–	–	–	–	34	7	1	32	29	317	17	5	52	–	51	10	–	1	5	–	4	–	–	–	–	–	3	–	–	10	257	–	3	33	85	11	128	–	1,095
24 RADIOS	–	–	–	–	–	–	–	–	–	–	–	–	–	–	–	*	1	–	13	–	–	4	8	243	95	19	15	4	–	–	–	–	–	3	1	–	–	*	23	–	–	2	74	–	–	56	113	83	296	639	1,692
25 OTHER ELECTRICAL MACHINERY	–	–	–	–	–	–	–	–	–	1	–	–	–	7	8	46	53	9	125	22	16	158	57	165	350	599	53	21	18	17	30	–	8	6	49	–	–	5	62	4	–	25	608	–	716	161	244	76	1,331	673	5,723
26 MOTOR VEHICLES	111	3	–	–	–	1	–	–	–	–	*	–	–	1	*	*	–	–	32	24	7	*	–	–	12	4,401	*	–	–	8	*	–	131	20	*	–	*	–	1,054	*	–	70	671	1	36	401	1,020	151	2,982	3,128	14,265
27 OTHER TRANSPORTATION EQUIPMENT	10	–	–	–	–	–	–	*	–	1	*	*	–	*	2	1	–	–	–	–	–	–	*	–	–	12	295	–	–	*	38	76	132	–	–	–	–	–	2	–	–	14	456	–	1	18	324	1,245	1,203	171	4,001
28 PROFESSIONAL & SCIENTIFIC EQUIPMENT	–	–	–	–	–	–	2	6	32	13	–	–	–	1	*	–	34	3	3	1	2	36	2	3	9	70	23	176	24	*	–	–	2	–	*	–	–	7	52	176	–	6	229	–	22	32	184	79	260	630	2,119
29 MISCELLANEOUS MANUFACTURING	4	11	–	4	256	1	16	15	–	29	–	*	22	9	5	*	1	1	18	*	1	45	20	30	61	22	3	26	156	2	4	5	4	10	*	–	–	149	164	46	53	112	638	21	32	43	187	85	511	1,934	4,756
30 COAL, GAS & ELECTRIC POWER	61	193	4	105	36	24	18	123	29	188	556	37	15	204	242	104	13	15	52	23	14	68	8	6	39	62	28	10	25	1,272	443	4	91	493	10	63	3,016	5	307	163	54	–	23	219	30	27	355	195	–	133	9,205
31 RAILROAD TRANSPORTATION	440	548	21	94	60	143	54	224	68	287	270	36	36	145	423	100	19	37	77	44	12	100	11	13	50	228	37	14	31	151	410	3	58	75	5	6	422	27	29	52	2	10	798	253	706	74	590	332	266	2,061	9,952
32 OCEAN TRANSPORTATION	73	126	3	13	11	9	*	16	*	44	94	*	1	14	30	52	*	*	*	*	*	*	–	*	*	1	*	2	10	*	–	218	–	–	–	–	–	–	–	–	–	5	2	–	–	–	1,340	126	–	102	2,292
33 OTHER TRANSPORTATION	553	367	16	79	25	138	40	117	25	95	470	7	21	70	140	19	6	5	17	10	3	29	3	8	19	67	13	5	14	35	195	35	253	311	3	4	125	29	14	190	2	6	1,102	97	572	38	314	186	103	3,860	9,855
34 TRADE	1,360	418	38	228	369	60	60	176	31	173	19	55	57	52	216	140	36	54	110	51	22	183	18	34	83	56	74	39	48	40	30	6	423	202	7	43	747	135	386	292	7	80	808	1,061	2,506	149	987	45	2,336	27,107	41,657
35 COMMUNICATIONS	2	41	1	9	19	10	6	8	39	23	15	6	5	10	16	6	3	6	13	6	4	23	3	4	13	16	10	6	9	18	18	2	42	326	66	85	62	29	123	66	11	–	83	11	44	–	38	148	–	1,269	3,173
36 FINANCE & INSURANCE	238	145	1	20	24	77	18	18	23	18	125	7	7	46	44	14	6	14	19	11	7	32	7	9	23	22	21	6	18	48	24	120	298	1,002	5	1,851	555	22	118	93	26	–	–	72	400	–	135	32	–	6,993	12,814
37 RENTAL	2,393	91	2	25	96	19	17	26	61	34	–	10	19	18	36	21	4	10	20	6	6	32	2	9	19	21	20	11	35	46	24	7	147	1,961	52	211	208	58	710	402	180	–	–	386	84	–	–	223	804	20,289	28,855
38 BUSINESS SERVICES	8	533	98	71	97	19	57	22	58	424	42	21	49	11	25	5	16	10	25	12	11	64	3	25	32	76	10	51	57	9	22	2	33	1,706	86	143	37	64	121	17	95	–	421	55	134	–	3	38	–	179	5,097
39 PERSONAL & REPAIR SERVICES	368	119	*	3	3	42	4	4	20	11	13	1	1	31	3	3	1	4	3	2	1	5	*	*	1	3	2	1	4	16	11	5	264	1,415	16	113	25	68	559	76	22	30	2,294	228	819	–	–	83	271	7,333	14,301
40 MEDICAL, EDUC. & NONPROFIT ORG'S.	–	–	–	–	–	–	–	–	–	–	–	–	–	–	–	–	–	–	–	–	–	–	–	–	–	–	–	–	–	–	–	*	*	–	–	16	–	–	–	85	–	–	350	–	–	–	–	5,078	–	7,856	13,385
41 AMUSEMENTS	–	–	–	–	–	–	–	–	–	–	–	–	–	–	–	–	–	–	–	–	–	–	–	–	–	–	–	–	–	–	–	–	–	–	–	–	–	–	–	7	392	–	14	–	–	–	128	–	–	2,403	2,944
42 SCRAP & MISCELLANEOUS INDUSTRIES	–	–	–	24	–	–	–	250	–	110	–	7	–	13	650	456	8	4	3	9	6	38	1	*	3	–	–	1	–	–	–	–	35	386	10	106	34	20	1	1	13	–	12	–	1	–	30	1	–	–	2,233
43 UNDISTRIBUTED	–	2,059	132	438	1,310	880	329	201	610	1,740	788	329	323	570	287	101	211	172	1,000	356	250	1,463	45	204	822	490	406	227	1,049	356	61	214	73	2,320	88	617	547	575	1,303	960	269	–	–	536	–	–	–	–	–	–	24,711
44 EATING & DRINKING PLACES	–	–	–	–	–	–	–	–	2	–	–	–	–	–	–	–	–	–	–	–	–	–	–	–	–	–	–	–	–	–	–	–	11	–	–	–	–	–	–	152	–	–	1,030	–	–	–	–	–	–	12,075	13,270
45 NEW CONSTRUCTION & MAINTENANCE	199	117	1	39	16	12	7	42	15	36	26	12	19	34	81	20	5	5	24	16	6	28	2	7	16	44	23	7	18	265	1,118	1	134	182	178	32	4,084	3	56	342	25	–	–	73	7	–	–	5,464	15,709	154	28,704
46 INVENTORY CHANGE (depletions)	2,660	402	1	120	185	*	14	87	26	140	8	3	33	2	3	102	–	*	3	*	*	4	–	*	2	7	8	47	157	*	–	–	–	–	–	–	–	–	–	–	–	851	–	–	–	–	22	–	–	–	4,887
47 FOREIGN COUNTRIES (imports from)	690	2,001	104	208	279	183	6	621	8	594	258	2	35	143	43	573	*	1	6	35	1	16	1	1	2	15	11	54	141	7	41	302	33	–	33	105	–	–	–	–	3	69	12	–	–	–	–	1,313	–	1,325	9,275
48 GOVERNMENT	813	1,134	104	639	376	338	112	497	335	762	780	114	136	323	573	245	86	113	277	167	86	514	64	62	274	656	120	134	191	1,142	1,075	256	766	3,750	344	1,111	3,997	212	503	170	318	74	2,176	1,410	470	73	831	3,458	216	31,308	63,685
49 GROSS PRIVATE CAPITAL FORMATION	DEPRECIATION AND OTHER CAPITAL CONSUMPTION ALLOWANCES ARE INCLUDED IN HOUSEHOLD ROW																–	–	–	–	–	–	–	–	–	–	–	–	–	–	–	–	–	–	–	–	–	–	–	–	–	–	–	–	–	–	–	–	–	–	–
50 HOUSEHOLDS	19,166	6,262	387	3,286	4,013	2,564	1,063	2,161	3,034	3,431	4,907	1,024	1,140	2,255	3,945	1,519	624	943	2,335	1,178	930	4,339	534	595	2,092	3,303	1,880	856	1,989	5,066	5,675	914	6,205	26,240	2,165	8,015	14,003	1,044	7,951	9,199	1,456	–	1,801	4,254	11,492	–	847	30,058	218	2,116	220,474
TOTAL GROSS OUTLAYS	44,263	37,636	2,663	9,838	13,321	6,002	2,892	7,899	6,447	14,050	13,670	2,825	3,810	4,844	12,338	6,387	1,745	2,316	6,445	3,292	1,833	10,312	1,095	1,692	5,723	14,265	4,001	2,119	4,756	9,205	9,952	2,292	9,855	41,657	3,173	12,814	28,855	5,097	14,301	13,385	2,944	2,233	24,711	13,270	28,704	4,802	17,320	51,060	33,514	191,625	769,248

* Less than $0.5 million.
NOTE: Each row shows distribution of output of producing industry named at left. Each column shows input distribution for purchasing industry named at top. All figures in millions of dollars.
SOURCE: Division of Interindustry Economics, U.S. Bureau of Labor Statistics.

adopted for both inputs and outputs. This symmetrical classification is quite different from the institutional and functional classifications that were used in the production statement. The two sides of the input-output account for the individual firm of course balance in the same way as all other accounts presented thus far.

The Input-Output Table for the United States, 1947

The aggregation of input-output data for individual production units is not carried out as it is in national income accounting. Instead of *consolidating* individual production statements by canceling out interfirm transactions so as to obtain a statement of output for the economy as a whole, the process of aggregation employed in the input-output accounts involves *combining* the accounts for all firms. No transactions cancel out. Since the classification system is symmetrical, it is possible to arrange all the data in a single table by listing the inputs of the industries in the columns and the outputs in rows. It is obvious that what is purchased from one industry as an input by another industry also represents an output which is sold by the first industry to the second industry. This fact is demonstrated by the arrangement of the data in Table 48, the input-output table for the United States in 1947.

In order to explain the implications of the data shown in Table 48, the data in the first column and the first row of the table, relating to agriculture, have been abstracted and are presented in account form in Table 49.

The first figure on both the input and the output sides of this account is the same, $10,856 million. It indicates that agriculture consumed $10,856 million of its own production. This self-consumed production was mostly feed and seed used in the further production of agricultural goods. When looked at from the input side, this body of goods represents purchases by agriculture from agriculture; and when looked at from the output side, sales by agriculture to agriculture. This treatment accents the fact that within an industry group there are many separate productive units buying and selling to each other. This total also includes, however, the production and consumption of agricultural goods in agricultural production within a single productive unit, even when no actual monetary transaction has taken place. If a farmer raises corn which he feeds to his hogs, the action is classified in this account as a purchase by the farmer of corn from himself and a sale of corn by the farmer to himself.

Agriculture also purchased goods and services worth $2,378 million from the food and kindred products industry. This total represents mainly prepared feeds for poultry and livestock. Fertilizer purchased for use on crops is classified as a purchase from the chemical industry.

Table 49. Input-Ouput Account for the Agriculture Industry, 1947
(In millions)

	Inputs	Outputs
1. Agriculture and fisheries............................	$10,856	$10,856
2. Food and kindred products........................	2,378	15,048
3. Tobacco manufactures.............................	—	783
4. Textile mill products..............................	64	2,079
5. Apparel..	44	19
6. Lumber and wood products........................	148	192
7. Furniture and fixtures.............................	—	—
8. Paper and allied products.........................	2	9
9. Printing and publishing............................	—	—
10. Chemicals.......................................	830	1,211
11. Products of petroleum and coal....................	457	—
12. Rubber products.................................	122	—
13. Leather and leather products......................	—	49
14. Stone, clay, and glass products....................	65	*
15. Iron and steel....................................	6	—
16. Nonferrous metals................................	—	11
17. Plumbing and heating supplies.....................	—	—
18. Fabricated structural metal products...............	—	—
19. Other fabricated metal products...................	83	—
20. Agricultural, mining, and construction machinery...	59	—
21. Metalworking machinery...........................	—	—
22. Other machinery (except electric).................	—	—
23. Motors and generators............................	—	—
24. Radios..	—	—
25. Other electrical machinery........................	—	—
26. Motor vehicles...................................	111	—
27. Other transportation equipment...................	10	—
28. Professional and scientific equipment..............	—	4
29. Miscellaneous manufacturing......................	4	4
30. Coal, gas, and electric power......................	61	—
31. Railroad transportation...........................	440	5
32. Ocean transportation.............................	73	1
33. Other transportation.............................	553	8
34. Trade...	1,360	—
35. Communications..................................	2	2
36. Finance and insurance............................	238	—
37. Rental..	2,393	—
38. Business services.................................	8	—
39. Personal and repair services.......................	368	—
40. Medical, educational, and nonprofit organizations...	—	116
41. Amusements.....................................	—	—
42. Scrap and miscellaneous industries.................	—	—
43. Undistributed...................................	—	250
44. Eating and drinking places........................	—	865
45. New construction and maintenance.................	199	92
46. Inventory change................................	2,660	1,008
47. Foreign countries................................	690	1,276
48. Government.....................................	813	569
49. Gross private capital formation................... }	19,166	21
50. Households...................................... }		9,785
Total........................	$44,263	$44,263

*Less than $0.5 million.

The purchases from transportation and trade recorded in the input column represent the transportation and distributive costs which are added to the goods and materials purchased by agriculture. Thus, for example, a bag of feed purchased for $10 is a product of the food processing industry, but this industry might receive only $7 of the total price the farmer pays. Transportation from the factory to the farmer might cost 50 cents, and the distributor's margin might be $2.50. Such costs as these are entered as purchases by agriculture from transportation and the distributive trades. Rental (item 37) as an input refers to the gross rent that producers in agriculture pay for their land and buildings. Inventory (item 46) shows the amount by which total sales of agricultural products exceeded production. The input entry for households (item 50) refers to wages, salaries, interest, depreciation, and entrepreneurial income derived from agriculture.

It should be noted that the purchases listed as inputs into the agriculture industry are only those that enter into the process of agricultural production. The expenditures of farmers and other individuals in this industry as consumers are not included in this account, but rather as a part of the outlay of households shown in column 50 of Table 48.

The agricultural outputs shown in Table 49 and the corresponding row in Table 48 show the product of the industry valued at what the producers in the industry receive for their products, i.e., before any transportation charges or trade margins have been added. The biggest purchaser of agricultural products is the food-processing industry, which purchased $15,048 million of agricultural goods. Households purchased farm produce in unprocessed form through normal trade channels or directly from farmers in the amount of $9,785 million. Other large purchasers of agricultural products were tobacco manufacturers, textile mills, the chemical industry, eating and drinking places, foreign countries, and the government.

The first forty-five columns and rows in Table 48 represent processing industries. For each of these industries the input column and the output row balance in exactly the same manner as is shown for agriculture in Table 49. (Column and row 43, labeled "undistributed," refer to production for which the source or destination could not be specifically identified.)

The last five columns and rows cover the remaining sectors of the economy, as follows. (1) Column and row 46 refer to inventory change, the depletion of inventories as an item of input and the additions to inventories as an item of output. (2) Column and row 47 refer to the foreign sector. Imports of a nature competitive to domestic industries are transferred to the domestic industries producing the same product and distributed as a part of the output of these industries, and other imports are treated as purchased by the industry using them. Both exports and imports include the invisible items of foreign trade and property income paid and received. (3) Column and row 48 refer to the government sector; they have much the same meaning and coverage as in national income accounting. (4) Column and row 49, "gross private capital formation," refer to the purchase of producers' durables and new construction. No entries are made in the gross capital formation row (outputs), since capital consumption allowances are included in the household row. (5) Column and row 50, "households," cover individuals in their role as income recipients and consumers. These last five sectors do not contain balancing items, so that their inputs do not equal their outputs. Thus personal saving is omitted from the household sector, the government surplus is omitted from the government sector, and the net borrowing from abroad is omitted from the foreign sector. The total of all rows and also of all columns for the complete table is $769,248 million. This total represents the sum of all transactions on current account in the economy.

Derivation of the national income aggregates from the input-output table is possible either by excluding from total transactions the transactions that do not enter into total output, or by building up separately the expenditures on final goods and services by households and government, gross domestic capital formation, net inventory change, and exports minus imports.

The Nature of Input-Output Information

The input-output table is intended to show primarily the detailed interdependence of industries. A change in any single cell of this table represents at the same time a change in output by one industry and a change in input by another. For example, let us assume that the cell shown in row 15, "iron and steel," column 26, "motor vehicles," increases by $100 million; this means that the steel output going to the motor vehicles industry has increased by this much.

A change in one single cell of the input-output table is not possible, since the system would not then be in balance. In the example above, one of two things must also happen in the iron and steel industry. Either the total amount of iron and steel produced must increase, or the amount of iron and steel going to other industries must be reduced. In the former case the increased output of iron and steel will require additional inputs into this industry to balance it. These additional inputs, furthermore, must be drawn from other industries whose output in turn must increase to take care of the increased requirements of the steel industry. In the second case, where steel output is reallocated from some other industry to the motor vehicle industry, the inputs of that other industry are correspondingly reduced, so that it can no longer sustain its previous level of output. It too, therefore, would be forced to reduce the output going to some of its customers, and another set of chain reactions would be set off. Similarly, for the motor vehicle industry the increased input of steel would result in greater output, which would have to be sold to other sectors of the economy as increased inputs, and these industries in turn would have to make appropriate adjustments. The interindustry relations described by this matrix thus dramatically reveal the high degree of interdependence among industries.

Comparison of input-output patterns over an extended period of time would demonstrate the direction in which the evolution of the economy was proceeding. The shifting patterns of supply and of distribution of output would show the impact of changing technology on the processes of production. In a finer industrial breakdown, for example, the introduction of rayon and nylon would appear in the form of repercussions on the input factors for the textile industry. Major innovations such as the introduction of the automobile, radio, and television would lead to rapid growth in some industries and consequent decline in others. The input-output patterns thus record the way in which the economy adjusts to changes in the structure of industry, and the relationship of the industrial sectors to such change.

Over a short period of time technology in many industries largely determines the relationship among the amounts of labor, materials, and machinery that are used. The steel industry, for example, employs processes that use fairly definite ratios of coke and ore. Over a longer period changes in technology will cause changes in the process, but as a general rule such changes are slow, and the input-output pattern does not shift violently from year to year.

This relative stability means that relationships derived from the input-output table can be used to show what can be expected to happen with changes in the output of specified final products in the economy. Given an input-output matrix for a particular year, it is possible to compute the technological input coefficients showing the direct purchases from each of the other industries that would be required per dollar of output in each industry, but this figure for direct purchases gives no information on the total effect of the expansion of one industry. Table 46 shows that about 8 cents out of every dollar's increase in output in the motor vehicle industry is spent directly upon iron and steel products, but for a dollar's worth of expansion of output, the motor vehicle industry would also have to purchase as much as 7 cents' worth of products from the electrical machinery industry, another 7 cents' worth from fabricated metal products, and additional amounts from many other industries that also use iron and steel. The total amount of iron and steel purchased directly by the motor vehicle industry for its own use, plus indirectly by its suppliers for their products that are in turn sold to the motor vehicle industry would amount to very much more than the 8 cents recorded as a direct purchase. Since the input-output table shows all the interindustry relations, however, it is possible by solving the appropriate equations to determine the total of the direct plus indirect requirements resulting from the expansion of a given industry. In the example in question the direct and indirect requirements of the motor vehicle industry for steel amount to approximately 24 cents for every dollar's worth of increase in output in the motor vehicle industry. The major use of input-output information historically has been associated with problems of this nature, although of course this is not the only purpose it could serve.

Because of this use there has been a tendency to expand the classification scheme of input-output accounting to obtain classifications that are as pure as possible, that is, classifications in which the firms and products embraced by a row and column classification have identical and fairly stable technological relations among their inputs. The derivation of input-output data conceived in this manner thus involves the study of production functions. Because the calculations necessary to derive the direct and indirect requirements for a given increase in dollar output for an industry are extremely complex when large numbers of industries are treated, it has become necessary to use electronic calculators to perform the necessary mathematical operations. In most of these operations, for the sake of simplicity, it is assumed that the relationships between inputs as given by the basic input-output table are constant and unchanging with changes in output. Such an assumption is not necessary to the analysis, and in cases where additional information is available on how these technological coefficients change either with time, with changes in the level of output, or with prices of various material inputs, such information can be fed into the calculations and will improve the results of the analysis. The effect of such refinement is, as would be expected, to make the amount of information required very much greater and the methods of calculation very much more complex.

The Uses of Analysis Based on the Input-Output Relationships

There are many different possible uses to which the information contained in input-output tables can be put, one general class of which is commonly termed "input-output analysis." For the purpose of this discussion only a few of the specific forms of "input-output analysis" will be considered.[1] These uses are (1) long-term projections of the changes

---

[1] The major study in the field of input-output accounting is Wassily Leontief, *The Structure of the American Economy* (Harvard University Press, Cambridge, Mass., 1951, 2d ed.).

in the economic structure of an economy; (2) the structural requirements of specific mobilization plans; (3) the impact of foreign trade upon the economy and the impact of the economy on foreign trade; (4) the effect of changes in factor prices and profits upon relative prices and the general level of prices in the economy; and (5) the effect of changes in productivity in given industries upon the structure and total output of the economy.

Long-term Projections of Changes in Structure. In a growing economy some industries can be expected to expand relatively more than others. Under a set of assumptions in which projections are made of population and of the kinds of final products that individuals, government, investors, and foreign countries are likely to want to purchase, it is possible on the basis of the interindustry relations shown in an input-output table to calculate the inputs that would be required, given present technological relationships. Such an analysis is really an examination of the long-term needs and resources of a country. For instance, it can, to at least a rough approximation, indicate the sort of power requirements that will be needed to support the growth of industry and to serve households. It can show the expansion that would be needed in such industries as steel, transportation, and agriculture. Even manpower requirements in various industries can be approximated. One of the earlier studies employing input-output analysis, "Full Employment Patterns, 1950," [2] carried out by the Bureau of Labor Statistics, was just such an analysis. Such studies as these can highlight the kinds of long-term investment that will be necessary in the basic industries to assure proper economic growth.

Requirements of Mobilization. A second use of input-output analysis is in the examination of the requirements implied by different types of defense mobilization plans. Given a list of final goods needed for defense, it is possible through input-output analysis to show what would be required in the way of raw materials, manpower, and industrial processing facilities to produce these goods. It is thus possible to check the feasibility of mobilization plans and to compare the relative cost in real terms of different kinds of defense production. For example, the cost, in terms of manpower, materials, and facilities, of producing a large air force could be compared with that of a smaller air force and increased naval power.

Foreign Trade. The impact of foreign trade upon the economy can be indicated by determining what industries would be affected with a given change in exports of final goods.[3] A decline in exports would show

[2] J. Cornfield, W. D. Evans, and M. Hoffenberg, "Full Employment Patterns, 1950," *Monthly Labor Review,* vol. 64, pp. 163–190 and 420–432, February and March, 1947.

[3] W. W. Leontief, "Exports, Imports, Domestic Output, and Employment," *Quarterly Journal of Economics,* vol. 60, no. 2, pp. 171–197, February, 1946.

up not only in a decline in the industries directly supplying the exported goods, but also in industries providing the inputs for the export industries. Similarly, projected increases in exports can be traced in terms of the kind and degree of industrial expansion they would involve. Conversely, the import requirements of the economy can be projected, given assumptions about changes in the level of economic activity. In this manner the effect of a mild recession or a boom upon other countries can be calculated and the changes in the balance of payments shown.

Factor Prices. Changes in factor prices and profits [4] will affect the relative prices in the economy and the level of prices as well. Under the assumption that increases in costs are directly passed on in terms of higher prices, it is possible to trace the effect of a change in factor prices in a given industry, in a group of industries, or for the economy as a whole in terms of the cumulative price repercussions that result when the output of one industry becomes input for another and thus the price changes are passed through the channels of production.

Productivity Changes. Finally, input-output analysis is useful in calculating the effect of changes in productivity upon the structure of the economy and the level of output. Because input-output accounting deals with the production relations of individual industries, it is particularly suited to the examination of the effect of changes in these input relations.

It bears repeating that the usefulness of input-output data presented in Table 46 is not limited to what is generally referred to as input-output analysis. Considerable contribution to factual knowledge is made by the presentation of transactions data in input-output form, and it reveals certain deficiencies and gaps in our knowledge about the economic system. As a framework for basic economic information, it provides considerable raw material for a wide variety of analytic purposes. The term "input-output analysis" is generally used to refer to specific uses of the data contained in an input-output table similar to those indicated in the preceding paragraphs. Other comprehensive and systematic methods of utilizing input-output data can be conceived of and are in fact discussed extensively in economic literature under such names as "linear programming" and "activity analysis." To date, however, input-output analysis has appeared to be the most practical and feasible method of utilizing input-output information.

All the forms of input-output analysis mentioned above assume that the technological coefficients yielded by the input-output table are in fact constant. This assumption implies (1) that there are constant returns to scale in the economy, i.e., that the economy is not characterized by either increasing or decreasing cost industries; (2) that there are no

---

[4] W. W. Leontief, "Wages, Profit, and Prices," *Quarterly Journal of Economics,* vol. 61, no. 1, pp. 26–39, November, 1946.

joint products in the economy; (3) that there are no shifts in the relative quantities of inputs used in specific industries due to the substitution of inputs under changing price conditions; (4) that no technological change occurs; and (5) that constancy of production coefficients is an appropriate concept for all industries in the economy, even where technological considerations are not determining, for example, certain service industries, trade, and finance. It should be emphasized, of course, that even the most ardent user of input-output analysis does not argue that these assumptions are true. In fact, it will generally be admitted by all concerned that these conditions are rarely, if ever, met. Rather, it is implied that the statistical accuracy of the analysis is not greatly impaired by making these assumptions instead of introducing all the complications that would be necessary to take into account all the changes in conditions. An immense amount of information would be required to include the actual shape of the production function in every industry and to allow for the production of joint products, product substitutability, and technological change. For each different projection into the future, furthermore, different assumptions would have to be made, and this would involve recomputing the inverse matrix, since each inverse matrix has frozen into it the structure of the data on which it was based. Even a 50×50 matrix, such as is shown in Table 48, requires 125,000 multiplications. The computational difficulty increases rapidly; a 400×400 table would require 90 million multiplications. Such a calculation job is not undertaken lightly. Thus for practical reasons input-output analysis must deal with simplified assumptions.

Early input-output analysis assumed a closed system, that is, that there was an input-output relationship for each nonindustrial sector of the economy, as well as for the various industries. Under this assumption the supply of labor (the output of households) depends upon consumers' expenditures (the input of households). In most more recent input-output analyses the inputs of the various nonindustrial sectors are considered to be autonomously determined, so that their expenditures are not unique functions of their incomes. In other words, the behavior of the expenditures of such sectors is assumed rather than derived from the input-output table. In the listing of the specific uses of input-output analysis above, for example, the final expenditures of individuals, government, investors, and even in some instances foreign trade, were taken as given, and the characteristics of the economy which followed from this given pattern were then derived. Input-output analysis thus concentrates on spelling out the implications of a given demand for final products rather than upon actually estimating final demand for goods and services in some future period.

Moneyflows and Flow-of-funds Accounting as a Form of Economic Analysis

In recent years a form of economic accounting has been developed which is referred to either as "moneyflows accounting" or as "flow-of-funds accounting." The term "moneyflows" was given to this type of accounting by Morris Copeland in his work on this subject; more recently the Board of Governors of the Federal Reserve System has presented information of essentially the same nature and has entitled it flow of funds.[5] In the following discussion these terms will be used interchangeably.

The Rationale of the Moneyflows and Flow-of-funds Accounting Procedures

In contrast with both national income and input-output accounting, moneyflows or flow-of-funds accounting does not focus its attention on the output of the economy. Instead, it sets forth the flow of payments and receipts, not only for goods and services but also for instruments of ownership and debt. The scope of moneyflows and flow-of-funds accounting is thus more comprehensive than just the transactions directly involved in the generation of current production and income. Many other types of transaction must be considered in the study of the role played by the flow of funds in the economic system. Existing capital assets are bought and sold. Individuals and businesses accumulate assets in the form of currency, deposits, real estate, etc. The government borrows money, and banks and insurance companies extend credit in the form of mortgages, commercial loans, and consumer credit. The moneyflows accounting system is designed to comprehend this entire complex of transactions in a systematic and informative manner.

The Consumer Sector in the Flow-of-funds Accounts

The basic difference between national income and input-output accounting on the one hand, and flow-of-funds accounting on the other hand, can be seen by examining the Sources and Uses of Funds Statement for the Consumer Sector in the flow-of-funds system. This statement is given in Table 50, for the years 1939 to 1953. The Sources and Uses of Funds Statement for the Consumer Sector in flow-of-funds accounting is considerably more comprehensive than the Personal Income Account in national income accounting or the household column and row

---

[5] Morris A. Copeland, *A Study of Moneyflows in the United States,* National Bureau of Economic Research, New York, 1952; Board of Governors of the Federal Reserve System, *The Flow of Funds in the United States, 1939–1953,* Washington, 1955.

in input-output accounting. In addition to the receipts of income, such as payroll, interest, dividends, and transfer payments, the sources of funds for the consumer sector also include such flows as insurance benefits and receipts of consumers from the sale of assets such as homes and automobiles. The net increases in consumer credit, mortgages, and other loans are also included as sources of funds for the consuming sector. Similarly, the uses of funds by the consuming sector include more than just consumer expenditures on goods and services, taxes, and personal saving. The purchase of homes, the payment of insurance premiums, and the increase in holdings of currency, bank deposits, and securities are all taken into account.

The System of Sector Accounts in Flow-of-funds Accounting

The flow-of-funds accounts also differ from the national income and input-output accounts in that they employ a different sector breakdown of the economy. Flow-of-funds accounting, because of its focus on the sources and uses of funds, is interested in setting up sector classifications that reveal the borrowing and lending taking place in the system as well as the income payments and purchases of goods and services. The sector classifications in national income accounting are far too consolidated to reveal these interrelationships satisfactorily. The sector classification of input-output accounting, although more detailed, uses the criterion of similarity of inputs and outputs for defining industry groupings, and is not suitable for revealing the sources and uses of funds in the system.

The Federal Reserve Board employs ten major sectors for its system of flow-of-funds accounting. These ten sectors are as follows: (1) consumers, (2) corporations, (3) nonfarm noncorporate, (4) farm, (5) Federal government, (6) state and local government, (7) banking, (8) insurance, (9) other investors, (10) rest of the world. In contrast with national income and input-output accounting, the flow-of-funds sectoring places considerable emphasis on financial institutions, e.g., banking and insurance, and on differences in institutional forms of business and government, e.g., corporate vs. noncorporate, and Federal vs. state and local.

For each of the sectors listed above, the flow-of-funds accounting system provides a sources and uses of funds account similar to that shown for the consumer sector in Table 50. These accounts can be presented in the form of one large cross tabulation for all sectors, after the manner of the input-output table. Such a table for the year 1953 is given in Table 51.

This table is unlike an input-output table in that only the columns make use of the sector classifications. The rows show the kind of transaction which took place. Not all sectors engage in the same transactions. Thus

Table 50. Sources and Uses of Funds Statement for the Consumer Sector *

(In billions)

Item no.	Sources of funds	1939	1940	1941	1942	1943	1944	1945	1946	1947	1948	1949	1950	1951	1952	1953
1	Nonfinancial sources	$72.6	$79.4	$95.1	$117.0	$144.2	$160.1	$167.2	$182.7	$199.8	$216.9	$218.1	$238.6	$265.0	$289.1	$303.9
2	Payroll	45.3	49.1	61.0	80.0	102.3	113.0	113.2	109.6	121.0	133.2	132.6	144.6	168.0	182.3	195.5
3	Interest	3.7	3.6	3.6	3.4	3.2	3.3	3.7	4.2	4.6	5.1	5.6	6.1	6.6	6.7	7.1
4	Dividends	3.7	4.0	4.4	4.2	4.4	4.6	4.6	5.7	6.4	7.1	7.3	9.0	8.9	8.9	9.2
5	Insurance benefits	4.3	4.6	4.4	4.4	4.2	4.6	5.6	7.0	7.3	8.0	9.8	13.1	12.6	13.9	15.8
6	Private	3.3	3.4	3.4	3.4	3.4	3.6	3.9	4.3	4.8	5.3	5.8	6.5	7.6	8.3	9.4
7	Life policies[a]	2.8	2.8	2.7	2.6	2.6	2.7	2.9	3.0	3.3	3.5	3.8	4.1	4.5	4.7	5.2
8	Other	0.6	0.6	0.7	0.8	0.8	0.9	1.1	1.2	1.5	1.8	2.0	2.4	3.1	3.6	4.2
9	Government	1.0	1.1	1.0	1.0	0.8	1.0	1.7	2.7	2.5	2.7	4.0	6.6	5.0	5.5	6.4
10	Grants and donations	2.0	2.1	2.2	2.2	2.2	2.8	4.6	9.7	9.6	8.5	8.6	8.7	7.9	8.1	8.1
11	Federal government	0.5	0.6	0.6	0.6	0.5	0.9	2.6	7.2	6.5	4.7	4.7	4.2	3.7	3.6	3.6
12	State and local government	1.1	1.0	1.0	1.0	1.0	1.0	1.0	1.3	1.9	2.5	2.5	3.0	2.4	2.6	2.5
13	Private	0.4	0.5	0.6	0.6	0.7	0.9	1.0	1.1	1.2	1.3	1.4	1.5	1.8	1.9	2.0
14	Tax refunds			[b]	[b]	0.3	0.3	1.3	1.7	1.7	1.8	2.4	1.7	1.8	2.1	2.6
15	Net withdrawals by proprietors	10.9	12.3	15.1	18.9	23.4	26.2	28.1	34.7	39.2	42.4	39.4	39.2	42.1	45.4	43.6
16	Nonfarm	8.9	10.1	11.9	14.2	15.9	18.3	19.4	24.3	26.5	30.9	29.3	29.3	31.4	35.9	34.3
17	Farm	2.0	2.2	3.2	4.7	7.5	8.0	8.7	10.4	12.7	11.6	10.2	9.9	10.7	9.4	9.3
18	Sales receipts	2.7	3.7	4.5	3.9	4.3	5.2	6.0	10.3	10.0	10.7	12.5	16.1	17.1	21.7	22.0
19	Homes	1.9	2.6	3.0	2.5	3.2	4.1	4.8	8.8	7.9	7.7	9.1	12.6	13.4	16.7	16.8
20	Automobiles, etc.[c]	0.8	1.1	1.5	1.5	1.1	1.1	1.1	1.4	2.2	3.0	3.4	3.6	3.7	4.9	5.3
21	Net increase in liabilities[d]	1.2	1.8	1.7	-3.2	-0.8	1.2	2.0	4.8	7.5	6.8	6.9	11.2	6.6	10.5	10.1
22	Consumer credit	0.9	1.1	0.8	-3.2	-1.1	0.2	0.6	2.7	3.2	2.8	2.7	3.7	0.7	4.4	3.1
23	Banks	0.1	0.4	0.5	-1.0	-0.4	0.1	0.3	1.2	1.3	0.9	1.0	1.6	0.1	1.9	1.4
24	Other[e]	0.8	0.7	0.3	-2.2	-0.7	0.1	0.3	1.6	1.9	1.9	1.7	2.1	0.6	2.4	1.7
25	Mortgages	0.6	1.1	1.2	0.4	0.2	0.5	0.9	3.6	4.2	4.0	3.6	6.5	5.8	5.9	6.2
26	Banks	0.2	0.3	0.4	0.1	[b]	0.1	0.3	1.5	1.8	1.3	1.0	2.2	1.6	1.6	1.7
27	Other	0.4	0.8	0.8	0.3	0.2	0.4	0.6	2.1	2.4	2.7	2.7	4.3	4.3	4.2	4.5
28	Security loans	-0.2	-0.3	-0.2	-0.1	0.4	0.8	0.7	-1.5	[b]	-0.1	0.3	0.8	-0.2	0.2	0.5
29	Banks	-0.1	-0.1	-0.1	-0.1	0.1	0.5	0.6	-0.7	-0.1	-0.1	-0.1	0.2	-0.1	0.1	0.1
30	Other[f,g]	-0.1	-0.2	-0.1	[b]	0.3	0.3	0.1	-0.7	0.1	[b]	0.4	0.6	-0.1	0.1	0.4
31	Policy loans[g]	-0.1	-0.2	-0.2	-0.2	-0.3	-0.3	-0.2	-0.1	[b]	0.1	0.2	0.2	0.2	0.1	0.2
32	Valuation adjustment	0.3	0.3	0.3	0.3	0.2	0.2	0.2	0.2	0.3	0.3	0.4	0.3	0.3	0.3	0.3
33	Total, above sources	$74.1	$81.5	$97.1	$114.1	$143.6	$161.4	$169.3	$187.7	$207.5	$224.0	$225.4	$250.2	$272.0	$299.9	$314.3

Item no.	Uses of funds	1939	1940	1941	1942	1943	1944	1945	1946	1947	1948	1949	1950	1951	1952	1953
1	Nonfinancial uses [h]	$73.1	$79.1	$91.3	$99.9	$121.3	$132.5	$148.0	$179.4	$203.7	$219.3	$219.7	$241.6	$265.6	$286.2	$301.8
2	Durable goods	7.5	8.9	11.1	8.4	7.7	7.9	9.2	17.3	22.8	25.3	27.0	32.2	30.9	31.7	35.0
3	Nondurable goods	33.9	35.9	41.4	48.3	54.7	60.1	67.6	81.7	91.8	97.8	96.3	99.6	109.4	114.6	118.0
4	Services	18.5	19.4	21.0	22.8	25.2	27.2	29.1	33.4	36.5	40.1	42.2	45.4	48.9	52.4	56.3
5	Payroll	1.0	1.0	1.0	1.2	1.4	1.7	1.7	1.9	2.1	2.1	2.1	2.3	2.5	2.5	2.7
6	Interest	1.4	1.5	1.6	1.5	1.3	1.3	1.3	1.6	2.0	2.5	2.9	3.5	4.0	4.6	5.5
7	Rents [i]	4.6	4.8	5.1	5.4	5.5	5.6	5.4	5.6	6.1	6.9	7.7	8.5	9.2	10.0	10.8
8	Other	11.6	12.1	13.2	14.7	17.0	18.7	20.4	24.3	26.3	28.6	29.5	31.1	33.2	35.3	37.4
9	Taxes	2.9	3.1	3.8	6.5	18.4	19.8	22.7	21.0	24.0	23.8	22.2	23.9	32.8	38.5	40.9
10	Income	1.1	1.3	1.9	4.4	16.3	17.5	20.2	18.4	20.9	20.4	18.5	19.9	28.2	33.4	35.2
11	Property	1.0	1.1	1.1	1.1	1.2	1.2	1.2	1.4	1.7	1.9	2.3	2.6	3.0	3.4	3.9
12	Other	0.8	0.8	0.8	1.0	0.9	1.0	1.2	1.2	1.4	1.5	1.4	1.4	1.6	1.7	1.9
13	Home purchases	3.8	5.0	6.3	5.4	5.3	6.3	7.2	13.3	14.9	17.3	16.7	23.2	24.5	28.0	28.8
14	New [j]	1.8	2.2	2.8	1.9	0.8	0.8	0.8	3.2	5.6	8.4	6.9	10.7	11.1	11.2	12.1
15	Existing	2.1	2.8	3.5	3.5	4.5	5.5	6.4	10.1	9.3	8.9	9.8	12.6	13.4	16.7	16.8
16	Grants and donations	1.3	1.4	1.9	2.3	2.9	3.1	3.2	3.4	3.7	4.1	4.0	4.4	4.4	4.9	5.2
17	Insurance premiums	5.2	5.4	5.7	6.2	7.2	8.2	8.8	9.2	10.1	10.9	11.4	12.8	14.4	16.1	17.6
18	Private	4.5	4.7	4.9	5.0	5.3	5.9	6.4	7.1	8.0	8.6	9.1	9.8	10.9	12.1	13.4
19	Life policies, etc. [k]	3.8	3.9	4.0	4.1	4.4	4.8	5.2	5.6	6.0	6.3	6.5	6.9	7.5	8.1	8.7
20	Other	0.7	0.8	0.9	0.9	1.0	1.1	1.2	1.6	1.9	2.3	2.5	2.9	3.4	4.0	4.7
21	Government [l]	0.6	0.7	0.8	1.2	1.9	2.3	2.4	2.0	2.2	2.2	2.3	3.0	3.5	3.9	4.1
22	Net increase in financial assets	2.5	2.4	5.8	14.7	22.7	27.8	24.7	9.0	6.8	4.9	4.4	4.9	8.5	14.8	13.3
23	Currency and deposits	2.7	2.1	3.5	6.3	10.5	13.9	14.2	7.8	2.7	-0.4	-1.1	1.2	4.1	7.4	4.4
24	Time deposits [m]	0.8	0.7	b	0.7	4.1	6.6	8.2	5.0	2.2	0.8	0.9	0.4	1.9	4.1	4.0
25	Federal obligations	0.2	0.5	2.5	8.7	11.9	13.3	9.5	0.4	1.8	1.1	1.3	0.2	-1.4	b	0.8
26	State and local obligations	-0.3	-0.4	-0.1	-0.3	-0.1	-0.1	-0.2	-0.2	0.5	1.2	0.6	0.7	b	0.9	2.0
27	Corporate securities	-0.5	-0.3	-0.7	-0.2	-0.3	-0.8	-1.2	-0.6	-0.3	1.1	1.1	b	2.4	2.2	1.2
28	Mortgages	0.1	0.1	0.1	-0.2	-0.2	b	0.3	0.7	0.5	0.6	0.6	0.6	0.6	0.7	0.6
29	Miscellaneous assets	0.3	0.4	0.6	0.4	0.9	1.5	2.1	0.9	1.6	1.4	1.8	2.3	2.4	3.4	4.4
30	Savings and loan shares	b	0.2	0.4	0.3	0.5	0.9	1.0	1.2	1.2	1.2	1.5	1.5	2.0	3.0	3.6
31	Credit balances at brokers	b	b	b	b	0.1	0.2	0.2	0.1	b	-0.1	0.1	0.4	b	-0.2	b
32	Other [n]	0.3	0.2	0.2	0.1	0.3	0.5	0.9	-0.3	0.4	0.3	0.3	0.4	0.5	0.7	0.8
33	Discrepancy [o]	-1.6	b	b	-0.5	-0.3	1.1	-3.3	-0.7	-3.1	-0.1	1.2	3.7	-2.2	-1.0	-0.8
34	Total, above uses	$74.1	$81.5	$97.1	$114.1	$143.6	$161.4	$169.3	$187.7	$207.5	$224.0	$225.4	$250.2	$272.0	$299.9	$314.3

* For footnotes to Table 50, see p. 203.

the consumer sector is the only one to receive payroll payments as a source of funds. Some types of transactions are common to all sectors, however; thus all sectors receive interest payments. In the section of the table referring to changes in liabilities and assets, currency and deposits is a liability only for the Federal government (currency is a promise to pay by the Federal government) and for the banking system (bank deposits are a promise to pay by the banks). The uses of funds employ the same transaction classifications as the sources of funds, and the total for each transaction class as a use of funds must exactly balance that shown as a source of funds. Thus payroll received by individuals as a source of funds ($195.5 billion) must exactly equal that paid out by the various sectors as a use of funds (also $195.5 billion). The net increase in the amount of currency and deposits held as assets ($6.5 billion) must balance exactly the increase in the amount of currency and deposits shown under liabilities ($6.5 billion).

Since the sources of any one class of transaction balance the uses of that class, it is also possible to record the information relating to one class of transaction in a separate account, which can be referred to as a transactions account. Thus, for example, it would be possible to show in a separate account the transactions in Federal obligations. Such an account for the years 1939 to 1953 is given in Table 52. Items 1 and 4 in this table show the increase (or if negative, the decrease) in total Federal obligations outstanding each year. Items 5 through 28 show the amounts by which the sectors and subsectors increased or decreased their holdings of government obligations during each year. Each pair of transaction rows shown in Table 51 could similarly be drawn up in the form of a separate transactions account.

With respect to assets and liabilities, the transaction accounts show the *changes* which have taken place. It would also theoretically be possible to show the *level* of these assets and liabilities existing at a particular time, according to either the sector classification or the asset classification. The sector classification would show, for the consuming sector, for example, the total holdings of currency, deposits, Federal obligations, etc., on the one hand, and the total liabilities, in the form of trade credit, mortgages, bank loans, etc., on the other hand. The transactions classification would show, for example, for Federal obligations, the total amounts held by each sector on the one hand, and the total amount owed by the Federal government on the other hand.

In actual practice very great difficulties arise in the valuation of total stocks of certain categories of assets and liabilities—notably corporate securities—the price of which varies considerably from time to time. In drawing up the tables relating to the level of total assets and liabilities, the Federal Reserve Board has not attempted to evaluate some of these categories of assets and liabilities. The accounts for individual sectors are therefore incomplete and no totals can be derived. The accounts for individual types of assets and liabilities, however, are either complete or entirely omitted.

Table 53 gives an example of the latter type of account; it shows the *level* of Federal obligations held by the various sectors and subsectors in specific years. It readily demonstrates the considerable rise in the level of Federal obligations during the years of World War II and the changing composition of the Federal debt holdings of the various sectors.

The Uses of Flow-of-funds Accounts

The flow-of-funds accounts concern themselves with the sources and uses of funds in each sector of the economy. Such information is extremely important for analyzing the effect that different monetary policies may be expected to have upon the general functioning of the economy. Thus in a period of boom it is important to know just how a restriction of bank credit would affect the different sectors of the economy. Aggregate statistics on many of the components of the flow-of-funds accounts have been available for many years, but the flow-of-funds accounts place the data in the context of the operation of specific sectors. Thus the data on new corporate security flotations and retirements become analytically more useful when considered in relation to the other sources and uses of funds by corporations.

The money and credit flows in the economy vitally affect the stability and growth potential of the system. These patterns of flows are highly sensitive to such factors as the legal forms of business organization which are dominant, the types of credit institutions and their regulations, and the nature of tax laws applying to business and to households. With

---

Footnotes to Table 50:

^a Includes benefit payments from private pension plans.

^b Less than $50 million.

^c Consumer receipts in flow-of-funds transaction category "other goods and services." Includes trade-in allowances associated with purchase of automobiles; also includes sale of furniture, clothing, and other consumer goods.

^d Includes a small amount of bank loans secured by hypothecated deposits not shown separately.

^e Trade debt owed to sales finance companies, credit unions, other nonbank financial institutions, and retail outlets.

^f Debit balances owed to brokers and dealers in securities.

^g These two items—debit balances owed to brokers and policy loans on life insurance policies—constitute consumer debt in the flow-of-funds category "miscellaneous financial liabilities."

^h The sum of lines 2, 3, 8, and 13 is equal to consumer expenditures in the flow-of-funds transaction categories, "other goods and services" and "real estate transfers."

ⁱ Contract rent.

^j Includes cost of land, a component of the flow-of-funds transaction category "real estate transfers."

^k Includes premiums and employee contributions to private pension plans.

^l Mainly premiums for veterans' life policies and government employee retirement programs.

^m Consists of time deposits with commercial and mutual savings banks, and the Postal Savings System.

ⁿ Consists of credit union shares, loans in process from savings and loan associations, deposit claims with life insurance companies, and trust and deposit liabilities of the Federal government.

^o Net uses (+) or net sources (−) not accounted for.

NOTE: Details may not add to total because of rounding.

SOURCE: Board of Governors of the Federal Reserve System, The Flow of Funds in the United States, 1939–1953, Washington, D.C., 1955.

Table 51. Structure of the Flow-of-funds Account, 1953
(In billions)

Item no.		Consumers	Corporations	Nonfarm noncorporate	Farm	Federal government	State and local government	Banking	Insurance	Other investors	Rest of world	Valuation adjustment + discrepancy	Total
1	Nonfinancial sources:												
2	Payroll	$195.5										—	$ 195.5
3	Interest	7.1	$ 1.7			$ 0.9	$ 0.5	$ 6.0	$ 3.0	$ 1.2	$ 0.1	—	20.7
4	Dividends and branch profits	9.2	3.0	$ 0.3	*	0.1	0.3	*	0.3	0.4	0.3	—	13.3
5	Rents and royalties		5.1	17.2	1.1	7.4	2.2	0.1	0.2	0.1	0.2	—	24.3
6	Insurance premiums		1.1		0.2	0.1	1.0	*	27.5	0.1	*	—	37.2
7	Insurance benefits	15.8	0.2	1.0	0.2	0.1			1.4	5.6	*	—	20.6
8	Grants and donations	8.1				0.1	8.8				2.0	—	25.0
9	Taxes and renegotiations					64.8	21.4					—	86.3
10	Tax refunds	2.6	0.5			*						—	3.1
11	Net withdrawals by proprietors	43.1										—	43.1
12	Real estate transfers	16.8	0.2	1.5	0.4		0.1		*	*		—	18.9
13	Other goods and services	5.3	538.3	195.8	29.8	5.0	5.8	0.8	0.5	4.9	15.8	—	802.0
14	Total nonfinancial sources	$303.4	$550.0	$215.9	$ 31.7	$ 78.4	$40.0	$ 7.0	$33.0	$12.3	$18.4	—	$1,290.0
15	Net increase in liabilities (financial sources):												
16	Currency and deposits					$ 1.6		$ 5.0				—	$ 6.5
17	Treasury currency					*						—	*
18	Gold stock							1.2				—	1.2
19	Trade credit	$ 2.2	$ -0.6	$ 1.0	$ -0.1	-0.1				$ 0.1		—	2.5
20	Bank loans other than mortgages	1.7		0.7	0.6							—	2.9
21	Federal obligations					5.2				0.2		—	5.4
22	State and local obligations					0.3	$ 3.6					—	3.9
23	Corporate securities		6.7	1.8				0.1		0.4	0.1	—	7.3
24	Mortgages	6.2	1.3	1.8	0.4					*		—	9.8
25	Miscellaneous	0.6	*	-0.1	0.2	0.3		0.2	0.3	4.5	0.9	—	6.9
26	Total net increase in liabilities	10.7	7.4	3.4	1.1	7.3	3.6	6.4	0.3	5.2	1.0	—	46.4
27	Valuation adjustment and discrepancy	0.3										—	0.3
28	Total sources	$314.4	$557.4	$219.3	$ 32.8	$ 85.7	$43.6	$13.5	$33.3	$17.6	$19.4	—	$1,336.7

204

Table (all figures in billions of dollars). Columns: Consumers, Corporations, Nonfarm non-corporate, Farm, Federal government, State and local government, Banking, Insurance, Other investors, Rest of world, Valuation adjustment + discrepancy, Total.

Item no.		Consumers	Corporations	Nonfarm non-corporate	Farm	Federal government	State and local government	Banking	Insurance	Other investors	Rest of world	Valuation adjustment + discrepancy	Total
	Nonfinancial uses:												
1	Payroll	$ 2.7	$118.7	$ 30.0	$ 2.6	$ 19.0	$13.5	$ 1.9	$ 2.6	$ 4.4	*	—	$ 195.5
2	Interest	5.5	3.9	1.7	0.9	5.2	0.8	1.5	*	0.7	$ 0.4	—	20.7
3	Dividends and branch profits	—	10.6	—	*	0.3	—	0.5	0.1	0.4	1.5	—	13.3
4	Rents and royalties	10.8	5.5	3.9	3.2	—	0.2	0.1	3.7	0.4	*	-0.1	24.3
5	Insurance premiums	17.6	10.7	2.9	0.4	—	1.4	0.3	—	0.4	0.1	*	37.2
6	Insurance benefits	—	—	—	*	5.7	1.8	—	13.0	1.0	0.1	*	20.6
7	Grants and donations	5.2	1.4	0.1	1.1	8.7	8.5	0.8	0.7	*	—	-0.2	25.0
8	Taxes and renegotiations	40.9	36.0	6.8		—	—	—	—		—		86.3
9	Tax refunds	—	—	—	8.8	3.1	—	—	—	—	—	—	3.1
10	Net withdrawals by proprietors	—	—	34.3	8.8	—	—	—	—	—	—	—	43.1
11	Real estate transfers	18.1	0.1	*	*	0.1	0.5	—	0.2	—	—	—	18.9
12	Other goods and services	201.1	368.4	136.2	15.7	42.9	13.6	0.8	3.5	5.1	14.3	0.4	802.0
13	Total nonfinancial sources	$301.8	$555.3	$215.9	$32.8	$ 85.1	$40.4	$ 5.9	$23.9	$12.4	$16.5	*	$1,290.0
14	Net increase in financial assets (financial uses):												
15	Currency and deposits	$ 4.4	$ 0.1	$ 0.4	*	—	$ 1.0	—	$ 0.2	$ 0.2	$ 0.3	*	$ 6.5
16	Treasury currency					*		$ 0.1				-0.1	*
17	Gold stock					$ -0.1						*	1.2
18	Trade credit		0.1	1.9						0.4	1.2	*	1.2
19	Bank loans other than mortgages		*					2.5		0.1	0.3	0.2	2.5
20	Federal obligations	0.3	1.1	0.6			1.8	0.9	*	*	0.6	*	2.9
21	State and local obligations	2.0	0.1	—		*	0.3	0.7	0.8	0.3	0.1	0.1	5.4
22	Corporate securities	1.2	0.2	-0.6				0.3	5.7	0.3	—	*	3.9
23	Mortgages	0.6	—	0.5		0.3	—	2.5	2.1	3.7	—	*	7.3
24	Miscellaneous	4.4		0.4	*	0.3	—	*	0.2	0.5	0.2	0.9	6.9
25	Total net increases in assets	12.9	1.6	3.2	*	0.5	3.0	6.9	9.1	5.2	2.7	1.3	46.4
26	Valuation adjustment and discrepancy	-0.2	0.5	0.2		—	0.2	0.4	0.3	-0.1	0.2	-1.2	0.3
27	Total uses	$314.4	$557.4	$219.3	$32.8	$ 85.7	$43.6	$13.5	$33.3	$ 17.6	$19.4	—	$1,336.7

* Less than $0.05 billion.

NOTE: Detail may not add to totals because of rounding.

SOURCE: See Table 50.

205

Table 52.* Transactions in Federal Obligations, 1939–1953 [a]

(Annual changes in billions)

Item no.		1939	1940	1941	1942	1943	1944	1945	1946	1947	1948	1949	1950	1951	1952	1953
1	Net change in liability of the Federal government	$ 2.1	$ 2.3	$11.4	$45.4	$52.9	$58.0	$41.6	$-22.5	$-6.3	$-6.8	$ 2.0	$-0.1	$-0.6	$ 4.4	$ 5.2
2	Issued for cash [b]	2.1	2.3	11.4	45.3	52.7	57.3	40.7	-22.7	-8.3	-6.7	1.7	-0.8	-1.2	3.7	4.5
3	Other [c]	d	d	0.1	0.1	0.2	0.8	0.9	0.2	2.0	-0.1	0.3	0.8	0.6	0.7	0.7
4	Net change in assets	2.2	2.4	11.3	45.3	52.6	58.5	41.9	-22.4	-6.3	-7.3	2.1	-0.2	-1.1	4.3	5.1
5	Consumer	0.2	0.5	2.5	8.7	11.9	13.3	9.5	0.4	1.8	1.1	1.3	0.2	-1.4	d	0.8
6	Issued for cash	0.2	0.5	2.4	8.6	11.7	13.0	9.3	-0.7	1.2	0.8	0.8	-0.3	-1.9	-0.6	0.2
7	Other [e]	d	d	0.1	0.1	0.2	0.3	0.2	1.0	0.7	0.3	0.5	0.5	0.5	0.7	0.6
8	Corporate business	—	-0.2	2.0	6.1	6.2	4.9	0.6	-6.7	-1.2	0.7	2.0	2.9	1.0	-0.3	1.1
9	Issued for cash	—	-0.2	2.0	6.1	6.2	4.5	-0.1	-5.6	-1.2	0.8	2.0	2.9	1.0	-0.4	1.1
10	Other [f]	—	—	d	—	—	0.5	0.6	-1.1	d	d	d	d	d	0.1	d
11	Nonfarm noncorporate business	0.1	—	0.5	1.6	1.8	2.7	1.9	-0.8	-0.8	-0.7	-0.3	-0.5	-0.2	-0.2	0.6
12	State and local government	—	0.1	0.2	0.3	1.1	2.2	2.2	-0.2	0.9	0.6	0.2	0.7	0.8	1.5	1.4
13	Banking	1.5	1.4	4.7	24.4	25.8	27.9	21.7	-15.3	-6.6	-6.2	-4.3	-3.5	0.8	2.2	0.9
14	Commercial banks	1.3	1.6	4.1	19.6	18.6	17.9	13.3	-15.3	-6.2	-6.5	-4.3	-4.6	-0.9	1.8	d
15	Mutual savings banks	0.2	0.1	0.5	0.9	1.5	2.2	2.4	1.1	0.2	-0.4	-0.1	-0.6	-1.0	-0.4	-0.2
16	Postal Savings System [g]	0.1	d	d	0.1	0.4	0.5	0.6	0.3	0.1	0.1	-0.1	-0.2	-0.2	-0.1	-0.2
17	Federal Reserve Banks	-0.1	-0.3	0.1	3.9	5.4	7.3	5.4	-0.9	-0.8	0.8	-4.4	1.9	3.0	0.9	1.2
18	Insurance	0.5	0.6	1.1	3.2	3.9	5.2	4.7	1.3	-0.7	-2.5	-0.7	-1.2	-2.3	-0.2	d
19	Life insurance companies	0.4	0.5	0.9	2.5	3.2	4.4	4.0	0.7	-1.6	-3.3	-1.5	-1.8	-2.4	-0.8	-0.4
20	Self-administered pension plans	d	d	d	0.1	0.1	0.2	0.2	0.3	0.3	0.2	0.3	0.2	0.2	0.2	0.2
21	Other insurance companies	d	0.1	0.2	0.5	0.5	0.6	0.4	0.2	0.7	0.5	0.4	0.4	d	0.4	0.2
22	Other investors	-0.2	-0.1	0.1	0.7	1.3	1.6	0.8	-0.6	-0.4	0.5	-0.1	-0.1	0.3	0.3	0.3
23	Nonprofit organizations	-0.1	d	d	0.3	0.6	0.4	0.3	d	d	d	d	d	-0.1	-0.1	-0.3
24	Savings and loan associations	d	d	d	0.2	0.5	0.8	0.7	-0.4	-0.3	-0.3	-0.1	d	0.1	0.2	0.1
25	Financial institutions n.e.c.	d	-0.1	d	0.2	0.5	0.4	-0.2	-0.2	-0.1	0.1	0.1	d	0.3	0.1	0.1
26	Rest of the world	—	—	0.1	0.4	0.6	0.6	0.6	-0.5	0.6	0.1	0.1	1.4	d	1.0	0.6
27	Issued for cash	—	—	0.2	0.4	0.6	0.6	0.6	-0.7	-0.7	0.4	0.3	1.2	-0.1	1.1	0.5
28	Other [h]	—	—	d	—	—	d	—	0.2	1.3	-0.4	-0.2	0.3	d	d	0.1
29	Discrepancy [i]	d	d	0.2	0.1	0.2	-0.5	-0.4	-0.1	d	0.5	-0.1	0.1	0.4	0.1	0.1

* For footnotes to Table 52, see p. 209.

Table 53.* Federal Obligations, 1939–1953 [a]

(Amounts outstanding at year end; in billions)

Item no.		1939	1940	1941	1942	1943	1944	1945	1946	1947	1948	1949	1950	1951	1952	1953
1	Liability of the Federal government	$43.2	$45.6	$57.0	$102.4	$155.3	$213.3	$254.8	$232.3	$226.0	$219.2	$221.2	$221.1	$220.5	$224.9	$230.1
2	Issued for cash [b]	42.9	45.2	56.6	101.9	154.6	211.9	252.5	229.8	221.6	214.8	216.5	215.7	214.5	218.2	222.8
3	Other [c]	0.3	0.4	0.4	0.5	0.7	1.4	2.3	2.5	4.4	4.3	4.6	5.4	6.0	6.7	7.3
4	Total assets	43.8	46.1	57.4	102.7	155.4	213.9	255.8	233.4	227.1	219.8	221.9	221.7	220.6	225.0	230.0
5	Consumer	8.7	9.2	11.7	20.3	32.2	45.5	55.0	55.4	57.2	58.2	59.5	59.7	58.3	58.4	59.1
6	Issued for cash	8.4	8.9	11.3	19.8	31.6	44.6	53.8	53.2	54.3	55.1	55.9	55.7	53.7	53.1	53.2
7	Other [d]	0.3	0.4	0.4	0.5	0.7	0.9	1.2	2.2	2.9	3.1	3.6	4.1	4.6	5.3	5.9
8	Corporate business	2.2	2.0	4.0	10.0	16.3	21.2	21.8	15.1	13.9	14.7	16.6	19.5	20.4	20.1	21.2
9	Issued for cash	2.2	2.0	4.0	10.0	16.3	20.8	20.7	15.1	13.9	14.6	16.6	19.5	20.4	20.1	21.2
10	Other [e]					f	0.5	1.1	f	f	f	f	f	0.1	0.1	0.1
11	Nonfarm noncorporate business	1.1	1.1	1.6	3.2	5.0	7.7	9.6	8.8	8.0	7.3	7.1	6.6	6.3	6.1	6.7
12	State and local government	0.4	0.5	0.7	1.0	2.1	4.3	6.6	6.4	7.3	7.9	8.1	8.8	9.6	11.2	12.5
13	Banking	23.6	25.0	29.8	54.2	80.0	108.0	129.7	114.4	107.7	101.5	101.2	97.6	98.5	100.7	101.5
14	Commercial banks	16.8	18.4	22.5	42.1	60.7	78.5	91.9	76.0	69.9	63.4	67.7	63.1	62.2	64.0	64.0
15	Mutual savings banks	3.1	3.2	3.7	4.6	6.1	8.3	10.7	11.8	12.0	11.6	11.5	10.9	9.8	9.5	9.2
16	Postal Savings System [g]	1.2	1.2	1.3	1.4	1.7	2.3	2.9	3.2	3.3	3.3	3.1	2.9	2.7	2.6	2.4
17	Federal Reserve Banks	2.5	2.2	2.3	6.2	11.5	18.8	24.3	23.4	22.6	23.3	18.9	20.8	23.8	24.7	25.9
18	Insurance	6.8	7.4	8.6	11.7	15.6	20.8	25.5	26.8	26.0	23.4	22.7	21.4	19.0	18.8	18.9
19	Life insurance companies	5.5	5.9	6.8	9.3	12.5	16.9	21.0	21.6	20.0	16.7	15.3	13.5	11.0	10.3	9.8
20	Self-administered pension plans	0.2	0.2	0.2	0.3	0.4	0.6	0.9	1.2	1.4	1.6	1.9	2.0	2.1	2.2	2.5
21	Other insurance companies	1.2	1.4	1.6	2.1	2.6	3.2	3.6	3.9	4.6	5.1	5.5	5.9	6.0	6.3	6.5
22	Other investors	0.9	0.9	0.9	1.7	3.0	4.6	5.4	4.8	4.5	4.1	4.0	4.0	4.3	4.6	4.3
23	Nonprofit organizations	0.1	0.1	0.1	0.3	0.9	1.3	1.6	1.7	1.7	1.7	1.6	1.5	1.5	1.5	1.1
24	Savings and loan associations	0.1	0.1	0.1	0.3	0.9	1.7	2.4	2.0	1.7	1.5	1.5	1.5	1.6	1.8	1.9
25	Financial institutions n.e.c.	0.8	0.7	0.8	1.0	1.2	1.6	1.4	1.2	1.1	1.0	0.9	0.9	1.2	1.3	1.3
26	Rest of the world	—	—	0.2	0.6	1.2	1.8	2.3	1.9	2.5	2.5	2.6	4.1	4.0	5.1	5.6
27	Issued for cash	—	—	0.2	0.6	1.2	1.8	2.3	1.6	0.9	1.4	1.6	2.8	2.7	3.8	4.3
28	Other [h]	—	—						0.2	1.5	1.2	1.0	1.3	1.3	1.3	1.3
29	Discrepancy [i]	-0.5	-0.6	-0.4	-0.3	-0.1	-0.6	-1.0	-1.1	-1.1	-0.6	-0.7	-0.6	-0.2	-0.1	0.1

* For footnotes to Table 53, see p. 209.

the evolution of an economy it is natural that the economic institutions, the legal framework, and other institutional arrangements will change. The flow-of-funds accounts reflect in measurable terms the effect of all such changes upon the structure of transaction flows in the system. Contemplated changes in basic institutions or regulations in the system should be considered from the point of view of how they will affect these transaction flows, and whether they will promote the stability and growth of the economy in an equitable manner. Similarly, alleged defects in the system should be examined in terms of what flows are involved and in what way attempts to remove such defects will affect individual sectors in the economy and the economy as a whole.

The problem of economic fluctuations is intimately bound up with the processes by which transaction flows expand and contract. Studying the structure of assets and liabilities of the different sectors will throw light upon the determinants of their behavior, or at least upon the range of possibilities. Thus, for example, the determinants of consumer behavior may not lie solely in the changes in consumers' income. The degree to which a contraction in disposable income will be reflected in a contraction in consumers' expenditures may depend on how much currency and deposits consumers have at their command or on their holdings in the form of government bonds or other securities. Similarly, the reaction of producers to contractions in demand may depend on the liquidity of the firms, whether they feel it is possible to weather the bad times by paying out more than they are taking in, or whether they will be forced into bankruptcy. It is such problems as these that flow-of-funds data can help to explain.

CONCLUSIONS

This discussion of different forms of economic accounting emphasizes the fact that no single system of economic accounting can serve all purposes. The attempt to put all the detail of all systems of economic accounting into a single system would vitiate the very purpose of economic accounting, that of the aggregation of detail into meaningful components and aggregates. Economic accounts must be designed to fit specific requirements.

Conversely, the progress of economic knowledge may well depend on the degree of success achieved in developing specialized forms of economic accounting that can probe various aspects of the economic system. The three systems that have been discussed here have very different purposes and refer to quite different aspects of the economic system.

National income accounting is designed (1) to measure production; (2) to show the uses of production in terms of the final purchasers in the economy; and (3) to show the types of factor income and other payments generated by economic activity. In an economic accounting system intended for such purposes, the sectoring must be designed in terms of the functional aspects of economic activity; thus producers, consumers, and government are distinguished, with additional accounts for foreign trade and for saving and investment transactions.

Input-output accounting focuses on the way in which the technological production functions of various industries affect interindustry relationships and thus determine the industrial structure of the economy. The sectoring here, therefore, highlights individual industries, classifying them in considerable detail by the type of product produced and by the industrial processes used, and showing for each industry the inputs consumed and the distribution of outputs produced.

Flow-of-funds accounting is perhaps more related to national income accounting than to input-output accounting, largely because it is not at all concerned with the technological aspects of the economic system. Instead, it focuses on the sources and uses of funds that are essential for the support of economic activity in a modern economy. Since money and credit flows are strongly influenced by the institutional and legal arrange-

---

Footnotes to Table 52:

ᵃ Consists of all security issues of the Federal government and its agencies held outside the Federal government sector. Includes direct issues of the Treasury and both fully guaranteed and not fully guaranteed issues of government corporations and agencies; includes both cash issues and noncash issues arising in public debt transactions; includes all transactions in government securities whether or not reflected in the Treasurer's account.

ᵇ Differs from the Treasury Net Cash Borrowing series in that it includes securities not handled through the Treasurer's account, excludes currency items in the public debt, and differs in coverage and timing in the amounts deducted for net purchases of Federal securities by government agencies.

ᶜ Consists of accrued interest on savings bonds and Treasury bills, Armed Forces leave bonds, notes issued as part payment for subscription to the International Monetary Fund and International Bank for Reconstruction and Development, adjusted service certificates, and excess profits tax refund bonds.

ᵈ Less than $50 million.

ᵉ Accrued interest on savings bonds, Armed Forces leave bonds, adjusted service certificates.

ᶠ Excess profits tax refund bonds and accrued interest on Treasury bills.

ᵍ Includes a small amount held by the Exchange Stabilization Fund.

ʰ Notes issued as part payment for subscription to International Monetary Fund and International Bank for Reconstruction and Development.

ⁱ Increase in excess liabilities. Primarily due to differences in valuation between obligor and holder records.

NOTE: Detail may not add to totals because of rounding.

SOURCE: See Table 50.

Footnotes to Table 53:

ᵃ Consists of all security issues of the Federal government and its agencies held outside the Federal government sector. Includes direct issues of the Treasury and both fully guaranteed and not fully guaranteed issues of government corporations and agencies; includes both cash issues and noncash issues arising in public debt transactions; includes all transactions in government securities whether or not reflected in the Treasurer's account.

ᵇ Differs from the Treasury Net Cash Borrowing series in that it includes securities not handled through the Treasurer's account, excludes currency items in the public debt, and differs in coverage and timing in the amounts deducted for net purchases of Federal securities by government agencies.

ᶜ Consists of accrued interest on savings bonds and Treasury bills, Armed Forces leave bonds, notes issued as part payment for subscription to the International Monetary Fund and International Bank for Reconstruction and Development, adjusted service certificates, and excess profits tax refund bonds.

ᵈ Accrued interest on savings bonds, Armed Forces leave bonds, adjusted service certificates.

ᵉ Excess profits tax refund bonds and accrued interest on Treasury bills.

ᶠ Less than $50 million.

ᵍ Includes a small amount held by the Exchange Stabilization Fund.

ʰ Notes issued as part payment for subscription to International Monetary Fund and International Bank for Reconstruction and Development.

ⁱ Increase in excess liabilities. Primarily due to differences in valuation between obligor and holder records

NOTE: Detail may not add to totals because of rounding.

SOURCE: See Table 50.

ments of the economic system, the classification of sectors and transactions in the flow-of-funds accounts is designed in terms of both functional and institutional classifications. As in the case of national income accounting, producers, consumers, and government are identified, but within the producing and government sectors further breakdowns are given to segregate certain financial sectors and show the different types of business organization involved. In flow-of-funds accounting, also, the scope of coverage is much broader than in national income accounting. All transactions involving money or credit flows, capital and current alike, are included in the accounts, the changes in assets and liabilities of each sector as well as the money and credit flows directly related to income.

Since these different forms of economic accounting have different purposes, they should not be compared in absolute terms but rather in terms of how efficiently they meet the purposes for which they were designed, and how important each of the various uses is in helping to solve the major economic problems facing the world today.

Part Two

Income Analysis

10. The Economic Setting of the Problem

Income analysis is concerned with analyzing the processes by which changes in income, output, and employment take place in the economic system. Economic change is a very complex phenomenon, reflecting the impact of all the cultural, technological, and institutional changes in a society as well as the more direct economic forces which may be at work. Before embarking upon the more abstract approach to income analysis, it will be useful to examine the context of the analysis: the kinds of economic change that take place, and the role of income analysis in the study of such change. This chapter and Chap. 11 will consider this context briefly. This chapter will concern itself with discussing in broad nontechnical terms the kinds of economic change that have occurred in the United States economy, and will indicate the kinds of economic change to which income analysis relates. Chapter 11 will examine the operation of the United States economy for the period from 1929 to 1954, in order to focus more sharply, still in nontechnical empirical terms, on the specific economic processes with which income analysis deals. The empirical information in these two chapters also will provide useful background material for later chapters, and will acquaint the reader with some of the changes that have been taking place in the United States economy.

THE GROWTH OF THE UNITED STATES ECONOMY, 1790 TO 1954

The past 170 years have seen the rise of the United States from a small colony to a nation unsurpassed in productive powers and wealth. In the early period of our history the economic system was relatively simple; its problems were those of overcoming the physical barriers imposed by nature. Land had to be cleared, shelter had to be erected, and protection had to be secured. Today the outlook is very different. The economy has developed into a complex and delicate mechanism; the problems are those of maintaining full employment and securing a proper allocation of resources. As a background for the study of the operation of the modern economy, it will be useful to trace in broad outline the evolution of the economy into its present form.

Population Growth in the United States

It is difficult to realize that the total population of the United States in 1790 was equal to less than half of the number of people who now live in New York City. Since 1790 the population has risen from about 4 million to over 165 million. When the United States was first formed, no city had as many as 50,000 people and only six had a population of over 8,000. The population was 95 per cent rural, and there was practically no manufacturing. The great growth in population since then has been essential to the achievement of the standard of living that now prevails in the United States. The building of the railroads and the opening up of the continent required a vast amount of manpower. The needs of a growing population and an expanding country forced the growth of the large heavy industries. The existence of mass markets permitted the development of industries that produced by mass methods and at the same time provided labor to supply these industries. The economic growth of the United States has been inseparably linked to the growth in population and territory, and the evolution of the system cannot be analyzed without taking both of these into account.

In future years population growth similar to that of the past 170 years cannot be expected. The growth in the past was the result both of a high birth rate and of continued immigration from Europe; the birth rate has declined, and immigration has been limited. Unless there is a marked change in immigration policy or measures are undertaken to increase the birth rate substantially, the population of the United States will probably not increase much longer and may even decline within a relatively short period. The future of the economic system thus cannot be forecast by extrapolating past trends. Far different basic forces will be operating in the future, and the growth that takes place will be quantitatively and qualitatively different.

The Growth in Production and Productivity

Production, obviously, has grown along with the growth in population. Measuring the amount of this growth, however, is difficult, both because the statistical evidence on past periods is fragmentary and because the conceptual problems involved in comparing different periods have no simple solutions. For periods prior to 1929 over-all data about the performance of the economy are very much less reliable and less complete than they are for periods since that date. From a conceptual point of view, the farther one goes into the past the more difficult meaningful comparison becomes. The general nature of this problem was discussed in Chap. 7, where the calculation of gross national product in constant prices was examined in greater detail. When the whole of the economic system changes, a mere summary quantitative measurement of this change cannot adequately portray what has taken place. The magnitude of the change shown also will vary considerably with differences in basic assumptions that must be made in the process of measurement, and with the extent to which such factors as quality changes, the introduction of new products, the change in social costs and benefits, and the increase or decrease in leisure are taken into account in the concept of total output.

Increases in Total Production—Gross National Product in Constant Prices. In spite of these difficulties, numerical calculations of the changes in gross national product in constant prices have been made for the period 1909 to 1954. These estimates are shown in Chart 1.

Gross national product in constant prices in 1954 was $3\frac{1}{2}$ times what it was in 1909. Furthermore, what fragmentary evidence does exist

Chart 1. Gross national product in constant prices, 1909–1954. **Source:** 1909–1928, supplied by U.S. Department of Commerce, National Income Division. 1929–1953, *National Income,* U.S. Department of Commerce, 1954 ed., pp. 216–217.

on earlier periods indicates that gross national product in constant prices in 1909 was at least five times greater than it had been thirty years earlier in 1879. No estimates exist for gross national product prior to 1879. Even if there had been no increase in productivity from 1790 to 1879, however, the population data indicate that gross national product in 1790 could not have been much over $1 billion.[1] If the goods and services produced in 1790 were sold on the market today, they would not bring a sufficient amount to keep today's population in cigarette money.

If anything, the gross national product series in constant prices probably understates the growth that has taken place in production. Most of the products that have passed from the market have done so because superior or cheaper products replaced them, and in many lines there has been a steady improvement in the quality or design of products that is not reflected in the statistical data.

Increase in Per Capita Production—Gross National Product in Constant Prices Per Capita. In view of the change in the size of the population of the United States, it would obviously be erroneous to consider the rise in total production a measure of the increase in the economic well-being of the people in the nation. Nevertheless, even when the estimates of the gross national product in constant prices are reduced to a per capita basis, the growth in production appears very sizable. Chart 2 shows that output per capita has almost doubled since 1909.

As was pointed out in Chap. 6, however, these comparisons should not be taken as indicators of economic welfare. These figures refer to production, not consumption. The other uses of output, such as government services and capital formation, may not have the same import for economic welfare as does the direct consumption of goods by individuals. Because the data are stated in gross terms, the role of capital consumption must also be considered; if capital consumption has increased as a percentage of gross output, the above figures would tend to overstate the true change. Per capita data also fail to take into account the changed age and family composition of the population, and this would of course be an important element in any calculation of economic welfare.

Furthermore, these aggregate figures conceal a great many dissimilarities between the periods, and these dissimilarities are difficult to evaluate. Consumers did not have the advantages of many modern appliances, but on the other hand the pattern of living in that period did not require so

---

[1] Output in 1790 was composed primarily of agricultural products, and for this reason the total is reasonably comparable to later figures. Although the change in quality of agricultural goods produced has been significant, it has been nowhere near so great as the change in quality and type of manufactured goods. If allowance were made for the change in the quality of agricultural produce, the figure for 1790 would necessarily be even smaller.

Chart 2. Gross national product per capita in constant prices, 1909–1954. **Source:** Derived from *National Income*, U.S. Department of Commerce, 1954 ed.; *Survey of Current Business*, February, 1955; *Business Statistics*, U.S. Department of Commerce, 1952 ed.; *Statistical Abstract*, 1950 and 1924; and data supplied by the National Income Division, U.S. Department of Commerce.

many. For example, the facilities for rapid and convenient transportation did not exist, but the need for them was not so great as it is now. People did not live at great distances from their jobs and commute to work every day. Cities were not so crowded that people were forced to live in the suburbs in order to have a house and a yard. A great many modern developments simply represent the attempt to keep up with the increasing requirements that accompany growth and change in society. For this reason even if it were possible to evaluate the net increase in the amount of goods provided to each person in the country, it would still be impossible to draw any conclusion as to the welfare of the economy as a whole. Also, welfare is to a large extent a relative rather than an absolute matter. Much of the consumption in the economy is carried out on a competitive basis by individuals attempting to live according to the standards set up by particular classes of society. As production increases, these standards also increase, so that the same relative position in society requires a higher standard of consumption.

Finally, the aggregate figures on gross national product per capita say nothing about the manner in which income and output were distributed among various groups in the economy. The economic welfare of a nation is highly related to the manner in which various groups share in the total output, and this has undoubtedly changed over time. To the extent also that economic welfare is a function of the degree to which individuals are able to improve their status, rather than the absolute level of what they receive, the important consideration is how the *increases* in output were distributed among the various groups in the nation.

Increase in Productivity—Gross National Product in Constant Prices Per Man-hour. Calculation of the change in productivity that has occurred in the economy requires a consideration of the change in the number of hours worked relative to total output.[2] For at least one sector of the economy such a comparison is not meaningful because of the assumptions made in the estimation of gross national product in constant prices. In the government sector gross product originating is calculated as equal to the compensation of government employees. In obtaining gross product originating in constant prices, any increase in the pay of government workers is considered a price increase rather than an output increase. The measurement of the change in gross product originating in government in constant prices obtained by deflating the compensation of government employees for price changes therefore comes out to be identical with the actual hours worked by government employees. By definition, therefore, gross product in constant prices per man-hour for the government sector is always unchanging over time. For this reason the consideration of government gross product must be eliminated from a study of productivity changes in the economy. Eliminating the gross product originating in government from gross national product merely requires the subtraction of the compensation of government employees from the total. The resulting concept is generally referred to as gross private product. Chart 3 shows the changes in gross private product in constant prices per man-hour that have taken place since 1909.

It is interesting to note that the increase of 127 per cent from 1909 to 1950 shown in this chart is greater than the increase of 88 per cent in per capita gross national product in constant prices shown in Chart 2. One of the major reasons for this difference is of course the shortening of the work week since 1909.

It is misleading to assume that all sectors of the economy enjoyed the

---

[2] Conceptually, the measurement of productivity should take capital goods and natural resources into account. Statistically, this does not appear to be feasible at present.

Chart 3. Gross private product per man-hour in constant prices, 1909–1950. **Source:** Derived from *National Income*, U.S. Department of Commerce, 1954 ed.; J. W. Kendrick, "National Productivity and Its Long-term Projection," in *Long-range Economic Projection*, Princeton University Press, Princeton, N.J., 1954.

same degree of productivity change over this period. Chart 4 shows the distribution of the gross private product in constant prices between farm and nonfarm gross product.

Farm gross product in constant prices per man-hour showed an increase of 268 per cent for the period, whereas that for the nonfarm sector increased by 239 per cent. It might appear at first glance that there is an inconsistency between these productivity figures and those given in Chart 3 for the whole of the private economy. The private economy as a whole apparently had a larger productivity increase than the sectors of which it is composed. This paradox can easily be explained, however, by taking into account the difference in absolute productivity between the farm and nonfarm sectors shown in Chart 4. The absolute productivity of the farm sector was lower throughout the whole period. Even if there had been no increase in productivity in either the farm sector or the nonfarm sector, productivity for the economy as a whole could have increased

Chart 4. Farm and nonfarm gross private product in constant prices, 1909–1953. **Source:** Derived from *National Income*, U.S. Department of Commerce, 1954 ed.; *Survey of Current Business*, August, 1954; J. W. Kendrick, "National Productivity and Its Long-term Projection," in *Long-range Economic Production*, Princeton University Press, Princeton, N.J., 1954.

if resources were shifted out of the farm sector and into the more productive nonfarm sector. This is of course precisely what happened. Chart 5 shows how the total man-hours used by the private sector were divided between the farm and the nonfarm sectors.

Although total man-hours in the private sector as a whole increased throughout most of the period, the number of man-hours used by the farm sector declined. In relative terms the farm sector accounted for 28 per cent of the total man-hours used in 1909 and only 16 per cent in 1950. Some of the productivity change in the economy as a whole therefore was achieved by the shift of resources from sectors having lower productivity to sectors having higher productivity.

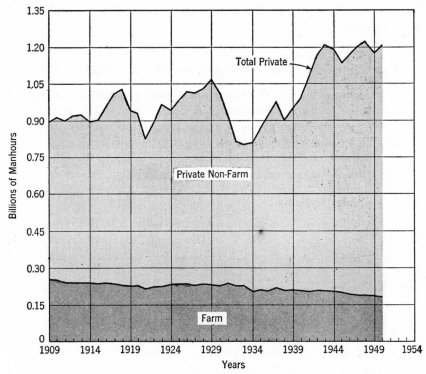

Chart 5. Use of man-hours by the farm and nonfarm sectors, 1909–1950. **Source:** J. W. Kendrick, "National Productivity and Its Long-term Projection," in *Long-range Economic Projection*, Princeton University Press, Princeton, N.J., 1954, Table 4, pp. 82–83.

In summary, both the growth in population and the growth in productivity have been very important in the development of the United States economy. The growth patterns within the different sectors of the economy of course differ. They are influenced not only by the different levels of productivity which may exist, but also by the change in consumers' needs and preferences as their incomes increase, and by the changing role of government and the nature of capital formation over time. Future growth patterns for individual industries cannot be expected to conform to the patterns of past growth, so that there is no reason why future growth for the economy as a whole will conform to the pattern of past growth; entirely different forces will be at work and the conditions that exist in the economy of the future will be entirely different. To forecast the direction of future growth it would be necessary to study the causal elements affecting growth at the present time and in the future. Simply extrapolating apparent trends is not a valid procedure; when causal relations cannot be determined, accurate prediction of future development is not possible.

Changes in the Level of Economic Activity, 1929 to 1954

The process of change described above was evolutionary in that it dealt with the long-run development of the economy. The economy is also subject to short-run changes in the level of its activity. It would be possible to select many periods in the history of the United States economy to illustrate this type of change, but in many ways it is best illustrated by the course of events from 1929 to 1954.

The Level of Employment

One of the best indicators of the level of activity in the economy in the short run is the percentage of the population that is employed. Over a longer period of time this measure will not reveal a great deal about the level of activity of the economy, since it is greatly altered by such long-run factors as change in the age distribution of the population, change in the groups in the economy normally entering the labor force, and changes in the concept of employment. A growing population will have a greater proportion of people in the younger age groups than will a declining population, so that a different percentage of the population will be available for employment. Furthermore, as the country has grown in wealth and life expectancy has increased, the groups in the population normally seeking employment have been greatly changed. In the early years of the United States children were employed in factories and on the farm at a much earlier age than they are now, and individuals did not so frequently survive to retirement age. Finally, the very definition of employment itself has caused apparent changes in the proportion of the population that is employed. Housewives, for example, are not considered part of the employed labor force, so that when they hire someone else to do their housework and take jobs in industry, the apparent result is that more people are employed although actually there may have been only a shifting of tasks among people. Keeping all these conditions in mind, it is still useful to examine the proportion of the population employed as an indication of the level of economic activity in the short run. Chart 6 shows how this proportion changed during the period 1929 to 1954.

In the year 1929 about 48 million people were employed; this constituted about 39 per cent of the population. There was some unemployment (about 1.5 million) due to normal labor turnover, but the economy was in general considered to be at "full employment." The unemployment that did exist was frictional: for most unemployed in-

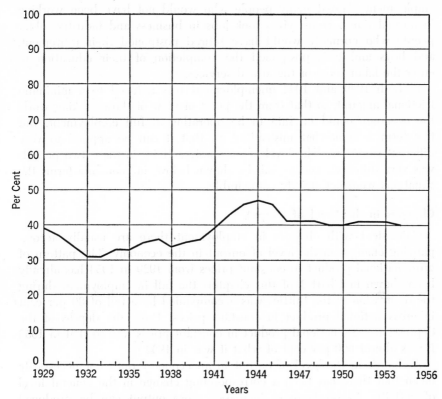

Chart 6. Percentage of the population employed, 1929–1954. **Source:** Derived from *Business Statistics*, U.S. Department of Commerce, 1952 ed.; *Statistical Abstract*, 1950 and 1924; *Survey of Current Business*, February, 1955; *Federal Reserve Bulletin*, December, 1954.

dividuals it was purely temporary and was due to changing jobs rather than to inability to find jobs. By 1932 and 1933, however, over 12 million people were out of work and were seeking employment. This unemployment was not frictional, since enough jobs did not exist to employ the number of people who wished to work. The percentage of the population employed dropped to 31 per cent. It did not get back to the 1929 level until 1941. The chart shows that the recovery from the depths of the depression was very slow, and the recession of 1938 appears very distinctly as a drop in the percentage of the population employed. In the year 1944 employment reached an all-time peak of 65 million (over 25 million above the depression level); this represented over 47 per cent of the population. Even at this time it is estimated that there was frictional unemployment of about 0.7 million. However, the extraordinary demand for labor in this period drew into employment a great many people who would not have been working in normal times. Housewives took jobs in business and industry, older people who normally would have retired postponed their retirement, and boys and girls postponed the completion of their education to enter the labor force or the armed services.

In both 1929 and 1944 unemployment was reduced to a minimum frictional amount, so that from the point of view of those seeking work, the economy could be said to be operating at full employment. But this term is somewhat misleading, in that it can be applied to very different situations. The level of economic activity in these two periods was very different; and as will be shown below, in economic terms the situations were not strictly comparable.

Changes in the Level of Output

Coincident with changes in employment there are usually accompanying changes in the level of output in the economy. The pattern of gross national product in constant prices from 1929 to 1954 has already been shown in Chart 1 of this chapter; the fall in employment during the depression of the thirties was accompanied by a fall of 30 per cent in gross national product in constant prices. From the depths of the depression gross national product in constant prices rose so that in 1953 it was almost 300 per cent of what it was in 1933.

A change in the level of output in an economy does not necessarily mean that there has been a corresponding change in the general level of activity. As productivity increases, more output can be produced with the same amount of activity. It has been pointed out in the earlier part of this chapter that changes in population and in productivity have had profound effects upon the economy. The action of these forces is by no means absent from the workings of the economy over a short period, but the effects of the long-run evolutionary changes cannot be separated from the effects of the short-run changes in the level of activity, since each influences and alters the other in the highly complex mechanism of the economy. Despite the fact that they cannot be isolated, however, both types of forces do exist.

In other words, it is not possible to say what gross national product would have been in 1940 if there had been no depression in the preceding period. If there had been no previous depression, many changes would have taken place and the economy in 1940 would have been quite different, but it is a matter of conjecture just how it would have been different. And conversely, the long-run changes in population and productivity that were in the process of taking place undoubtedly had some effect on the level of activity in the depression, but it is impossible to say what the level of activity would have been if these forces had been absent or had been of a different type. The evolutionary change of the economy and the fluctuations in the level of economic activity are so completely intermingled and interact with each other in such a way that it is not possible to look back over a period and separate the influence of each type of change.

In the short run, nevertheless, the level of economic activity, the level of employment, and the level of gross national product are all closely linked. During the depression of the thirties people were unemployed and so obtained less income; as a counterpart to this on the production side, less was produced and sold to consumers. A large segment of the labor force sat idle in dire need of the goods that they could have produced had they been employed. From a technical point of view there was no bar to production. Both manpower and industrial capacity were present—yet the economic mechanism was unable to bring together the ability to produce and the need for the product. To a very large extent the analysis developed in Part Two of this book is centered around this paradox of scarcity and plenty. Study of the economic mechanism in more detail will demonstrate how such a condition can exist.

Price Changes in the Economy

Every good or service produced in the economy can be thought of in terms of a price and a quantity, and almost all transactions have a price element in them. The wage rate is the price of labor, railway fare is the price of rail transportation, and the interest rate is the price of borrowing money. The prices of one producer often become the costs of another producer—as, for instance, when a lumber dealer sells lumber to a contractor or a farmer sells grain to a miller. These transactions among producers create a structure of price-cost relationships that are very important in explaining how a reaction takes place in the economy. Prices are most commonly used in connection with actual finished products that appear on the market; it is often assumed that these finished goods prices reflect the prices of the labor, transportation, interest, etc., that have gone into them, so that a study of commodity prices will give a true picture of the level of prices in the economy. This view is very much oversimplified, since it does not take into account the relationship of prices to each other, but for some purposes it is useful to show how a given group of commodity prices has changed.

An average picture of how prices in the economy have changed can be obtained by a method directly related to that employed in showing how on the average the quantity of output has changed. Gross national product in constant prices was used to show the changes in the quantity of output; in the process of making this calculation it was necessary to classify the gross national product in current prices into as fine a product breakdown as possible and then divide each of these series by appropriate price indexes in order to eliminate from the current dollar estimates all price changes that had taken place. Many different price indexes are used in such a calculation, but a measure of how prices changed on the average for all products can be obtained by making a comparison between the series of gross national product in current prices and the derived series of gross national product in constant prices. The measure of price change for the economy as a whole so derived is referred to as the implicit price deflator of the gross national product. This index for the years 1929 to 1954 is shown in Chart 7.

With the decline in the activity of the economy from 1929 to 1933, prices on the average fell about 23 per cent. After 1933 they rose slowly until the recession of 1938. In the early part of the war prices rose fairly

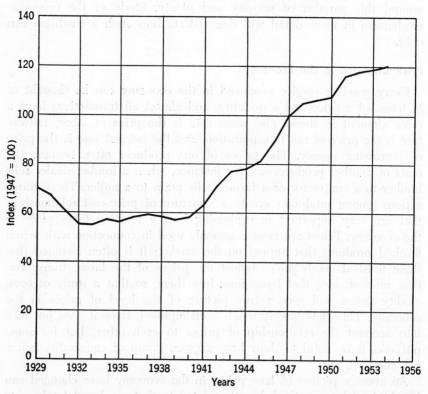

Chart 7. The implicit price deflator of the gross national product, 1929–1954. Source: 1929–1953, National Income, U.S. Department of Commerce, 1954 ed., pp. 216–217. 1954, Survey of Current Business, February, 1955, pp. 7–8.

sharply, but with the advent of price control the rise was slowed down. After the removal of price control, prices again rose sharply.

In an uncontrolled economy prices are highly related to the level of economic activity. They are not merely a resultant of the forces operating within the system; they are an active part of the mechanism that determines the level of activity. Any study of that level, therefore, must of necessity analyze the function of prices in the system.

Prices and Income. Income in the economy is, as has been pointed out above, in large part dependent on prices. The wage rate of employees is the price at which the employees are selling their labor, and the amount of their income depends solely upon this wage rate and the amount of labor they perform. In this sense income is the result of the price of labor and the amount of employment, and reflects in one magnitude the total effect of these two elements. Similarly, the prices of agricultural goods in conjunction with the amount produced and farm costs determine the income of the farmer, and the prices of manufactured goods in conjunction with the volume of output and manufacturing costs determine manufacturing profits. There can be no change in either prices or output without someone's income being changed.

Income is very greatly dependent on the level of activity in the economy. The laborer who is unemployed does not get any income, and even those who are employed get less when the wage rate declines. The farmer receives less when the prices of agricultural goods fall, and the manufacturer makes no profit if he cannot produce at a cost less than the price for which he can sell his product. Gross national product in current prices and disposable income both vary greatly as the level of economic activity changes. The drop in both (Chart 8) from 1929 to 1933 was about 45 per cent. By 1954 they had risen 540 per cent and 450 per cent respectively.

Part of the variation in gross national product and disposable income over the period from 1929 to 1954 was undoubtedly due to basic changes that were taking place in economic institutions, population, and technology, but these elements alone cannot explain all the changes that took place. The fluctuations in gross national product and disposable income are a reflection of the changes in prices, output, and employment that have taken place within the framework of the economic mechanism. In order to understand these fluctuations it is necessary to analyze the process by which changes in the level of both gross national product and disposable income come about in terms of prices, output, and employment. Gross national product and disposable income are the resultants of these elements; an understanding of the place of each of them in the mechanism that determines the level of income is essential to an adequate explanation of the process of change in the economy.

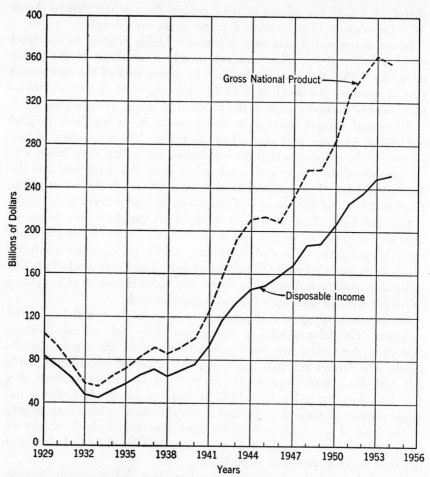

Chart 8. Gross national product and diposable income in current prices, 1929–1954.
Source: 1929–1953, *National Income,* U.S. Department of Commerce, 1954 ed., pp.
164–165. 1954, *Survey of Current Business,* February, 1955, p. 7.

Prices and Purchasing Power. The disposable income received by individuals is very important in determining the amount they can spend on
goods and services. The prices of these goods and services, however, determine how much can be purchased with a given amount of expenditure. It is quite feasible, for example, that even during a period of increasing expenditures the amount of goods purchased may decline if
prices are rising faster than expenditures. Prices, output, and expenditure
are by definition so related that if output remains the same and expenditure increases, prices must rise equivalently so that the amount of goods
and services that can be bought will remain the same. The previous sec-

tion pointed out the linkage of prices and output with income from the point of view of the determination of payments of income; the linkage here is from the point of view of the purchase of goods—the demand for output. The level of prices not only influences the amount of income available in the economy; it also affects the quantity of output that can be purchased.

Prices thus have a dual aspect in the economic mechanism. On the one hand, together with output and employment, they are reflected in the amount of income in the economy. On the other hand, together with income and personal saving, they are reflected in the amount of available purchasing power and so provide a link between income and output. Behind the level of economic activity reflected in the national income accounts there is thus a system of interrelated prices, outputs, and employment, which by its repercussions both to external changes and to changes within the system produces fluctuations in the level of economic activity. The study of changes in the level of economic activity is thus the study of prices, output, and employment in the short run, or, more briefly, the study of income and employment.

Patterns of Changes in Prices, Output, and Employment

The previous sections have attempted to show that violent changes in prices, output, and employment occur over relatively short periods of time, and for this purpose general statistics have been given that refer to the economy as a whole. These statistics do not reveal the extent to which various parts of the economy differ from each other. Agriculture and manufacturing, for instance, react quite differently to a change in the level of economic activity, and these reactions in turn have a further effect upon the economy.

Agricultural Prices, Output, and Employment, 1929 to 1954. The position of the farmer in the economy is quite different from that of other producers. The actual outlay of money costs in agriculture is usually a small percentage of the total market value of the commodities produced, and the major portion of the cash return goes to pay the farmer for the labor he has expended in production. This situation is quite different from that of the manufacturer, who makes large expenditures for materials and labor and receives as his return the margin that exists between these costs and the selling price. Agricultural output will not be curtailed when the price of the commodities produced drops sharply. As long as the farmer gets some return for his labor, he will prefer to produce for whatever he can get rather than sit idle and get nothing. In almost all instances the point of maximum return for the individual farmer will be the largest amount he can produce irrespective, within very broad limits, of price. This phenomenon is clearly shown in Chart 9, which shows prices, output, and employment for agriculture in terms of index numbers. The fluctuations in prices are very marked, but the changes in employment are not very great, except for the continuous downward trend. Output

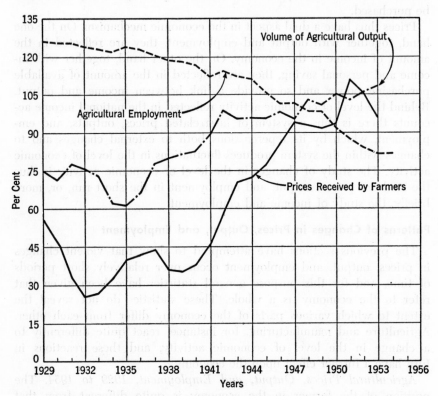

Chart 9. Prices, output, and employment in agriculture, 1929–1954. 1947–1949 = 100.
Source: Derived from *Survey of Current Business,* August, 1954; *Business Statistics,* U.S. Department of Commerce, 1952 ed.; *Federal Reserve Bulletin,* August, 1954; *Historical Statistics,* U.S. Department of Commerce.

increased considerably during the war period, but this increase is due to increased productivity per worker rather than to any increase in employment. Employment and output in agriculture are not affected to any very great degree by the level of activity of the economy. Weather creates some year-to-year fluctuation in the total output, and during the mid-thirties the policies of the AAA caused some drop in output. As a result of the lack of response of output to prices, when individuals in the economy have less income and the demand for agricultural products declines, prices must bear the brunt. Although there is less income to buy farm products, about the same quantity of such products is produced and sold. Their prices must therefore fall correspondingly, so that the same quantities can be bought with the lowered level of income. Correspondingly, when incomes increase, there is a rise in demand for agricultural goods that may be greater than the increase in output due to productivity increases. When this happens, prices must rise so that the increased amount of money available for purchase of agricultural products will equal the amount of agricultural goods available for purchase. Increases and decreases in the demand for agricultural products caused by changes in the level of activity of the economy are thus translated almost entirely into price changes, and employment and output are relatively unaffected.

Manufacturing Prices, Output, and Employment, 1929 to 1953. The pattern of prices, output, and employment for the manufacturing sector of the economy is very different from that for agriculture. The manufacturer must pay for the cost of wages and materials from the proceeds of the sale of his product. When demand for the product falls, the producer frequently finds that he would lose money if he were to keep on producing at the same level. The cost of the labor and materials might well exceed the total amount for which the final product could be sold were production to be maintained. A price will therefore exist below which the producer will not be willing to sell, and he will not produce more than will be bought at this price. A decline in activity (and incomes) in the economy leading to a fall in the demand for manufactured products will thus be translated partly into a decline in price and partly into a decline in output. Chart 10 shows the pattern of prices, output, and employment for the manufacturing sector of the economy. The fluctuation in output and employment is very much greater than the fluctuation in prices. The effect of increasing productivity can be seen in the greater rise in output than in employment after the depression. It should be noted, however, that the index of employment does not accurately reflect the true decline and increase in the amount of labor used in the economy. During the depression many people were employed on a part-time basis, whereas during the war not only were people fully employed but a great deal of overtime work was put in. For this reason the actual amount of labor utilized by the manufacturing industries fluctuated more than the employment index indicates.

The Interrelation among Industries in the Economy

Just as differences exist between agriculture and manufacturing in the pattern of their reactions to changes in the level of activity in the economy, so also within these industries and in other industries such

Chart 10. Prices, output, and employment in manufacturing, 1929–1953. 1947–1949 = 100. **Source:** Prices: 1929–1950, *Federal Reserve Bulletin*, March, 1952, p. 311. 1951–1953, *Federal Reserve Bulletin*, December, 1954, p. 1312. Employment: *Federal Reserve Bulletin*, December, 1954, p. 1297. Production: *Federal Reserve Bulletin*, December, 1954, p. 1297.

as trade and service, still different patterns result from the institutional organization of the economy. Public utilities and railroads, for example, behave differently from either the farmer or the manufacturer because of the problems involved in rate making and the existence of many different markets for their services. The corner grocery store may have a great deal in common with the farmer in that the proprietor has no employees beside himself so that employment cannot change, but on the other hand, changes in the cost of the goods sold may sometimes render infeasible the maintenance of a constant volume of sales.

No matter how differently the various sectors of the economy may react, however, it should not be forgotten that all the sectors are interrelated and form a part of one unified economic system. The wage earner in manufacturing purchases the agricultural goods produced by the farmer. The manufacturers themselves purchase agricultural goods as raw materials to use in their production. The farmers' income, derived from these purchases, is in turn spent on goods produced by the manufacturers and sold by the retailers. During a depression when prices of farm products fall greatly, wage earners need to spend less on food and so have more money left to spend on manufactured products. On the other hand, the fall in farm income means that farmers' ability to buy manufactured products is sharply curtailed. It is sufficient here to point out that these interrelationships do exist and should be kept in mind. Their importance and meaning can be evaluated only within a relevant framework of analysis. It is to the function of such a framework of analysis that attention shall now be directed.

The Meaning and Function of Income Analysis

The preceding section has served to point out that an economy may have short-run changes in the level of its activity fully as well as changes of a more evolutionary nature. Separation of the two types of changes is neither possible nor desirable; nevertheless, the illustration of these two aspects of change serves to show the setting of the problem of income analysis and helps to indicate what its role is conceived to be.

Income Analysis as Related to National Income Concepts

The term "income analysis" was used before the variety of national income concepts had been developed. It referred to the development of a theory relating the income of the economy to the level of economic activity. With the development of the national income concepts this theory has become an analysis of the process and mechanism by which the gross national product (or national income) changes level in the economy. Alternatively, such a theory has been called "income and employment theory" or the "theory of prices, output, and employment." All these titles serve to accent one fact: the elements to be analyzed are those which are contained in the national income accounts. Gross national product, for example, can be broken down into both the market value of current output and the allocations of such market value; implicit in both of these aspects are the prices, output, and employment of the economy. At different levels of economic activity, both the level of gross national product and the interrelation among the various elements in the economic system will be different. Income analysis attempts to describe the mechanism by which the gross national product changes with changes in economic activity and the way in which this mechanism in turn reacts on the level of activity.

The Relation between Income Analysis and the Causes of Changes in the Level of Economic Activity

Income analysis does not attempt to ascertain why a change in economic activity has taken place. During the period from 1942 to 1945, for instance, the level of activity in the economy changed primarily because of production for war purposes. But as far as income analysis is concerned, this knowledge of the underlying cause for the increased activity does not afford the desired answer. Questions still remain as to how the increased activity came about, how it affected the various elements in the economy, and how the level of increased activity was shaped by the economic mechanism. The problem of income analysis is one of explaining the operation of the mechanism of the economy rather than one of digging back to find the basic causes. There are many explanations of the causes of the depression of the thirties. Income analysis does not attempt to explain these causes, but rather it explains the process by which the economy went further into the depression and the way in which it recovered. The study of the causes of booms and depressions belongs to the field of business cycle theory, not to income analysis. This separation of business cycle theory from income analysis is useful, since the former is controversial and speculative whereas the latter is confined to the mechanistic aspects of the economic system about which economists in general are in agreement.

The Importance of Income Analysis

Analysis of the mechanism of economic change is important because of the well-recognized fact that any change in the level of activity, once started, may become cumulative. Income analysis would not be of very great importance if the economy were at all times entirely controlled by forces independent of itself. But this is far from being true; the economic mechanism may reinforce or limit the effects of any changes due to independent forces. Income analysis focuses attention on the nature of the economic mechanism and the role that this mechanism plays in the change in the level of economic activity; it is useful because it produces an understanding of how the economy operates. Such an understanding is essential if the implications of proposed policies are to be clear and if contradictory measures are not to be undertaken.

11. The United States Economy in Operation, 1929 to 1954

Before income analysis is introduced as a theoretical system, some consideration of what has taken place in the economy over the past twenty-five years will be useful. This presentation will not be a weighty consideration of all the detailed workings and ramifications of the economic system, but rather will try to paint in broad outline the history of the economy over the period. Furthermore, accent will not be laid on why things happened but instead on how they happened. By using such an approach this chapter will provide a background for the theoretical structure that will be given in the following chapters and at the same time will give empirical substance to the theory. Most of the material presented here is purely of a descriptive nature; for that reason it will have relevance after as well as before the presentation of income theory.

THE UNITED STATES ECONOMY IN THE TWENTIES

The Pattern of Economic Change

Many of the changes that took place in the economy after World War I graphically portrayed the nature of the evolutionary forces that were at work. Almost all sectors of the economy moved forward with improved technology and increased productivity. Gross national product in constant prices rose 46 per cent from 1920 to 1929. The people of the nation felt that the new era had dawned and that the future held only continued advances in wealth and abundance. The times were progressive in the sense that they were forward-looking and were willing to permit the forces of change and innovation to take hold. But reform was not carried out by correcting basic elements in the system; rather, the principles of "soundness" and mercifulness were followed. The nation was self-confident and felt that its growing wealth was justly due it. Harding, Coolidge, and Hoover all served their terms in quick succession—all assuring business that the government was its guardian and servant. Such a picture, however, does not adequately portray the course of economic development. The growth of the nation was not simply a general increase in everything; subtle changes were occurring, such that by 1929 the economy was strikingly different from that which existed in 1920.

Agriculture. Not all sectors of the economy responded to the new technology and increased productivity in a way that benefited those who worked in the industry. In agriculture the use of farm machinery, new fertilizers, and improved grains and stock had been increasing for some time. Abstracting from the price changes involved, the intermediate products consumed by the farm sector as a percentage of the value of output had increased from about 20 per cent in 1910 to 25 per cent in 1929. This of course meant that the value of farm output was rising faster than the gross product originating in the farm sector. Farmers were thus more dependent on the rest of the economy in their attempt to increase their productivity, but this process had not brought prosperity to the farmer. Ever since 1910 the movement of people from the farm to the city had been reducing the actual number of farmers, yet the smaller number of farmers had produced more agricultural goods than ever before. The cry of oversupply was raised, since consumers were not willing to purchase this larger amount of agricultural products unless the prices fell. Certainly from the consumers' point of view there were not too many agricultural goods; they were very happy to pay the lower prices and get more for their money. But from the farmers' point of view the situation was far from satisfactory; in comparison with industrial workers the farmers were underpaid for their efforts. Many farmers would have been more productive to society—and would have received higher incomes—had they been employed in other industries. The economy could use all the agricultural goods produced, but consumers would have preferred to have the resources used in producing these goods employed in other ways. Although consumers welcomed the lower prices and greater quantities of food, they would have welcomed lower prices and greater quantities of other goods even more. The depressed earnings of the farmers were not due to an actual oversupply of agricultural products but rather to a misallocation of the available resources of the country.

The shift of people away from agriculture did not provide very much relief to those remaining in the industry, since it was not rapid enough to keep pace with the increasing productivity. The amount supplied increased faster than the amount wanted at the going prices, so that prices had to fall. World War I, furthermore, delayed adjustment in agriculture by creating an abnormally high demand for its products, which increased the standard of living of farmers during the war period and shortly thereafter. After this abnormal demand had vanished, a substantial number of farmers who normally would have left the industry still remained in it—and the share of each was thereby made smaller than ever. The only satisfactory solution to the problem lay in an exodus of people from agriculture, but adjustment of this nature was difficult. People clung tenaciously to their past ways and endured hardship rather than take jobs in industry or business. As a result, agriculture remained on the whole unprofitable for those employed in it, in spite of the improving technology and productivity.

Manufacturing. In manufacturing the changes in technology and productivity had different repercussions. These repercussions were strikingly illustrated by the automobile industry, where new improvements were introduced in quick succession and output per man-hour rose by 40 per cent between 1923 and 1929. When allowance is made for the improved quality of the automobiles, production in this industry rose by 70 per cent, with the use of only 25 per cent more labor over this same period. The workers in the automobile industry did not benefit directly from the increased productivity; their average hourly earnings in money terms did not rise appreciably. Rather, with the fall in costs due to greater productivity, the manufacturers increased the quality of the product and reduced prices. The continued prosperity of the economy was reflected by the willingness of consumers to spend more and more money on automobiles, so that despite the huge increase in output, the demand for automobiles was not satiated.

Other manufacturing industries, though differing in detail, behaved in general quite similarly to the automobile industry. Employment increased slightly (less than 10 per cent), but the increase in productivity was such that output went up by about 30 per cent. The wage rate increased somewhat, but the major effect of this increased productivity was the gradual reduction of prices. The prosperity existed side by side with falling prices due to the increased productivity of the industries. The benefits were partly passed on to the workers in the form of new products and somewhat lower prices but not to any large extent in the form of increased wages.

Trade and Services. Under the impact of the increased productivity and output of agriculture and manufacturing other profound changes took place in the economy. There was a very considerable growth in the number of white-collar workers. With the huge increase in the amount of goods available, the economy permitted, and the increased output perhaps necessitated, a very large increase in the distributive trades. Between 1920 and 1930 sales forces almost doubled; this was due partly to an increase in the number of stores and partly to the increased size of stores. The professional and clerical white-collar groups also increased rapidly. More teachers, lawyers, engineers, and nurses were trained. Business hired more bookkeepers, secretaries, and cashiers. To a very large extent the white-collar classes absorbed the population increase and contributed their services to the increasing output of the nation.

It is interesting to speculate about the origins of these new classes and how they developed in the economic system. Many of the new services—distribution, packaging, advertising, etc.—were made possible without causing either an increase in prices or a lowering of earnings, because increased productivity had caused a sharp decrease in other costs of producers. Others of the services provided by these groups were rendered to the increasing number of higher income families; the number of domestic servants doubled, and there were extraordinarily large increases in the number of restaurants, laundries, insurance agents, and stockbrokers. America was coming of age.

Short-run Changes in the Twenties

In addition to the evolutionary changes that were taking place in the economy during the twenties, there were other changes that, though of a more short-run character, were nevertheless a very important part of the picture of the times. During World War I and immediately following it a sharp price inflation occurred. Prices in 1919 were almost double what they had been in 1914, and in 1920 they were driven even higher by people who expected even more price increases and attempted to increase their stocks of goods. The end to this process came in 1921, when prices fell and activity declined simultaneously. Prices dropped almost 50 per cent, and manufacturing output contracted 30 per cent, although the gross national product in constant prices did not drop more than about 10 per cent. The recession was short, however, and within a year output was back at its former level. The net effect of the fluctuation was only the readjustment of prices. After 1922 the period was one of prosperity; the slight fluctuations in activity in 1925 and 1927 went almost unnoticed. In agriculture weather conditions and world markets continued to vary the fortunes of farmers. Abundant crops forced the price of agricultural goods so low that there was hardship in the midst of plenty, and scarce crops sent it up again.

In keeping with the changed nature of the economy, the business sphere also took on new aspects during the twenties. The continued growth of corporations and holding companies created an intricate network of financial structures. In retrospect the stock-market dealings seem best to typify the spirit of the times. Except for the depression of 1921, the stock market moved continually upward throughout the period. To the vast majority of investors the purchase of securities was only partially a gamble. The problem seemed to be not one of choosing stocks that would go up; instead, it was one of choosing those which would go up most. Over this period almost all purchasers of securities gained; this gain was attributed at the time to the natural growth of the economic system. It is difficult to assess the importance of the stock market in the economy. During the boom economists and businessmen alike ascribed the rise in stock prices to the sound progress that the industrial firms were making in the economy. After the crash in 1929 the same people claimed that the depressed level of the stock market had little to do with the functioning of the economy. In all probability this last analysis is the more correct of the two. The stock-market phenomenon was an outgrowth of the period, but it was not necessarily a part of the basic evolution of the system. The dominant influences in the twenties were those forces which changed the nature of the economy; by 1929 the economic system of the United States was very different from what it had been ten years earlier.

THE DESCENT INTO DEPRESSION: 1930 TO 1932

The Process of Decline

Few signs existed in the first part of 1929 to indicate that the economy was on the brink of a disastrous depression. Manufacturing production had been rising fairly steadily throughout 1928 and early 1929. In the second half of 1929, however, distinct signs of the setting in of a decline appeared: from June to December there was a 20 per cent decline in the output of manufacturing industries, and in October the greatest stock-market crash in history occurred.

The Original Impetus. It is not the purpose of this description to suggest a cause for the initial decline that set off the depression. There are a great many conflicting explanations of the basic causes of the depression, but there is general agreement as to the course followed by the decline. The fall in manufacturing output was a reflection of the decline in purchases from manufacturers. In large part, manufacturers produce according to the orders that they receive from distributors. When jobbers, wholesalers, and retailers reduce their purchases, the manufacturer, afraid of being overstocked with output that is not in demand, curtails the level of his production to the amount that can be sold. The jobbers, wholesalers, and retailers in turn try to act as middlemen between the producers and the final purchasers. If the final purchasers stop buying a product, the jobbers, wholesalers, and retailers will stop ordering it for fear of an oversupply of goods that do not sell. With a fall of goods purchased fewer goods will be needed to replenish stocks, so that orders will be smaller. When a distributor looks forward to an additional decline in sales, furthermore, he may decide actually to reduce the volume of his stock in the expectation of a fall in prices.

The decline in manufacturing output thus reflects the decline in the amount of goods removed from the markets by the final purchasers. Final purchasers have already been defined in Part One of this book; they are (1) consumers, (2) government, (3) purchasers of producers' durables and inventories, and (4) foreign purchasers. A change in the amount these groups purchase is capable of having repercussions on the level of output in the economy. It does not follow from this, however, that observing the amount of goods which each of these groups purchased will indicate what caused the initial decline. All these groups, with the possible exception of the government, were highly sensitive to changes in the level of activity in the economy. The change in the amount each purchased might be either the cause or the result of the over-all change in level.

The Cumulative Decline. Although the origins of the depression can perhaps not be discovered, the immediate repercussions can be traced. In 1930 purchases contracted. The inventories of manufacturers did not increase so much as they had in 1929, and the inventories of both wholesalers and retailers contracted. The contraction in output was thus greater than the contraction in purchases. Goods did not pile up and so provide a lag between the decline in purchases and the corresponding decline in output; rather, the decline was more than passed on by the decline in inventories.

Production of fewer goods meant that less labor was needed, so payrolls were smaller. In 1930 disposable income was $74.4 billion, as contrasted to $83.1 billion the previous year. Consumers had less money to spend, so that consumers' expenditures dropped from $79.0 billion to $71.0 billion. The contraction of output thus contracted people's income; the cut in income decreased people's expenditures; and this in turn was translated into a further cut in output as demand dropped still further. This process obviously is self-perpetuating in that every decline in output reduces income and expenditures, which in turn further reduces the level of output and income. The result was that from $74.4 billion in 1930, disposable income dropped to $63.8 billion in 1931 and $48.7 billion in 1932. Consumers' expenditures also dropped, but not quite so much; in 1932 consumers' expenditures were actually in excess of disposable income. Before the depression consumers as a whole had saved almost $4 billion from their income each year; but as their incomes fell, they were forced to dig into their past savings and spend more than they received. In 1932 they dissaved almost $1 billion; i.e., they spent this much more than they received. To some extent this dissaving tended to limit the momentum of the downward movement.

Once it became apparent to business that a depression had set in, a further reaction took place. Many producers had been purchasing machinery and equipment to expand their plants or make new products. The decline in all parts of the economy and the lack of purchasing power in the hands of consumers made such expansion ill-advised. The depression was forcing producers to operate at far below their capacity, so additional capacity was unnecessary. Even replacements of machinery and equipment were postponed as much as possible. The construction industry also declined very sharply; businessmen could not be persuaded to erect new plants, and the market for houses was at a low ebb. The effect of all this was to reduce purchases of durable goods by producers from $15 billion in 1929 to about $3 billion in 1932, and as a result, both output and employment in these industries were sharply curtailed.

The price declines that took place as production contracted further intensified the movement downward because of their effect on inventories. Producers and distributors are very reluctant to purchase goods in the face of declining prices. Any goods that they hold decrease in value as prices go down, and by postponing purchases as long as possible, they can buy their materials and products more cheaply. For this reason demand fell still more and production was cut still further, so that more unemployment resulted and still less disposable income was available.

The Nature of the Economy in the Depression

For three long years economic conditions in the nation grew continually worse—not by gradual degrees but in a cumulative crash. By 1932 the economy was at a low ebb; unemployment had swelled to 13 million, and gross national product had dropped from the 1929 level of $104.4 billion to $58.5 billion. The effects of the depression had penetrated the economy to its core and presented many difficult problems of adjustment that had not existed in 1929.

Financial Problems of the Economy. The crash of the stock market in 1929 had carried with it a wave of bank suspensions, such that in 1931 over 1,500 banks were forced to close their doors. The economy was trying to get into a liquid position, and the only way that such liquidation could occur under the existing system was by a contraction of the huge credit structure which had been built up in the twenties. Bankruptcies and foreclosures were so widespread that it seemed as if the system would break down into chaos. In order to stem the disastrous effects of this liquidation, Hoover's administration in 1932 created the Reconstruction Finance Corporation. This organization had the power to make loans to banks, railroads, farmers, and business. The Federal Reserve System sought ways to make advances to banks that needed liquid funds by enlarging the discount facilities of the Federal Reserve banks to include the discounting of commercial paper, which until then had not been eligible. Efforts were made to forestall foreclosure and forced liquidation of business. Without doubt, the measures that were taken did help the economy to adjust to the contraction and upheaval taking place, but it is not at all evident that these measures did much to prevent the further financial complications of the deflationary process.

Patterns of Decline. Not all the economy was equally affected by the decline. As has been pointed out, agricultural output did not contract; as a result, the prices of agricultural goods collapsed, since consumers no longer had sufficient income to spend the same amount of money on food. Prices of farm products found their new level at the place where price was low enough for the total amount produced to be purchased by consumers with their reduced incomes. At this low level agricultural income was less than half of what it had been in 1929.

Different types of manufacturing responded quite differently. Some industries, such as steel and machine-tool production, were greatly affected by the very sharp decline in the demand for producers' durable goods. The output of steel fell by more than 75 per cent between 1929 and 1932, and the production of machine tools fell by about 85 per cent. Consumers' durable goods similarly declined sharply, since consumers could postpone their purchases of durable goods much more easily than they could do without food and shelter. Automobile production fell 70 per cent, and clock and watch production fell by 50 per cent. In the nondurable consumers' goods industries two different factors were at work. (1) The goods were very much more necessary than were consumers' durable goods. Consumers needed food and clothing more than they needed new automobiles and household appliances. (2) The decline in agricultural raw material prices reduced costs in the nondurable goods industries so that they were in a better position to lower their prices and thereby attract consumers' expenditures. The fall in boot and shoe production, for instance, did not exceed 17 per cent during the depression, and the fall in cotton-goods production was about 33 per cent.

The period from 1930 to 1932 thus was one of sharply declining output and employment. It demonstrates very well the manner in which an initial decline in output can produce a cumulative movement downward. The decrease in employment and income that accompanies a curtailment of output will lead to further reductions in output, and this in turn will have its repercussions, so that a continuous series of reactions are set in motion. In addition, the decline in output discourages the purchase of producers' durable goods, and this in turn has its repercussions on output and employment. Finally, the price decline, with a prospect of further decline, induces producers and distributors to reduce their holdings of goods and materials to a minimum. The economy attempts to use up goods produced in the past rather than produce currently all that it uses. All these elements help to produce the cumulative movement of the economy. The decline in output generates further declines in output by causing unemployment; once a decisive movement downward is started, the contraction in purchases of producers' durable goods and inventories will further accentuate the decline.

THE GRADUAL RECOVERY: 1933 TO 1940

The Turning Point: 1933

The depression continued into 1933. In many lines of production output declined through the first quarter of this year, but by the latter part of 1933 the path upward had definitely started. By the end of 1933 output and employment in manufacturing had increased by 30 per cent over their lowest level and reached the level at which they had been in mid-1931. Total employment did not increase so fast, and with the growth of the labor force, actual unemployment was reduced by only 1 or 2 million. Nevertheless, disposable income increased from $45.7 billion in 1933 to $52 billion in 1934, so that more income was available for consumers' expenditures. The rise in consumers' income increased the demand for agricultural products, so that there was a substantial rise in their prices. The cumulative process of the upward movement had started.

Although the exact causes underlying this change in the level of activity cannot be identified, it should be realized that by this time many of the forces which had been depressing the economy had lost their strength. Primary among these forces was the decline in purchases of producers' durables. The amount of the nation's output that was purchased by producers had dropped from $16 billion in 1929 to less than $1 billion in 1932. Producers practically stopped buying machinery and equipment, construction was at a low ebb, and inventories declined. The time came, however, when producers' purchases on capital account were so near zero that they could not decline further and inventories were so low that they could not be reduced any more. When this happened, a very great deflationary force in the economy ceased to exist. Declining purchases of producers' durables could not reduce output further, since for all practical purposes these purchases had ceased to exist. If total expenditures in the economy were to decline any more, either the expenditures of the government or the expenditures of consumers would have to decline. There had been relatively little change in government expenditures. Consumers' expenditures had declined almost entirely because of the decline in disposable income. As the depression became more severe, people used their past savings to maintain to some extent the level of consumers' expenditures, and the cumulative movement downward was to some degree slowed down.

Other sources of expenditures had a regenerative influence on the economy in 1933. Producers had postponed all possible expenditures during the period 1930 to 1932, and a point was finally reached when further postponement of maintenance and replacements was not feasible if production was to continue even at the existing low level. During 1933 there were increases in the sales of such producers' durable equipment as mining machinery, metalworking machinery, farm machinery, railroad and transit equipment, and business motor vehicles. In all probability these increased purchases represented necessary maintenance rather than actual improvement in the industry. Other producers' durable equipment continued to decline in 1933. Less construction machinery, electrical apparatus, and office equipment was purchased; these were lines of goods in which maintenance was not so important. Also, by 1933 producers had contracted their inventories to the point beyond which sales could no longer be made from goods on hand. After stocks had been reduced to a minimum, the maintenance of the same volume of sales required an increase in the orders to producers and to sellers of raw materials, so that a definite stimulus to increased activity was provided.

In discussing the turning point of 1933, or for that matter any turning point of activity, it should be kept in mind that many other influences will affect the operations of the economy. The size of agricultural crops, the political climate and its effect on businessmen's expectations, and the many different aspects of government actions, among other things, will all be important for the economic outlook of the country, and any explanation that does not consider these is not complete. However, since this chapter is not intended to explore the causal forces behind the changes that took place in the economy but instead to examine the economic processes of change, no attempt will be made to take forces of this nature into account.

The Initial Recovery: 1934 to 1937

The recovery after the beginning of the upturn was not so rapid as the descent into the depression had been. Although by the middle of

1937 both industrial production and the number of persons employed were as high as they had been in 1929, there still remained 5 million unemployed in the country, and the economy was not operating at full capacity. Productivity in manufacturing had increased by about 20 per cent, but the growth of the labor force resulting from the increase in population had not yet been absorbed.

As early as 1933 the government had made attempts to help the economy out of the depression, but the part these efforts played in the upward movement is not entirely clear. The bank holiday of 1933 and the subsequent measures taken to support the banking system were probably of very real aid in creating confidence. The National Industrial Recovery Act was an attempt to help business stave off the deflationary price slump and keep wages up. Although it had a turbulent existence, its effectiveness as a recovery measure is doubtful. The Agricultural Adjustment Act of 1933 attempted to curtail agricultural output, so that the farmer would receive higher prices for his output. Since a small contraction in the supply of agricultural products would cause a relatively large price increase, it was reasoned —probably correctly—that the total income of the farmer would be increased if the total supply of farm products were smaller. Such action would give the farmer more money to spend, but at the same time it must be remembered that consumers in general would have to pay higher prices for food products, so that they would have less to spend on other goods. It is extremely doubtful if this program actually stimulated recovery, although it did improve the position of the farmer relative to that of the wage earner. The Works Progress Administration, finally, was a program of work relief. In that it gave people income they would not otherwise have had, it stimulated consumers' expenditures. This program was insignificant in size until 1936, when it amounted to somewhat over $2 billion. In evaluating its importance as an aid to recovery at that time, the effect of the program on wage rates and on businessmen's expectations must also be considered.

The actual mechanism of recovery was strikingly similar to that of the decline, except that, of course, the mechanism worked in reverse. When new orders induced producers to expand their level of output, they hired more labor, more income was made available to consumers, and consumers in turn increased their expenditures. The increase in consumers' expenditures caused an increase in orders from producers, and producers were induced to expand further and hire still more labor. The process is a cumulative one, which continues to grow of its own momentum in just the reverse of the way that it did when the descent downward was in progress.

Once the movement upward was started, some industries were enabled to expand their capacity profitably in spite of the fact that industry as a whole was still operating at far below capacity. This was especially true of industries such as the electric refrigerator industry, which had scarcely existed in 1929. At the beginning of the upward movement this industry felt strongly the impact of increased demand resulting from the increase in consumer purchasing power. In some fields certain purchases of capital equipment were necessary with any revival of activity. In other fields the advance in technology forced the purchase of new equipment to meet the competition of other producers.

In the face of growing demand there were, inevitably, price rises, especially in agricultural goods. Just as inevitably, producers and distributors altered their attitudes about the holding of inventories. With rising prices and increasing demand there seemed to be good reason to order more goods than were currently being purchased. Merchants who had previously been disgorging goods and glutting the market began to order goods in expectation of future increases in demand and future price rises. The rate of production thus exceeded the current rate at which goods were being taken from the market. In this way inventory accumulation provided a stimulus to output and employment over and above that induced by current expenditures.

The analogies between the processes by which an economy descends into a depression and the processes by which it recovers from a depression cannot be extended to the length of time that these processes take. The descent that occurred from 1930 to 1932 was much sharper than was the partial recovery that took place from 1934 to 1937. One factor that would at least partially explain this difference is the psychology of individuals' reactions. Conservative business practice and the policy of playing safe make people attempt to consolidate their position during the descent into a depression with much greater rapidity than they would be induced to seek gain aggressively in the recovery period. Fear of loss produces a faster reaction than the hope of gain. It is therefore not always justifiable to consider the forces influencing the descent into a depression and those influencing the recovery from it as symmetrical.

The Recession of 1938 and the Prewar Period 1939 to 1940

The recovery that had started in the latter half of 1933 was interrupted in the third quarter of 1937 by a convulsive movement downward. In two months unemployment rose from 5 million to over 9 million. In the early months of 1938 it reached almost 12 million. Manufacturing output fell off by 40 per cent from the peak it had reached in 1937. In many ways the economy was back where it had been in 1934. The same process of descent that had occurred before repeated itself, but there were some differences. Producers reduced their expenditures on durable goods, and inventories declined, but disposable income was only 8 per cent lower than it had been at the peak in 1937. This peculiarity is partly explainable by the fact that in most industries hourly earnings continued to rise throughout the recession, so that the increased rates of pay compensated somewhat for the reduction in the number of hours worked.

As has been indicated earlier, it is not the purpose of this description to suggest causes for the 1938 recession or explain all its individual peculiarities. There is a considerable amount of controversy among economists as to the initiating factors in this contraction, but the way in which the economy reacted is generally undisputed. The contraction that occurred between the third quarter of 1937 and the middle of 1938 operated by much the same mechanism as that of 1930 to 1932. Unemployment, resulting from a decline in output, made less income available for consumers. Consumers' expenditures therefore declined, and this decline in consumers' expenditures resulted in further cutbacks in production. The period of descent into the recession was shorter and did not result in so sharp a contraction; but it should be remembered that, unlike 1929, the economy was still not operating at full employment in 1937.

In the period from mid-1938 until the latter part of 1940 economic conditions improved gradually; throughout this whole period unemployment never dropped to the level it had reached in 1937. The size of the labor force and productivity had increased, however, so that gross national product in 1947 dollars was $172 billion in 1940, in comparison with $149 billion in 1929 and $154 billion in 1937; the economy was not at full capacity, yet it was producing more goods than ever before. Although the population had increased so that per capita disposable income was significantly lower, this smaller amount represented more real goods per capita because of the fall in the cost of living. The farmer, as well as the employed wage earner, was better off than he had been in 1929. There were 15 per cent fewer farmers than there had been in 1929, and these farmers were producing about 10 per cent more farm products. Farm prices generally were lower than they had been in 1929, but these lower prices were partially compensated for by the fact that prices of manufactured commodities were also somewhat lower.

Thus the economy, even though it was not operating at full capacity, had achieved just before World War II a higher level of output than ever before. The high level of output was the result of the evolutionary changes that were taking place in productivity; with regard to the short-run changes in the level of activity, the economy still had not recovered fully from the depression.

THE ECONOMY IN WORLD WAR II AND THE POSTWAR PERIOD: 1941 TO 1954

The industrial mobilization of the United States economy during World War II was unparalleled in its vast productive achievement. In order to bring about such mobilization unprecedented changes in the economic and governmental structure were necessary. So large a change in the level of activity and the capacity of the nation had never before occurred in so short a time, and the manner in which it took place reveals a great deal about the operation of the economy. Although the war production was carried out on the initiative of the government, it still had to be fitted into the framework of the economic system.

The Early Defense Program

As early as 1939 significant steps were taken toward national defense. In September of that year the War Resources Board was created to review the Army and Navy plans for defense. By May, 1940, after the successful offensives of the Germans, it became evident that preparation for national defense and support of the Allies was imperative, and the National Defense Advisory Commission was formed to help carry out the defense program. The duty of the commission was primarily to help the Army and Navy obtain their requirements from the peacetime economy. By January, 1941, it was obvious that this informal arrangement would be inadequate for the increasing magnitude of the program. There was no integration between the Army and Navy defense programs and the munitions orders that had been placed by the British and other Allied countries. In certain lines bottlenecks due to insufficient raw materials and plant capacity began to appear, and with them they brought the problems of priorities and coordination. For this reason the Office of Production Management was established, and the real task of mobilizing the economy was begun.

During 1941 there was a constant acceleration of war expenditures, and these increasing expenditures provided a great stimulus to the economy. The government spent more than $13 billion for war purposes; this was more than the total amount spent in the previous year for producers' durable equipment. These war expenditures not only stimulated producers directly by providing increased orders; they further provided an indirect stimulus through the increased disposable income that resulted from them. Because consumers had more income, they spent more money, and this increased expenditure had the usual cumulative expansionary effect.

Early in 1941 the production of some goods became insufficient to meet both the government demand and the increasing current demand of the private sector of the economy. This was especially true of the production of basic metals, where capacity was quickly reached and expansion was a slow process. Such a situation naturally led to a rise in prices, since the supply of the commodity was limited while the demand for it increased rapidly. The purchasers bid against one another for the limited supply until those who were not able to pay the higher price dropped from the market. The OPM material distribution system proved to be incapable of coping with this problem, and in August, 1941, the Supply Priorities and Allocations Board was set up in addition. The function of this new organization was to allocate resources among the military, defense aid, and civilian portions of the economy and to provide greater integration among the already existing government controls. In conjunction with this, price controls were extended to certain scarce commodities to prevent price rises that would have occurred in the face of the then current shortages. For different commodities the problem was handled in different ways. Where it was apparent that the increase in prices would not stimulate increased supply, price ceilings were adopted. In other situations premium payment plans were designed so that producers were paid the ceiling price for all output up to a certain amount and an additional premium for output in excess of this amount. In one or two instances (such as in aluminum production) price ceilings were actually adjusted downward when the increased output of the plants caused costs to drop off sharply. The first restriction of civilian goods production occurred in the automobile industry, where the increasing rate of production had been consuming more and more scarce steel. Early in 1941 the automobile industry consented to restrict its production by 20 per cent on a voluntary basis, but by August it was apparent that a cut of at least 45 per cent would be needed, and mandatory curtailment was adopted. Shortly after this time curtailment of production in order to conserve steel was extended to the farm-machinery and equipment producers.

It is very significant that the economy was not at full employment by the middle of 1941, yet bottlenecks and shortages in certain lines were so prevalent that complicated methods of control and allocation had to be instituted. Basic metals production was not the only bottleneck; the shortage of machine tools prevented the rapid expansion of the aircraft industry, and priority systems had to be set up in this field at a very early stage. The volume of defense production rose rapidly during 1941, but the increasing requirements made output lag far behind what was needed. The production schedules that were adopted did not reflect the potential productive power of the economy but rather the fact that growth could not take place overnight. Bottlenecks had to be removed and capacity had to be extended before the nation could move further in the direction of specialized war production.

The Growth of War Production

After Pearl Harbor an intensive program of war production was laid out. With the creation of the War Production Board, an attempt was made to provide more complete controls over the allocation of goods and to set in force a program of expanding plant facilities in the economy. The rapidly growing fabricating industries made necessary considerable expansion in the facilities for producing raw materials. Besides the very large expansion in the steel industry, tremendously increased facilities for the production of aluminum were needed to supply the material for the air armada that had been scheduled. Synthetic rubber plants were needed to make up the deficiency caused by the curtailment of natural rubber supplies, and aviation gasoline had to be produced on a scale hitherto unanticipated. In addition, other types of facilities had to be constructed or converted for carrying out the fabrication aspects of the munitions program. Dry docks and ship-construction facilities were needed for the scheduled shipbuilding program. Aircraft assembly plants had to be constructed, and many subcontractors throughout the country had to convert to war production. The army needed to build camps, bases, and supply depots. During 1942 over half of the government expenditure on war production was in the form of construction, facilities, and equipment. The impact of the war program was felt first by those sectors of the economy which were concerned with construction and the production of machines and equipment.

Employment reacted somewhat more slowly to the increased war expenditures, although by the middle of 1942 civilian employment equaled the total number in the labor force before the war. This is all the more remarkable because the Army had by this time already drafted a part of the labor force, and over 2 million people were still unemployed. The answer to this paradox lies in the fact that there was a substantial increase in the number of people who were induced to enter the labor force. Under the stimulus of changed conditions by mid-1942, over 3 million people had entered the labor force who had not been in it before. Housewives took jobs in factories, retired people went back to work, and those who were about to retire continued work. The war conditions had made many more people willing to work. Some were induced to work for patriotic motives; others were induced to work by the ease of getting a job and the high rate of pay. The wives of drafted soldiers often took jobs that they would not have held were it not for the fact that their husbands were away from home. The expansion of civilian employment continued in 1943, in spite of the increased number of men being drafted into the Army. By the end of 1944 civilian employment plus the number of men in the armed services exceeded the total prewar labor force by 11 million people, and unemployment had been reduced to about half a million.

During the war the number of people that were willing to work increased very sharply with the increase in the level of activity of the economy. For this reason it is difficult to say just when the economy reached full employment or if it was operating at more than a full employment level during the peak of the war production. In a less pronounced way it is probably true that the number of people willing to seek employment in the economy is always somewhat dependent on the availability of jobs and the rate of pay. Since the level of activity in an economy in itself is a factor affecting the size of the labor force, the term "full employment" loses precision in its meaning.

The Change in Gross National Product

The magnitude of the war production program at its peak can be appreciated only by viewing it in over-all terms. Examination of specific munitions items does not throw much light on the productive ability of the nation at peak war production in comparison with the volume of civilian production prior to the war. By 1944 gross national product in 1947 prices had risen to $268 billion, as compared with about $172 billion in 1940. Consumers were getting fewer durable goods, but they were getting more nondurable goods and services, so that their total expenditures expressed in constant dollars rose by about 11 per cent. The government had increased its expenditures (in 1947 dollar terms) from about $24 billion to $127 billion—an amount greater in magnitude than the whole of the gross national product in the depression years of 1932, 1933, and 1934.

It is important to note, however, that in spite of the huge demand created by the war, gross national product did not reach its peak until the last quarter of 1944. It took the economy three years to reach peak output. It was not sufficient that the demand for goods existed in the economy; it took time to bring about the greatest possible fulfillment of this demand.

The magnitude of war production sharply reveals the limited extent to which the prewar economy was utilizing its potential capacity. Chart 11 shows that the war production was primarily an addition to, rather than a substitution for, the civilian production that had been taking place in the prewar period. This chart shows the level of the various components of expenditure for gross national product in constant

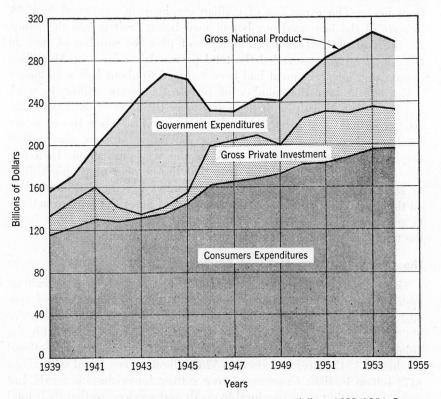

Chart 11. Components of gross national product in constant dollars, 1939–1954. **Source:** 1939–1953, *National Income*, U.S. Department of Commerce, 1954 ed., pp. 216–217. 1954, *Survey of Current Business*, February, 1955, p. 8.

dollars for the period 1939 to 1954. Total consumers' expenditures rose almost continually throughout the period, and government nonwar expenditures decreased very little if at all. Private capital formation declined almost to nothing during the peak of the war production, but here it must be remembered that much of what is classified as war outlay was expenditure for durable producers' goods. All in all, in spite of the price rise, the economy continued to be almost as well off in terms of nonwar production and, in addition, turned out the huge volume of war production.

In many ways war production is not comparable to civilian production. Before the war many workers were employed in agriculture and service industries, where machinery and mass-production techniques are not used to any large extent. In producing war munitions they were employed at tasks that utilized such techniques, so their output per man-hour rose substantially. In a peacetime economy, however, it may well be more desirable to employ these people at their former tasks, even though the apparent output per man-hour may be lower. An economy organized for civilian production may not afford the same opportunity for the use of mass-production techniques that is present in the tremendous volume of war output. In other words, technical processes may permit a larger amount of munitions output than of civilian goods output. Nevertheless, it is still true that the level of activity during World War II was at an all-time high.

War Finance, Price Control, and Rationing

The need for financing the war expenditures, together with the cumulative repercussions of the change in the level of activity in the economy, brought with it a host of complicating problems during this period. The level of Federal government expenditures in current dollars in 1944 was $89 billion, compared with the prewar expenditures of about $5 billion. Funds to finance these expenditures had to be obtained, and the two possible sources were taxation of producers and consumers and the borrowing of money through the sale of government bonds. The government used taxation to procure a large part of the needed funds, and the remainder was borrowed. Consumers were urged to purchase as many war bonds as they could; a substantial quantity were sold to businesses; and the rest were sold to banks, which through the expansion of credit created sufficient funds.

When the government made expenditures on war goods, individuals received a great deal more money as income. More people were employed, and it became necessary to pay higher wages to attract workers into the war industries. The total amount of wages and salaries paid in the nation increased steadily. In 1941 individuals received about $62 billion in wages and salaries. This increased to $82 billion in 1942, to $106 billion in 1943, and finally to $117 billion in 1944. The income of proprietors and property owners rose from $21 billion in 1941 to $35 billion in 1944. Thus both employees and owners received more income. The production of civilian goods could not increase similarly, so that the quantity of goods available to be purchased was limited. The normal reaction in such a situation would have been for prices to have risen until all expendable income had been absorbed. The price increase would not have been restricted only to an amount sufficient to absorb the increased income that actually existed in 1942, 1943, and 1944. Had the price increases been permitted, the sellers of consumers' goods would have had a great deal more income, which would have become available for further purchases, so that a cumulative price rise over and above the initial price rise would have been started. Such a reaction not only would have permitted some individuals to profiteer at the expense of others but might very well have endangered the war effort as well.

In order to prevent the increasing volume of war expenditures from having such a disastrous inflationary effect on the economy, the government undertook four basic programs: (1) heavy taxation, (2) bond selling, (3) price control on consumers' commodities, and (4) rationing of some consumers' commodities. Heavy taxation took a much larger portion of individuals' income during the war than it had before; in 1941 personal tax receipts ($3 billion) were only 3 per cent of individuals' income, but by 1944 these receipts ($19 billion) had increased to 13 per cent of individuals' income. By this means the government hoped to absorb a portion of the newly created income and thus narrow the gap that existed between the value of the goods available at existing prices and the value of the funds that consumers had to spend. The selling of bonds, especially to consumers, was another way of absorbing some of this increased purchasing power. By absorbing individuals' income the payroll savings plan left less income in their hands to spend. To reduce inflationary pressures it was preferable to sell bonds to people who would have otherwise spent that much more. Selling bonds to banks and to people with higher incomes who would have saved the money anyway gave the government funds, but it did not reduce consumers' expenditures and so did not aid in suppressing inflation. But these two measures were not sufficient to remove enough funds from the hands of the consumers to prevent commodity shortages. There was still more income in the hands of consumers than there were goods available to be bought with this money at the existing prices. Price control was therefore necessary in order to prevent the cumulative effects of price rises. Rationing was instituted to make sure that each consumer would get his fair share of those goods which were available, since there were not enough to give everyone as much as he could buy. Under these conditions the personal saving of individuals mounted rapidly. In 1941 disposable income ($93 billion) had been only $11 billion in excess of consumers' expenditures, but in 1944 disposable income ($147 billion) was $37 billion in excess of consumers' expenditures; personal saving had increased from 12 per cent of disposable income to over 25 per cent. The war economy was a controlled economy, but such controls were necessary in order to obtain the allocation of resources to war production in sufficient volume and to prevent the cumulative reactions of the change in the level of activity from causing a major economic upheaval. Knowledge of the basic processes and mechanisms by which the economy operates was essential to intelligent control of the war economy.

The Period of Reconversion and the Postwar Economy

The problems that had accompanied the increases in war production caused many people to fear the reconversion period, when the government's war expenditures would be cut down. It was felt that the stoppage of production in the war plants would cause so much unemployment that, via the cumulative effects on disposable income and consumers' expenditures, a depression would necessarily follow. In spite of the fact that the government cut war production drastically in the last quarter of 1945, however, the anticipated decline did not occur. The major reasons probably lay in the extreme shortages of consumers' goods and the accumulated purchasing power of consumers, which provided a strong market for such goods.

The period of reconversion did not immediately let loose a flood of consumers' goods upon the economy. Producers had to change over their factories and obtain materials with which to start production. In many cases the higher stages of production could not take place until there were sufficient supplies at the more basic levels. But because producers immediately embarked on reconversion programs, the decline in employment was small and was mostly limited to the frictional unemployment caused by the shift. Disposable income and consumers' expenditures continued to increase steadily. The increased consumers' expenditures and the increased volume of producers' expenditures on durable goods in large measure substituted for the decline in government expenditures. The decline in gross national product in constant dollars was less than 15 per cent from its wartime peak, and the amount of goods purchased by consumers increased steadily.

With the end of the war came a demand that the various wartime controls be relaxed. The need for operating a war economy had passed, and it was argued that the controls prevented the establishment of a free economy. Rationing on most items had been abolished as the particular commodities had become more plentiful, but price control still remained on most consumers' commodities. The removal of price control in the middle of 1946 was followed by a very sharp price rise; food prices increased by one-third in six months, and clothing and house furnishings increased by one-eighth. Although production of consumers' goods increased during this period, it did not increase fast enough to absorb the large volume of purchasing power that was available.

The removal of price control did not immediately lead to a spurt in production. Gross national product in constant prices was no higher in 1947 than it had been in 1946. The 2 per cent gain in the volume of consumers' goods purchased was offset by the decline in government expenditures. Disposable income continued to rise sharply in the immediate postwar period, but this did not bring with it an increased volume of personal saving. In 1944 personal saving had totaled almost $37 billion out of a total disposable income of $147 billion; by 1947, however, individuals were saving only $4 billion out of a disposable income of $169 billion. Higher prices and greater availability of goods had either forced or induced consumers to spend more of their incomes. Many individuals were probably using the savings that they had accumulated during the war to purchase consumers' durable goods which they had been unable to buy, or to meet the higher costs of living. Veterans just starting out had to make heavy outlays for clothing and household goods, and these outlays may well have exceeded their current incomes. By 1948, however, personal saving again rose as the cash balances of many individuals were depleted and they were forced to live within their incomes.

In 1949 the rapid rise in prices that had been taking place came to an end, and in its stead there was a slight fall in prices accompanied by a significant decline in gross national product in current prices. Each quarter in 1949 showed some decline over the previous quarter, but the cumulative decline did not amount to more than 5 per cent, and gross national product in constant prices did not show any appreciable change. The number of full-time equivalent employees dropped by over 1 million between 1948 and 1949, from 47.8 million to 46.6 million. Although personal income actually decreased in this period, personal taxes and personal saving also decreased, with the result that consumers' expenditures continued to increase. Government expenditures also showed an increase; the major decline was in inventories. During 1948 inventories had increased by over $4 billion; in 1949 inventories decreased by almost $3 billion. The decline in the level of economic activity has thus been considered by many to have been an inventory readjustment.

By 1950 production was on its way up again. In June, 1950, the outbreak of hostilities in Korea triggered increases in consumers' expenditures, government expenditures, and purchases of producers' durables. Prices as well as production increased over the next few years; gross national product in current prices rose 39 per cent, and gross national product in constant prices 12 per cent, over the period from 1949 to 1954.

It is not possible to predict just what the future course of economic events will be. Minor declines in the level of economic activity continue to occur in our economic system. Whether such declines will always be of a minor nature, to be followed by a continued expansion of a peace-time economy, or whether they may result in a significant decline in the level of economic activity such as that of the thirties, cannot be told in advance. The one fact they do indicate, however, is that the course of economic events in the future will not be without its uncertainties and fluctuations. Furthermore, the very nature of political instability in the present period may bring many pressures from outside forces to bear upon the economy.

Summary

Changes in the level of economic activity may be brought about by a variety of causes, but the repercussions of all such causes on the economy will always operate through prices, output, and employment. Furthermore, the process by which an economy changes level will in turn have cumulative repercussions on itself, so that once started, it may continue in the same direction by feeding on itself. The period 1929 to 1954 amply illustrates the meaning of changes in the level of economic activity, and the examination of this period reveals the inter-dependence among income, expenditures, output, and employment. The following chapters will attempt to weave all these elements into a coherent explanation of the economic processes involved.

12. The Basic Concepts of Income Analysis

Income analysis, as has been indicated previously, does not attempt to explain the causes of changes in the level of economic activity. Rather, it explains the process by which such changes take place. In this chapter attention will be focused upon the nature and role of the economic mechanism in income analysis. Certain reactions and relationships in the economy must be understood before it is possible to explain fully what takes place during a downswing or upswing.

THE EFFECT OF CHANGES IN EXPENDITURES ON THE PRICES AND OUTPUT OF PRODUCERS

The Producers' Account and Changes in Expenditure

A logical starting point for the study of economic processes is the Gross National Income and Product Account that was developed in Part One. The totals in this account are the gross national income and the gross national product; they are equal to the total market value of all goods produced in the economy. The two sides of this account show two different aspects of total production. On the right-hand side the sales made to various groups in the economy and the change in inventories are shown; the change in inventories represents the difference between the production that has taken place and the total amount that has been sold. The left-hand side shows the costs and profits related to the creation of the gross national product: the allocation of the total market value of production. Table 54 shows the Gross National Income and Product Account for 1953 as it was given in Table 26, Chap. 5.

The sales to the various groups shown on the right-hand side of the Gross National Income and Product Account have a significance beyond that of simply showing the disposition of part of the total production. Expenditures by these groups may to a very large extent determine the magnitude of the gross national product. The reason for their im-

Table 54. Gross National Income and Product Account, 1953

(In billions)

Allocations		Sources	
1. Payments by producers to individuals...........................	$281.9	6. Consumers' expenditures........	$229.6
2. Income retained by producers....	35.1	7. Government expenditures (net)..	77.2
3. Tax payments by producers......	54.4	8. Gross expenditures on producers' durables...............	51.6
4. Minus: Subsidies and government interest......................	7.6	9. Net change in inventories.......	1.5
5. Statistical discrepancy...........	1.0	10. Exports and property income received......................	21.3
		Subtotal......................	$381.2
		11. Minus: Imports and property income paid....................	16.4
Gross national income............	$364.9	Gross national product............	$364.9

SOURCE: See Table 21.

portance lies in the reaction of producers to changes in expenditures and the resulting effect on inventories. When expenditures on goods and services contract, it does not follow that the inventories in the hands of producers will increase. For the most part, producers hold inventories as a necessary part of their business; inventories are not simply the goods produced in excess of what people wish to buy. With a contraction in expenditures for specific goods, producers holding inventories of these goods, far from allowing these inventories to pile up, may even try to contract their holdings if they anticipate worse conditions in the future. They can accomplish this either by cutting output or by reducing prices to induce purchasers to buy more. Similarly, an increase in expenditures for specific goods above the level of current production will not necessarily result in a drain of the stock of these goods in the hands of producers; the increase in expenditures may well convince producers that the market for such goods is very strong, so that they will be led to increase output or to raise prices. When the volume of expenditures changes, therefore, inventories will not necessarily reflect the change. The change in expenditures will have a direct effect on the level of gross national product, and the change in inventories will tend to reinforce this effect rather than to reduce it. If the amount spent by various groups in the economy is reduced, the gross national product will fall by the same amount and, in addition, by any decline in inventories.

The Reaction of Producers to Changes in Expenditures

Since gross national product is the total output of the economy valued at market prices, it follows that when gross national product declines, prices and/or output must have declined. In actual practice it can be shown that when there is a fall in expenditures, both prices and output will decline. The factors governing the specific reactions of producers are quite different for different parts of the economy.

Farm Products. A fall in expenditures for farm products will not ordinarily result in a contraction of output. The impact of the decrease in the volume of expenditures will be absorbed by a decline in prices, and output will be maintained. Two circumstances account for this reaction on the part of the farmer. (1) An individual farmer usually produces only a very small part of the total output of a given agricultural product, and any contraction of his output would have practically no effect on the going market price. The farmer is thus forced to accept this going market price; he can only decide how much he will produce at that price. (2) The cost conditions under which the farmer produces are such that it will be to his advantage to maintain his output even though prices for his products may fall quite far. The amount that a farmer produces does not influence his costs very much. Were he to reduce his output to half, he might save some money on seed, fertilizer, and gasoline for his tractor; but since these out-of-pocket costs are such a small percentage of the value of his product, the amount he would thus save would not compensate him for cutting the total value of his production by 50 per cent. The farmer will maintain his output because any curtailment in it would reduce his income more than it would reduce his costs. Prices could fall a great deal before the farmer would be forced to sell his crops for an amount below his out-of-pocket costs; and as long as he gets some return above these costs, he will keep his output up.

Even for farmers who raise livestock or do dairy farming a decline in expenditures will tend to cause prices to fall far more than it will restrict output. The mechanism in this case is somewhat more elaborate, since the feed costs of dairy farmers and livestock raisers represent a large percentage of the total market value of their products, and it would seem at first glance that prices could not fall very far before the farmer would be paying out more for feed than he would be receiving for his products. However, if these livestock and dairy farmers were to contract the amount of feed they purchase, their action would have immediate repercussions on the price of grain. As was pointed out above, when expenditures on grain decline, its production will be maintained but its price will fall to the point where the total supply will be consumed by the economy. A fall in the price of grain is a fall in the costs of livestock and dairy farmers, so they can continue production at lower prices than they could before. The output of livestock and dairy farmers will thus tend to be maintained at a constant level in the face of a decline in expenditures, because the price of feed (their chief out-of-pocket cost) will fall as low as is necessary to secure the consumption of a relatively constant amount of it.

When there is an increase in expenditures on agricultural products, the major reaction similarly centers about price. Agricultural prices rise to the point at which all the increased expenditures are absorbed by the price rise; the purchasers merely pay higher prices for the same amount of agricultural products. The farmer does not expand his output when prices rise; he was already producing all he could, and he will continue to do so.

The long-run effects of changes in expenditures for agricultural products may be different from those described above. If expenditures on agricultural products contract over a long period, the depressed state of prices and consequently of farmers' income will drive people away from the farm and into other industries; and similarly, when there is an increase in demand, the high income of the farmer will induce people to leave less well-paid employment in other industries to take up farming. These reactions do not occur in the short run for several reasons. (1) There is a considerable amount of immobility between occupations that are as different as farming and, say, manufacturing; the shift of individuals from one occupation to another occurs only slowly over a long period of time. (2) The lowest prices for agricultural products and thus the lowest farm incomes occur in depressions, when it is not possible for farmers to leave the farm and get jobs elsewhere. In a depression unemployment is widespread in the economy; and if the farmer left his farm, he would only add to the mass of the unemployed. He is better off to continue farming; for although his income from farming may be low, it is higher than it would be if he were totally unemployed. In prosperous times, on the other hand, there are corresponding forces that prevent an increase in the number employed in agriculture. Employment opportunities in other industries are numerous, and wages are rising, so that the marginal workers may not be any more attracted by the relatively high income in farming than they are by other opportunities that present themselves. In the short run, therefore, a change in expenditures on agricultural products will not change the number of people engaged in agriculture greatly. It will have its impact largely on agricultural prices rather than on agricultural output.

Manufactured Products. A fall in expenditures for manufactured products usually does not produce the same reaction that a fall in expenditures for agricultural products does. The manufacturer is ordinarily in a position quite different from that of the producer of farm products. In contrast to the farmer, the manufacturer frequently sells in a market where the price for which he can sell his product bears a direct relation to the amount of his output. He can increase his output only at the expense of lowering his price; and if he contracts his output, he may be able to sell all of it for a higher price. When there is a decline in expenditures for his product, therefore, he has the alternative either of maintaining his price and contracting his output or else of lowering his price and maintaining his output. The cost situation of the manufacturer, again in contrast to the farmer, is usually such that he will be led to a price-output policy involving some lowering of price, together with some contraction of output. The out-of-pocket costs of most manufacturers are much higher than those of farmers. If a manufacturer were to maintain output in the face of a large decline in expenditures for his product, he would usually find that, in order to sell all his output, the market price of the product would have to fall below his out-of-pocket costs. In other words, he would be paying more for the materials and labor going into the product than his customers would give him for the finished good. Under these circumstances he would reduce his losses if he lowered output. The price he could get for his product would then not fall so far, and he would reduce his costs more than he would reduce his income. No producer will sell for a price below his out-of-pocket costs; instead, production will be cut until the entire output can be sold for a price at least equal to these costs. In many manufacturing firms the cost of labor and raw materials (the principal out-of-pocket costs) may constitute as much as 85 or 90 per cent of the market value of the product. For these products the market price will not be reduced more than 10 or 15 per cent unless costs also fall, so that the major impact of a decrease in expenditures on these products must necessarily fall on output.

This situation may be modified somewhat if, when expenditures on the finished product decrease, the costs of producing the product also fall. This may occur when agricultural raw materials are used. When the output of an industry using agricultural materials is cut, the producers' expenditures for these agricultural raw materials will fall. As has been pointed out above, this reduction in expenditures will cause the price of the agricultural raw materials to decline. If raw materials are important as a part of the costs of the manufacturer, he will then produce more than he would have if his costs had not fallen. An example of this type of reaction is found in the cotton-textile industry. When expenditures on cotton textiles decline, textile manufacturers curtail their production and with it their use of cotton, thus causing a sharp fall in the price of cotton. This reduction in the cost of cotton to the manufacturers encourages them not to cut production so much as they otherwise would have. The final result is that output declines less and prices decline more because agricultural products are used as raw materials.

When a producer uses a large amount of hired labor or uses raw materials that were produced by employing relatively large amounts of hired labor, the results may be quite different. Unlike the price of agricultural goods, the wage rate will not fall as much in the face of a decreasing demand for labor. When a producer contracts his output, wage rates will fall somewhat, but wages are sticky, and they will rarely fall far enough to induce the producer to maintain employment. As a result, in industries where a large amount of labor is hired directly or raw materials that have been produced by large amounts of hired labor are consumed, out-of-pocket costs for the producer will not be forced down much by the contraction of output. Prices in such industries will not fall so far and output will contract more than in industries that are more highly related to agriculture.

With an increase in expenditures for manufactured products, similarly, producers may expand their output without increasing the prices of their products, or they may prefer to raise the prices of their products and maintain the same output. The latter may occur even though excess capacity exists in the industry, and it must necessarily occur when a plant or industry reaches capacity. In periods when there is little unemployment, the hiring of additional labor by one firm in the attempt to increase output may only bid it away from other firms. When this happens, the increase in expenditures will merely shift labor around in the economy, resulting in higher costs and higher prices without any appreciable increase in the total amount of labor employed. Likewise, as industries attempt to expand under the impact of increased expenditures, they will need more raw materials. When the raw materials are agricultural products, the attempts by manufacturers to buy more of them will cause a sharp rise in raw material costs, and this in turn will make the manufacturers raise their prices instead of increasing output as much as they otherwise would have.

Summary

Changes in the level of expenditures will thus cause a change in the level of gross national product with which will be associated both price changes and output changes. Not all parts of the economy react in the same way to changes in gross national product. In the agricultural sector the characteristic reaction will be one of changing price with the level of output remaining constant, but in the manufacturing sector both price and output changes will occur, the extent of each depending on the capacity of the industry, the amount of unemployment in the economy, the nature of raw materials used by the manufacturers, and the price policies of the manufacturers. Every change in the level of gross national product will involve price and output changes in an interrelated pattern, with different reactions taking place in the different sectors. Only when activity in each industry reaches a stage above which it is difficult to go because of bottlenecks or limitations of capacity and available labor will the predominant reaction throughout the economy be one of increasing prices rather than of increasing output.

These basic reactions in different parts of the economy are extremely important in analyzing what takes place as the economy goes into a depression or starts off into an inflationary spiral. But an explanation of exactly how prices and output change in each part of the economy would, of necessity, have to take into account simultaneously all the considerations that have been mentioned in the above sections. In discussing income analysis, therefore, little additional attention will be given to the exact price-output patterns that will result from a change in the level of gross national product; for convenience it will be assumed that if the economy is operating at less than full capacity, an increase in expenditures on manufactured products will cause additional output and employment and an increase in expenditures on agricultural products will merely increase their prices. When a point of relatively full employment is reached, it will be assumed that prices in general will rise.

The remaining part of this chapter will be concerned with tracing the sources and examining the determinants of the expenditures for goods and services. This will involve on the one hand relating current expenditures to current income, and thus analyzing the nature of saving; and on the other hand showing how gross domestic investment fits into the economic process and how it in turn is related to gross saving.

THE DETERMINANTS OF TOTAL EXPENDITURE IN THE ECONOMY

The expenditures for the gross national product by the different sectors of the economy can be viewed not only as a part of the gross national product but also in terms of how they relate to the current income received and the current saving carried on by each sector. This section will discuss these relationships for each of the major sectors in turn: the consuming sector, the government sector, and the producing sector; and also for the Foreign Trade and Payments Account. It will then be possible to consider further the economic significance of the Gross Saving and Investment Account.

Consumers' Expenditures and Personal Saving

The Personal Income and Outlay Account for the consuming sector was developed in Part One; it is shown in abbreviated form in Table 55.

Table 55. Personal Income and Outlay Account, 1953

(In billions)

Allocations		Sources	
1. Consumers' expenditures.........	$229.6	5. Payments by producers to individ-	
2. Tax payments by individuals.....	44.6	uals...........................	$281.9
3. Transfer payments to abroad.....	0.5	6. Transfer payments by government	12.8
4. Personal saving.................	20.0	7. Transfer payments from abroad..	0.0
Personal outlay and saving.........	$294.7	Personal income...................	$294.7

SOURCE: See Table 21.

Consumers' expenditures as shown in this table is the same as was shown on the sources side of the Gross National Income and Product Account in Table 54. It is within the consuming sector that the determinants of the magnitude of consumers' expenditures lie. The context is the total income received by consumers and the taxes which consumers are required to pay out of their income. The income left over after taxes is disposable income; consumers divide this disposable income between spending and saving. Given the level of disposable income, the amount of saving that individuals decide to do out of their disposable income is by definition the determinant of the level of consumers' expenditures. Personal saving, in the sense in which the term is used in the Personal Income and Outlay Account, should not be confused with the accumulated savings of individuals in the form of cash, bonds, or other assets. Personal saving represents that part of the personal income of individuals that is not used either for tax payments or for consumers' expenditures; it indicates that at least some individuals in the economy have refrained from consuming a part of what was available to them for consumption. Some individuals of course will have incomes that are smaller than the sum of their tax payments and consumers' expenditures. When this happens, these individuals must either use up past accumulated savings or borrow to meet their current outlays. This process constitutes personal *dissaving* equal to the difference between their consumers' expenditures and their disposable income. At any one time some individuals in the economy will be saving and others will be dissaving. Total personal saving for all individuals equals the excess of personal saving over personal dissaving. Ordinarily, total personal saving will be a positive amount; during the depression of the thirties, however, the amount of dissaving was in some years greater than the amount of saving, so that for consumers as a group personal saving was negative; consumers' expenditures exceeded disposable income.

Government Expenditures and Government Surplus or Deficit

The Government Receipts and Outlay Account is given in abbreviated form in Table 56. This table shows government receipts and outlays in

Table 56. Government Receipts and Outlay Account, 1953

(In billions)

Allocations		Sources	
1. Government expenditures (net)....	$77.2	7. Tax payments by producers.......	$54.4
2. Subsidies and government interest	7.6	8. Tax payments by individuals......	44.6
3. Capital grants to government enterprises.......................	1.7	9. Transfer payments from abroad...	0.1
4. Transfer payments to individuals..	12.8		
5. Transfer payments to abroad......	6.5		
6. Surplus........................	−6.6		
Government outlay and surplus......	$99.1	Government receipts...............	$99.1

SOURCE: See Table 21.

much the same manner that the Personal Income and Outlay Account shows the income and outlay flows for the consuming sector. The government surplus or deficit is the difference between the total amount received by the government and the total amount of the government's outlays. When government receipts exceed its outlays, the government is withdrawing income from the economy much in the same way that individuals who do not consume all of their disposable income withdraw income in the form of personal saving. A government surplus thus is saving by the government, and a government deficit is government dissaving.

The economic actions of the government with respect to saving and spending are not determined by the same set of forces as those which guide individuals. Individuals decide to refrain from spending all of their income for reasons such as a desire to provide future resources in case of sickness or for old age, for the education of children, or for the purchase of a home or consumers' durables. In some cases individuals may have so much income that saving automatically results from the failure to spend as much as is received. For the government, however, decisions to tax or spend are made on quite different bases. The government requires payments from the other sectors so that it can make certain outlays without disrupting the economy. Both tax schedules and appropriations are determined by political bodies. An exactly balanced budget is almost an impossibility, since only tax rates, not tax receipts, can be legislated. The receipts of the government will depend both on the tax rates and on what these tax rates yield at the level of activity at which the economy is operating. In practice the forecasts of tax yields and the actual tax yields often differ by substantial amounts. Furthermore, situations often arise when it is reasoned that the attempt to finance current outlays needed for war or depression from current receipts would create greater economic ills than would the borrowing of funds through the mechanism of credit creation. The present size of the national debt is an indication of the extent to which government deficits have exceeded government surpluses in the history of the nation.

Gross Domestic Investment Expenditures and Gross Business Saving

The producing sector does not make any current expenditures that appear in the gross national product, since all current expenditures of producers are canceled out in the process of consolidation by which gross national product is obtained. Producers do make another kind of expenditure which appears on the Gross National Income and Product Account, however; this is gross domestic investment expenditures. The most obvious types of investment expenditures are those made by producers for buildings, machinery, equipment, or other producers' durables. These expenditures do not appear on the buyer's books as allocations of current receipts; they are recorded instead as a change in the form of assets or an increase in both assets and liabilities on the capital account of the buyer. Thus the balance sheet of the buyer is changed but his income statement is not. For the seller of the producers' durable goods, however, the transactions are on current account, since they represent receipts from current sales. The transactions thus do not cancel out in the process of consolidation, and so they appear as a part of the total expenditures for goods and services on the Gross National Income and Product Account.

Some of the expenditures on durable goods made by producers serve to replace productive capacity that has been used up or become obsolete. This replacement is necessary if the economy is to keep its productive power intact, and such replacement expenditures do not represent any net addition to the stock of capital goods in the economy. Gross domestic investment expenditure, which includes these replacement expenditures, therefore does not equal the net gain in the stock of capital goods in the economy. Rather, it shows the gross amount of capital goods created in the current period, with no allowance for those which are used up in the current period. The net increase in capital goods (net investment expenditure) would be measured by the investment expenditures over and above those required for replacement. Such net current investment expenditures are made by producers to create or extend productive capacity in anticipation of greater expenditures on their products or in the light of technological change. Basically, a producer makes investment expenditures in the hope of future profits. He thinks that consumers' expenditures on the product will be such that he can produce and sell it at a margin of profit sufficient to compensate him for the risk and bother involved in the undertaking. A number of factors can produce such a situation. Consumers' expenditures on goods in general might be high. Their expenditures on a new type of product might be increasing. On the cost side, technical advance or other gains in productivity might produce such a fall in costs that it would be more profitable to produce increased quantities of the product at lower prices. Any or all of these things can create a situation favorable to investment expenditures.

The change in inventories also represents investment expenditure when inventories are increasing, and disinvestment when inventories are decreasing. In a modern economy inventories serve a definite function. Their size over the long run depends upon the conscious design of producers; it is not simply the difference between what is produced and what is sold.[1] Retailers and wholesalers need stocks of goods to carry out their business; the stock of goods on their shelves is as essential to them as any of the rest of their equipment. Producers similarly need stocks of raw materials and goods in process in order to carry out production. When inventories increase, the economy is holding more goods in the pipeline of production, and this pipeline is for producers a type of capital good of the same general nature as their buildings and machines. Producers whose inventories increase have incurred costs greater than those which appear as a part of the cost of the goods they have sold. These additional costs do not appear on their current income statements. (They will appear on their future income statements when the inventories are again reduced through the sale of the goods.) For this reason they are expenditures on capital account. A decrease in inventories constitutes the reverse of this situation. Goods produced in the past are being used up in the present, and this is current disinvestment.

Since gross domestic investment expenditures do not come out of

[1] In the short run inventories will be affected by fluctuations in sales of goods in the economy.

current income, it is necessary to examine the source of the funds with which they are made. The process of investment does not use up savings, since the amount of assets is the same after the purchase is made as it was before. The amount of cash, for example, might be lower, but the amount of equipment would be increased by an equivalent amount. For saving to have been used up, some type of consumption has to occur; but when an investment is made, there is no consumption. The supply of funds for investment expenditures, therefore, need not be drawn from the saving of the economy but may come from a variety of other sources. Credit may be created to cover the investment expenditure: the banking system may have idle reserves, which it brings into use when funds are required for investment expenditure. Or firms may have idle balances of cash on hand, which they draw down to make capital outlays. These idle balances, furthermore, do not necessarily bear any relation to the saving that a firm has done in the past; it is possible for a firm that is making a loss (and so dissaving) to be in a highly liquid state, and similarly for a firm that is making and retaining huge profits (and so saving) to have practically no liquid funds. The firm that is making the loss may strive to maintain its liquidity by not selling on credit, by cashing in its securities, and by buying on credit rather than paying out cash. On the other hand, the firm whose assets are increasing faster than its liabilities may find that little or none of this increase in assets is in the form of cash. Other firms may owe it more money, or its inventories may have increased. For these reasons it would be naïve to assume that in the complexities of the modern economy the cash which some people accumulate as saving is itself loaned out to those who wish to make investment expenditures. Current saving and the supply of funds available for investment expenditures are not necessarily directly related in this way; the link between current saving and current investment must be approached from a different direction.

The gross saving carried out by a producer does appear in his current account, and for all producers as a group the gross saving will be derivable from the Gross National Income and Product Account in a manner similar to the derivation of personal saving and government surplus or deficit from the accounts for these sectors. Gross national product is the gross current income that producers have to allocate among the various elements of costs, taxes, and profits. What producers pay out to individuals and the government becomes income to these latter groups; the total of these payments can be considered the current expenditure of the producing sector. The amount of the gross national product that producers do not pay out as income to either individuals or the government is their gross saving. This gross saving of producers is the difference between what producers as a group receive from the other sectors and what they pay out to individuals and the government; it represents a part of the gross current income of the economy that cannot result in consumption expenditures. The more producers refrain from passing on either to individuals or to the government, the less of the gross income of the economy will be available for current expenditures. In this way producers can bring about saving in the economy. The term "gross" is used here because the income retained by producers includes depreciation allowances as well as undistributed profits. The income retained by producers therefore does not all represent additional accumulation of assets. To the extent that capital goods have been used up in the process of production, the gross saving of producers will exceed the net increase in their assets. The income retained, and thus the gross saving of producers, has already been shown in the Gross National Income and Product Account given in Table 54.

Foreign Trade Expenditures and Net Borrowing from Abroad

Both exports and imports are included on the sources side of the Gross National Income and Product Account; imports are shown as a deduction from the total. The Foreign Trade and Payments Account shows on one side the receipts of foreigners and on the other side the payments which foreigners make to the domestic economy. Net foreign borrowing is positive when the imports purchased and transfer payments made by the domestic economy exceed the exports sold and the transfer income received. These relations are shown in Table 57. If foreign

Table 57. Foreign Trade and Payments Account, 1953

(In billions)

Allocations		Sources	
1. Exports and property income received................	$21.3	5. Imports and property income paid	$16.4
2. Transfer payments to individuals..	0.0	6. Transfer payments from individuals	0.5
3. Transfer payments to government	0.1	7. Transfer payments from government................	6.3
4. Net borrowing from abroad......	1.9		
Receipts from abroad..............	$23.2	Payments to abroad..............	$23.2

SOURCE: See Table 21.

countries provide goods to the domestic economy in excess of what they receive in return, this is in effect a loan of the goods, and thus saving by the foreign countries. This saving in the Foreign Trade and Payments Account represents a contribution of goods or income to the domestic economy, and as such represents a part of the total current saving in the system.

If the domestic economy exports more than it imports, it is engaging in net lending to abroad, and so is dissaving in exactly the same sense that personal dissaving and government deficits are dissaving.

The Equality of Saving and Investment

The expenditures on goods and services by the various sectors in the economy generate income which in turn is available to the sectors for disbursement in the form of additional expenditures on goods and services, tax payments, or transfer payments to other sectors; or for retention within the sector as saving. Tax payments and transfer payments among the sectors do not alter the total amount of income available to all sectors as a group for spending on goods and services and for saving; these intersectoral flows are merely redistributions of the existing income already generated by productive activity. If one sector gives income to another sector, the income which remains to the first sector for spending and saving is reduced, and the income available to the second sector is increased by an identical amount. The gross national income is the amount of income generated by economic activity, and constitutes the income available to all sectors as a group for spending and saving.

In each of the accounts discussed in the previous sections, saving has been defined as that portion of the current income of a sector that is not passed on as an expenditure or outlay to any other sector. Gross saving for the economy as a whole is the amount of current income that the various sectors as a group do not spend. Looked at from the point of view of the gross national product and the gross national income generated, gross saving is that portion of the total that is not absorbed by the current expenditure of sectors. The gross national income minus gross saving equals the current expenditures on goods and services made by the various sectors, and gross national product minus the current expenditures on goods and services made by the various sectors is equal to gross saving. Gross saving is that portion of total output that is not consumed by the various sectors; it is output that the economy has refrained from using up and so has saved for use at some later time.

Gross domestic investment, on the other hand, represents those purchases of output that are made in addition to the current expenditures for goods and services by the various sectors. Since gross national product is equal to the total expenditures for the goods and services that have been produced, gross domestic investment plus the current expenditures for goods and services by the various sectors is by definition equal to the gross national product. But gross national product minus the current expenditures on goods and services made by the various sectors is also equal to gross saving. From this it follows that gross saving must always be equal to gross domestic investment. The Gross Saving and Investment Account shown in Table 58 demonstrates this equality.[2]

Table 58. Gross Saving and Investment Account
(In billions)

Allocations	Sources

1. Gross expenditures on producers' durables...................... $51.6	3. Personal saving.................. $20.0
2. Net change in inventories........ 1.5	4. Income retained by producers..... 35.1
	5. Capital grants to government enterprises........................ 1.7
	6. Government surplus.............. −6.6
	7. Net borrowing from abroad....... 1.9
	8. Statistical discrepancy........... 1.0
Gross domestic investment.......... $53.1	Gross saving...................... $53.1

SOURCE: See Table 21.

[2] The complete set of sector accounts can be presented with slight rearrangement in the form of a transactions matrix. This is given below for the year 1953.

(In billions of dollars)

	Producers	Consumers	Government	Foreign countries	Gross investment	Total outlay and saving
Payments to producers	X	229.6	84.8	21.3	53.1	388.8
Payments to individuals	281.9	X	12.8	0.0	0.0	294.7
Payments to government	54.4	44.6	X	0.1	0.0	99.1
Payments to foreign countries	16.4	0.5	6.3	X	0.0	23.2
Gross saving	36.1	20.0	−4.9	1.9	X	53.1
Total allocations of receipts	388.8	294.7	99.1	23.2	53.1	X

This transactions matrix is on the same consolidated basis as are the sector accounts, so that no intrasectoral flows are shown. The row and column for each

For the economy as a whole, therefore, saving represents that portion of total output that is saved and not consumed, and investment represents that portion of output that is not consumed but is, as investment, put in the form of producers' durables to be used in future periods. Thus saving and investment are one and the same thing looked at from different points of view, and must under all circumstances be identical in amount.

The obvious equality of the concepts of saving and investment from the point of view of the economy as a whole, however, does not satisfactorily explain the whole situation. The decisions to refrain from consuming income and the decisions to make capital outlays on producers' durable goods are still made by different groups; it has not yet been explained why these two should coincide, since the supply of available funds for capital outlays is not necessarily related to saving. To explore this relationship further, the processes of saving and investment must be studied in detail.

THE PROCESS OF SAVING

The processes by which the saving of consumers, government, and producers, and the saving originating in foreign trade, are integrated into economic activity are all quite similar; the analysis that applies to the saving of one group is equally applicable to the saving of other groups. In the following discussion, therefore, major attention will be focused on the process by which consumers save and how this personal saving affects the economy. Examples of saving by the other sectors will be given only to indicate the basic similarity in the analysis from sector to sector.

Personal Saving

Since personal saving is the difference between personal income and consumers' expenditure, it is obvious that personal saving will be affected by either a change in income or a change in expenditures. When an individual receives an increase in income and his expenditures do not change, personal saving will automatically increase by the same amount that income has increased. This repercussion of a change in income on saving is important because it emphasizes that changes in personal saving need not be entirely voluntary; they may occur simply because of

---

sector equal the sources of receipts and the disposition of outlays respectively. For producers these totals exceed the gross national product by the amount of imports, subsidies, and government interest. Government gross saving in this account is the sum of government surplus and capital grants to government enterprise. For the rest of the sectors the flows and the totals are as presented in the sector accounts.

changes in income to which an individual has not had opportunity to adjust. An increase of $1,000 in an individual's income will increase his saving by the same $1,000 until he has time to increase his rate of expenditure. Similarly, a decrease in an individual's income would have the immediate effect of cutting his rate of saving until he can adjust his expenditures downward. Income changes will thus have immediate repercussions on personal saving, and it is only by adjustment over a period of time that an individual can bring his expenditures into line so that his rate of saving is actually the rate he wants.

The current expenditures of consumers are a part of the current receipts of producers, so that any change in an individual's expenditures not only will change his own saving and consumption but also will affect the current receipts of producers. It was pointed out in Chap. 3 that every transaction has four aspects, two of them in the accounts of the buyer and two in the accounts of the seller. When an individual contracts his consumption in order to increase his current rate of saving, the reduction in his expenditures will show up not only in his own current accounts but also in the current accounts of producers. In order to show just how the current accounts of business will be affected, it will be necessary to be more specific with respect to the type of consumption that the individual cuts in his efforts to save more.

Expenditures on Commodities. When an individual contracts his purchases of commodities, sales of commodities will, of course, be contracted simultaneously. Until producers have an opportunity to adjust their rate of production to this new situation, inventories in their hands will increase. For simplicity in this initial change, examination of the contraction in consumers' expenditures will be confined to those commodities for which no excise or sales taxes apply. In this instance, therefore, the increased saving of the individual has had the simultaneous effect of increasing inventories, and this is a form of investment. This result is shown in Table 59 in terms of changes in the sector accounts. The reduction in consumers' expenditures is assumed to be ten units.

The reduction in consumers' expenditures appears both in the Personal Income and Outlay Account and in the Gross National Income and Product Account. Before producers can react by changing the level of their output and their payments to individuals, government, and themselves, goods will accumulate and inventories will increase by the amount of the reduction in consumers' expenditures. This increase in inventories appears both on the Gross National Income and Product Account and on the Gross Saving and Investment Account. Up to this point there has been no net change in gross national product (the market value of goods produced), and the allocations of gross national product have not changed. Personal income therefore has not changed. Since consumers' expenditures have fallen, more of personal income must have been retained as saving; this increase is shown both in the Personal Income and Outlay Account and in the Gross Saving and Investment Account. All the sector accounts are therefore in balance, and investment has increased (at least temporarily) as much as the increase in saving.[3]

This situation is not necessarily stable, however, since producers will probably want to make some adjustment to it. Inventories are now probably larger than the producers want them to be. They can be reduced to the previous level by either cuts in prices or cuts in production. In either case gross national product will fall as inventories are brought back to their previous level. There is now a smaller gross national product to be allocated, so that one or more of the specific categories of allocations must receive less. In practice it can be expected that all the allocations of the producer would suffer somewhat. Profits would normally be lower, so that, until changes in dividend policy could be made, undistributed profits would be lower. Payments of wages and salaries to individuals would drop, thus lowering personal income. Tax liability would fall, thus

[3] It is also possible to arrange the sector accounts and their changes in the form of the transactions matrix shown on pp. 276 and 277 as follows:

	Pro-ducers	Con-sumers	Gov-ern-ment	For-eign coun-tries	Gross invest-ment	Total outlays by sectors
Payments to producers	X	−10			+10	0
Payments to consumers		X				0
Payments to government			X			0
Payments to other countries				X		0
Gross saving		+10			X	+10
Total allocations of receipts by sectors	0	0	0	0	+10	+10

Table 59
(In billions)

I. Gross National Income and Product Account

1.1. Payments by producers to individuals (2.5)	1.6. Consumers' expenditures (2.1) −$10
1.2. Income retained by producers (5.4)	1.7. Government expenditures, net (3.1)
1.3. Tax payments by producers (3.7)	1.8. Gross expenditures on producers' durables (5.1)
1.4. Minus: Subsidies and government interest (3.2)	1.9. Net change in inventories (5.2) +10
1.5. Statistical discrepancy (5.8)	1.10. Exports and property income received (4.1)
	Subtotal
	1.11. Minus: Imports and property income paid (4.5)
Gross national income	Gross national product

II. Personal Income and Outlay Account

2.1. Consumers' expenditures (1.6) −$10	2.5. Payments by producers to individuals (1.1)
2.2. Tax payments by individuals (3.8)	2.6. Transfer payments by government (3.4)
2.3. Transfer payments to abroad (4.6)	2.7. Transfer payments from abroad (4.2)
2.4. Personal saving (5.3) +$10	
Personal outlay and saving	Personal income

III. Government Receipts and Outlay Account

3.1. Government expenditures, net (1.7)	3.7. Tax payments by producers (1.3)
3.2. Subsidies and government interest (1.4)	3.8. Tax payments by individuals (2.2)
3.3. Capital grants to government enterprises (5.5)	3.9. Transfer payments from abroad (4.3)
3.4. Transfer payments to individuals (2.6)	
3.5. Transfer payments to abroad (4.7)	
3.6. Surplus (5.6)	
Government outlay and surplus	Government receipts

IV. Foreign Trade and Payments Account

4.1. Exports and property income received (1.10)	4.5. Imports and property income paid (1.11)
4.2. Transfer payments to individuals (2.7)	4.6. Transfer payments from individuals (2.3)
4.3. Transfer payments to government (3.9)	4.7. Transfer payments from government (3.5)
4.4. Net borrowing from abroad (5.7)	
Receipts from abroad	Payments to abroad

V. Gross Saving and Investment Account

5.1. Gross expenditures on producers' durables (1.8)		5.3. Personal saving (2.4)	
5.2. Net change in inventories (1.9)	+$10	5.4. Income retained by producers (1.2)	
		5.5. Capital grants to government enterprises (3.3)	
		5.6. Government surplus (3.6)	
		5.7. Net borrowing from abroad (4.4)	
		5.8. Statistical discrepancy (1.5)	
			+$10
Gross investment	+$10	Gross saving	+$10

causing a fall in government revenue. Even the volume of raw materials imported for use in production would probably be cut back, thus making the payments to foreign countries smaller. In each of these sectors the reduction of income automatically affects the allocations side of the sector account. In the Personal Income and Outlay Account the reduction in income will immediately reduce the taxes that the government receives from individuals, since less will be withheld by the producers for the government. Before individuals have an opportunity to adjust their consumers' expenditures in accord with the new level of income, the saving of individuals will decrease. Government revenue will decline initially, both because producers pay less taxes and because less is withheld from individuals' incomes, and before the government can react to the changed situation, its surplus will decrease or its deficit will increase. Finally, a decrease in imports in the Foreign Trade and Payments Account will decrease the amount of foreign borrowing necessary or will increase the amount of foreign lending required. When all the increases and decreases noted above are recorded in the various accounts, it will be found that the decrease in inventories has been exactly offset by the decrease in the amount of saving in all the accounts. These new changes are shown in Table 60.

The contraction in inventories by producers under these assumptions has thus reduced the gross national product and the income of each one of the sectors in the economy. This latest set of transactions, however, still does not bring the economy into equilibrium. The repercussions could, of course, be traced still further. The reduction in personal income would probably lead some individuals to reduce their expenditures again, so that a new series of changes would be set in motion. This new reduction in consumers' expenditures will have an effect similar to that of the original reduction. Thus the original increase in saving by individuals has set in motion a series of reactions. Throughout this series of reactions, saving and investment will always be equal, just as they were in the reactions traced in detail above. The reactions resulted in a lowering of the value of total output in the economy, through the successive adjustments of producers and consumers to the successive new situations in which they found themselves.

Expenditures on Services. When an individual contracts his purchases of services rather than commodities, the initial reaction may be somewhat different. A decrease in expenditures on bus rides, for example, cannot produce an increase in inventories, since no inventoriable commodity is involved. Instead, there will be an immediate reduction in the amount of bus services sold and a corresponding immediate fall in the gross national product. On the allocations side of the Gross National Income and Product Account the immediate effect will be to reduce the profits of the bus company and its tax liability. The amounts which the bus company pays in wages and salaries and other expenses will not decline until the company attempts to adjust to the new situation. The sector flows involved before any adjustments can take place are shown in Table 61.

The reduction in sales to consumers causes a fall in the gross national product of an equivalent amount; and before payments to individuals can be adjusted, producers will have less left over in the form of gross saving (undistributed profits in this case) and will owe less to the government in taxes. Payments to individuals have not changed, and therefore personal income will not have changed. Personal saving must therefore have increased by the amount that consumers' expenditures have decreased. The decrease in the saving of producers and the government balances the increase in personal saving, and total gross saving remains unchanged. From this point on, reactions will be similar to those discussed above; the adjustment of producers to the reduced purchases of consumers might involve a reduction of payments to individuals, and a continuous series of reactions might be set in motion.

An attempt by individuals to increase their saving will thus increase the total saving of the economy only as long as the involuntary accumulation of inventories by producers continues. As long as producers do not want to increase the amount of gross investment, attempts by individuals to save will eventually lead either to a reduction in the amount of saving done by other sectors or else to a fall in the level of personal income. In the first case the increase in personal saving will be offset by a reduction in the saving of the other sectors. In the second case the fall in personal income will offset the cut in consumers' expenditures, so that the attempt to save will have been abortive for individuals as a group. An increase in saving by one individual, therefore, will not necessarily result in an increase in saving in the economy; it may only force someone else to dissave an equal amount.

Government Surplus and Deficit

Changes in either government receipts or government outlays will be reflected in the government surplus or deficit. Examination of both types of change will illustrate the manner in which the various sectors of the economy are affected by the saving and dissaving of the government.

Government Receipts. Government revenue is for the most part derived from taxation, and a change in the receipts from taxation can occur either through changes in the incomes and expenditures of those who are taxed or through changes in the tax rates that are applied to this income and expenditure. Changes in tax rates are usually accomplished by legislative procedure, so that producers are aware in advance just how a change may affect them. Unlike the situation discussed above for changes in the

Table 60
(In billions)

I. Gross National Income and Product Account

1.1. Payments by producers to individuals (2.5)	— $ 7		1.6. Consumers' expenditures (2.1)	
1.2. Income retained by producers (5.4)	— 1		1.7. Government expenditures, net (3.1)	
1.3. Tax payments by producers (3.7)	— 1		1.8. Gross expenditures on producers' durables (5.1)	— $10
1.4. Minus: Subsidies and government interest (3.2)			1.9. Net change in inventories (5.2)	
1.5. Statistical discrepancy (5.8)			1.10. Exports and property income received (4.1)	
			Subtotal	— $10
			1.11. Minus: Imports and property income paid (4.5)	— 1
Gross national income	— $ 9		Gross national product	— $ 9

II. Personal Income and Outlay Account

2.1. Consumers' expenditures (1.6)	— $ 1		2.5. Payments by producers to individuals (1.1)	— $ 7
2.2. Tax payments by individuals (3.8)			2.6. Transfer payments by government (3.4)	
2.3. Transfer payments to abroad (4.6)			2.7. Transfer payments from abroad (4.2)	
2.4. Personal saving (5.3)	— 6			
Personal outlay and saving	— $ 7		Personal income	— $ 7

III. Government Receipts and Outlay Account

3.1. Government expenditures, net (1.7)	— $ 1		3.7. Tax payments by producers (1.3)	— $ 1
3.2. Subsidies and government interest (1.4)	— 1		3.8. Tax payments by individuals (2.2)	— 1
3.3. Capital grants to government enterprises (5.5)			3.9. Transfer payments from abroad (4.3)	
3.4. Transfer payments to individuals (2.6)				
3.5. Transfer payments to abroad (4.7)				
3.6. Surplus (5.6)	— $ 2			
Government outlay and surplus	— $ 2		Government receipts	— $ 2

IV. Foreign Trade and Payments Account

4.1. Exports and property income received (1.10)	4.5. Imports and property income paid (1.11)	–$ 1
4.2. Transfer payments to individuals (2.7)	4.6. Transfer payments from individuals (2.3)	
4.3. Transfer payments to government (3.9)	4.7. Transfer payments from government (3.5)	
4.4. Net borrowing from abroad (5.7) –$ 1		
Receipts from abroad –$ 1	Payments to abroad	–$ 1

V. Gross Saving and Investment Account

5.1. Gross expenditures on producers' durables (1.8)	5.3. Personal saving (2.4)	–$ 6
5.2. Net change in inventories (1.9) –$10	5.4. Income retained by producers (1.2)	–1
	5.5. Capital grants to government enterprises (3.3)	
	5.6. Government surplus (3.6)	–2
	5.7. Net borrowing from abroad (4.4)	–1
	5.8. Statistical discrepancy (1.5)	
Gross investment –$10	Gross saving	–$10

Table 61

(In billions)

I. Gross National Income and Product Account

1.1. Payments by producers to individuals (2.5)			1.6. Consumers' expenditures (2.1)	−$10
1.2. Income retained by producers (5.4)	−$ 5		1.7. Government expenditures, net (3.1)	
1.3. Tax payments by producers (3.7)	−5		1.8. Gross expenditures on producers' durables (5.1)	
1.4. Minus: Subsidies and government interest (3.2)			1.9. Net change in inventories (5.2)	
1.5. Statistical discrepancy (5.8)			1.10. Exports and property income received (4.1)	
			Subtotal	
			1.11. Minus: Imports and property income paid (4.5)	
Gross national income	−$10		Gross national product	−$10

II. Personal Income and Outlay Account

2.1. Consumers' expenditures (1.6)	−$10		2.5. Payments by producers to individuals (1.1)	−$10
2.2. Tax payments by individuals (3.8)			2.6. Transfer payments by government (3.4)	
2.3. Transfer payments to abroad (4.6)			2.7. Transfer payments from abroad (4.2)	
2.4. Personal saving (5.3)	+10			
Personal outlay and saving			Personal income	

III. Government Receipts and Outlay Account

3.1. Government expenditures, net (1.7)			3.7. Tax payments by producers (1.3)	−$ 5
3.2. Subsidies and government interest (1.4)			3.8. Tax payments by individuals (2.2)	
3.3. Capital grants to government enterprises (5.5)			3.9. Transfer payments from abroad (4.3)	
3.4. Transfer payments to individuals (2.6)				
3.5. Transfer payments to abroad (4.7)				
3.6. Surplus (5.6)	−$ 5			
Government outlay and surplus	−$ 5		Government receipts	−$ 5

IV. Foreign Trade and Payments Account

4.1. Exports and property income received (1.10)	4.5. Imports and property income paid (1.11)
4.2. Transfer payments to individuals (2.7)	4.6. Transfer payments from individuals (2.3)
4.3. Transfer payments to government (3.9)	4.7. Transfer payments from government (3.5)
4.4. Net borrowing from abroad (5.7)	
Receipts from abroad	**Payments to abroad**

V. Gross Saving and Investment Account

5.1. Gross expenditures on producers' durables (1.8)	5.3. Personal saving (2.4)	+$10
5.2. Net change in inventories (1.9)	5.4. Income retained by producers (1.2)	−5
	5.5. Capital grants to government enterprises (3.3)	
	5.6. Government surplus (3.6)	
	5.7. Net borrowing from abroad (4.4)	−5
	5.8. Statistical discrepancy (1.5)	
Gross investment	**Gross saving**	

level of consumers' expenditures, it is quite possible for producers and individuals alike to react to a change in taxes even before it takes place. For example, assume that the government announced a tax reduction to take place three months hence. Individuals would realize that they would have more income available to them in the future. In such a situation they might anticipate the tax reduction by making purchases on the installment plan, or by using up some of their cash holdings which they would not otherwise have spent. Producers likewise might decide to purchase durable goods in anticipation of greater consumer demand and in view of the increased funds that they would expect to have after the tax reduction went into effect. Thus even prior to the actual tax reduction the changes shown in Table 62 might take place.

In this example both consumers and producers are assumed to have increased their expenditures. Consumers are assumed to have increased their expenditures by six units, producers by three units. It is further assumed that this increase in expenditures resulted in some increase in imports and an increase in payments of income to individuals, payments of taxes to government, and income retained by producers. Personal saving will not drop by the entire amount of the increase in consumers' expenditures, since personal income also rises. Government revenue and government surplus actually increase, due to the increased level of income in the economy. The new investment of producers and the decrease in personal saving are balanced by increases in the saving of producers and government and in the foreign trade account.

When the actual tax reduction goes into effect, the major adjustments of spending and investment may already have taken place, so that only individuals who previously were hampered by an actual lack of funds will increase their outlays. In Table 63, which shows the new changes after the tax reduction goes into effect, it is assumed therefore that rather minor changes in consumers' expenditures will accompany the actual tax reduction, and that no increase in total investment expenditures will take place.

The reduction in government revenue results in a decrease in the government surplus (or an increase in the deficit) of an equal amount. The slight rise in consumers' expenditures is for the sake of simplicity assumed to result in an equivalent amount of income paid out to individuals; the tax reduction to individuals therefore results in an increase in personal saving equal to the tax reduction, and the same situation is also true for producers. The Gross Saving and Investment Account shows how this saving and dissaving balances for the economy as a whole.

Government Outlays. An increase in government outlays such as an increase in unemployment benefits would immediately on payment increase personal income. Before individuals could spend their unemployment checks, the transaction would appear in the sector accounts as an increase in government transfer payments, an equal offsetting decrease in government surplus, and increases in personal income and personal saving. These initial entries are shown in Table 64.

As soon as individuals have an opportunity to spend their unemployment checks, however, consumers' expenditures will rise and a whole new set of transactions will need to be recorded in the accounts. Since the rise in consumers' expenditures will cause a rise in income payments to individuals, personal income will rise, and this in turn will provide more income for individuals to spend. Throughout each stage of the process of adjustment, however, the transactions made by the different sectors can be recorded, and at every point in time there will be a balance of saving and investment.

Net Borrowing or Lending Abroad

Changes in the Foreign Trade and Payments Account will have the same sort of effect upon the economy as that shown above for changes in the consuming and government sectors. An increase in exports, for example, will cause an inflow of funds into the economy, and will reduce the amount of foreign borrowing and at the same time increase exports on the Gross National Income and Product Account. If there is a sudden demand for certain particular goods by foreign countries, the initial result might be a decrease in inventories in the hands of producers. Such a situation is shown in Table 65.

Producers will attempt to regain their desired level of inventories. The repercussions that are involved will be very similar to the inventory adjustments shown in Table 60. In that particular example producers were attempting to reduce their inventories, whereas in the repercussions which will follow from the situation shown in Table 65 the changes will be increases, since producers will be attempting to increase their inventories back to the desired level.

Some of the changes that may occur in the Foreign Trade and Payments Account may prevent repercussions in the rest of the economy, rather than force them to take place. Suppose, for example, that a foreign country has a balance of payments problem and cannot borrow additional funds, and so is faced with curtailing sharply the volume of goods purchased from the United States. In such an instance a transfer payment in the form of foreign aid by the United States to the foreign country might prevent the contraction of exports which would otherwise have to take place, and which would entail a whole series of readjustments within the United States economy. In the sector accounts the transaction would be recorded as shown in Table 66. In this situation the lending to abroad is reduced by the amount of the government trans-

Table 62
(In billions)

I. Gross National Income and Product Account

1.1. Payments by producers to individuals (2.5)	+$5	1.6. Consumers' expenditures (2.1)		+$6
1.2. Income retained by producers (5.4)	+2	1.7. Government expenditures, net (3.1)		
1.3. Tax payments by producers (3.7)	+1	1.8. Gross expenditures on producers' durables (5.1)		+3
1.4. Minus: Subsidies and government interest (3.2)		1.9. Net change in inventories (5.2)		
1.5. Statistical discrepancy (5.8)		1.10. Exports and property income received (4.1)		
		Subtotal	+$9	
		1.11. Minus: Imports and property income paid (4.5)	+1	
Gross national income	+$8	Gross national product		+$8

II. Personal Income and Outlay Account

2.1. Consumers' expenditures (1.6)	+$6	2.5. Payments by producers to individuals (1.1)	+$5
2.2. Tax payments by individuals (3.8)	+1	2.6. Transfer payments by government (3.4)	
2.3. Transfer payments to abroad (4.6)		2.7. Transfer payments from abroad (4.2)	
2.4. Personal saving (5.3)	−2		
Personal outlay and saving	+$5	Personal income	+$5

III. Government Receipts and Outlay Account

3.1. Government expenditures, net (1.7)		3.7. Tax payments by producers (1.3)	+$1
3.2. Subsidies and government interest (5.5)		3.8. Tax payments by individuals (2.2)	+1
3.3. Capital grants to government enterprises		3.9. Transfer payments from abroad (4.3)	
3.4. Transfer payments to individuals (2.6)			
3.5. Transfer payments to abroad (4.7)			
3.6. Surplus (5.6)	+$2		
Government outlay and surplus	+$2	Government receipts	+$2

IV. Foreign Trade and Payments Account

4.1. Exports and property income received (1.10)			4.5. Imports and property income paid (1.11)	+$1
4.2. Transfer payments to individuals (2.7)			4.6. Transfer payments from individuals (2.3)	
4.3. Transfer payments to government (3.9)			4.7. Transfer payments from government (3.5)	
4.4. Net borrowing from abroad (5.7)		+$1		
Receipts from abroad		+$1	Payments to abroad	+$1

V. Gross Saving and Investment Account

5.1. Gross expenditures on producers' durables (1.8)	+$3	5.3. Personal saving (2.4)		−$2
5.2. Net change in inventories (1.9)		5.4. Income retained by producers (1.2)		+2
		5.5. Capital grants to government enterprises (3.3)		
		5.6. Government surplus (3.6)		+2
		5.7. Net borrowing from abroad (4.4)		+1
		5.8. Statistical discrepancy (1.5)		
Gross investment	+$3	Gross saving		+$3

Table 63

(In billions)

I. Gross National Income and Product Account

1.1. Payments by producers to individuals (2.5)	+$ 1	1.6. Consumers' expenditures (2.1)	+$ 1
1.2. Income retained by producers (5.4)	+2	1.7. Government expenditures, net (3.1)	
1.3. Tax payments by producers (3.7)	−2	1.8. Gross expenditures on producers' durables (5.1)	
1.4. Minus: Subsidies and government interest (3.2)		1.9. Net change in inventories (5.2)	
1.5. Statistical discrepancy (5.8)		1.10. Exports and property income received (4.1)	
		Subtotal	+$ 1
		1.11. Minus: Imports and property income paid (4.5)	+$ 1
Gross national income	+$ 1	Gross national product	+$ 1

II. Personal Income and Outlay Account

2.1. Consumers' expenditures (1.6)	+$ 1	2.5. Payments by producers to individuals (1.1)	+$ 1
2.2. Tax payments by individuals (3.8)	−8	2.6. Transfer payments by government (3.4)	
2.3. Transfer payments to abroad (4.6)		2.7. Transfer payments from abroad (4.2)	
2.4. Personal saving (5.3)	+8		
Personal outlay and saving	+$ 1	Personal income	+$ 1

III. Government Receipts and Outlay Account

3.1. Government expenditures, net (1.7)		3.7. Tax payments by producers (1.3)	−$ 2
3.2. Subsidies and government interest (1.4)		3.8. Tax payments by individuals (2.2)	−8
3.3. Capital grants to government enterprises (5.5)		3.9. Transfer payments from abroad (4.3)	
3.4. Transfer payments to individuals (2.6)			
3.5. Transfer payments to abroad (4.7)			
3.6. Surplus (5.6)	−10		
Government outlay and surplus	−$10	Government receipts	−$10

IV. Foreign Trade and Payments Account

4.1. Exports and property income received (1.10)	4.5. Imports and property income paid (1.11)
4.2. Transfer payments to individuals (2.7)	4.6. Transfer payments from individuals (2.3)
4.3. Transfer payments to government (3.9)	4.7. Transfer payments from government (3.5)
4.4. Net borrowing from abroad (5.7)	
Receipts from abroad	Payments to abroad

V. Gross Saving and Investment Account

5.1. Gross expenditures on producers' durables (1.8)	5.3. Personal saving (2.4)	+$ 8
5.2. Net change in inventories (1.9)	5.4. Income retained by producers (1.2)	+2
	5.5. Capital grants to government enterprises (3.3)	
	5.6. Government surplus (3.6)	−10
	5.7. Net borrowing from abroad (4.4	
	5.8. Statistical discrepancy (1.5)	
		———
Gross investment	Gross saving	

Table 64

(In billions)

I. Gross National Income and Product Account

1.1. Payments by producers to individuals (2.5)	1.6. Consumers' expenditures (2.1)
1.2. Income retained by producers (5.4)	1.7. Government expenditures, net (3.1)
1.3. Tax payments by producers (3.7)	1.8. Gross expenditures on producers' durables (5.1)
1.4. Minus: Subsidies and government interest (3.2)	1.9. Net change in inventories (5.2)
1.5. Statistical discrepancy (5.8)	1.10. Exports and property income received (4.1)
	Subtotal
	1.11. Minus: Imports and property income paid (4.5)
Gross national income	Gross national product

II. Personal Income and Outlay Account

2.1. Consumers' expenditures (1.6)	2.5. Payments by producers to individuals (1.1)	
2.2. Tax payments by individuals (3.8)	2.6. Transfer payments by government (3.4)	
2.3. Transfer payments to abroad (4.6)	2.7. Transfer payments from abroad (4.2)	+$10
2.4. Personal saving (5.3)	+$10	
Personal outlay and saving	+$10	Personal income +$10

III. Government Receipts and Outlay Account

3.1. Government expenditures, net (1.7)	3.7. Tax payments by producers (1.3)	
3.2. Subsidies and government interest (1.4)	3.8. Tax payments by individuals (2.2)	
3.3. Capital grants to government enterprises (5.5)	3.9. Transfer payments from abroad (4.3)	
3.4. Transfer payments to individuals (2.6)	+$10	
3.5. Transfer payments to abroad (4.7)		
3.6. Surplus (5.6)	−10	
Government outlay and surplus		Government receipts

290

IV. Foreign Trade and Payments Account

4.1. Exports and property income received (1.10)	4.5. Imports and property income paid (1.11)
4.2. Transfer payments to individuals (2.7)	4.6. Transfer payments from individuals (2.3)
4.3. Transfer payments to government (3.9)	4.7. Transfer payments from government (3.5)
4.4. Net borrowing from abroad (5.7)	
Receipts from abroad	**Payments to abroad**

V. Gross Saving and Investment Account

5.1. Gross expenditures on producers' durables (1.8)	5.3. Personal saving (2.4)	+$10
5.2. Net change in inventories (1.9)	5.4. Income retained by producers (1.2)	
	5.5. Capital grants to government enterprises (3.3)	−10
	5.6. Government surplus (3.6)	
	5.7. Net borrowing from abroad (4.4)	
	5.8. Statistical discrepancy (1.5)	
Gross investment	**Gross saving**	—

Table 65
(In billions)

I. Gross National Income and Product Account

1.1. Payments by producers to individuals (2.5)	1.6. Consumers' expenditures (2.1)
1.2. Income retained by producers (5.4)	1.7. Government expenditures, net (3.1)
1.3. Tax payments by producers (3.7)	1.8. Gross expenditures on producers' durables (5.1)
1.4. Minus: Subsidies and government interest (3.2)	1.9. Net change in inventories (5.2)
1.5. Statistical discrepancy (5.8)	1.10. Exports and property income received (4.1) −$10
	Subtotal +10
	1.11. Minus: Imports and property income paid (4.5)
Gross national income	Gross national product

II. Personal Income and Outlay Account

2.1. Consumers' expenditures (1.6)	2.5. Payments by producers to individuals (1.1)
2.2. Tax payments by individuals (3.8)	2.6. Transfer payments by government (3.4)
2.3. Transfer payments to abroad (4.6)	2.7. Transfer payments from abroad (4.2)
2.4. Personal saving (5.3)	
Personal outlay and saving	Personal income

III. Government Receipts and Outlay Account

3.1. Government expenditures, net (1.7)	3.7. Tax payments by producers (1.3)
3.2. Subsidies and government interest (1.4)	3.8. Tax payments by individuals (2.2)
3.3. Capital grants to government enterprises (5.5)	3.9. Transfer payments from abroad (4.3)
3.4. Transfer payments to individuals (2.6)	
3.5. Transfer payments to abroad (4.7)	
3.6. Surplus (5.6)	
Government outlay and surplus	Government receipts

IV. Foreign Trade and Payments Account

4.1. Exports and property income received (1.10)	+$10	4.5. Imports and property income paid (1.11)	
4.2. Transfer payments to individuals (2.7)		4.6. Transfer payments from individuals (2.3)	
4.3. Transfer payments to government (3.9)		4.7. Transfer payments from government (3.5)	
4.4. Net borrowing from abroad (5.7)	−10		
Receipts from abroad		Payments to abroad	

V. Gross Saving and Investment Account

5.1. Gross expenditures on producers' durables (1.8)		5.3. Personal saving (2.4)	
5.2. Net change in inventories (1.9)	−$10	5.4. Income retained by producers (1.2)	
		5.5. Capital grants to government enterprises (3.3)	
		5.6. Government surplus (3.6)	
		5.7. Net borrowing from abroad (4.4)	−$10
		5.8. Statistical discrepancy (1.5)	
Gross investment	−$10	Gross saving	−$10

Table 66
(In billions)

I. Gross National Income and Product Account

1.1. Payments by producers to individuals (2.5)	1.6. Consumers' expenditures (2.1)
1.2. Income retained by producers (5.4)	1.7. Government expenditures, net (3.1)
1.3. Tax payments by producers (3.7)	1.8. Gross expenditures on producers' durables (5.1)
1.4. Minus: Subsidies and government interest (3.2)	1.9. Net change in inventories (5.2)
1.5. Statistical discrepancy (5.8)	1.10. Exports and property income received (4.1)
	Subtotal
	1.11. Minus: Imports and property income paid (4.5)
Gross national income	Gross national product

II. Personal Income and Outlay Account

2.1. Consumers' expenditures (1.6)	2.5. Payments by producers to individuals (1.1)
2.2. Tax payments by individuals (3.8)	2.6. Transfer payments by government (3.4)
2.3. Transfer payments to abroad (4.6)	2.7. Transfer payments from abroad (4.2)
2.4. Personal saving (5.3)	
Personal outlay and saving	Personal income

III. Government Receipts and Outlay Account

3.1. Government expenditures, net (1.7)	3.7. Tax payments by producers (1.3)
3.2. Subsidies and government interest (1.4)	3.8. Tax payments by individuals (2.2)
3.3. Capital grants to government enterprises (5.5)	3.9. Transfer payments from abroad (4.3)
3.4. Transfer payments to individuals (2.6)	
3.5. Transfer payments to abroad (4.7)	+$10
3.6. Surplus (5.6)	−10
Government outlay and surplus	Government receipts

IV. Foreign Trade and Payments Account

4.1. Exports and property income received (1.10)	4.5. Imports and property income paid (1.11)
4.2. Transfer payments to individuals (2.7)	4.6. Transfer payments from individuals (2.3)
4.3. Transfer payments to government (3.9)	4.7. Transfer payments from government (3.5) +$10
4.4. Net borrowing from abroad (5.7) +$10	
Receipts from abroad +$10	Payments to abroad +$10

V. Gross Saving and Investment Account

5.1. Gross expenditures on producers' durables (1.8)	5.3. Personal saving (2.4)
5.2. Net change in inventories (1.9)	5.4. Income retained by producers (1.2)
	5.5. Capital grants to government enterprises (3.3)
	5.6. Government surplus (3.6) −$10
	5.7. Net borrowing from abroad (4.4) +10
	5.8. Statistical discrepancy (1.5)
Gross investment	Gross saving

fer payment to abroad, and this is shown by an increase in the "net borrowing from abroad" item in the account.

THE PROCESS OF INVESTMENT

Gross domestic investment embraces expenditures on a wide variety of producers' goods, such as the construction of homes and apartment houses, the erection of plants, and the installation of machinery, together with the change in inventories. The decisions which call investment into being are quite different from those responsible for the saving taking place in each of the sectors. Yet from a national income accounting point of view, the gross investment in the economy will at all times be equal to the gross saving that is taking place. Examination of the process of saving has shown how the mechanism operates from the point of view of decisions to save; examination of the process of investment is still necessary, however, to show just how increases or decreases in investment will by their very occurrence simultaneously create or destroy the saving which accompanies them.

An increase in purchases of producers' durable goods may have the immediate effect of removing goods from the inventories of the dealers in such equipment. The increase in investment represented by the increased purchase of durable goods is thus offset by a simultaneous decrease of the same amount in the sellers' inventories; thus the new investment is temporarily balanced by an equal disinvestment on the part of the sellers of producers' durable goods. This is shown in Table 67. But this disinvestment on the part of the sellers is involuntary, since it will reduce their stocks below the level they prefer. They will therefore either raise their prices or increase their output in order to regain the inventory position that they want. In either case the result will be an increase in the value of total output in the economy, so that the gross national product will increase. The repercussions that occur when producers attempt to regain their desired inventory positions are the same as those discussed with reference to the adjustments shown in Table 60, except that the changes here will be positive, since producers are attempting to increase rather than reduce their inventories.

An increase in expenditures on capital goods need not always have its effect through involuntary changes in inventories. Instead, it may directly increase payments to individuals, payments to government, or income retained by producers. This would occur, for instance, if the increase in expenditures took the form of new construction. As the expenditure on new construction is made, the wages and salaries paid to employees, taxes paid by producers, and income retained by producers will increase simultaneously with the value of construction work in process and the gross national product. Until the workers have a chance to spend their new pay checks, and other sectors also adjust to the new situation, the saving for all sectors taken together will be increased by the exact amount of the new investment. The subsequent reaction of the construction workers and other groups to the new level of income will cause additional consumption expenditures, and another chain of adjustments will be set in motion. The process by which changes in the level of investment are integrated into the system is thus identical with the process by which changes in saving and current expenditure are integrated.

An increase in the rate of gross domestic investment expenditures will give rise to a cumulative increase in the level of gross national product. Similarly, a decrease in the rate of gross domestic investment expenditures will lead to a cumulative fall in the level of gross national product. There are a number of factors that will influence the cumulative movements set up by changes in saving and investment. Some of these factors will reinforce the movements upward or downward, and others will tend to limit the changes in gross national product. An understanding of the changes in the level of activity in the economy will require an examination of these factors and an analysis of the meaning of equilibrium in the economy. These questions will be examined in the following chapters.

THE CIRCULAR FLOW OF INCOME BETWEEN PRODUCERS AND CONSUMERS

In order to emphasize the interdependence of producers and consumers, it will be useful to examine briefly the nature of the flow of income between these two groups. In this discussion the Government Receipts and Outlay Account, the Foreign Trade and Payments Account, and the Gross Saving and Investment Account will not be treated as representing decision-making sectors in the same sense as producers and consumers. The government will be viewed as an outside agency, withdrawing income at certain stages of the economic process and injecting income at other stages. The decisions with respect to how much is to be withdrawn from the system (taxation) and how much is to be injected into the system (government outlays) may be quite unrelated. Wars, depressions, and inflations all have the effect of causing the government to seek to regulate its taxation and outlays in such a way as to promote the welfare of the economy, and it does not always follow in these instances that an equality between the removal of income from the economy and the addition of income to the economy will lead to economic stability. For these reasons it will be useful to consider the actions of the government essentially as those of an outside agency rather

Table 67

(In billions)

I. Gross National Income and Product Account

1.1. Payments by producers to individuals (2.5)	1.6. Consumers' expenditures (2.1)
1.2. Income retained by producers (5.4)	1.7. Government expenditures, net (3.1)
1.3. Tax payments by producers (3.7)	1.8. Gross expenditures on producers' durables (5.1) +$10
1.4. Minus: Subsidies and government interest (3.2)	1.9. Net change in inventories (5.2) −10
1.5. Statistical discrepancy (5.8)	1.10. Exports and property income received (4.1)
	Subtotal
	1.11. Minus: Imports and property income paid (4.5)
Gross national income	Gross national product

II. Personal Income and Outlay Account

2.1. Consumers' expenditures (1.6)	2.5. Payments by producers to individuals (1.1)
2.2. Tax payments by individuals (3.8)	2.6. Transfer payments by government (3.4)
2.3. Transfer payments to abroad (4.6)	2.7. Transfer payments from abroad (4.2)
2.4. Personal saving (5.3)	
Personal outlay and saving	Personal income

III. Government Receipts and Outlay Account

3.1. Government expenditures, net (1.7)	3.7. Tax payments by producers (1.3)
3.2. Subsidies and government interest (5.5)	3.8. Tax payments by individuals (2.2)
3.3. Capital grants to government enterprises (5.5)	3.9. Transfer payments from abroad (4.3)
3.4. Transfer payments to individuals (2.6)	
3.5. Transfer payments to abroad (4.7)	
3.6. Surplus (5.6)	
Government outlay and surplus	Government receipts

IV. Foreign Trade and Payments Account

Receipts from abroad	Payments to abroad
4.1. Exports and property income received (1.10)	4.5. Imports and property income paid (1.11)
4.2. Transfer payments to individuals (2.7)	4.6. Transfer payments from individuals (2.3)
4.3. Transfer payments to government (3.9)	4.7. Transfer payments from government (3.5)
4.4. Net borrowing from abroad (5.7)	

V. Gross Saving and Investment Account

Gross investment	Gross saving
5.1. Gross expenditures on producers' durables (1.8) +$10	5.3. Personal saving (2.4)
5.2. Net change in inventories (1.9) −10	5.4. Income retained by producers (1.2)
	5.5. Capital grants to government enterprises (3.3)
	5.6. Government surplus (3.6)
	5.7. Net borrowing from abroad (4.4)
	5.8. Statistical discrepancy (1.5)

than of a subjective participant. In similar manner the Foreign Trade
and Payments Account may, for the purpose at hand, be split into two
separate parts, one part showing exports as injections of income into the
economy, the other part showing imports as withdrawals of income from
the economy. Finally, since the decisions involving saving are quite
different from those involving investment, it will be quite proper to
consider saving as a withdrawal of income from the economic system and
investment as an injection of income into the system.

Given this general view of the economic system, a picture of income
flows can be constructed that will show (1) the income that producers
receive from consumers, plus the additional injections made by government, gross domestic investment, and foreign trade; (2) the income
that does not get back to consumers because of the leakages of tax payments to government by producers and the income retained by producers; (3) the income received by consumers from producers, plus the
injections of government transfer payments; and (4) the income that is
not passed back to producers by consumers due to the leakages of personal saving and personal taxes. A diagrammatic presentation of this
flow of income and expenditure with the injections and leakages is given
for the United States economy in 1953 in Chart 12.

As in the sector accounts, the sources of income are equal to the
allocations, both for producers and consumers. By definition, also, the
total of all injections into the system (i.e., subsidies, government interest,
exports, net change in inventories, gross domestic investment expenditures, government expenditures on goods and services, and government
transfer payments to individuals) is equal to the total of all the leakages
from the system (imports, tax payments by producers, income retained
by producers, personal taxes, and personal saving). Any new injection
into either sector which does not result in an increased flow of income
must by definition be matched by an equivalent leakage.

Changes in the level of consumers' incomes or producers' receipts can
come about only because of a change in the amount of injections or leakages. An increase in the amount of injections will in the first place cause
an increase either in consumers' incomes or in producers' receipts. If the
sector receiving the injection balances it with an increase in leakages of
equal amount, the other sector will not be affected. As was pointed out
in the discussion of the process of saving and investment, the equal
leakage may exist only because no adjustment time has elapsed. If in the
process of adjustment the initial leakages become smaller or cease to
exist, the injection will also result in an increase in the income or receipts of the other sector. Again it is necessary to examine the process
of adjustment to determine how the new increase in income or receipts

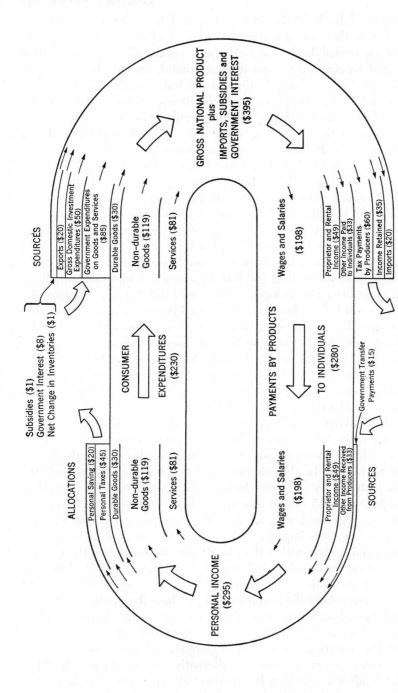

Chart 12. Circular flow for the United States economy in 1953. (In billions.)

will be passed back to the first sector, and how much will now be siphoned off in the form of leakages. An initial injection into an economy thus will be passed back and forth between the sectors, raising their income and receipts each time it goes around, and at the same time being siphoned off gradually in the form of leakages. The rise in income due to an injection is thus a cumulative process involving successive increases in income and outlay by the two sectors. The cumulative process ends when all of the original injection ends up in the form of leakages and each sector is allocating its resulting income as it wishes.

Taxation, in this presentation, is treated as a leakage, that is, a withdrawal of income from the system. As the income and receipts of the economy increase, more and more will be siphoned off in the form of taxes. This will slow the rise in income, and would, if other injections did not increase, have a major role in halting the rise. Government expenditures and transfer payments, on the other hand, are injections of income into the system. If these injections were not accompanied by taxation or other leakages in the system, continued government injections might result in a cumulative rise in income that would develop into a hyperinflation. It does not follow, however, that equal increases in taxes and government expenditures will neutralize each other. Referring to the circular flow shown in Chart 12, suppose the government increases both its expenditures and personal income taxes by $10 billion. Producers' receipts from the government would increase by $10 billion, but in spite of the increase in personal taxes, consumers' expenditures would probably decrease by considerably less than $10 billion. Many individuals would reduce their saving as well as their expenditures, so that the increase in personal taxes might initially cause personal saving to drop by as much as $5 billion, with consumers' expenditures dropping only the remaining $5 billion. In this circumstance the government expenditure, although matched by an equal increase in taxes, would be equivalent to net injection of $5 billion into the system, since producers' receipts would rise by this much as a result of the government's action. For this reason, therefore, it is important to consider the total effect of government taxes and outlays rather than to attempt to summarize the government's effect on the economy in terms of its surplus or deficit alone.

Exports of domestic production may vary because of the changed economic conditions in the countries that purchase the products. Prosperity or inflation abroad may result in an increase in the demand for domestic products, and similarly, a recession or depression abroad may force foreign countries to curtail their purchases. Exports may also fluctuate with declines or increases in alternative sources of supply. Thus immediately after World War II exports of all types were very large, but this volume of exports declined somewhat as the countries recovered from the effects of the war and began to offer their own products on the world market.

Imports, viewed as a leakage, may fluctuate both in response to the general level of domestic output and in response to changes in the relationship of domestic and foreign prices. If the prices of specific raw materials sold in world markets fall, it may be advantageous for domestic producers using such raw materials to purchase their supplies abroad rather than from domestic producers. This would have the effect of increasing the volume of imports, and in many instances correspondingly reducing the amount of income paid out as wages and salaries to the employees of the domestic producers of the raw materials. Insofar as the increase in the volume of imports supplies funds to foreign countries that permit them to increase their purchases from the domestic economy, however, the decrease in income caused by the decreased use of domestic raw materials may be partially or wholly offset by an increase in exports.

Foreign trade and payments thus may have considerable effect upon the operation of the domestic economy. In countries where the size of imports and exports is large relative to the gross national product (e.g., in the Netherlands exports have amounted to 50 per cent of gross national product), the domestic economy may be subjected to severe fluctuations as a result of changes in the world export and import markets.

In conclusion, the importance of the role of leakages and injections of all kinds in the economic system cannot be stressed too much. The decisions behind these leakages and injections are complex and involved. However, they in large part determine the reaction of the economy to income changes, and through their own changes are at times responsible for initiating many of the cumulative changes in income and output that occur.

13. The Mechanism of Income Analysis I: Consumers' Expend- itures and Disposable Income

The previous chapters have shown that the level of activity in the economy depends upon the expenditures that are made for goods and services, but the exact process by which the level of gross national product is determined still remains to be analyzed. It has been shown that an attempt to change the level of gross saving or investment expenditures can start a cumulative change in the level of gross national product, but the explanation is incomplete until the limits of the cumulative movement are determined. The problem is complicated by the fact that both current saving decisions and current investment decisions are themselves highly related to the level and the rate of change of gross national product. The process of cumulative adjustment initiated by a change in saving or investment decisions, therefore, will itself have repercussions upon future saving and investment decisions. The first step in unraveling these relationships must therefore be an attempt to understand the determinants of these saving and investment decisions.

It should be emphasized once more that the purpose of this analysis is not to determine causes or to predict the future course of events but rather to bring about an understanding of the mechanism by which change takes place. It frequently is not possible to determine exactly what repercussions a given event will have. It is possible, however, to discuss the process of change in terms of specific elements and the factors that bear upon them, breaking the total process down into its component parts. For example, a rise in wages would lead producers to expect higher prices, but at the same time it would raise their costs. Just exactly how they would behave in such a situation cannot be determined empirically. But the repercussions that would follow each of the possible reactions of producers can be traced. Income analysis cannot in this case choose between the possible responses of producers, but given their behavior it can lay bare the mechanism by which the change will be integrated into the economic system.

The amount an individual will spend on goods and services is by definition dependent on the amount of his income and the decisions he makes with respect to the division of this income between spending and saving. Different individuals possessing equal incomes will divide this income quite differently, depending on such factors as age, family composition, and even personality. In analyzing total consumers' expenditures and the personal saving for the economy as a whole, however, it is not necessary to know all the determinants of each individual's personal saving. If on the average individuals as a group behave in a predictable manner with respect to their spending and saving decisions, it is possible to omit from the analysis many of the more random factors that will influence specific individuals.

Personal Saving and the Distribution of Income

As a starting point in explaining consumers' spending and saving, it may be asked whether there are significant and systematic differences in the division of income between spending and saving by groups of individuals having different incomes. A good deal of light can be thrown upon this question by the examination of consumer budget data. Table 68 shows how consumers with different levels of income spent these incomes in the year 1935 to 1936; it covers all the 40 million families in the country. It is quite evident that families receiving low incomes saved a different amount from families with higher incomes. Those receiving $2,000 a year or less (two-thirds of the 40 million) paid out as a group more than they received as income. On the average, therefore, more than two-thirds of the families in the United States were dissaving. Families with incomes higher than $2,000 did all the personal saving carried out by individuals, and the personal saving of those receiving incomes above $15,000 amounted to almost half of the total. Of all the families in the United States, 99.5 per cent had incomes of less than $15,000, so that less than 1 per cent of the families in the country were currently doing half of the total personal saving.

If the data contained in Table 68 are recast in terms of average consumers' expenditures and average disposable income, as is done in Table 69, it becomes evident that the amount of income which individuals receive is a very important factor in determining how much they will save, and it is a useful generalization to observe that individuals with higher incomes save more than individuals with lower incomes. This generalization can be framed in a slightly different form by saying that although individuals with higher incomes have more money to spend, they do not use all this extra money for the purchase

Table 68. Consumers' Income and Expenditure, by Income Group, 1935–1936

(Dollar items in millions)

Income group	Number of families, thousands	Personal income	Personal taxes *	Disposable income	Consumption expenditures	Current personal saving
Under $780	13,153	$ 6,190	$ 171	$ 6,019	$ 7,226	−$1,207
$ 780–$ 1,450	13,153	14,154	516	13,638	13,890	−252
1,450– 2,000	5,974	10,035	409	9,626	9,164	462
2,000– 3,000	4,434	10,577	465	10,112	9,043	1,069
3,000– 5,000	1,818	6,644	343	6,301	5,125	1,176
5,000– 15,000	749	5,839	413	5,426	3,529	1,897
$15,000 and over	178	5,820	750	5,070	2,237	2,833
Total..............	39,458	$59,259	$3,067	$56,192	$50,214	$5,978

Percentage Distribution

Income group	Number of families, thousands	Personal income	Personal taxes *	Disposable income	Consumption expenditures	Current personal saving
Under $780	33.3	10.4	5.6	10.7	14.4	−20.2
$ 780–$ 1,450	33.3	23.9	16.8	24.3	27.7	−4.2
1,450– 2,000	15.2	16.9	13.3	17.1	18.3	7.7
2,000– 3,000	11.2	17.9	15.1	18.0	18.0	17.9
3,000– 5,000	4.6	11.2	11.2	11.2	10.2	19.6
5,000– 15,000	1.9	9.9	13.5	9.7	7.0	31.8
$15,000 and over	0.5	9.8	24.5	9.0	4.4	47.4
Total..............	100.0	100.0	100.0	100.0	100.0	100.0

* Includes some gifts.

SOURCE: National Resources Committee, *Consumer Expenditures in the United States. Estimates for 1935–36*, 1939, p. 48.

Table 69. Average Consumers' Expenditures and Personal Saving by Average Disposable Income Classes 1935–1936

Income group	Average disposable income	Average consumer expenditures		Average personal saving		Per cent of increase in disposable income saved
Under $780	$ 458	$ 549	120.1%	−$109	−20.1%	
$ 780–$ 1,450	1,037	1,056	101.8	−19	−1.8	12.4%
1,450– 2,000	1,611	1,534	95.2	77	+4.8	16.7
2,000– 3,000	2,281	2,039	89.4	242	+10.6	24.6
3,000– 5,000	3,466	2,819	81.3	647	+18.7	34.2
5,000– 15,000	7,244	4,712	65.0	2,532	+35.0	49.9
$15,000 and over	28,483	12,567	44.1	15,916	+55.9	63.0
All income groups...	$ 1,424	$ 1,273	89.4%	$ 251	10.6%	

SOURCE: Computed from Table 68.

of consumers' goods. Individuals with higher incomes tend to have a larger absolute amount of saving than those with lower incomes, and in Table 69 even the relative amount saved is greater for the high-income groups than it is for the low-income groups. Families with an average disposable income of $458 in 1935 to 1936 on the average spent 120 per cent of their disposable incomes, whereas families with an average disposable income of $28,483 spent only 44 per cent of their disposable incomes.

The Propensity to Consume for Individuals

This relationship between the level of income and the amount of consumption expenditures by individuals is extremely important in explaining the mechanism of income change. For this reason it will be useful to develop the concept of the propensity to consume. The propensity to consume will be defined as the schedule showing the amount of his disposable income that an individual will spend at various different disposable income levels. Knowledge of an individual's propensity to consume will, of course, simultaneously reveal the amounts that he will be willing to save at these different disposable income levels. No two individuals can be expected to have identical propensities to consume. Just because two individuals receive the same disposable income and spend the same amount is no indication that they would continue to react identically at other levels of disposable income; more likely, were

they both to receive equal increases in disposable income, their reactions
would be different. An individual's propensity to consume changes whenever there is a change in any part of the schedule. For example, as mentioned above, a change in family size or in the age of the children in the
family would undoubtedly alter the family's propensity to consume.
When the family is small or the children are young, the amounts that
would be spent at various levels of disposable income would be quite
different from the amounts that would be spent when the family is
larger or the children older.

Although little or no empirical evidence exists about the exact form
of propensity to consume schedules for specific individuals, it is usually
assumed that as the level of an individual's disposable income increases,
his consumption expenditures will not increase as fast. In other words,
an individual's personal saving in absolute terms will be larger when he
has a high level of disposable income than it will be when his disposable
income is at a lower level. The logic upon which this assumption is based
is simple: when an individual receives an increase in disposable income,
he will be able to divide this increase between spending and saving; he
will increase his consumers' expenditure somewhat, but he will probably
also increase his personal saving (or decrease his dissaving). Similarly,
an individual who receives less disposable income will decrease both his
spending and his saving in order to be able to live within his lower income. Table 69 demonstrates that this relation of saving to disposable
income is true for different individuals receiving different incomes, but
it does not show that it would also be true for the same individual at
different disposable income levels. It obviously will have certain exceptions for specific individuals, but it is believed to apply to most individuals.

The fact that an individual who received $2,000 ten years ago saved
more out of this income than he saves out of $5,000 today is no dis-
proof of this assumption about the propensity to consume. To disprove
it, it would be necessary to show that the individual's saving would
have been smaller than it actually was had he received $5,000 ten years
ago instead of $2,000, and similarly, that his current rate of saving would
increase if today he were to receive $2,000 instead of $5,000. There
are many reasons why individuals may save less at one time than they
did at another even though their disposable income may have increased.
Prices may have gone up, the amount of savings that individuals have
accumulated may have increased, or the standard of living that they
are trying to maintain may have risen; all these would cause a change
in their propensity to consume schedules, so that the observed change
in an individual's saving frequently is more the result of forces that
change the propensity to consume than of the shape of the schedule

itself. The pattern of saving that has taken place during the history of the economy illustrates well the existence of such shifts in the propensity to consume schedules of individuals. It is probably true that the majority of people today are receiving far more real income than their ancestors did, yet they consume a much higher proportion of this real income. An individual's propensity to consume is greatly influenced by many factors in the culture, and in no two periods of history will people be subject to identical forces.

For short periods of time with no great change in the economic and social setting, however, individuals' propensities to consume are relatively stable. Under these conditions an increase in an individual's disposable income will tend to increase the amount he wants to save as well as increasing his ability to spend, and a decrease in his disposable income will decrease the amount he wants to save as well as decreasing his ability to spend.

The Marginal Propensity to Consume for Individuals

Once an individual's propensity to consume schedule is known, it is possible to determine how much of a given increment of disposable income he will spend at any given level of disposable income. For example, if the data shown in Table 69 were applicable to the spending and saving habits of particular individuals as their incomes changed, it would be possible to examine what percentage of a given increment of income they would spend at various income levels. Using these data as an example, if an individual's disposable income were to increase from $458 to $1,037, he would spend 87.6 per cent of the increase in disposable income, and would save 12.6 per cent of it. However, if an individual were at the $7,244 disposable income level, and his disposable income were increased to $28,483, he would spend only 37 per cent of the increase in disposable income, and would save 63 per cent of it. From the data contained in Table 69 it is evident that the higher the level of disposable income, the smaller the percentage of a given increment of disposable income that will be spent. The ratio between the increment of an individual's disposable income and the increment of consumers' expenditure to which it gives rise, i.e.,

$$\frac{\Delta \text{ consumers' expenditure}}{\Delta \text{ disposable income}}$$

is called the marginal propensity to consume. The marginal propensity to consume shows the percentage of a given increment of income that will be spent at a given level of disposable income. If the focus of interest is on the change in consumers' spending that can be expected to result from a given change in disposable income, the marginal propensity to consume is the specific measure needed.

The Consumption Function for Consumers as a Group

Having postulated the relation between an individual's consumption and his income, it is natural to ask about the relation between total consumers' expenditures and total disposable income in the economy. Empirically this relation can be found for any year by looking at the

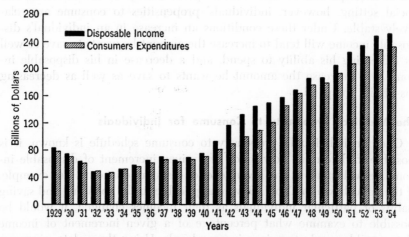

Chart 13. Disposable income and consumers' expenditures, 1929–1954. **Source:** 1929–1953, *National Income*, U.S. Department of Commerce, 1954 ed., pp. 164–165. 1954, *Survey of Current Business*, February, 1955, p. 14.

personal income account. Chart 13 shows total disposable income and total consumers' expenditures for the period 1929 to 1954.

From this chart it seems to be true that the higher the level of disposable income, the greater the amount of personal saving. Many economists have attempted on the basis of the empirical data to establish a relationship that will give the amount of personal saving that can be expected in the economy for different levels of disposable income. One of the most usual procedures in such analyses is to plot the data showing the amount of consumers' expenditures that have been made at different levels of disposable income in the form of a scatter diagram. This has been done in Chart 14.

Some explanation of the mechanics of this chart is in order. The level of disposable income is measured in the horizontal direction, and the level of consumers' expenditures is measured in the vertical direction. The data for 1947, for instance, can be plotted by measuring along the horizontal base line to $169.0 billion, the amount of dis-

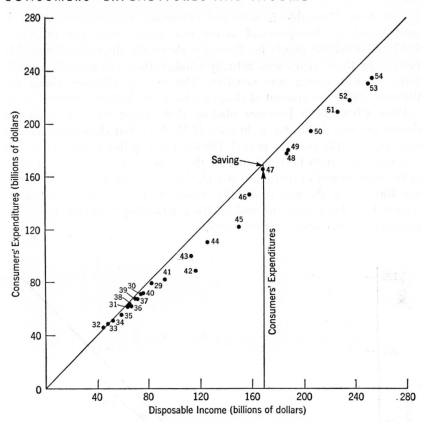

Chart 14. Disposable income and consumers' expenditures, 1929–1954. **Source:** 1929–1953, *National Income*, U.S. Department of Commerce, 1954 ed., pp. 164–165. 1954, *Survey of Current Business*, February, 1955, p. 14.

posable income in 1947, and then erecting a perpendicular at this point to the height of $165.0 billion, the amount of consumers' expenditures. This procedure is shown in Chart 14. For the other years only the points are plotted; the lines of consumers' expenditures are not drawn. The diagonal line on the chart has been drawn in as a guideline to show the points where the horizontal and vertical distances are equal. If disposable income and consumers' expenditures were exactly equal, the plotted point would fall on this diagonal. For 1947 it will be noted that the plotted point fell considerably below the diagonal line. This means that consumers' expenditures were less than disposable income. The vertical distance from the plotted point to the diagonal line (shown by the dotted line) represents the amount of personal saving; it amounted to $4.0 billion ($169.0 minus $165.0) in 1947. The point for 1934, in contrast, lies almost on the diagonal line.

In this year disposable income and consumers' expenditures were almost equal, so that personal saving was nearly zero. For the years 1932 and 1933 the points lie distinctly above the diagonal. Disposable income in these years was actually smaller than consumers' expenditures, so that saving was negative. The vertical distance above the diagonal shows the amount of dissaving by individuals as a group.

From Chart 14 it becomes obvious that saving was much greater during the war than after it, in spite of the fact that disposable income was larger in the postwar period. During the war the amount of saving was unusually high both because of the scarcity of goods and because of the government's program of stimulating saving by selling war bonds. For this reason the war period has generally been excluded when attempts have been made to analyze the relationship between disposable income and consumers' expenditures.

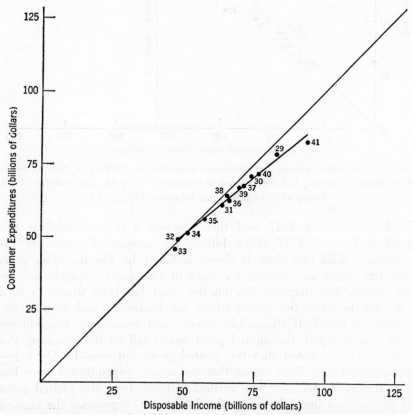

Chart 15. Disposable income and consumers' expenditures, 1929–1941. **Source:** *National Income,* U.S. Department of Commerce, 1954 ed., pp. 164–165.

The period from 1929 to 1941 appears to indicate the existence of a more general relationship between the level of disposable income and the amount of consumers' expenditures. A straight line can be drawn almost through the points that have been plotted. Such a line has been drawn in Chart 15.[1]

[1] This line is the regression line of best fit. A straight line has been fitted in this particular case; it does not necessarily follow that a straight line is best for all cases. Furthermore, no such line should be considered to apply over a range greater than that represented by the points to which it is fitted; the line should not be extended either upward or downward. Fitting a line such as this to the data is objectionable on a number of grounds, but it does serve to emphasize some important points. In the first place it seems to be true that the larger the disposable income of individuals the greater (as a group) their current personal saving has been. But, and this is more important, the computed relationship does not hold exactly for all the years to which the regression line is fitted. Attempts have frequently been made to refine and adjust the data in order to obtain a regression line that fits better. In most cases the process of obtaining a more adequate fit has involved the introduction of additional variables or special explanations of why particular years are not "normal." For example, it will be noted that the points which lie above the regression line generally refer to periods when income was declining, whereas those which are below the regression line are more apt to represent years in which income was increasing. This might logically be expected if people had difficulty adjusting their standards of living downward in a depression and/or did not react immediately to increase their expenditures when their incomes rose. Diligent rationalization or the experimental adding of variables can always lessen the discrepancy between the consumption function and actual consumers' expenditures, but this procedure is not necessarily very helpful for explaining the relation that may occur between disposable income and consumers' expenditures in the future. Furthermore, the national income statistics themselves are estimates and as such are subject to error, so that the discrepancies which are being eliminated may be different from those which actually exist. The data without any adjustments reveal quite a close relationship between disposable income and consumers' expenditures, but it is not close enough so that anything can be predicted from it with respect to saving beyond a very general indication of magnitude. The table on p. 314 shows the difference between actual personal saving and personal saving as estimated from the computed relation for the years 1929 to 1941.

It is apparent from this table that the change in saving resulting from a given change in disposable income cannot be estimated very accurately from this computed relation. For example, in 1937 disposable income was $71.0 billion, and in 1938 it was $65.7 billion. According to the consumption function (the fitted regression line), a decrease in personal saving of $1.0 billion would have been expected to accompany this change in income. Actually, however, saving decreased by $2.6 billion in this period, from $3.7 billion to $1.1 billion.

The reasons for the failure of the computed consumption function to explain fully the changes that take place in personal saving may be divided into two general groups: changes in the distribution of disposable income among individuals, and changes in the propensities to consume of individual consumers. Were it not for changes either in the income distribution or in individuals' propensities to consume, a consumption function could be fitted to the data that would truly represent

The line that has been drawn in Chart 15 is often referred to as the consumption function. Assuming this line to be an adequate guide to consumers' expenditures, it can be used to indicate the amount that people can be expected to spend for any level of disposable income. At any level of disposable income this amount can be estimated by the length of the perpendicular from the base line to the consumption function. The consumption function is thus a schedule of how much individuals as a group may be expected to spend at different levels of disposable income.

The Marginal Consumption Ratio. Just as the propensity to consume schedule for an individual implies a given set of marginal propensities to consume, so the consumption function for the economy implies a set of marginal consumption ratios. These ratios indicate the percentage of a given aggregate increment of disposable income that will be spent by individuals as a group at various levels of aggregate disposable income. In the case of the straight-line consumption function shown in Chart 15, the marginal consumption ratios would be the same for all levels of aggregate disposable income. That is, according to the consumption function given in Chart 15, 80 per cent of an increment in aggregate dis-

	Actual personal saving	Personal saving as estimated from the regression line of best fit
1929	$ 4.2	$8.3
1930	3.4	4.4
1931	2.5	2.3
1932	−0.6	−0.8
1933	−0.6	−1.4
1934	0.1	−0.1
1935	2.0	1.2
1936	3.6	2.8
1937	3.7	3.7
1938	1.1	2.7
1939	2.9	3.6
1940	4.2	4.8
1941	11.1	8.2

the relationship between disposable income and consumers' expenditures, i.e., all the points in Chart 15 would lie on the regression line. Either of these types of change, however, can shift the consumption function from year to year, so that no one relation can be computed for the whole series of years.

posable income would be spent by individuals as a group irrespective of the level of aggregate disposable income in the economy. Should a consumption function of the type described by the data contained in Table 69 obtain for the economy, however, the marginal consumption ratio would decrease with an increase in the level of disposable income. Just as the consumption function can be thought of as an aggregation of individual propensities to consume, so also the marginal consumption ratio can be thought of as an aggregation of individual marginal propensities to consume.

The Distribution of Income as Related to the Consumption Function. From the data presented in Table 69 it is apparent that any change in the distribution of personal income among individuals would probably cause a change in the total amount of personal saving that would accompany a given level of disposable income in the economy. If income were taken from the upper income groups, for example, and given to the lower income groups, personal saving would probably decrease: the lower income groups would spend more of this income than the upper income groups had. Conversely, if the income of the lower income groups is decreased and that of the upper income groups increased by the same amount, personal saving would probably increase. What is involved in this example is the redistribution of income between income groups having a relatively low marginal propensity to consume (high-income groups) and those having a relatively high marginal propensity to consume (low-income groups). If all individuals had the same marginal propensities to consume, the redistribution of income in the economy would have no effect on spending and saving. The data shown in Tables 68 and 69, however, strongly suggest that the marginal propensities to consume of different income groups are in fact quite different. For this reason the way in which income is distributed among individuals is probably an important factor in determining the amount of saving. With different distributions of income, different amounts of saving would accompany the same level of disposable income. This idea is represented graphically in Fig. 2.

The point X on this diagram represents the amount of consumers' expenditures that would accompany a given level of disposable income, for one specific income distribution. Point Y, below point X, shows the amount of consumers' expenditures that might result if the distribution of income existing at X were altered by taking income away from the lower income groups and giving it to the upper income groups. Under such circumstances it is reasonable to assume that the lower income groups would be forced to reduce their consumption. The upper income groups might increase their consumption somewhat, but they would probably save more of this income than the lower in-

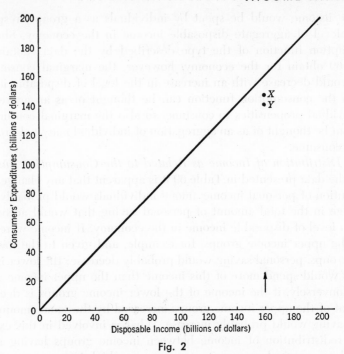

Fig. 2

come groups had. Therefore total consumers' expenditures accompany-ing this level of disposable income would be reduced by the redis-tribution of the income. This is another way of saying that the amount of consumers' expenditures that can be expected with a given level of disposable income will in large part depend upon the way in which that income is distributed among individuals.

By extending this argument to apply to more than one level of dis-posable income, it can be demonstrated that a different consumption function must exist for each different type of income distribution. This is shown graphically in Fig. 3.

Line *Y* on this chart represents the consumers' expenditures to be expected at different levels of disposable income with a distribution of income that probably would be somewhat more equal than that represented by line *X*. There is, of course, no reason why the con-sumption functions that would accompany the different income dis-tributions should be parallel. Two different types of income distribu-tion might yield the same amount of consumers' expenditures at one level of disposable income and different amounts of consumers' ex-penditures at other levels of disposable income. The consumption functions might then actually cross each other.

An increase in the level of income without any change in the rela-

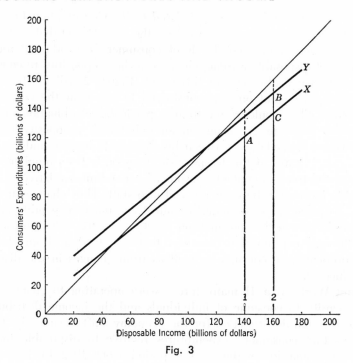

Fig. 3

tive distribution of income would be equivalent to moving along the particular consumption function, but a change in the type of income distribution would be equivalent to moving to a different consumption function. A change in the level of disposable income in the economy may also change the distribution of income, so that the point which is finally reached is not only at a different level of income but also on a new consumption function. In terms of Fig. 3, for example, the economy may start out at point A, at a given level of income and with a particular income distribution. As the level of income changes, the distribution of this income may also shift, and consumers' expenditures at the new level of income will fall on a new consumption function at point B, instead of at point C, where they would have been if the income distribution had not changed.

In practice it has been found that over short periods of time the distribution of income in the economy is relatively stable, so that the consumption function applicable to one year will not for this reason differ greatly from that for the next. Yet between longer periods of time or during periods of violent change, differing income distributions may well cause consumers' expenditures to fall on different consumption functions.

The Propensity to Consume as Related to the Consumption Function.
Differing income distributions are not the only force that will lead
to the existence of different levels of consumers' expenditures for the
same level of disposable income; changes in the propensities to consume
of individuals can also lead to this result. Figure 2 will illustrate this
situation if each point on it is considered to represent the consumers'
expenditures that would result from a particular combination of propensities to consume. A change in an individual's propensity to consume changes the relation between his disposable income and his consumers' expenditures; if this happens simultaneously for a number of individuals, the total amount of consumers' expenditures relative to total
disposable income in the economy will also shift. Thus changes in individuals' propensities to consume that affect consumers' expenditures will
result in changes in the consumption function. Figure 3 therefore represents differing consumption functions that might result from changes
in the propensity to consume as well as from changes in the distribution of income.

During World War II many forces were operating to change both
the propensity to consume of individuals and the income distribution,
and the consumption function for the economy shifted violently. Chart
14 shows that consumers' expenditures relative to disposable income
were very much lower during the period from 1942 to 1945 than
they might have been expected to be on the basis of prewar experience. Because of rationing and the shortages of consumers' goods, individuals found it difficult to buy the quantities of goods that, with
their wartime incomes, they would have liked to buy. In ordinary circumstances prices of consumers' goods would have risen until at the
new prices the total quantity of goods available would have exactly
equaled the amount that consumers wished to spend, but during the
war such price rises were prevented by price controls. Consumers
therefore were led to save a larger portion of their incomes than they
otherwise would have. Furthermore, great efforts were made during
this period to induce individuals to increase their savings in the form
of war bonds. The consumption function therefore shifted downward.
After the war the consumption function continued to shift under the
impact of changes in surrounding circumstances. Consumers' goods that
had been scarce became more plentiful; soldiers who were discharged
from the army had to buy civilian clothes; and many similar postwar
adjustments took place.

The stability of the consumption function is to a very large extent
dependent upon the stability of the propensities to consume of individuals. Anything that alters the latter will alter the consumption
function based upon them; and for this reason whenever the con-

sumption function is used to predict the level of consumers' expenditures that will accompany a given level of disposable income, close attention must be given to the possibility of changes in the propensities to consume of individuals.

The Theory of the Multiplier

The consumption function for the economy is one of the key elements in the mechanism of income analysis. But since it is only one of the factors that are important, certain simplifying assumptions are necessary to demonstrate its role. Only after other elements such as the relation between disposable income and gross national product and the role of investment expenditures, government expenditures, and foreign trade have been discussed can the whole mechanism be fully understood. The analysis can be simplified, however, by taking these factors up one at a time. In order to demonstrate the role of the consumption function alone, the additional factors will be eliminated by making the assumptions that (1) gross national product equals disposable income, and (2) investment expenditures, government expenditures, and foreign trade together are a fixed absolute amount determined by forces outside the system. Both of these assumptions are of course very unrealistic, and will be removed in turn in the following two chapters, so that the operation of the economy under more realistic conditions can be examined.

One of the simplest national income accounting models conforming to these assumptions would be one in which there were no taxes, no income retained by producers, and foreign trade was in balance. Such a situation is shown in Table 70. In this example gross national product is $300 billion, and since there are no producers' tax payments, no income retained by producers, and no transfers received by individuals, all of gross national product flows into personal income, so that personal income equals gross national product. Since individuals pay no taxes either, disposable income in turn is equal to personal income, and therefore also to the gross national product. Personal saving in this model is assumed to be $40 billion, government expenditures $20 billion, and investment expenditure $20 billion. Since the government collects no taxes in this example, it has a deficit of $20 billion, and thus is dissaving. In the Gross Saving and Investment Account, therefore, the gross saving for the economy is $20 billion, balancing the gross investment expenditures.

It is now possible to examine the chain of repercussions and the final effect upon the level of gross national product and disposable income of an arbitrary change in the level of investment expenditures. The change assumed in this example will be $20 billion. Initially, therefore, investment expenditures will increase by $20 billion, leading to simultaneous

Table 70
(In billions)

I. Gross National Income and Product Account

1.1. Payments by producers to individuals (2.5)	$300	1.6. Consumers' expenditures (2.1)	$260
1.2. Income retained by producers (5.4)	0	1.7. Government expenditures, net (3.1)	20
1.3. Tax payments by producers (3.7)	0	1.8. Gross expenditures on producers' durables (5.1)	20
1.4. Minus: Subsidies and government interest (3.2)	0	1.9. Net change in inventories (5.2)	0
1.5. Statistical discrepancy (5.8)	0	1.10. Exports and property income received (4.1)	5
		Subtotal	$305
		1.11. Minus: Imports and property income paid (4.5)	5
Gross national income	$300	Gross national product	$300

II. Personal Income and Outlay Account

2.1. Consumers' expenditures (1.6)	$260	2.5. Payments by producers to individuals (1.1)	$300
2.2. Tax payments by individuals (3.8)	0	2.6. Transfer payments by government (3.4)	0
2.3. Transfer payments to abroad (4.6)	0	2.7. Transfer payments from abroad (4.2)	0
2.4. Personal saving (5.3)	40		
Personal outlay and saving	$300	Personal income	$300

III. Government Receipts and Outlay Account

3.1. Government expenditures, net (1.7)	$ 20	3.7. Tax payments by producers (1.3)	$ 0
3.2. Subsidies and government interest (1.4)	0	3.8. Tax payments by individuals (2.2)	0
3.3. Capital grants to government enterprises (5.5)	0	3.9. Transfer payments from abroad (4.3)	0
3.4. Transfer payments to individuals (2.6)	0		
3.5. Transfer payments to abroad (4.7)	0		
3.6. Surplus (5.6)	−20		
Government outlay and surplus	$ 0	Government receipts	$ 0

IV. Foreign Trade and Payments Account

4.1.	Exports and property income received (1.10)	$ 5	4.5.	Imports and property income paid (1.11)	$ 5
4.2.	Transfer payments to individuals (2.7)	0	4.6.	Transfer payments from individuals (2.3)	0
4.3.	Transfer payments to government (3.9)	0	4.7.	Transfer payments from government (3.5)	0
4.4.	Net borrowing from abroad (5.7)	0			
	Receipts from abroad	**$ 5**		**Payments to abroad**	**$ 5**

V. Gross Saving and Investment Account

5.1.	Gross expenditures on producers' durables (1.8)	$ 20	5.3.	Personal saving (2.4)	$ 40
5.2.	Net change in inventories (1.9)	0	5.4.	Income retained by producers (1.2)	0
			5.5.	Capital grants to government enterprises (3.3)	0
			5.6.	Government surplus (3.6)	−20
			5.7.	Net borrowing from abroad (4.4)	0
			5.8.	Statistical discrepancy (1.5)	0
	Gross investment	**$ 20**		**Gross saving**	**$ 20**

Table 71

(In billions)

I. Gross National Income and Product Account

1.1. Payments by producers to individuals (2.5)	+$20	1.6. Consumers' expenditures (2.1)	+$20
1.2. Income retained by producers (5.4)		1.7. Government expenditures, net (3.1)	
1.3. Tax payments by producers (3.7)		1.8. Gross expenditures on producers' durables (5.1)	
1.4. Minus: Subsidies and government interest (3.2)		1.9. Net change in inventories (5.2)	
1.5. Statistical discrepancy (5.8)		1.10. Exports and property income received (4.1)	
		Subtotal	+$20
		1.11. Minus: Imports and property income paid (4.5)	
Gross national income	+$20	Gross national product	+$20

II. Personal Income and Outlay Account

2.1. Consumers' expenditures (1.6)	+$20	2.5. Payments by producers to individuals (1.1)	+$20
2.2. Tax payments by individuals (3.8)		2.6. Transfer payments by government (3.4)	
2.3. Transfer payments to abroad (4.6)		2.7. Transfer payments from abroad (4.2)	
2.4. Personal saving (5.3)	+$20		
Personal outlay and saving	+$20	Personal income	+$20

III. Government Receipts and Outlay Account

3.1. Government expenditures, net (1.7)		3.7. Tax payments by producers (1.3)
3.2. Subsidies and government interest (1.4)		3.8. Tax payments by individuals (2.2)
3.3. Capital grants to government enterprises (5.5)		3.9. Transfer payments from abroad (4.3)
3.4. Transfer payments to individuals (2.6)		
3.5. Transfer payments to abroad (4.7)		
3.6. Surplus (5.6)		
Government outlay and surplus		Government receipts

IV. Foreign Trade and Payments Account

4.1. Exports and property income received (1.10)	4.5. Imports and property income paid (1.11)
4.2. Transfer payments to individuals (2.7)	4.6. Transfer payments from individuals (2.3)
4.3. Transfer payments to government (3.9)	4.7. Transfer payments from government (3.5)
4.4. Net borrowing from abroad (5.7)	
Receipts from abroad	Payments to abroad

V. Gross Saving and Investment Account

5.1. Gross expenditures on producers' durables (1.8)	+$20	5.3. Personal saving (2.4)	
5.2. Net change in inventories (1.9)		5.4. Income retained by producers (1.2)	
		5.5. Capital grants to government enterprises (3.3)	
		5.6. Government surplus (3.6)	
		5.7. Net borrowing from abroad (4.4)	
		5.8. Statistical discrepancy (1.5)	
Gross investment	+$20	Gross saving	+$20

increases in gross national product, personal income, disposable income, and personal saving of the same amount. The immediate changes are shown in Table 71, pp. 322–323.

The general reaction to be expected as a consequence of these changes was described in Chap. 12. When individuals attempt to adjust to their new level of disposable income by increasing their consumers' expenditures in accord with their marginal propensities to consume, it would at first glance seem that their consumers' expenditures should increase and their personal saving decrease. But in the particular situation described by the accounts shown in Table 70 this cannot happen. As long as the two simplifying assumptions that were made above hold, any increase in consumers' expenditures will result in an immediate and equal increase in gross national product, personal income, and disposable income.[2] Personal saving thus will not be affected by the increased consumers' expenditures of individuals. The more people as a group spend, the more (by exactly the same amount) they will receive as disposable income. The gap between their disposable income and their consumers' expenditures cannot be changed by the process of increasing consumers' expenditures—and this gap is, of course, personal saving. No matter how hard individuals may try, therefore, in this simplified situation they cannot as a group change the amount of personal saving. The more they spend, the more income they will have; the absolute amount of personal saving will remain the same.

It does not follow, however, that in response to an arbitrary increase in investment expenditures individuals will continue to increase their consumers' expenditures (and so their incomes) indefinitely. Although consumers cannot change the absolute amount of their personal saving, the change in their incomes will change their desire to save. As their disposable incomes rise, individuals as a group will be willing to save a larger absolute amount. The actual saving that they are doing will remain the same, but a larger part of it will be voluntary, and a smaller part will be involuntary. Eventually a level of disposable income will be reached at which all of individuals' saving is voluntary; at this level of disposable income the actual amount of personal saving will be exactly what individuals want it to be. When this point is reached, individuals will no longer try to increase their consumers' expenditures, since they are spending and saving in exactly the proportions they prefer. When consumers' expenditures stop increasing, personal incomes will also stop

[2] As previously described, it would be possible for the increase in consumers' expenditures to result in an involuntary decline of producers' inventories, so that gross national product would not rise in this initial instance. For simplicity this particular possibility has been omitted in the following discussion, although it can easily be carried through in the accounts and diagrams as an alternative possibility.

rising and the series of repercussions will come to an end. Throughout the whole process the actual amount of personal saving has changed only once, in response to the initial increase in investment expenditure. The chain of reaction comes to an end not when consumers adjust their personal saving to the level they wish, but rather when their disposable incomes have risen to the point where they are satisfied to continue the amount of saving they are doing.[3] Diagrammatically, this is shown in Fig. 4.

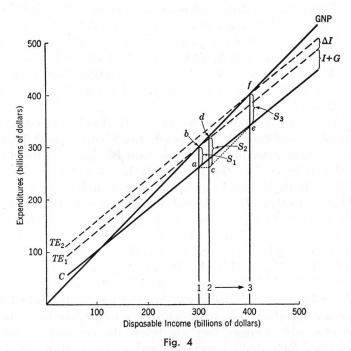

Fig. 4

This diagram is of the same general nature as those already shown in Charts 14 and 15 and Fig. 3, except that it has been adapted to the conditions described in Tables 70 and 71. The initial situation (Table 70) where gross national product and disposable income both equal $300 billion, is shown at the point of the vertical line 1 on the chart. This line cuts the consumption function (C) at point a, indicating consumers' expenditures of $260 billion, and meets the 45-degree line at point b, indicating gross national product of $300 billion. Since gross national product and disposable income are equal in this example, the distance from point a to point b ($40 billion) equals the sum of investment and gov-

[3] In this situation it is implicitly assumed that with the rise in disposable income prices will not change enough to bring about a change in the consumption function.

ernment expenditures,[4] and also equals personal saving (S_1). On the one hand, the diagram shows that consumers' expenditures (a) of $260 billion, plus the assumed investment and government expenditures $(I + G)$ of $40 billion, equals the gross national product (b) of $300 billion. On the other hand, it also shows that disposable income of $300 billion (b), minus the consumers' expenditures (a) of $260 billion, equals personal saving (S_1) of $40 billion. The broken line TE_1, which is above the consumption function by the amount $I + G$, is called the total expenditures function. Its shape and position conform to the condition that both investment and government expenditures are determined by factors outside the system, so that the total expenditures in the economy under equilibrium conditions will in fact be equal to the volume of desired consumers' expenditures, as given by the consumption function (C), plus the assumed fixed amount of investment and government expenditures of $40 billion $(I + G)$.

When the assumed $20 billion increase in the level of investment and government expenditures is introduced, two changes must be made. First, a new total expenditures function must be shown; in the diagram this is shown by adding the increase in investment expenditures ΔI ($20 billion) to the old total expenditures function, forming a new total expenditures function (TE_2). Second, the change in disposable income, equal in amount to the increase in investment expenditures of $20 billion, must also be shown; in the diagram this is indicated by the vertical line 2. At this point it will be seen that personal saving (S_2) has risen to $60 billion, since there has been no opportunity as yet for individuals to increase their consumption, and consumers' expenditures, shown by point c, are the same as they were at point a. Individuals, however, are not spending and saving what they would like to at the new level of disposable income; they are below the consumption function that describes their desired spending and saving relationship. In the attempt to get back to the consumption function and thus regain the desired relation between spending and saving, individuals will increase their consumers' expenditures. This will result, under the given assumptions, in an increase in disposable income that is exactly equal to the increase in consumers' expenditures. The path of adjustment of consumers' expenditures is therefore shown by the dotted line parallel to the 45-degree (GNP) line. As individuals expand their spending, their disposable income will rise equally, leaving their personal saving unchanged. Since the consumption function slopes at an angle of less than 45 degrees, and the path of adjustment is at the 45-degree angle, there will be a point where the path of adjustment does catch up with the

---

[4] Since exports equaled imports in this simple example, foreign trade does not appear as an element in the gross national product.

consumption function; in the diagram this is point e, on vertical line 3. At this point the absolute amount of personal saving (S_3) is equal to the absolute amount of personal saving (S_2), $60 billion, that existed immediately after the change in investment, and throughout the whole process of adjustment personal saving has remained the same. The final situation described by the vertical line 3 is stable not because personal saving has adjusted, but rather because individuals are now willing to do this absolute amount of personal saving because of the increase in the level of their disposable incomes.

The amount by which disposable income must rise before the equilibrium position is reached obviously will depend upon the shape of the consumption function. If the consumption function is nearly parallel to the diagonal, a considerable rise in disposable income may be necessary before individuals will voluntarily save what is required of them by the economy. On the other hand, if the consumption function diverges rapidly from the diagonal, only a small increase in disposable income need occur before individuals will voluntarily save the necessary amount.

Even without explicit knowledge of the slope of the dotted adjustment path of consumers' expenditures, the point of stable equilibrium for gross national product and disposable income can be determined by the intersection of the total expenditures function with the disposable income function. The intersection of the original total expenditures function (TE_1) and the disposable income function (GNP) is at point b ($300 billion), and after the increase in investment expenditures ΔI, the intersection of the new total expenditures function (TE_2) with the disposable income function (GNP) is point f ($400 billion). The reason that these points are actually points of equilibrium lies in the definition of the total expenditures function. It represents the amount of consumers' expenditures individuals desire at a given level of disposable income, plus the amount of investment and government expenditures that will be forthcoming at this level. Therefore when gross national product and disposable income, as indicated by the disposable income function (GNP), actually crosses the total expenditures function (TE), the economy will have no reason to change the level of expenditures, and so equilibrium will be achieved.

The ratio of the total change in the level of disposable income to the original change in investment that set it off is termed the multiplier. With a stable consumption function and with the simplifying assumptions described above, this ratio can be determined quite simply either graphically or statistically. Graphically, the multiplier can be derived from Fig. 4 by relating the initial change in investment expenditures and disposable income of $20 billion (line 2 minus line 1) to the total change that finally took place in disposable income of $100 billion (line 3 minus line 1). The total change in this instance turned out to be five times the initial change, so that the initial change had a multiplier of five. Statistically, the multiplier can be computed by taking into account the marginal consumption ratio. As pointed out above in connection with the marginal propensity to consume, it is the spending decisions of individuals with respect to the *increment* of disposable income they receive that is important in determining their behavior. Similarly, for the individuals as a group it is the marginal consumption ratio that is important in the analysis of changes. In Fig. 4 the marginal consumption ratio is constant for all levels of disposable income, and as drawn comes out to be .80. This means that individuals as a group tend to consume 80 per cent of any increment of disposable income they receive. The multiplier can be calculated by the simple formula $1/(1 - \text{MCR})$, which in this case would be $1/(1 - .80)$, or five.[5] This of course is the same

[5] This formula can be developed quite simply from the definitions and relationships given by the national income accounts and by the concepts of income analysis that have been developed. The changes in the relevant national income aggregates and components are defined as follows:

$$\Delta DI = \text{change in disposable income}$$
$$\Delta I = \text{change in investment expenditures}$$
$$\Delta C = \text{change in consumers' expenditures}$$

The income analysis concepts that have been developed thus far expressed in these terms are

$$\frac{\Delta C}{\Delta DI} = \text{marginal consumption ratio (MCR)}$$

$$\frac{\Delta DI}{\Delta I} = \text{the multiplier}$$

The accounting definition under the assumptions postulated in the above example would result in the following equation:

$$\Delta I + \Delta C = \Delta DI$$

If each side of this equation is divided by $1/\Delta DI$, the equation becomes

$$\frac{\Delta DI}{\Delta I} \text{ (i.e., the multiplier)} = \frac{\Delta DI}{\Delta DI - \Delta C}$$

Dividing the numerator and denominator of the second half of the equation by ΔDI, this becomes:

$$\text{The multiplier} = \frac{1}{1 - \dfrac{\Delta C}{\Delta DI}}$$

By definition this is the same as

$$\text{The multiplier} = \frac{1}{1 - \text{MCR}}$$

as the value of the multiplier derived graphically from Fig. 4. From this formula it can be seen that the higher the marginal consumption ratio, the larger the multiplier will be. If the marginal consumption ratio were .90, the multiplier would be 10, and if it were .99, the multiplier would be 100. If the marginal consumption ratio were 1.00, no stable equilibrium could ever be reached under the simplifying assumptions postulated above.

Just as the arbitrary increase in investment expenditures postulated above led to a cumulative upward movement of disposable income, so also an arbitrary decrease in investment expenditures will lead to a similar chain of reactions in the opposite direction. The decrease in investment expenditures under the simplifying assumptions made above will produce an equal decrease in disposable income. Until consumers have a chance to adjust their expenditures, personal saving will necessarily decrease (or personal dissaving increase). Individuals will then cut their consumers' expenditures in the attempt to bring their personal saving back up to the level they want, but this cut in consumers' expenditures will have the effect only of decreasing disposable income once more, so that personal saving of the group as a whole will not change. This process will continue until disposable income has fallen to the point where the actual amount of personal saving being done is all that individuals want to do; at this point the chain of reactions will cease. Figure 5 illustrates this process.

The original situation described in Table 70 is again shown by vertical line 1, and the situation immediately after the decrease in investment expenditures (the same as Table 71 but with negative items instead) is shown by the vertical line 2. With the decrease in investment expenditures of $20 billion, disposable income will fall by the same amount, and before consumers can adjust their expenditures, personal saving will fall by the same $20 billion, from the original $40 billion ($S_1$) to $20 billion ($S_2$). Now consumers find themselves spending more than they want to (i.e., saving less) in relation to their disposable income, so they attempt to get back to the consumption function by cutting their consumers' expenditures. As a result, however, under the assumptions postulated, disposable income will fall by exactly the same amount, so that personal saving will stay the same. A stable situation will be reached when disposable income falls sufficiently so that the volume of personal saving being done is in fact in line with what individuals want to save as indicated by the consumption function. As in the previous example, the new equilibrium position is given by the intersection of the new total expenditures function (TE_2) with the disposable income function (GNP) at point f. The multiplier of five is the same as that shown for the

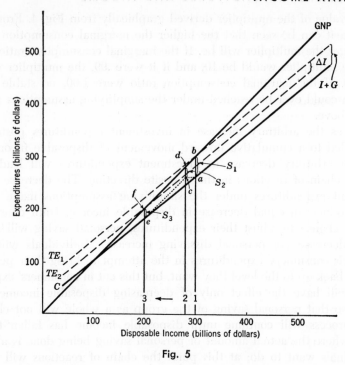

Fig. 5

previous example; the reason for this is of course that the same linear consumption function, having a marginal consumption ratio of .80, was used.

The Effect of Shifts in the Consumption Function

Cumulative changes in the level of disposable income can be brought about by shifts in the consumption function as well as by changes in the level of investment expenditures. As has already been pointed out, shifts in the consumption function may occur for a variety of reasons. Family size may change, the distribution of income among income groups may shift, new consumers' durables may come on the market, and such factors as unemployment insurance and pensions may alter saving decisions. These are all primarily long-run considerations. From a short-run point of view also there are many factors that can cause shifts in the consumption function. During the war, for example, individuals could not obtain goods, and they were influenced by patriotic motives to refrain from spending and to buy war bonds instead. This caused the consumption function to shift downward from its normal position. After the war the greater availability of goods, the backlog of demand, and the existence of liquid funds in the hands of individuals led to an upward shift in the consumption function to a position probably higher than would have existed under normal conditions. After a few years of such spending, much of the liquid funds was used up and the stock of consumers' durables in the hands of individuals had increased, so that it is probable that another downward shift in the consumption function occurred.

The repercussions of a downward shift in the consumption function are shown in diagrammatic terms in Fig. 6.[6] The original equilibrium position

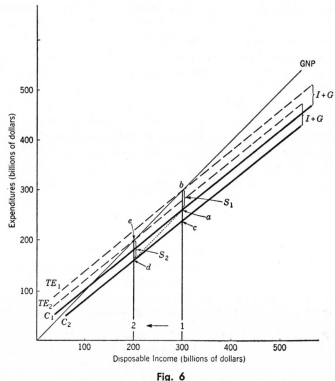

Fig. 6

is assumed to be identical with that given in Figs. 4 and 5. The impetus to cumulative movement in this case is the downward shift of the consumption function, from position C_1 to position C_2. This shift in the consumption function causes a corresponding and equal downward shift in the total expenditures function, from TE_1 to TE_2. Personal saving in the original situation was $40 billion ($S_1$). The new consumption function

---

[6] The shift of the consumption function need not necessarily be a parallel shift as depicted in Fig. 6. The parallel shift has been used in this example for diagrammatic simplicity. A nonparallel shift would mean that the marginal consumption ratio had changed.

(C_2) indicates that in the new situation individuals would like to save $60 billion at the existing level of disposable income. Consumers' expenditures are therefore cut back. But the process of adjustment does not result in a decrease in personal saving. Instead, what happens is that disposable income declines by exactly the same amount as consumers' expenditures, so that personal saving remains unchanged. Equilibrium will be reached when the process of adjustment brings individuals to point d, where the amount of personal saving that is being done matches the amount which the consumption function indicates is desired. This position is of course where the new total expenditures function (TE_2) crosses the disposable income function (GNP) at point e.

One more practical consideration should be brought out in connection with the process of adjustment and the magnitude of the multiplier. Throughout the analysis of the impact of a change in investment expenditures it was implicitly assumed that the consumption function would not shift. This assumption is not necessarily warranted. Changes in the distribution of income, changes in prices, and/or changes in the expectations of consumers may result from changes in the level of disposable income, and any of these may cause shifts in the consumption function that will alter the actual multiplier.[7] Such a reaction is shown in Fig. 7.

This diagram portrays the same situation that was shown in Fig. 4, except that in this case the consumption function also shifts in an upward direction. The initial increase in investment expenditures of $20 billion (ΔI) caused an increase in disposable income of an equal amount as shown by vertical line 2, and an equal rise in the total expenditures function, from (TE_1) to (TE_2). In this situation the personal saving of individuals (S_2) exceeded the amount of personal saving individuals

[7] Since a change in the level of disposable income invariably causes changes in the distribution of income and in relative prices, it is probably impossible for the economy actually to move along a particular consumption function. Instead, the consumption function itself will shift continually throughout the process of adjustment. For this reason the empirical consumption function shown in Chart 15 actually represents points on a number of different consumption functions, since both movements along the consumption function and shifts of the consumption function itself would have occurred over the years. In order to eliminate the effect of prices on the consumption function, some economists prefer to consider consumers' expenditures a function of real income rather than a function of money income. The major difficulty with this alternative procedure, however, is that for large segments of the population, where saving either is minimal or takes the form of such things as insurance, changes in consumers' expenditures may not in the short run be determined by real income nearly as much as by money income. For the economy as a whole, furthermore, the rise in prices will force groups with relatively fixed incomes to cut down on their expenditures in real terms, even though for all individuals as a group income in real terms may not have changed.

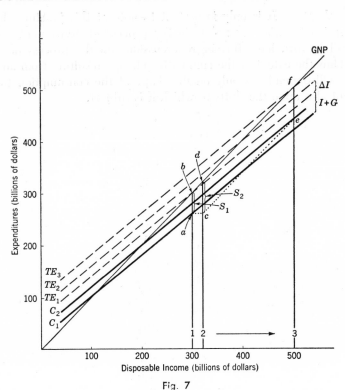

Fig. 7

wished to do at this level of disposable income. As in the example shown in Fig. 4, individuals would increase their consumers' expenditures, and this would simultaneously increase disposable income by an exactly equal amount. The path of adjustment of consumers' expenditures as shown by the dotted line is parallel to the 45-degree (GNP) line. In Fig. 7, however, it has been assumed that this process of adjustment causes the consumption function to rise from C_1 to C_2, and of course this also causes an equal rise in the total expenditures function, from TE_2 to TE_3. The equilibrium position under these conditions becomes point f, $500 billion, where the new total expenditures function (TE_3) intersects the disposable income function (GNP). At this level of gross national product and disposable income, consumers are spending exactly what they want to, as shown by point e. The resulting multiplier has risen to ten times the original investment expenditures of $20 billion, instead of the five times shown in Fig. 4.

There are of course many other possible repercussions of shifts in the consumption function. Some of these will be examined in greater detail in later chapters. It is only important to note at this juncture that the consumption function may shift in the process of adjustment and this shift will in turn have further repercussions on the process of adjustment. Thus the extent of the cumulative change resulting from an initial change will depend not only on the shape of the consumption function itself but also upon the shifts to which it is subject.

14. The Mechanism of Income Analysis II: Disposable Income and Gross National Product

The role of the consumption function and the multiplier were discussed in the last chapter in terms of two simplifying assumptions: (1) that gross national product and disposable income were equal, and (2) that investment expenditures, government expenditures, and foreign trade were fixed in amount and determined by factors outside the system. The purpose of this chapter is to remove the first of these assumptions and to examine the effect of such removal upon the mechanism of income change.

THE CONCEPTUAL AND STATISTICAL DIFFERENCES BETWEEN GROSS NATIONAL PRODUCT AND DISPOSABLE INCOME

The gross national product is composed of the total expenditures for final goods and services produced in the economy. The income generated by the gross national product, plus subsidies and government interest payments, is paid partly to individuals for their services and partly to the government as taxes, and partly is retained by producers themselves. The disposable income of individuals is composed of what individuals receive from producers and what they receive from the government as transfer payments,[1] minus the amount individuals pay to the government in the form of taxes. The differences between the two concepts for the United States in 1953 were as follows:

[1] Transfer payments to individuals from abroad and transfer payments by individuals to abroad are not considered explicitly in the following analysis since they are included in consumers' expenditures in the United States definition of disposable income. In any case, their effects for the United States would be very small.

Gross national product............................ $365 billion
Minus: 1. Tax payments to government...............   97
         a. Excise and other taxes................ $30
         b. Corporate profits taxes.............. 21
         c. Personal income taxes............... 36

    2. Income retained by producers...............   36
         a. Capital consumption allowances....... $27
         b. Undistributed profits.................   9

Plus: 1. Subsidies and government interest............   6
         a. Subsidies......................... $1
         b. Government interest................   5

    2. Government transfer payments to individuals..   13
                                                                                     —
Equals: Disposable income........................... $251 billion

Statistically, the difference between gross national product and disposable income thus comes out to be over $100 billion. Disposable income is almost one-third smaller than gross national product.

For the period for which statistics are available, there has always been a significant difference between the gross national product and the disposable income. Chart 16 shows the gross national product and disposable income for the years 1929 through 1954. This chart is of the same nature as Charts 14 and 15. Since gross national product is the total expenditure on final goods and services in the economy, it is plotted on the vertical axis in exactly the same manner as consumers' expenditures were in Charts 14 and 15. Disposable income is shown on the horizontal axis. The 45-degree line in this diagram designates the points where gross national product and disposable income would be equal. The vertical differences between this line and the plotted points above it therefore represent the actual differences between the gross national product and disposable income. The distance between the points and the 45-degree line appears to be greater for higher levels of gross national product and disposable income. In fact, if the data are converted to percentage terms, it is found that in the year 1933, when the gross national product and disposable income were at their lowest levels, disposable income amounted to 84 per cent of the gross national product, whereas in the year 1953, when they were at their highest levels, disposable income amounted to only 68 per cent of the gross national product.

The relationship between the gross national product and disposable income for given levels of gross national product may be termed the disposable income function, just as the relation between consumers' expenditures and disposable income in the last chapter was termed the

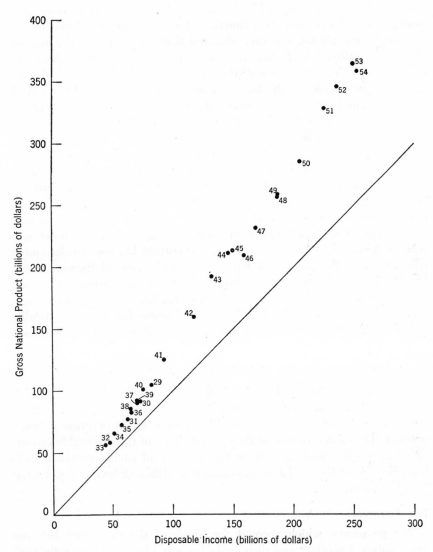

Chart 16. Disposable income and gross national product, 1929–1954. **Source:** 1929–1953, *National Income*, U.S. Department of Commerce, 1954 ed., pp. 164–165. 1954, *Survey of Current Business*, February, 1955, p. 14.

consumption function.[2] There are, however, significant differences in nature between the disposable income function and the consumption function. For the consumption function, a straight line was fitted to the empirical data, although it was admitted that such a procedure was of doubtful validity. The fitting of a straight line to the data shown in Chart 16 in order to derive a disposable income function would also be quite possible mechanically, but the resulting function would not reflect a relationship between gross national product and disposable income that could be expected to hold in the future at various levels of gross national product. The reason for this is that, unlike the consumption function, the disposable income function is in large part determined by tax laws rather than by the voluntary behavior of individuals. Past behavior of individuals may be relevant to their future behavior patterns, but the tax laws in 1933, for example, have little to do with tax laws today. The data given in Chart 16 therefore represent a historical pattern rather than a true functional relationship. To build up a true functional relation it would be far more valid to use current tax laws to determine how much of the gross national income and personal income would have to be paid in taxes at various levels of income, instead of relying on time series data that were the result of tax laws existing in the past. Rather than to approach the disposable income function statistically, therefore, it will be more useful to examine its theoretical determinants.

The Determinants of the Disposable Income Function

The disposable income function is the composite result of several different elements which behave quite differently. These elements, furthermore, differ in relative importance at different levels of gross national product. Thus a description of the general shape of the disposable income function requires analysis both of the behavior of each component individually and of their relative importance at different levels of gross national product.

Tax Payments

Tax payments, which account for much of the difference between gross national product and disposable income, change significantly with changes in the gross national product.

Excise and Sales Taxes. Excise and sales taxes are levied upon the sales value of certain goods, so that if the total value of sales increases, either

[2] It would be customary to show the independent variable (gross national product) on the horizontal axis and the dependent variable on the vertical axis. This procedure is not followed here, however, in order to keep the same axis orientation as that shown for the consumption function, so that the different diagrams may more easily be integrated.

because of prices or because of volume of sales (or both), total tax payments will rise by the same proportion. But because all goods and services are not covered equally by sales and excise taxes, it will make a great deal of difference, for any given increase in gross national product, exactly which expenditures increase. If, for example, the increase in gross national product comes about through investment and government expenditures, excise and sales taxes would not increase very much, but if the increase is due to an increase in consumers' expenditures on durable goods and luxuries, excise and sales tax payments might increase a great deal. Where the increase or decrease in gross national product is such that all categories of expenditure increase or decrease by about the same amount, the excise and sales tax payments would remain about the same *percentage* of the gross national product.

Corporate Profits Tax. The corporate profits tax depends on the volume of corporate profits, and, generally speaking, an increase in the gross national product will result in an increase in corporate profits and thus an increase in corporate profits taxes. Because profits tend to be very sensitive to fluctuations in the level of business activity, even a moderate increase in gross national product may result in a very significant change in corporate profits. Therefore in periods of rising gross national product, corporate profits taxes can be expected to become a larger *percentage* of the gross national product, and conversely, in periods of falling gross national product they can be expected to become a smaller *percentage* of the gross national product. It should be noted in this connection that corporate profits taxes are probably not as much related to the level of gross national product as they are to the change in gross national product. What might have been considered a high level of gross national product in the early forties, and associated with high corporate profits, would by the standards of the fifties be considered a low level of gross national product, and would be associated with very low or even negative corporate profits. In other words, the level of gross national product and the level of corporate profits are not uniquely related. Large corporate profits may accompany a given level of gross national product if an upward movement is taking place, and small or even negative corporate profits may accompany this same level of gross national product if a downward movement is taking place.

Personal Income Tax. Personal income taxes are a higher percentage of income for higher income groups than they are for lower income groups, both because exemptions are a larger percentage of income at lower levels of income and because tax rates are lower. An increase in personal income results in many individuals moving into income classes where more of their income is taxed and where they are taxed at a higher rate; similarly, a decline in personal income will mean that many individuals will move into lower income classes, where exemptions become a larger portion of income and where they will be taxed at a lower rate. As a result of exemptions and progressivity in the tax structure, income tax payments will thus become a larger percentage of the gross national product as gross national product increases, and a smaller percentage as it decreases.

Income Retained by Producers

Capital Consumption Allowances. Capital consumption allowances are in large part determined by the amount of investment expenditures that occurred in the past, together with the tax laws regarding depreciation and obsolescence charges. In situations where increases in the gross national product represent growth in the physical volume of production, it is probably true that the increase in the stock of capital goods will keep capital consumption allowances at approximately the same percentage of gross national product. However, in situations where a rise in the gross national product is primarily the result of a price rise, capital consumption allowances will decline as a percentage of the gross national product, since they are largely calculated in original cost rather than in current prices.

Undistributed Profits. Undistributed profits are even more sensitive, relatively, to changes in the gross national product than total corporate profits, since many corporations make an attempt to keep dividend payments at a fairly constant level, so that the undistributed profits remaining after dividend payments must absorb most of the fluctuation in corporate profits. In periods of rising gross national product, therefore, undistributed profits will tend to increase as a percentage of gross national product, and in periods of falling gross national product they will tend to decrease as a percentage of gross national product.

Additional Income Payments

Subsidy and interest payments by the government, and transfer payments by the government to individuals, unlike the factors discussed above, narrow the gap between gross national product and disposable income, since they are included in disposable income but not in gross national product.

Subsidies and Government Interest Payments. Subsidies are a very minor item and are probably more related to political developments than to the changes in the gross national product. Similarly, interest payments by the government are determined by past expenditures and the rate of interest rather than by current changes in the level of gross national product. When a rise in gross national product is associated with a higher interest rate, the refunding of the debt that is continually going on may have to be carried out at higher interest rates so that interest payments will rise somewhat. Even so, however, it is probable that the interest payments will be a smaller percentage of the gross national product as gross national product rises and a larger percentage as the gross national product falls.

Government Transfer Payments. Government transfer payments to individuals are largely the result of social security programs relating to old-age pensions and unemployment relief. These two elements may behave quite differently with changes in the gross national product. Paradoxically, if an economy is at relatively full employment, a change in either direction may increase the absolute, if not the relative, amount of government transfer payments to individuals. A rise in the gross national product at full employment will not significantly lessen the level of unemployment payments, and it may increase the pressure to enlarge old-age pension payments to keep pace with the rise in prices. Any such increases in pension payments will lag behind the price rise, however, so that government transfer payments as a whole will be a smaller percentage of the gross national product. If a significant decline in the gross national product takes place, however, unemployment payments will cause government transfer payments to become a larger percentage of the gross national product.

The General Shape of the Disposable Income Function

On the basis of this examination of the behavior of the individual components it is possible to make some generalizations about the general shape of the disposable income function. All components were found to increase in absolute amount with increases in gross national product.[3] This means that the gap between gross national product and disposable income will grow wider as gross national product rises. A number of the major components, such as corporate profits taxes, personal income taxes, and undistributed profits, were found to become an increasing *percentage* of gross national product as gross national product increased. Excise and sales taxes probably remain about a constant percentage of gross national product. The additions to income (subsidies, government interest, and government transfer payments) were found to be a smaller *percentage* of gross national product with increases in gross national product, so that they would be a smaller offset to the other components, and thus accentuate the difference between gross national product and

---

[3] An increase in the last category of additional income payments would of course tend to cause a decrease in the difference between gross national product and disposable income. However, these items and their probable increases with increases in gross national product are relatively small.

disposable income. The only element that does not operate in such a manner as to increase the percentage difference between gross national product and disposable income is capital consumption allowances in periods of rising prices rather than rising output. This item, however, would be outweighed by the other components. For increases in gross national product, therefore, it would appear that the percentage difference between gross national product and disposable income could be expected to increase.

For decreases in the gross national product, most of the components described above would operate exactly in reverse, causing the percentage difference between gross national product and disposable income to decline. There is also an additional element that reinforces this tendency. If large-scale unemployment accompanies a decline in gross national product, there will be a significant percentage rise in unemployment benefits, and this, as an offset to the other components, will cause further reduction in the difference between gross national product and disposable income.

The relationship illustrated by Chart 16, therefore, probably is not misleading with respect to the general shape that the disposable income function can be expected to take. It should be remembered, however, that the difference between the gross national product and disposable income depends not only on the level of gross national product but also, and probably more strongly, upon whether the gross national product, prices, and employment are rising or falling.

The Role of the Disposable Income Function in Income Analysis

Once the concept of the disposable income function has been developed, it can be integrated into the mechanism of income analysis to remove the unreal assumption that gross national product and disposable income are equal. The following discussion will still retain the second assumption, namely, that investment expenditures, government expenditures, and foreign trade are arbitrarily determined by factors outside the system and do not react to the processes of adjustment that take place in the economy. This second assumption will be removed in the next chapter.

Table 70 in the last chapter gave an example of an economy that conformed to the assumption that gross national product and disposable income were equal. In removing this assumption it will be necessary to change the example by adding income retained by producers, tax payments by producers, subsidies and government interest payments, transfer payments by government to individuals, and tax payments by individuals. These changes have been made in Table 72. Consumers' expenditures and personal saving, and thus disposable income, have all been retained at the amounts shown in Table 70, but tax payments by individuals of $50 billion have been introduced. This increases personal income to $350 billion from the original $300 billion. On the income side of the Personal Income and Outlay Account, transfer payments to individuals have been set at $10 billion, leaving $340 billion as the amount paid by producers to individuals. On the allocations side of the Gross National Income and Product Account, additional payments of taxes of $70 billion, income retained of $40 billion, and subsidies and government interest of $10 billion have been added, yielding a gross national income of $440 billion. On the sources side of the Gross National Income and Product Account, the two categories that have been changed are government expenditures (now $100 billion) and gross expenditures on producers' durables (now $80 billion); foreign trade is left unchanged. When these transactions are recorded in the other accounts, it is found that government receipts and government outlays total $120 billion, with zero surplus. The Gross Saving and Investment Account balances, with personal saving of $40 billion, and income retained by producers of $40 billion, equaling gross expenditures on producers' durables of $80 billion.

These are the accounts for an economy in which a difference exists between gross national product and disposable income. It is now possible to analyze the repercussions of an increase in investment expenditures in such a situation. The initial entries resulting from an increase in investment expenditures are given in Table 73. In these accounts the increase in investment expenditures of $80 billion is distributed on the allocations side of the Gross National Income and Product Account such that $55 billion is paid out to individuals, $10 billion is retained by producers, and $15 billion is paid to the government in taxes by producers. In the Personal Income and Outlay Account $10 billion of the $55 billion increase goes into personal taxes, and the other $45 billion is recorded as personal saving. This increase in personal saving is of course involuntary, since it exists at this level of disposable income only because individuals have not had an opportunity to spend their increase in income. These entries result, in the Government Receipts and Outlay Account, in an increase of $25 billion in receipts, and therefore an equal increase of $25 billion in government surplus. The Gross Saving and Investment Account balances, since the increases of (1) personal saving of $45 billion, (2) income retained by producers of $10 billion, and (3) government surplus of $25 billion equal the increase in gross investment expenditures of $80 billion. These entries record only the first set of transactions that take place as a result of the increase in investment expenditures, and because individuals are not saving and spending what they want to for

Table 72
(In billions)

I. Gross National Income and Product Account

1.1. Payments by producers to individuals (2.5)	$340	1.6. Consumers' expenditures (2.1)	$260
1.2. Income retained by producers (5.4)	40	1.7. Government expenditures, net (3.1)	100
1.3. Tax payments by producers (3.7)	70	1.8. Gross expenditures on producers' durables (5.1)	80
1.4. Minus: Subsidies and government interest (3.2)	10	1.9. Net change in inventories (5.2)	0
1.5. Statistical discrepancy (5.8)	0	1.10. Exports and property income received (4.1)	25
		Subtotal	$465
		1.11. Minus: Imports and property income paid (4.5)	25
Gross national income	$440	Gross national product	$440

II. Personal Income and Outlay Account

2.1. Consumers' expenditures (1.6)	$260	2.5. Payments by producers to individuals (1.1)	$340
2.2. Tax payments by individuals (3.8)	50	2.6. Transfer payments by government (3.4)	10
2.3. Transfer payments to abroad (4.6)	0	2.7. Transfer payments from abroad (4.2)	0
2.4. Personal saving (5.3)	40		
Personal outlay and saving	$350	Personal income	$350

III. Government Receipts and Outlay Account

3.1. Government expenditures, net (1.7)	$100	3.7. Tax payments by producers (1.3)	$ 70
3.2. Subsidies and government interest (5.5)	10	3.8. Tax payments by individuals (2.2)	50
3.3. Capital grants to government enterprises (5.5)	0	3.9. Transfer payments from abroad (4.3)	0
3.4. Transfer payments to individuals (2.6)	10		
3.5. Transfer payments to abroad (4.7)	0		
3.6. Surplus (5.6)	0		
Government outlay and surplus	$120	Government receipts	$120

IV. Foreign Trade and Payments Account

4.1. Exports and property income received (1.10)	$ 25		4.5. Imports and property income paid (1.11)	$ 25
4.2. Transfer payments to individuals (2.7)	0		4.6. Transfer payments from individuals (2.3)	0
4.3. Transfer payments to government (3.9)	0		4.7. Transfer payments from government (3.5)	0
4.4. Net borrowing from abroad (5.7)	0			
Receipts from abroad	$ 25		Payments to abroad	$ 25

V. Gross Saving and Investment Account

5.1. Gross expenditures on producers' durables (1.8)	$ 80		5.3. Personal saving (2.4)	$ 40
5.2. Net change in inventories (1.9)	0		5.4. Income retained by producers (1.2)	40
			5.5. Capital grants to government enterprises (3.3)	0
			5.6. Government surplus (3.6)	0
			5.7. Net borrowing from abroad (4.4)	0
			5.8. Statistical discrepancy (1.5)	0
Gross investment	$ 80		Gross saving	$ 80

Table 73

(In billions)

I. Gross National Income and Product Account

1.1. Payments by producers to individuals (2.5)	+$55	1.6. Consumers' expenditures (2.1)		
1.2. Income retained by producers (5.4)	+10	1.7. Government expenditures, net (3.1)		
1.3. Tax payments by producers (3.7)	+15	1.8. Gross expenditures on producers' durables (5.1)	+$80	
1.4. Minus: Subsidies and government interest (3.2)		1.9. Net change in inventories (5.2)		
1.5. Statistical discrepancy (5.8)		1.10. Exports and property income received (4.1)		
		Subtotal	+$80	
		1.11. Minus: Imports and property income paid (4.5)		
Gross national income	+$80	Gross national product	+$80	

II. Personal Income and Outlay Account

2.1. Consumers' expenditures (1.6)	+$10	2.5. Payments by producers to individuals (1.1)	+$55
2.2. Tax payments by individuals (3.8)		2.6. Transfer payments by government (3.4)	
2.3. Transfer payments to abroad (4.6)		2.7. Transfer payments from abroad (4.2)	
2.4. Personal saving (5.3)	+45		
Personal outlay and saving	+$55	Personal income	+$55

III. Government Receipts and Outlay Account

3.1. Government expenditures, net (1.7)		3.7. Tax payments by producers (1.3)	+$15
3.2. Subsidies and government interest (1.4)		3.8. Tax payments by individuals (2.2)	+10
3.3. Capital grants to government enterprises (5.5)		3.9. Transfer payments from abroad (4.3)	
3.4. Transfer payments to individuals (2.6)			
3.5. Transfer payments to abroad (4.7)			
3.6. Surplus (5.6)	+$25		
Government outlay and surplus	+$25	Government receipts	+$25

IV. Foreign Trade and Payments Account

4.1. Exports and property income received (1.10)	4.5. Imports and property income paid (1.11)
4.2. Transfer payments to individuals (2.7)	4.6. Transfer payments from individuals (2.3)
4.3. Transfer payments to government (3.9)	4.7. Transfer payments from government (3.5)
4.4. Net borrowing from abroad (5.7)	
Receipts from abroad	Payments to abroad

V. Gross Saving and Investment Account

5.1. Gross expenditures on producers' durables (1.8) +$80	5.3. Personal saving (2.4)	+$45
5.2. Net change in inventories (1.9)	5.4. Income retained by producers (1.2)	+10
	5.5. Capital grants to government enterprises (3.3)	
	5.6. Government surplus (3.6)	+25
	5.7. Net borrowing from abroad (4.4)	
	5.8. Statistical discrepancy (1.5)	
Gross investment +$80	Gross saving	+$80

their present level of disposable income, the situation is unstable and will result in a cumulative movement upward. The process of adjustment is shown in Fig. 8.

This diagram is quite similar to those presented in Figs. 4–7, except that here it is not assumed that gross national product and disposable

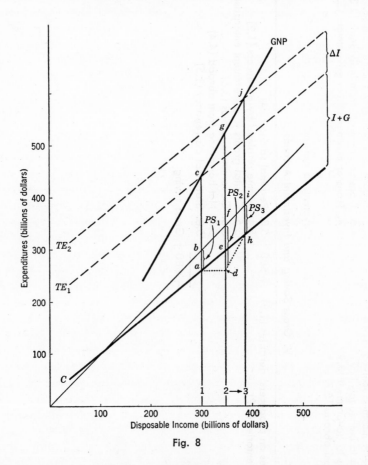

Fig. 8

income are equal. Instead, the disposable income function, labeled GNP in Fig. 8, has been introduced to show the relationship which does exist. The other lines have the same meaning as in the previous diagrams. Vertical line 1 represents the situation described by Table 72. This line starts at the point where disposable income equals $300 billion, and intersects the consumption function at point a, indicating consumers' expenditures of $260 billion; it intersects the 45-degree line at point b, indicating personal saving of $40 billion ($b$–$a$); and finally, it intersects the disposable income function (GNP) at point c, indicating a gross national product of $440 billion. These figures are the same as those recorded in Table 72.

The introduction of an increase in investment expenditures of $80 billion ($\Delta I$ in the diagram) is shown by the new total expenditures function (TE_2). The new initial situation is shown at vertical line 2. The increase in investment expenditures of $80 billion results in an increase in the gross national product of $80 billion, so it is possible to plot the position of line 2 by moving up the disposable income function (GNP) from the original position of $440 billion (point c) to the new level of $520 billion (point g). Disposable income as given by the disposable income function is at this point increased by $45 billion. Consumers' expenditures as shown by the dotted line a–d have not had an opportunity to rise. The difference between gross national product and disposable income has increased by $35 billion. The process of adjustment by consumers to the new level of disposable income is shown by the dotted line d–h. In Figs. 4–7 this path of adjustment was parallel to the 45-degree line, since all consumers' expenditures resulted in an equal increase in disposable income. In Fig. 8, however, it is recognized that an increase in consumers' expenditures will not result in an equal increase in disposable income; some of it will be siphoned off into such items as taxes paid by producers and consumers and income retained by producers. The disposable income function (GNP) gives the relation between an increase in gross national product and the increase in disposable income. Since the increase in consumers' expenditures is assumed to cause an equal increase in gross national product, the relation between changes in consumers' expenditures and changes in disposable income will be the same as that shown by the disposable income function (the GNP line). For this reason the dotted line showing the process of adjustment in consumers' expenditures and disposable income will be exactly parallel to the disposable income function. Because the angle of the adjustment line is steeper than 45 degrees, the consumption function will be reached with a smaller rise in income than was true in Figs. 4–7. The level of disposable income that is reached is, of course, also the equilibrium position indicated by the intersection of the new total expenditures function (TE_2) with the disposable income function (GNP).

The multiplier in this diagram, if defined in terms of $\Delta DI/\Delta I$, would be smaller than that indicated graphically in Fig. 7. If the multiplier is defined in terms of $\Delta GNP/\Delta I$, it becomes approximately 1.8. This can be seen graphically in Fig. 8, since gross national product rose by about $145 billion (from point c, $440 billion, to point j, $585 billion), with the original increase in investment expenditures of $80 billion.[4]

[4] The value of the gross national product multiplier can be computed statistically by multiplying the slope of the disposable income function (the GNP line) by the

The multiplier is thus considerably reduced by the leakages of consumers' expenditures into such things as taxes and income retained by producers. In Fig. 8 the process of adjustment has caused personal saving to decrease from PS_2 to PS_3, compensated by an exactly equal increase in the difference between gross national product and disposable income.

THE EFFECT OF SHIFTS IN THE DISPOSABLE INCOME FUNCTION

Like the shifts in the consumption function discussed in Chap. 13, shifts in the disposable income function can cause cumulative adjustments. Inasmuch as the disposable income function is made up of a number of different components that are subject to different determinants, there will be a variety of reasons why shifts occur. Primary among these determinants, however, is the action of the government with respect to taxes on producers, taxes on individuals, and transfer payments to individuals. The effect of changes in each of these elements upon the level of income will be examined in turn.

Taxes on Producers

It is difficult to forecast exactly what the effect of a change in taxes on producers will be. In the case of excise and sales taxes, a reduction in the tax rate may cause prices to consumers to fall; if this happens, a greater volume of goods would probably be sold, more income would be paid to individuals, and more profits would accrue to producers. A reduction in the corporate profits tax would in all probability increase undistributed profits, but it might also lead to an increase in dividends paid out, and even in the long run to lower prices to consumers. For simplicity it will be assumed that as a result of a reduction in taxes on producers (1) both income retained by producers and disposable income will increase, (2) the marginal disposable income function will remain the same as it was before (i.e., the shift in the disposable income function leaves it parallel to the old function); and (3) the tax reduction and the process of adjustment do not cause the consumption function to shift. Figure 9 shows the repercussions of such a reduction in taxes on producers.

---

slope of the consumption function (C), and treating their product in the way the marginal consumption ratio was used in the last chapter. These slopes are in fact the marginal disposable income ratio and the marginal consumption ratio. In the particular case above they are equal to .57 ($4/7$) and .80 ($4/5$) respectively. The product of these is .45; if this is inserted in the multiplier formula, it becomes $1/(1-.45)$, or 1.8.

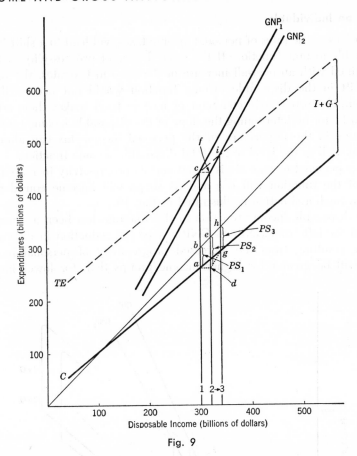

Fig. 9

The shift in the disposable income function from GNP_1 to GNP_2 results in an increase in disposable income of about $20 billion. This is shown at vertical line 2. Individuals will now want to increase their consumers' expenditures. The new equilibrium position where the total expenditures function (TE) intersects the new disposable income function (point i) indicates that the rise in disposable income that finally takes place is approximately $40 billion, whereas the increase in gross national product is nearer $30 billion.[5] In this case the change in disposable income is larger than that in gross national product, since the tax reduction resulted in an initial increase of $20 billion in disposable income before any change took place in the gross national product.

[5] Computed according to the slopes of the disposable income and consumption functions, the changes come out to be $36.4 billion for disposable income and $28.8 billion for gross national product.

Taxes on Individuals

Changes in the rates of personal income taxes will lead to a shift in the disposable income function. If the same degree of progressivity of taxes is retained with an over-all increase or decrease in tax rates, the resulting shift in the disposable income function would not necessarily be parallel. The progressive character of income taxes makes them an important factor in determining the slope of the disposable income function. A change in the importance of the personal income tax can alter the slope as well as the level of the total disposable income function.

If the personal income tax is raised and its progressivity increased, the level of the function will rise and its shape will become considerably steeper. Such a situation is illustrated in Fig. 10.

The disposable income function in this diagram has been assumed to shift to the left from GNP_1 to GNP_2. Since the reduction in disposable income resulting from the increased progressivity of personal income taxes will be greater for higher income groups than for lower income

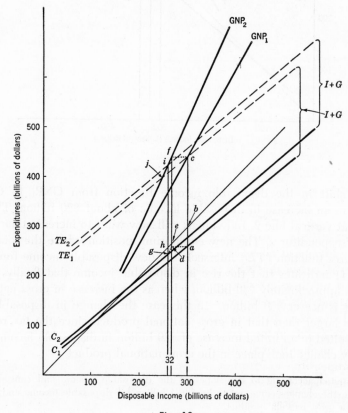

Fig. 10

groups, the tax increase will reduce personal saving more than normally would be true for this reduction in disposable income. In this situation, in other words, a redistribution of income has accompanied the reduction in disposable income, so that the higher marginal propensities to consume of the lower income groups become relatively more important. The shift in the consumption function from C_1 to C_2, and the corresponding shift in the total expenditures function from TE_1 to TE_2, is in line with such reasoning. This shift is greater for higher levels of disposable income than for lower levels. The original situation is again shown at vertical line 1. The situation immediately after the increase in the progressivity of personal tax rates is shown at vertical line 2. The gross national product of $440 billion, which formerly yielded a disposable income of $300 billion, under the new tax rates yields a disposable income of $260 billion. Individuals will now find that their personal savings are drastically reduced before they have an opportunity to alter their consumers' expenditures. In the process of adjustment it is the new consumption function (C_2) and its corresponding total expenditures function (TE_2) that are relevant. In Fig. 10 the adjustment process has been shortened by this upward shift in the consumption function, and equilibrium is established at point i, where the gross national product is about $430 billion, rather than at point j, where it is about $395 billion, which would have been the point of equilibrium if no upward shift in the consumption function had taken place.

Transfer Payments by the Government to Individuals

Since transfer payments to individuals do not affect the gross national product directly but do increase disposable income, they make the gap between the gross national product and disposable income smaller. An increase in old-age pensions, for example, would cause a downward shift in the disposable income function. This is shown in Fig. 11.

A parallel shift in the disposable income function from GNP_1 to GNP_2 is shown, since it is assumed that this increase in pensions would be constant in amount at all levels of disposable income. As in the case of the increase in personal income tax rates, an increase in pensions would be expected to cause a redistribution of income in favor of lower income groups, and this would cause the consumption function to shift in an upward direction. In this instance, however, it would be expected that the upward shift in the consumption function would be greater at lower levels of income than at higher levels of income, since individuals' marginal propensities to consume are higher at low levels of income. This is shown in Fig. 11 by the shift in the consumption function from C_1 to C_2, and in the total expenditures function from TE_1 to TE_2. The increase in pensions in this example is assumed to amount to $40 billion. The situa-

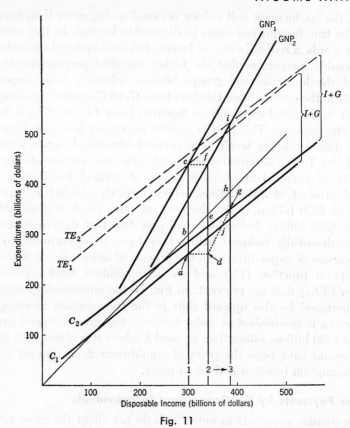

Fig. 11

tion immediately after the pensions are paid is illustrated at vertical line 2, and the new equilibrium position is given at vertical line 3 by the intersection of the new total expenditures function (TE_2) and the new disposable income function (GNP$_2$) at point i.

For other types of government transfer payments the shape of the disposable income function as well as its level might be changed. For example, an increase in the coverage or amount of unemployment benefits would alter both the slope and the level of the disposable income function at lower levels of disposable income. This would mean that the disposable income function would have a steeper slope at higher levels of disposable income than at lower levels, and the function therefore would not be a straight line. It has been shown as such in the preceding examples purely for reasons of diagrammatic simplicity. For any realistic analysis, in fact, there is excellent reason for believing that, as indicated above, the slope of the line will vary at different levels of disposable income.

15. The Mechanism of Income Analysis III: Investment Expenditures, Government Expenditures, and Foreign Trade

In the previous chapters on the mechanism of income analysis it was assumed that investment expenditures, government expenditures, and foreign trade were determined not by the operation of the economic system but rather by factors outside the system. This chapter will remove this assumption, insofar as possible. Each category of these expenditures will be examined in terms of its determinants and its reaction to the processes of cumulative adjustment.

THE DETERMINANTS OF INVESTMENT EXPENDITURES

One of the outstanding characteristics of investment expenditures is their extremely wide fluctuation from year to year. Furthermore, although high levels of investment tend to be generally associated with high levels of gross national product, examination of the statistical relationship reveals a considerable amount of variance. This is shown in Chart 17. During the war years investment expenditures were seriously affected by the regulations required for war mobilization, so that any relationship existing in the prewar period could not be expected to continue. Even omitting the war period, however, there does not appear to be a very valid relationship between the gross national product and investment expenditures. If the relationship that apparently existed in the prewar period is projected to the postwar period, investment expenditures would have to be fantastically high. In the postwar period, furthermore, different years which had about the same level of gross national product had widely differing levels of investment, and conversely, years

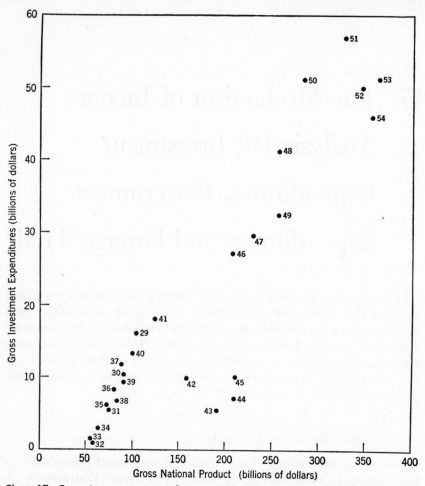

Chart 17. Gross investment expenditures, 1929–1954. **Source:** 1929–1953, *National Income,* U.S. Department of Commerce, 1954 ed., pp. 162–163. 1954, *Survey of Current Business,* February, 1954, p. 14.

which had approximately the same level of investment had wide differences in the level of gross national product. Thus the gross national product for both 1948 and 1949 was about $257 billion, but investment expenditures in the former year were $41 billion, in contrast with $33 billion in the latter year. Similarly, investment expenditures in 1950, 1952, and 1953 were all about $51 billion, whereas gross national product in these years was $285 billion, $346 billion, and $365 billion respectively.

There does not therefore appear to be any reasonable sort of investment expenditure function that can be postulated for different levels of gross national product. Instead, income analysis makes use of two theoretical concepts to explain the level of investment expenditures. These are (1) the acceleration principle, and (2) the marginal efficiency of capital.

The Acceleration Principle

The acceleration principle is the name given to the effect that certain changes in the volume of consumers' expenditures may be expected to have upon the level of investment expenditures. According to this principle, increases in consumers' expenditures may through the process of derived demand cause even greater increases in investment expenditures. An increased rate of output of consumers' goods may make investment expenditures necessary, either to expand the capacity of the expanding consumers' goods industries or to provide additional stocks of goods for the inventories of manufacturers and distributors.

The Nature of Derived Demand. If every industry in the economy were operating at capacity, and if this capacity were neither increasing nor decreasing, investment expenditures for producers' durable goods would consist solely of the replacements of worn-out machinery that would become necessary each year. Suppose, for example, that the cotton textile industry was using machinery which lasted ten years; under these conditions it would need to buy for replacement each year an amount of textile machinery equal to 10 per cent of the total quantity in use. The producers of textile machinery would be geared to a level of output equal to this replacement rate. Under these circumstances an increase in expenditures of consumers for cotton textiles might induce textile manufacturers to increase their capacity, and such an extension of capacity would require expenditures for textile machinery in excess of those needed simply for replacement during the year. These increased expenditures for textile machinery are derived from the increased volume of expenditures on cotton textiles and so can be said to be the result of derived demand. On the basis of a given increase in consumers' expenditures textile manufacturers might decide to expand capacity by 10 per cent. The machinery required for the increased capacity would then be exactly equal in amount to that which is currently needed for replacement. The total amount of machinery purchased would be equal to 20 per cent of the machines in use, and the producers would have to double their output to meet both requirements.[1] Textile machinery producers

[1] A relatively small change in consumers' expenditures may thus cause a relatively large change, in percentage terms, in investment expenditures. This is the source of the name "acceleration principle." It is also true, of course, that an increase in capital goods production will cause acceleration in other capital goods production in exactly the same manner as is caused by the increase in consumers' goods expenditures.

could continue to produce at this double level of output, however, only as long as increasing consumers' expenditures continued to cause the same amount of expansion each year in the cotton textile industry. For instance, textile manufacturers, after they had expanded their capacity by 10 per cent the first year, might find in the second year that consumers' expenditures on textiles were still increasing, but only fast enough to warrant an increase in their capacity of an additional 5 per cent instead of 10 per cent as in the first year. Their purchases of textile machinery would then amount to the 10 per cent required for replacement plus 5 per cent for expansion, or a total of 15 per cent—less than in the previous year. The output of textile machinery producers would actually drop below the level of the previous year, even though consumers' expenditures on cotton textiles were still increasing. Investment expenditures will thus decline in spite of increases in consumers' expenditures if the rate of expansion slows up. This phenomenon was well illustrated by the wartime experience of the United States economy. In Chap. 11 it was pointed out that machine-tool producers and the construction industry were called upon to build war capacity at a very early stage of the war effort but that once such capacity was created, the major task of these sectors of the economy was accomplished and their output declined, while the rest of the economy went on to greater heights of production.

The principle of derived demand applies to inventory accumulation, as well as to producers' durable goods. Inventories are a necessary part of the economic process. When the volume of production grows, producers will need additional stocks of raw materials to be able to produce this larger volume. More goods will be in the pipeline of the manufacturing processes, so that a part of current production of the economy must be set aside to fill this need. Finally, goods in the hands of wholesalers and retailers will increase with the increased volume of production, and this accumulation will absorb goods out of the stream of current production. As was true for producers' durable goods, the amount of additional inventories that are accumulated is dependent upon the continued increase in the volume of consumers' expenditures. A slowing down of the expansion process means that a smaller quantity of goods will have to be dedicated to this use; when a level rate of output is reached, no further investment at all in inventories will be necessary. Investment expenditures for inventory accumulation will increase as the rate of expansion of production increases; but when the expansion slows down, such investment expenditures will actually decline.

The Rate of Acceleration. The amount of derived expenditures for investment goods that will result from a given change in the volume of consumers' expenditures will differ considerably not only among different industries but also in the same industries with differing attendant circumstances. The derived demand resulting from an increase in consumers' expenditures for the products of some industries might be negligible; this would be especially true in those industries which react to an increase in expenditures by allowing price to rise rather than by increasing output. Even in industries that do expand output, however, there are a number of factors that may serve to keep the expansion of investment expenditures relatively small. (1) The industry may be operating at less than capacity, and a considerable increase in output may occur before an increase in capacity would be required. An increase in consumers' expenditures in such an industry might have no effect on investment expenditures. (2) The industry might be one that uses very little capital equipment, so that an increase in output could be achieved by hiring more labor and buying more materials. This would be especially true of industries in which a major part of the work is assembly. (3) The needed expansion in capacity might be obtained through the installation of machinery that increases productivity, so that the amount of investment expenditures normally required for replacement alone might be sufficient in some periods to provide for an actual expansion of the industry.

Even within the same industry the willingness of producers to expand under the impact of increasing consumers' expenditures will vary considerably at different levels of economic activity. Forces that at one level of activity would induce producers to make a given volume of investment expenditures might at another level call forth either a smaller or a larger volume. A businessman invests in increased capacity with an eye to the future. During the early stages of an upward movement he may be very sensitive to increases in expenditures on his product and try to expand so that he can capture a larger share of the increasing market. On the other hand, when the level of activity has been rising for some time, he may be reluctant to expand further in spite of increased expenditures on his product, feeling that this additional capacity would go unutilized in the future and so would not pay for itself. The investment expenditures that are derived from increases in consumers' expenditures are thus conditioned by a large number of other factors, but their reactions must be taken into account in analyzing the process of income change.

It is similarly difficult to predict the derived effect upon investment expenditures of a decrease in consumers' expenditures. A decline in output may to some extent permit an industry to consume its capital, instead of maintaining it completely. But this process cannot continue indefinitely, with further decreases in consumers' expenditures on the product of the industry continually causing greater reductions in the amount of replacement expenditures that are being made. Machinery will eventually become obsolete, so that producers are forced to purchase new equipment in order to meet competition. Outlays on producers' durable goods in 1932 were 25 per cent of the total amount needed for replacement, even though excess capacity existed in almost all industries. On the other hand, expenditures for inventory accumulation may actually become negative; i.e., producers and distributors may sell goods out of stock without replacing them. Thus with a contraction in consumers' expenditures, the derived effect on investment expenditures will not necessarily be exactly the opposite of that which results when consumers' expenditures expand.

The Marginal Efficiency of Capital

Before attempting to integrate the acceleration principle into the theory of the multiplier, it will be helpful to consider the other elements influencing the level of investment in the economy. When this has been done, it will be possible to see how changes in the level of investment—whatever their cause—fit into the process of income change.

The factors that influence the level of investment expenditures can conveniently be grouped under the heading of the marginal efficiency of capital. The marginal efficiency of capital may be defined as the expected rate of return that an additional investment expenditure would yield over and above its costs, aside from the cost of interest.[2] The marginal efficiency of capital minus the interest rate that a producer must pay for the use of this capital is the expected profit rate on the investment expenditure. For instance, a marginal efficiency of capital rate of 6 per cent combined with an interest rate of 4 per cent would leave 2 per cent as the expected net profit rate. Not all investment expenditures in the economy will yield the same rate of return, of course; and, if risk is taken into account as a part of cost, businessmen will naturally prefer to make those investment expenditures which have the highest expected rate of return, since they will yield the highest net profit. But as long as the expected rate of return on a given project is higher than the interest rate, the producer can always make a profit by undertaking that investment expenditure. For this reason, after the most desirable investment opportunities have been used up, producers will continue to make further expenditures in less profitable areas until finally they have left only those investment outlets which will not yield them sufficient return to cover the interest rate. At this juncture producers will not make any more investment expenditures.

[2] The marginal efficiency of capital thus is the rate of discount that would make the present value of the expected net returns from the investment equal to its cost.

The Marginal Efficiency of Capital Schedule. This relationship between the expected profitability of investment expenditures and the
interest rate can be put into the form of a schedule showing the annual
rate of investment expenditures that would take place with given interest rates. This has been done in Fig. 12.

On the vertical axis of Fig. 12 are interest rates, and on the horizontal
axis are rates of investment expenditures per year. The schedule re-

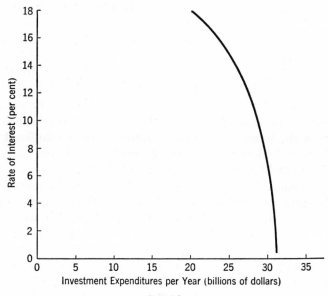

Fig. 12

lating the rate of investment expenditure that business would be willing to make to the rate of interest is the marginal efficiency of capital
schedule, since it shows the marginal rate of return that would accompany various rates of investment expenditure. With this schedule, for
instance, businessmen would be willing to make investment expenditures at the rate of about $28 billion a year when the interest rate is
8 per cent. It follows from this that the marginal rate of return on
the least profitable investment, i.e., the marginal efficiency of capital,
at a level of investment expenditure of $28 billion per year must be
8 per cent. Were all investment expenditures yielding higher returns
than 8 per cent, businessmen would be willing to make additional
investment expenditures above the $28 billion level. On the other hand,
all the investment expenditures that businessmen are willing to make
at this point must be expected to yield at least 8 per cent, since this
return is required to cover the existing interest rate.

In a modern economy a change in the interest rate from 4 to 6 per cent would be considered a large change, yet on a marginal efficiency of capital schedule such as the one shown in Fig. 12 this increase in the price of capital would only decrease the rate of investment expenditures from a level of $30 billion to a level of $29 billion. In other words, a large increase in the interest rate (50 per cent) might decrease capital expenditures by a relatively small amount (less than 5 per cent). A marginal efficiency of capital schedule of this shape does not seem unreasonable when it is recalled that the interest rate is only a minor part of the costs of most producers, so that even a large change in it would not affect total costs very significantly. There is, however, one major exception to this generalization. Certain capital goods such as factory buildings and housing last a great many years, so that their decline in value each year is small relative to their total original cost. For these assets interest charges are relatively more important and often constitute a major portion of the total costs of the investment. A change in the interest rate may therefore cause a significant change in the cost of building and housing services, and this in turn will change the profitability of the construction industry.

Although changes in the interest rate thus do not in general greatly affect the rate of investment expenditures, these expenditures are highly sensitive to other influences, changes in which will shift the position of the entire marginal efficiency of capital schedule. The national income statistics reveal that the rate of investment expenditures varies widely from period to period. In 1929 the volume of investment expenditures amounted to about $16 billion, whereas in the depression of 1932 it was less than $1 billion. In the period after World War II it rose as high as $57 billion per year. These violent fluctuations are attributable to shifts in the entire marginal efficiency of capital schedule in one direction or the other rather than to movements along the schedule in response to changes in the interest rate. Such a situation is illustrated in Fig. 13.

This chart shows a number of different possible positions of the marginal efficiency of capital schedule. Those at the extreme left would apply to periods when producers did not expect very much investment expenditure to be profitable, irrespective of what the interest rate might be. The schedules at the right of the diagram, on the other hand, apply to periods when producers' hopes of profit are high enough to cover even a high rate of interest. Producers' expectations of profits from identical investments differ violently from period to period, and these changes in turn change the rate of investment expenditures that producers are willing to undertake.

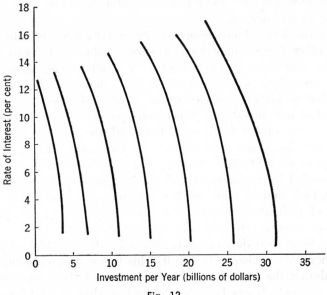

Fig. 13

Factors Affecting Expectations of Producers. Producers' expectations of profits are highly related to the past and current conditions in the economy. In a period when consumers' expenditures are increasing and producers find the sales of their products rising, expectations will tend to be high; on the other hand, when consumers' expenditures are falling and causing cutbacks in prices and output, producers will be extremely skeptical about the profitability of any investment expenditures or any attempts to expand. The actual level at which the economy is operating as well as the rate and direction of change in gross national product will also be taken into account. An increase in consumers' expenditures at a level of income such that the economy evidently is on the road to recovery will be interpreted very differently from an equivalent increase in consumers' expenditures when producers are wondering whether a depression is about to follow an inflationary boom. A slight decrease in consumers' expenditures at the top of a boom might cause producers to start a policy of retrenchment and make them hesitate about any but very necessary investment expenditures. This large element of instability is all the more important since a decrease in the rate of investment itself may be instrumental in lowering disposable income and so causing a contraction in consumers' expenditures. A slight decline in the level of investment expenditures could easily generate a situation in which the expectations of producers would quickly be reversed and a sharp cumulative decline would be set into motion.

Besides the level of economic activity and its rate and direction of change, other factors may have a strong influence on expectations. Inventions and changes in technology can either encourage or discourage investment expenditures. An invention may be of such a nature that it makes previous stocks of capital obsolete, so that a great deal of new investment is necessary, or it may develop processes that use more capital equipment than did the processes previously in use. But inventions and changes in technology may also be of types that increase productivity in such a way that fewer capital goods will be needed for replacement and plant expansion; these changes are capital saving and require smaller investment expenditures. Finally, the rate of technological change at times may be so rapid that producers are reluctant to make investment expenditures for fear that further technological developments will make their equipment obsolete before they have a chance to use it. This factor was undoubtedly important during the early stages of the growth of the television industry; radio manufacturers hesitated to start production of television receivers because it was obvious that new developments would occur before their models could be put on the market, and they would run the risk of having some other producer come out with a vastly superior model.

The labor situation in the economy may have a very strong influence on the investment expenditures of producers. If it is evident that, by the time additional capacity is built, there will be a labor shortage with high wage costs, producers will probably not feel that the time is a good one for expansion. On the other hand, rising labor costs may induce producers to install laborsaving devices to cut their costs. These considerations will have opposite effects upon investment expenditures, so that although it is clear that the labor situation will influence investment expenditures, it is impossible to predict exactly what effect a given change will have.

The political climate also has an important bearing upon producers' expectations and the rate of investment expenditures. Changes in tax rates or in the regulations regarding industry will have a bearing on producers' actions in building for future capacity. High taxes will deter some producers, who may feel that the profit which they expect to make after the payment of taxes is not large enough to compensate them for the risk and responsibility involved. Other producers may react to high taxes by maintaining their plants in excellent condition and spending money on advertising, research, and other such costs, which are considered nontaxable current expenditures in the tax law but which from the point of view of the producer are investment expenditures. Here again it is difficult to analyze the effect of any specific political action, but it can almost certainly be said that an unsettled political situation will be a positive deterrent to investment expenditures. Producers have a tendency to wait and see what will happen in an unsettled period; and if the unsettled state continues for any length of time, it will probably result in a very low level of investment expenditure.

Finally, there are many influences exogenous to the economy that can have a very great effect upon investment expenditures. Conditions in foreign countries that lead foreign purchasers to make heavy expenditures may create a net export balance for the country from which the goods and services are bought. A change in weather conditions that alters the size of crops will have repercussions on both national and international conditions, and these in turn may influence the level of investment expenditures. Investment expenditures are always made in the light of existing or expected future conditions; and as these conditions change owing to external forces, the level of investment expenditures itself will change.

Investment Expenditures and the Multiplier

It is now possible to consider how the mechanism of income analysis and the multiplier will be affected by removing the second of the two simplifying assumptions that were adopted in Chap. 13. These two assumptions, it will be recalled, were (1) that gross national product equaled disposable income, and (2) that investment expenditures, government expenditures, and foreign trade were determined by factors outside the system and did not change throughout the process of adjustment. It has already been shown in Chap. 14 that the removal of the first assumption through the introduction of a disposable income function tends to limit the magnitude of the multiplier; in a period of increasing gross national product leakages will cut down the amount of the increase in consumers' expenditures that will return to individuals as disposable income, and in a period of falling gross national product leakages will prevent disposable income from falling as much as gross national product. With respect to the second assumption, the effect of a change in the level of investment expenditures in bringing about cumulative changes in disposable income has already been treated, but the final step—the analysis of the manner in which investment expenditures will react to the process of cumulative change and in turn again alter disposable income—has not yet been taken. This step is necessary if the relation of investment expenditures to the multiplier is to be explained.

The Interaction of the Acceleration Principle and the Multiplier. The influence of derived demand upon the multiplier will be different at different levels of employment of manpower and industrial capacity in the economy, and at different points in the process of adjustment. The acceleration principle becomes a significant factor influencing investment expenditures during the upswing only when an expansion of capacity results from an increase in consumers' expenditures. It is therefore not possible to introduce an investment function that is similar in its meaning to the consumption function and the disposable income function discussed above. What can be done, however, to demonstrate the role of the acceleration principle is to introduce additional assumptions with respect to the initial employment and capacity levels at which the economy is operating, and then see under these conditions what effect the acceleration principle would have upon the multiplier. Such a situation is shown in Fig. 14.

It is assumed in this diagram that vertical line 1 represents full utilization of capacity by the economy, such that increases in consumers' expenditures will induce additional investment expenditures. This is illustrated diagrammatically by the total expenditures function (TE), which is no longer parallel to the consumption function but rather rises more steeply. Government expenditures and foreign trade in this diagram are still assumed to be determined by factors outside the system, and to be equal to the magnitudes shown on Table 70 in Chap. 13. A shift in the disposable income function from GNP_1 to GNP_2 is assumed to increase disposable income by $20 billion, as depicted at vertical line 2. The intersection of the total expenditures function (TE) with the new disposable income function at point i indicates the new position of equilibrium (at vertical line 3). What has happened in this situation is that consumers' expenditures stimulated additional investment expenditures and a greater increase in disposable income resulted than would otherwise have occurred. For this reason, therefore, the dotted line d–g will no longer be parallel to the disposable income function (GNP_2). The fact that the total expenditures curve (TE) is steeper than the consumption function means that more expenditures will be funneled back into disposable income so that the adjustment line will be less steep. Viewed in terms of the multiplier, the original injection of $20 billion of disposable income has increased to $80 billion, so that the multiplier is four. Thus the effect of introducing the acceleration principle under the given assumptions has been to increase the magnitude of the multiplier.

The analysis given in Fig. 14 is somewhat unrealistic in that it does not take into account the fact that the acceleration principle may be in-

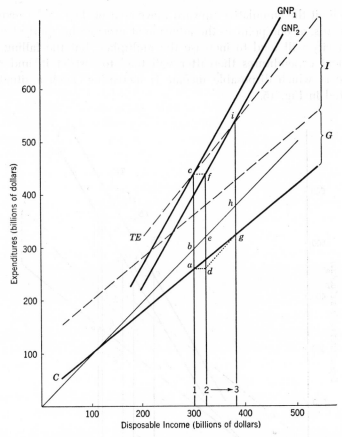

Fig. 14

operative at various phases in the adjustment process. As has been pointed out above, an increase in consumers' expenditures may result only in a price rise or in an increase in the utilization of already existing capacity; and furthermore, when considerable capacity has already been added to the economy, producers may not respond to an increase in consumers' expenditures by even maintaining their previous rate of investment expenditures. For these reasons the acceleration principle may be inoperative or unimportant in many periods of increasing consumers' expenditures, and obviously will then have no effect upon the multiplier. When a rise in the level of consumers' expenditures does result in an increase in capacity, the acceleration principle will reinforce the cumulative changes in disposable income, and so will increase the multiplier effect. But in the later stages of adjustment derived demand will fall off, and a decline in the level of investment expenditures will result; in these later stages, therefore, the acceleration principle will tend to limit the cumulative upward movement of disposable income. In other words, at one point in the adjustment process the spurt of extending capacity will tend to increase the multiplier, but the falling off of investment expenditures thereafter will tend to restrict it, and reduce the rate at which disposable income is increasing. Such a situation is illustrated in Fig. 15.

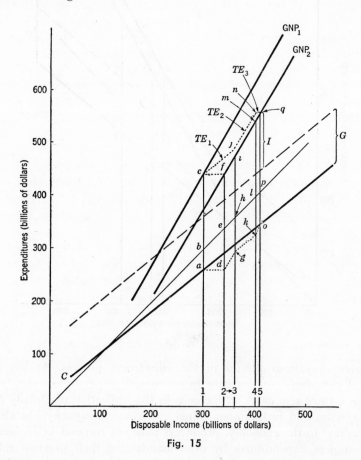

Fig. 15

Vertical line 1 again illustrates the original situation. The impetus to change is provided by a shift in the disposable income function from GNP_1 to GNP_2, increasing disposable income by $40 billion as shown at vertical line 2. In the initial phase of the adjustment process, i.e., from vertical line 2 to vertical line 3, it has been assumed that the acceleration principle is inoperative, and that the increase in consumers' expenditures results in increased utilization of existing capacity. The relevant total expenditures function (TE_1) therefore is parallel to the consumption function at this time, and the path of adjustment of consumers' expenditures is parallel to the disposable income function (GNP_2). At vertical line 3, however, it is assumed that the economy reaches full utilization of capacity, so that additional consumers' expenditures will have a strong accelerative effect upon investment expenditures. This is shown in Fig. 15 by a change in the total expenditures function from TE_1 to TE_2. From vertical line 3 to vertical line 4, it is assumed that the acceleration principle is operative, in accordance with total expenditures function (TE_2). The path of adjustment shown by the dotted line g–k has been flattened out, since the increased expenditures are being funneled back into disposable income. At vertical line 4, however, it is assumed that the influence of the acceleration principle falls off, and that investment expenditures no longer react to the upward movement in consumers' expenditures. This is illustrated by the new total expenditures function (TE_3), which indicates that investment expenditures are actually declining slightly. The effect of the third total expenditures function is to make the path of adjustment k–o rise sharply, and intersect the consumption function at point o. Equilibrium is determined by the intersection of the total expenditures function (TE_3) with the disposable income function (GNP_2) at point q.

It would be quite possible for the falling off in investment expenditures in the later stages of adjustment actually to cause a fall in disposable income. In such a situation the new point of equilibrium would be at a level below that which income had already attained. A cumulative movement downward would then be initiated, instead of the tapering off of the movement upward described in Fig. 15.

The interaction between the acceleration principle and the multiplier will thus be very different at different phases of the cumulative adjustment. In certain periods derived demand for investment goods will reinforce the multiplier, but in other periods it may do just the reverse. Only careful examination of each situation can indicate clearly the connection between the acceleration principle and the multiplier.

Expectations and the Multiplier. Investment expenditures will react to changes in consumers' expenditures and so affect the multiplier not only because of the acceleration principle, but also because of repercussions on the expectations of producers. Changes in the expectations of producers at some points in an upswing or downswing will have a reinforcing effect upon the multiplier, heightening the cumulative change in either direction. A rise in consumers' expenditures may lead producers to expect better business conditions so that they will increase their investment expenditures, and similarly, a fall in consumers' expenditures may make them feel that they should contract their expenditures. But expectations ordinarily will not continue to react this way when consumers' expenditures have increased or decreased over a prolonged period. In a period of upswing producers may become cautious and even expect a depression in spite of continued increases in consumers' expenditures; past increases in income may have created an inflation that producers do not think can continue, so that they may even decrease their investment expenditures. The opposite situation may develop in a depression. Producers who are still feeling the effects of contraction in consumers' expenditures may decide that the bottom of the depression is near and increase their investment expenditures either because the cost of capital equipment is low or because they hope to get ahead of their competitors in the coming upswing by being ready to expand output. Thus again, expectations will increase the multiplier in some periods and decrease it in others. The exact relation for any particular phase of the upswing or downswing is difficult to predict because of the numerous factors that condition and shape these expectations.

Figure 15 can also serve to illustrate the effect of producers' expectations. In the initial phase, i.e., from vertical line 2 to vertical line 3, the initial rise in consumers' expenditures might not immediately heighten producers' expectations. However, from phase 3 to 4, producers' expectations might lead to large increases in investment. Finally, from phase 4 to 5, the expansion that had already taken place might make producers somewhat hesitant about further increasing their investment expenditures.

In any practical sense the effects of expectations upon the level of investment expenditures cannot be separated from the effects of the acceleration principle. The acceleration principle is based upon producers' expectations of the level of future expenditures, and at the same time the influence of expectations on the level of investment depends on the extent of the derived demand that a desired expansion in output will call forth. Thus viewed, investment expenditures are a combined result of the operations of the acceleration principle and of expectations; at times the reaction of investment to changes in consumers' expenditures will serve to reinforce the multiplier so that the cumulative change in gross national product is greatly heightened, but in other periods gradual or sudden changes in investment expenditures will limit or even reverse the cumulative movement of gross national product.

THE DETERMINANTS OF GOVERNMENT EXPENDITURES

In addition to the effects of war and long-run social, political, and economic change, government expenditures will react in the short run to both inflation and depression. Each of these factors needs to be discussed separately.

Effects of Inflation on Government Expenditures

The prices of the goods and services that are purchased by the government will of course be affected by an inflationary price rise in the economy much in the same way as the prices of other goods and services are affected. As the cost of living rises, the government will find itself forced (although somewhat tardily) to raise the wages of its employees. Similarly, goods purchased from business on the market will contain the effect of the increased costs and wages which business has to pay, plus perhaps an increased profit margin which business can require in a period of high demand for its products. Since government expenditures are determined by the requirements of the nation for such things as education, health, and other government services, it is not to be expected that the actual quantity of services provided will diminish in a period of inflation. The money value of expenditure by the government on goods and services will therefore increase by about the same amount as prices increase.

In a period of war mobilization or defense expenditure, when the government is taking an appreciable part of the goods that the economy produces, the situation may arise that the more the government spends, the more prices will rise, and therefore the greater the volume of government expenditures that will be required in order for the government to obtain the same quantities of goods and services; in this way the inflation that is caused by government expenditures may reinforce itself. Such a situation is shown in Fig. 16. In this diagram it is assumed that at vertical line 1 the economy is at full employment, so that any increase in the gross national product will mean an increase in the price of goods and services. As will be pointed out in Chap. 16, this assumption is somewhat unrealistic, since the point of full employment is not a point but rather shades off into an area in which both price and output increases take place. However, for simplicity it has been assumed in Fig. 16 that the new amount of goods and services to be purchased by the government (G_2) would appear as a continually increasing money volume of government expenditures with changes in prices, gross national product, and disposable income, and that investment expenditures and foreign trade are constant. The new expenditures for war purposes are shown at vertical line 2. In this situation a multiplier effect would be created; equilibrium would occur at vertical line 3, where the total expenditures function (TE_2) intersects the disposable income function (GNP) at point j.

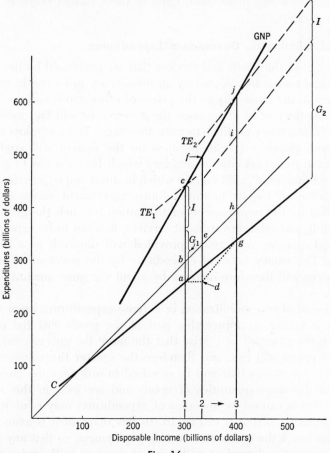

Fig. 16

The Effect of Depression

In a depression it is probably true that the prices of goods purchased by the government will fall, but this fall will be offset by the additional government expenditures required in a period of underemployment. The burden of many government agencies would be increased, and additional agricultural price supports (e.g., the purchase of farm products by the government) would be required. In addition, many local and state governments and some parts of the Federal government may undertake public works to alleviate conditions where unemployment is particularly severe. As a result, with declines in gross national product and disposable income from full employment levels, the actual volume of government expenditures might be expected to increase. This situation is shown in Fig. 17.

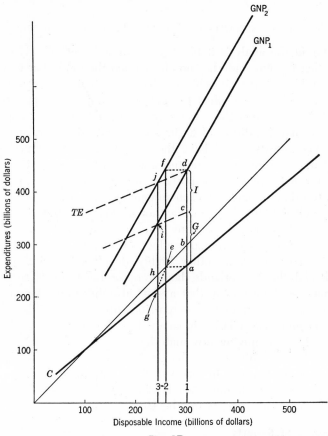

Fig. 17

In this diagram it is again assumed that the $440 billion level of gross national product represents full employment, and that a rise in the disposable income function has caused a cumulative process of adjustment downward. The decline in gross national product and disposable income, however, is mitigated by the fact that government expenditures increase as unemployment increases.

Thus either increases or decreases in the gross national product and disposable income from the level of full employment may in fact cause an increase in the volume of expenditures by the government. This situation was not always so. In the 1929 to 1932 period, for example, although government expenditures did increase in 1930 and 1931, they declined in 1932, even though the economy went into deeper depression. It does not seem probable, however, given the current knowledge of income analysis and the political temper of the country, that such a situation would again occur.

The Determinants of Foreign Trade Expenditures

Thus far in the analysis it has been assumed that exports equal imports, so that foreign trade has no effect upon the multiplier or the position of equilibrium that is achieved. To the extent that exports exceed imports they will in fact affect the process of adjustment and the point of equilibrium in much the same way as either investment expenditure or government expenditure of a similar amount. Similarly, an excess of imports over exports would have the same effect as a reduction in investment or government expenditures. In order to derive the determinants of the net amount of exports or imports, it will be necessary to examine the determinants of each independently.

In the United States economy neither exports nor imports assume as important a role as they do in many other countries. Relative to the other major elements in gross national product, exports and imports have been relatively minor. In some other highly developed countries such as Denmark and the Netherlands, however, foreign trade is such an important part of the economy that a shift in either imports or exports is capable of having very great repercussions upon the equilibrium of the domestic economy. Similarly, in many less developed countries whose major activity is supplying raw materials such as minerals, oil, or food products to other countries, a change in the export market can bring about violent fluctuations in prices and/or output. Such differences as these should be borne in mind in the following discussion of the determinants of exports and imports for the United States.

Determinants of Exports

The quantity of goods exported by the United States depends in large part upon the level at which other countries are operating, and the relative prices of United States goods and similar goods on the world market. Abstracting from the effect of the United States economy upon foreign economies, changes in the level of the United States gross national prodduct will affect the volume of exports mainly through its effect on the relative prices of United States export goods. It would be expected that as prices rose in the United States, the volume of goods exported would decline, and as prices fell, the volume of goods exported would increase. However, changes in the level of activity in the United States are in fact very apt to be reflected also in world conditions, and in such a case fewer goods will be demanded by foreign countries at lower levels of gross national product than at higher levels.

Determinants of Imports

Goods imported by the United States from other countries are primarily either raw materials or relatively finished goods intended for resale to consumers. With increases in the gross national product, the volume of goods imported will tend to increase for two reasons. First, the higher level of economic activity and production will require more goods for use as raw materials and for resale to consumers. Second, the increase in prices that accompanies increases in the gross national product will mean that foreign goods are cheaper than domestic goods, so that there will be some substitution of foreign suppliers for domestic suppliers. With declines in gross national product, these factors of course work in the reverse direction. Again, it should be noted that to the extent that world prosperity and depression correspond with United States prosperity and depression, the price substitution factor may be much less important. Also, in countries where much of the industry of the economy is involved in exporting raw materials, the major determinant of imports will not be so much the need of domestic industry for goods and services as the availability of the necessary funds provided by the sale of exports.

The Net Effect of Exports and Imports upon Cumulative Movements

If changes in gross national product in the United States were not accompanied by similar changes in the level of economic activity elsewhere in the world, exports would decrease and imports would increase with a rise in gross national product, and conversely, exports would increase and imports would decrease with a fall in the gross national product. This situation is shown diagrammatically in Fig. 18.

At the equilibrium position, where gross national product equals $440 billion, it is assumed that exports equal imports. Increases in the gross national product show net exports $(X - M)$ becoming negative; decreases show them becoming positive. Such a relation between gross national product and foreign trade tends to cause the total expenditures function to be flatter than it otherwise would be, and thus to reduce the cumulative movement involved with a given change in the domestic economy. Under such conditions the fact that the United States is not a closed economy means that the process of cumulative change is dampened. However, if the rest of the world parallels the economic movements of the United States, such a dampening effect may not exist.

With respect to foreign countries, it is apparent that an increase in imports by the United States or a reduction in exports would have an inflationary effect, causing a cumulative rise in those countries. This is in fact the manner in which cumulative adjustments in one country are passed on and become cumulative adjustments in other countries. Thus

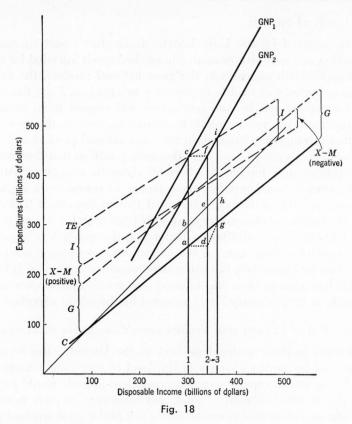

Fig. 18

countries that are highly dependent upon the United States as a purchaser of output will find that their fortunes vary directly with those of the United States. An increase in goods sold to the United States would mean a cumulative adjustment upward for those countries, and a decline in goods sold would mean a cumulative adjustment downward.

SUMMARY

The Consumption Function

The propensity to consume schedule for an individual records the amount which that individual would spend for consumption at different levels of income. From such a schedule, obviously, it is also possible to find out how much an individual would save at any given level of income. For most individuals it is probably true that the higher the income the greater the amount of saving the individual will wish to do. Spending habits of individuals may change for many reasons; some of these changes are brought about by such psychological factors as changes in tastes, but many of them are due to changes in the situation confronting the individual. When prices rise or fall, individuals may decide to change the amounts they spend. Similarly, such things as the accumulation of savings over a period of time, changes in the general standard of living in the economy, changes in provisions for social security, and shifts in expectations about future economic and political conditions all may lead to shifts in the propensity to consume schedules of individuals.

The consumption function for the economy as a whole is the schedule showing the total amounts of consumers' expenditures that would be made at various levels of disposable income. The consumption function depends not only upon the propensity to consume schedules of all of the individuals in the economy but also upon the way in which the total amount of disposable income is distributed among these individuals. If neither of these factors changes, the consumption function will show what the level of consumers' expenditures will be at any given level of disposable income, but any shift either in the propensities of individuals to consume or in the distribution of income will lead to a corresponding shift in the consumption function itself. There is some evidence that in periods which are generally considered "normal" the consumption function is relatively stable and does not shift without apparent reason.

The Theory of the Multiplier

Any change in the level of disposable income in the economy will set into motion a process of adjustment of consumers' expenditures to this change. When the level of disposable income is lowered, individuals must readjust their budgets to their lowered incomes, and they therefore will contract their expenditures on consumers' goods. When individuals receive more income, correspondingly, they will want to spend a part of the increase and will raise their expenditures. These changes in consumers' expenditures resulting from a change in the level of disposable income will in turn have repercussions upon the level of disposable income itself. When one individual reduces his purchases of goods, some other individual's disposable income, which had been derived from the sale of these goods, is immediately cut down. When spending is increased, more money is immediately received as disposable income by those individuals who sell the goods upon which the increased expenditures are made. These sellers of goods whose incomes have been changed will then in turn adjust their expenditures, and a cumulative process of adjustment will be set into motion. An initial change in the level of disposable income thus through the process of cumulative adjustment will finally cause a very much greater change in the level of such income in the economy.

The mechanism and limits of the process of adjustment can best be understood if two basic assumptions are made. Although both of these assumptions are unreal and must later be removed, they will serve to show how the cumulative process of change is related to the consumption function for the economy. It will be assumed (1) that gross national product equals disposable income, and (2) that investment expenditures, government expenditures, and foreign trade are determined by factors outside the system and will not react to the processes of adjustment.

With these assumptions, it necessarily follows that any change in expenditures for goods and services will involve a simultaneous and equal change in disposable income. An increase in the level of investment expenditures, therefore, will increase disposable income by an equal amount. Until individuals have time to adjust their consumers' expenditures to their new level of disposable income, personal saving will also increase by the amount of the investment. As individuals attempt to adjust to the new situation by increasing their expenditures, their incomes (as a group) will again rise by the amount of the increase in consumers' expenditures. Personal saving in the economy therefore will remain unchanged, no matter how much consumers' expenditures are increased. The more individuals as a group spend, the greater by the same amount their disposable income will be; the difference between disposable income and consumers' expenditures will remain unchanged. As the level of disposable income increases, however, individuals will want to save a larger and larger amount, and finally the process of adjustment will bring disposable income and consumers' expenditures to the point where they again lie on the consumption function. At this point the cumulative reaction will stop because consumers will be spending and saving the proportions of their incomes that they want to and they have no reason to increase their consumers' expenditures further.

The amount by which an initial increase in expenditures will be multiplied in its effect by the cumulative process of adjustment is of great importance. The ratio of this initial increase to the total increase in disposable income that it brings forth is called the multiplier. For example, if an increase in investment expenditures of $20 billion finally resulted in an increase in disposable income of $100 billion, the multiplier would be 5. The multiplier is obviously determined by the marginal consumption ratio as given by the consumption function. If in the process of adjustment disposable income and consumers' expenditures reach a level that lies on the consumption function after only a slight increase, the multiplier will be very low; but if a large increase in disposable income is required before the consumption function is reached, the multiplier will be large.

A decrease in the level of investment expenditures similarly will start a cumulative movement downward. Individuals with lowered disposable incomes will decrease their expenditures, and a cumulative decrease in income and expenditures will follow. This progressive movement downward will eventually reach the consumption function again, at the point where individuals are spending and saving the amounts they wish with the level of disposable income that they have, and the cumulative decline will cease. The multiplier downward need not be of the same magnitude as the multiplier upward, since, of course, the consumption function need not be a straight line (i.e., the marginal consumption ratio need not be constant) for all levels of disposable income.

The Multiplier in Practice

The theory of the multiplier is not invalidated by the removal of the two assumptions that were made above. The process of adjustment that takes place and the magnitude of the multiplier that results will be somewhat altered, but the principle remains the same. Relaxation of the first assumption means that a part of any increase in expenditures may be siphoned off by income retained by producers and by taxes, or counteracted by a fall in transfer payments such as unemployment insurance, so that not all the increased expenditures will result in an increase in disposable income. During the upward cumulative process consumers' expenditures will rise faster than income, therefore, and the consumption function will be regained with a smaller increase in disposable income than would otherwise have been the case. In a downward cumulative adjustment a decline in consumers' expenditures will similarly bring about a smaller decline in disposable income; both undistributed profits and taxes will shrink, so that disposable income will not decrease as much as consumers' expenditures. In other words, the existence of undistributed profits and of taxes in the economy decreases the multiplier effect and acts to limit the extent of the cumulative movements.

The second assumption involves primarily the reaction of investment expenditures to changes in consumers' expenditures. There are two ways in which investment expenditures may be altered by changes in consumers' expenditures: through the operation of the acceleration principle and through repercussions upon the expectations of producers. The acceleration principle is based upon the fact that an increase in consumers' expenditures may induce an expansion of productive capacity, and a decrease in such expenditures may permit a lapse in the maintenance of capacity. The acceleration effect is not always operative with a change in consumers' expenditures; and when it is operative, it may lead to very different results at different stages in the upswing or downswing; a strong acceleration of derived demand during one part of a cumulative movement may lead to exactly the opposite reaction upon investment in the immediately following stage. Thus the acceleration principle may at one point in the cumulative movement have no effect upon the multiplier at all; at another point it may increase the multiplier by adding additional investment expenditures; and finally, at still another point it may decrease the multiplier through the cessation of these additional investment expenditures. All these effects must be considered in the analysis of any particular situation.

The expectations of producers similarly will react quite differently to changes in consumers' expenditures at different points in a cumulative movement. The net result of changes in producers' expectations may be either reinforcement or limitation of the multiplier. Expectations obviously are a factor that must be taken into account in explaining the process of adjustment, even though in any particular circumstance it may be impossible to predict exactly what their influence will be.

Income analysis is thus an explanation of the process of cumulative adjustment in the economy. Knowledge of the mechanism of income analysis does not ensure an ability to forecast the future; empirically, few facts are known about the specific reactions of producers and consumers, and accurate prediction would involve a vast knowledge of economic facts and the psychology of human behavior. For any given set of economic facts and reactions of individuals it would be possible to explain the pattern of subsequent events, but the main value of income analysis does not lie in its attempt to explain the future. Rather, its value lies in its usefulness as an analytical tool. From the mass of changing events in the economy it can abstract particular forces and explain the way in which these forces will influence the level of economic activity. Perhaps its greatest usefulness is in the field of economic policy, for it leads to an understanding of the economic processes involved and delineates the various different ways that a given policy can affect the economy.

16. The Nature of Equilibrium and Full Employment

In the theory of income analysis the term "equilibrium" connotes the fact that no cumulative process of adjustment is occurring in any sector of the economy; it does not necessarily imply that full employment exists. In equilibrium individuals have no incentive to change the level of their consumers' expenditures or producers to change the level of their investment expenditures. Individuals are saving what they want to out of their disposable incomes, and investment expenditures of producers are at the level they want. Since actual personal saving and actual investment expenditures in the economy are always equal, equilibrium will exist when the economy voluntarily wishes to save and to invest the amounts that it actually is saving and investing, and there is no attempt on the part of either individuals or producers to change the level of their expenditures. Disequilibrium exists when either individuals or producers are dissatisfied with the level of their expenditures and are attempting to adjust them to a new level. Such adjustment will bring into play a cumulative series of reactions that will alter the level of gross national product until equilibrium is reached.

Equilibrium in Relation to Prices, Output, and Employment

When the level of gross national product changes, prices and/or output must of necessity also change. During any particular phase of the cumulative movement the reaction may be predominantly one or the other of these; which reaction is forthcoming is dependent upon the industrial organization of the economy and the degree to which resources are being utilized. For the moment equilibrium will be considered the limit of a cumulative movement in either direction. This limit for a cumulative movement downward will be very different in nature from that for a cumulative movement upward.

The Cumulative Movement Downward

The process of contraction in the economy will lead to a lower output in some sectors and to a fall in prices in other sectors. Manufacturers faced with semirigid costs are forced to contract output when consumers reduce the amount of their expenditures. Agricultural producers, on the other hand, may continue to produce the same amount, so that the market prices of their products will fall. The cumulative decline in disposable income and consumers' expenditures will be accentuated by the fall in the level of investment expenditures that will accompany it. Producers will be reluctant to extend or even maintain productive capacity in light of the contraction in consumers' expenditures, and they will try to reduce their inventories before they lose still more through the decline in the value of the goods they hold. In a deep, sharp depression such as that of 1932 investment expenditures may fall almost to

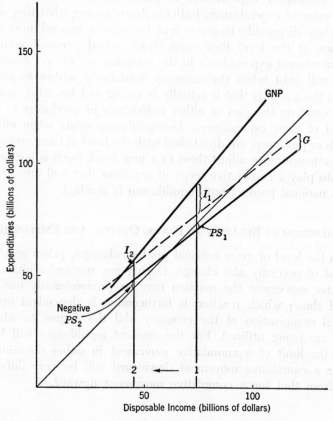

Fig. 19

zero; in 1929 they had stood at about $16 billion, but by 1932 they had dropped to less than $1 billion. This situation is illustrated by Fig. 19.

Vertical line 1 depicts the economy in the predepression period (1929), and vertical line 2 depicts it in the depths of the depression (1932). The result of the decline in investment expenditures was a very sizable drop in gross national product and disposable income. Government expenditures in the depression were about the same in absolute magnitude as they were in the predepression period, and individuals as a group spent somewhat more than their disposable income. It is interesting to note that the economy declined in 1932 about as far as possible, given the level of government expenditures and the consumption function. Even if investment had dropped to zero, the decline in gross national product would not have been more than a few billion more than it was, and except for fairly temporary inventory declines, it is not possible for the level of investment expenditures to go below zero.

Not every cumulative decline in income will continue until total investment and total saving drop to near-zero levels. During the recession of 1938 producers reduced their investment expenditures, but only from $11.7 billion to $6.7 billion. Gross business saving continued at about the same level ($6.9 billion), and personal saving dropped from $3.7 billion to $1.1 billion. There were many factors that made this recession less sharp and less deep than the 1932 depression. (1) The economy in 1938 still had not recovered completely from the shortages created by the 1932 depression; the need for replacement of equipment that had not been maintained during the depression had not yet been fully met, and investment expenditures could not be cut back so far. (2) There was a substantial increase in net exports from the United States, and this compensated somewhat for the decline in domestic markets. (3) The government increased its outlays by $1.8 billion without increasing its tax receipts. All these factors tended to offset the decline to some extent and to make it less severe, so that the downswing did not go so far as it had in 1932. This situation is illustrated by Fig. 20. Vertical line 1 depicts the economy in 1937, and vertical line 2 depicts the economy in 1938.

The limit of the cumulative movement downward, therefore, may come anywhere between the point at which it originates and a level of income at which both gross investment expenditures and gross saving in the economy are zero. The greater the decline in the level of gross national product, the greater will be the decline in prices, output, and employment. Under certain circumstances, as in 1932, the decline will not be stopped until almost the zero level of investment and saving is reached. But in other circumstances, when the economy starts from a situation of acute labor shortage, a short downward movement might

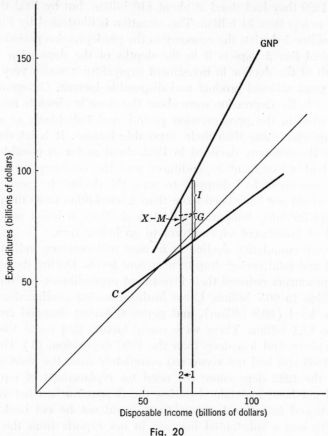

Fig. 20

possibly bring about a fall in prices and an alleviation of the labor shortage without causing more than frictional unemployment in the economy. Any prophecy as to how far a decline will continue, therefore, must at least implicitly consider the action of the government, the change in foreign trade balances, the immediate past history of the economy, and its current position.

The Cumulative Movement Upward

A cumulative movement upward can start at any level of gross national product. When unemployment exists, it is probable that an increase in the level of consumers' expenditures will involve a rise in output and employment as well as in prices. Even in the manufacturing sector, however, the existence of serious impediments to increasing employment may after a certain point make a large portion of the upward movement take the form of price rises. The problem of defining the point where this will happen—the so-called level of full employment—has already been discussed. At different levels of economic activity different numbers of individuals will be willing to work. Possibly, with the level of gross national product rising, higher and higher wage rates might continue to elicit a larger labor force and permit more employment in the economy. Even if this does not occur, however, there is no reason why a cumulative movement upward should cease when full employment has been attained. The sharp rise in prices that would follow the attainment of the limit of employment might well be an incentive for producers to increase the level of their investment expenditures. In all probability, however, a point will eventually be reached beyond which producers will hesitate to attempt to increase capacity or to accumulate additional inventories, and at this point gross national product will have reached its greatest height.

The rise in output from the pre-World War II period to the peak of war production is an instance in which a substantial cumulative movement upward took place in a very short time. In 1939 gross national product was about $91 billion, and there were 9 million unemployed. The upward cumulative movement was sharp, but full employment was not reached until 1942. At that time unemployment had dropped to about 2.5 million, which is about the level that can always be expected to exist due to frictions in the labor market. Gross national product continued to rise, from a level of about $160 billion in 1942 to $211 billion in 1944. The actual number of people employed continued to increase markedly after 1942, as more individuals were drawn into the labor force. Furthermore, gross national product in constant dollars rose by 20 per cent and prices by 11 per cent, indicating that some of the cumulative rise that took place after the attainment of so-called full employment actually was due to a rise in output, and only part of it was due to the rise in prices. This situation is shown in Fig. 21.

Vertical line 1 represents the economy in 1939. In the upward cumulative movement vertical line A, which indicates the "full employment" level of 1942, was reached and passed. The continued demand by the government for goods and services forced the gross national product up to the level shown at vertical line 2, representing the year 1944. After the war the cumulative movement upward continued, with slight downward interruptions in the years 1946 and 1949. The downward movements did not develop into substantial cumulative movements due to the backlog of consumers' and investment demand caused by the war. By 1953 gross national product had risen to $365 billion; this is indicated in Fig. 21 at vertical line 3. The cumulative movement upward during the war and postwar years often caused the economy to operate at levels of gross national product beyond the full employment level. But all of

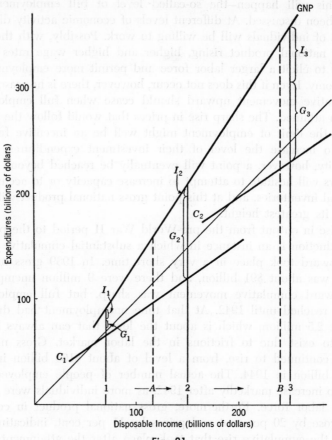

Fig. 21

the increase above the 1942 full employment level is not due to overfull employment; the full employment level itself moves upward. In other words, even a small decline from the gross national product level shown at vertical line 3, say below the level shown at vertical line B, might in 1953 have meant less than full employment. Thus the level of gross national product that corresponds to full employment will itself shift upward with cumulative upward movements.

In Fig. 21 line A represented a full employment level of activity, but the process of adjustment went beyond this point. On the other hand, the cumulative rise from a low level of employment need never attain a level of full employment. The history of the period from 1932 to 1937 is an example of such a situation. The slow cumulative rise from 1932 to 1937 reached its peak while the economy was still at less than full employment. There may have been special factors that brought this particular period of cumulative rise to a close, but nonetheless it was brought to a close, and in the latter part of 1937 a cumulative decline set in. It is conceivable that the desire of producers to make investment expenditures might be so constituted that no cumulative movement upward by an economy would ever reach full employment. As was true for the cumulative movement downward, the level of investment expenditures desired by producers will be conditioned by many factors, and this in turn will affect the height that a given cumulative movement will reach.

The Absence of Cumulative Movement

Since so many factors give rise to or condition the extent of cumulative movement, it is likely that at any given moment some forces will be pushing the economy up and other forces pushing it down. It is quite possible that the forces which tend to produce an upward cumulative movement will be exactly balanced by forces which tend to produce a downward movement, and no cumulative adjustment will take place. Such an absence of cumulative movement might be highly desirable at relatively high levels of economic activity; but if it occurs when the economy is at a low level of activity, the absence of change prevents a return to prosperity.

Although such an exact balance may be rare, the existence of a multitude of sometimes opposing forces will make the fluctuations in gross national product much less violent than the swings in the underlying forces themselves. The consumption function for the economy undoubtedly possesses greater stability than do the propensity to consume schedules of particular individuals. When one group of individuals in the economy decides to spend less of its income, the decrease may be partially or completely matched by other groups in the economy who decide to spend more, so that the change in the consumption function itself will be much less than the changes in individual propensities to consume. Similarly, a change in the distribution of income may be offset by changes in individuals' propensities to consume that have an opposite effect leaving the consumption function unchanged. For example, in a period of high and rising prices the distribution of income might be altered in such a way as to shift the consumption function downward. At the same time, however, many individuals would be unable to save as much out of their incomes as they had been accustomed to when prices were lower. These two reactions would tend to balance each other, and the consumption function might remain unchanged. Investment expenditures, similarly, are made by different groups of producers in different industries. At any one time investment in some industries may be stimulated while investment in other industries is dampened. This is especially true of competing industries; the development of a new product such as nylon will stimulate investment in certain chemical industries, but at the same time it will have a depressing effect upon the silk industry. The rise and fall of industries in the economy is at least in part a compensatory system of change, and it may take place without any appreciable change in the total level of investment expenditures. Even when the total level of consumers' expenditures or private domestic investment expenditures does change, there still may be no cumulative adjustment. A fall in expenditures of these types may be offset by an increase in the foreign trade balance or by a change in taxes or government expenditures. Continual change takes place in all sectors of the economy, and a cumulative movement will occur only when there is a balance of forces in a given direction. No one change in the economy can be said by itself to bring about a cumulative adjustment; such an adjustment occurs only because the balance of all forces leads in one direction. Past history reveals, however, that there have been few periods in which such a preponderance of forces in one direction or the other has been absent. The forces of growth alone have in the past produced a generally upward movement in gross national product, but this upward movement has been broken periodically by intervals when downward forces have prevailed.

THE ECONOMY AS AN EXPLOSIVE SYSTEM

The discussion so far has implicitly assumed that every upward or downward movement will have a limit. In actual practice, however, there have been periods when such a limit was not operative, and the cumulative movement continued until the economic system collapsed and the conventional standard of value was repudiated. After World War I such an inflation took place in Germany and resulted in a forced abandonment of the existing monetary system. The primary impetus to this inflation was the fact that the German government was spending greatly in excess of its revenues, thus producing a continual upward pressure. The upward movement to a large extent took the form of a price rise, and there came a point where individuals and businessmen alike expected these price rises to continue indefinitely. In such a situation money would buy less and less the longer it was held. Consumers therefore tried to spend their incomes as soon as they received them, so that it was no longer true that they became willing to save more as their incomes rose. Businessmen similarly wanted their assets in the form of goods rather than cash. No one in the economy wanted to hold money, but businessmen and individuals as a group could not reduce their holdings of money, since the quantity of money in circulation was being increased all the time. The more people spent in the attempt to get rid of money and obtain goods instead, the more they found that they were receiving as income. The more they received as income, the more they had to spend. It was impossible for everyone to reach a satisfactory adjustment at the same time, and the attempt to reach an impossible goal set off the explosive price spiral upward. This spiral eventually led to a situation in which people refused to give up goods or services for money but resorted to barter instead. Money was repudiated as a medium of exchange and became worthless.

In terms of income analysis this phenomenon reflects either rapid upward shifting of the various functions or a total expenditures function that is steeper than the disposable income function, so that continued expansion merely drives the system further from equilibrium. This latter situation is shown in Fig. 22.

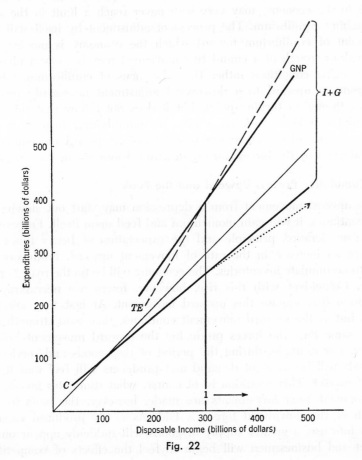

Fig. 22

It is also theoretically possible for a downward cumulative movement to be explosive, but no such situation is recorded in the annals of recent history. Should a continued fall in prices take place, expectation of further fall might increase the desire of individuals to save, leading them to postpone all possible expenditures in order to take advantage of later lower prices. Similarly, producers would have little incentive to invest, since by holding money they would expect to be able to buy more with it in the future. These circumstances are just the opposite of those discussed in the upward explosive spiral but are not so apt to take place in a modern economy with its existing social and economic institutions.

THE ECONOMY AS AN UNSTABLE SYSTEM

Quite apart from the problem of explosive spirals, cumulative movements in the economy may very well never reach a limit in the sense of reaching equilibrium. The process of adjustment by itself will alter the point of equilibrium toward which the economy is moving, and the peak or trough of a cumulative movement may be only a phase in the changing conditions rather than the locus of equilibrium. Changing from an upward to a downward adjustment necessarily involves passing through a turning point, but it does not follow that this turning point can be considered a place of equilibrium. Instead, it may simply be the place where the forces causing upward movement are overbalanced by the forces causing downward movement.

The Cumulative Process Upward and the Peak

The upward movement from a depression may start out slowly; but as it continues, it will gain momentum and feed upon itself. Forces such as the acceleration principle and the expectation of better times will produce an increase in the rate of movement upward. Producers will wish to accumulate inventories. The economy will be on the road to prosperity. Coincident with this rise, however, forces are necessarily set in motion that oppose this upward movement. At first they are very weak; but as the upward movement continues, they gain strength, and at the same time the forces producing the upward movement become weaker. For example, during the period of rise, goods and services of all kinds will be in great demand and producers will feel that it is a sellers' market. This condition is, of course, what stimulates investment. The moment such investments are made, however, the basis for the growth of the downward forces is laid, As newly produced capacity comes into use, a greater supply of goods will suddenly appear on the market and businessmen will begin to feel the effects of competition.

In some industries—food processing, for instance—this result will occur faster than in others, since these industries are able to expand production more quickly. If the expansion of capacity has been large, producers will find that they cannot sell all their expanded output at the going prices. They may be selling more than ever before, but still not so much as they can now produce. The level of investment expenditures in these industries will fall off rapidly even though investment may still be increasing in other parts of the economy. As the upward movement progresses, more and more industries will feel the market go soft under them and less and less expansion will be carried on. Finally a point will be reached where the decline in investment expenditures will more than match the increase in consumers' expenditures and in investment expenditures in those industries which are still expanding, and an absolute decline will set in for all the economy.

There are many factors that condition the duration and height of a cumulative movement upward. Basic among these is the so-called period of gestation of investment—the length of time that elapses between the making of an expenditure on producers' goods and the actual purchase by consumers of products which have been made with these producers' goods. If this period is long, the movement upward will be prolonged, since the increase in actual output of goods will be postponed for some time, although the increase in profits, wage rates, and employment—all leading to increases in disposable income—will occur immediately. The duration of the upward movement will also depend upon the time lags that exist between a change in conditions and the reaction of consumers and producers to it. For consumers this period may be very short; a fall in disposable income may be accompanied almost simultaneously by a cut in consumers' expenditures, and even with an increase in disposable income only a very short time is probably needed for consumers to increase their expenditures. Producers, on the other hand, cannot control their output or the rate of their investment expenditures with anywhere near the same facility. Once the construction of a building has been started, for instance, it may be better to finish it even though the producer's expectations have worsened in the meantime. A great many projects, once they have been started, must be finished; the producer often is not free to change his mind once he has made the original decision. A change in the rate of output of a plant may also require time. Plans have to be altered, labor must be notified, and the inflow of materials must be stopped. Until direct costs can be stopped, it is usually not profitable to contract output even if expectations do change radically. There is considerable evidence that output continues for a while at the same rate and that the accumulation of inventories is subject to a substantial lag behind changes in expectations. Commitments that have already been made will continue to supply deliveries even when it might be preferable from the point of view of the recipient to have less on hand. In other words, when consumers' expenditures contract, producers and distributors may involuntarily be forced to invest in inventories for a time before they are able to adjust. This sluggishness in reaction may well help to explain why at the peak of a cumulative movement upward the change in expectations does not always cause an immediate and precipitous drop in the level of income. During the period before producers can adjust, the economy will be in precarious balance or else in gradual decline; it may even continue upward slightly further. Only after adjustment can take place will the downswing occur.

The Cumulative Process Downward and the Trough

The cumulative movement downward will not necessarily be symmetrical with the movement upward. During a rapid decline there may or may not be forces that will put a floor under the fall before the economy reaches the point of zero investment expenditures. In the decline after 1929 no real floor existed; the decline stopped because the forces producing it played themselves out. The trough of 1932 was a period in which there were no very significant forces pressing for adjustment either way. The downward forces had reached their limit (virtually no investment and saving), and the upward forces had not yet begun to make themselves felt. Yet even this situation was not equilibrium, for the economy could not remain at this low level indefinitely. The process of inventory disinvestment obviously could not continue indefinitely; there would come a time when stocks would be exhausted. The replacement of some capital goods would eventually become necessary, when further postponement would impair the existing level of output. Barring an explosive situation, it was inevitable that forces would develop which would produce a cumulative movement upward even in the absence of external stimulating conditions. Therefore it seems proper to consider the trough of the 1932 depression as a phase in the continuous process of adjustment rather than an equilibrium. The existence of the low level of output in conjunction with other conditions planted the seeds for the cumulative movement upward. Although it might have taken much longer, this cumulative movement upward would eventually have occurred even in the absence of any external stimulation.

The recession of 1938 was quite different in nature from the 1932 depression. By 1937 the economy had not yet reached full employment. Many of the forces that had helped to produce the cumulative movement upward were not completely overridden by the recession, so that there were strong forces opposing the downward movement. The failure of the expansive forces to disappear eased the immediate impact of the decline and provided a cushion that forestalled the complete collapse of expectations. It provided a floor so that economic activity did not have to fall to the level of zero investment expenditures. The period was one of fluctuation in the strength of opposing forces. The natural development of cumulative forces downward plus the effect of external conditions combined to produce a situation in late 1937 in which the magnitude of the downward pressure exceeded that of the existing upward pressures. But in the latter part of 1938 the upward forces again became dominant and an upward movement again set in. Neither the peak of 1937 nor the trough of 1938 was in any sense an equilibrium position; instead, they were stages in a continuous process of change.

Cumulative Change and External Conditions

Although cumulative change in the economy may take place solely as a result of interrelated economic elements acting in sequence, the magnitude, duration, and direction of change in the economy will continually be altered by external conditions. One of the most spectacular of such external occurrences is war. Both World War I and World War II provided an extraordinary stimulation for the economy and in large measure were responsible for the duration and height of the upward movements in these periods. The course of economic events is completely altered by such major events. Even the postwar period bears the imprint of the war situation; the fact that there was a war will continue to affect the economy for a long period of time after it is over.

Other changes that are external to the economic process may be less spectacular than wars, but, as noted above, they are nevertheless very important in explaining the path of economic changes. Economic conditions in foreign countries may have repercussions through changes in imports and exports. For example, during the depression of the thirties many agricultural countries were brought to a low level of economic activity because foreign countries were no longer willing or able to purchase the amount of food products that they had been accustomed to. Within an economy a large number of noneconomic forces can also condition or alter the economic change that is taking place. The importance of inventions, and changes in laws, institutions, and social attitudes has already been mentioned. The establishment of a minimum-wage law will have important economic effects, even though these effects may be difficult to ascertain in any empirical study. A change in the composition of the Supreme Court or the passage of such a law as the

National Industrial Recovery Act will have very definite repercussions. The economist may not be able to predict their effects, but they are nonetheless important elements in the process of change.

THE ECONOMY AS A GROWING SYSTEM

The mechanism of income analysis as discussed in previous chapters looked at the economic system from a short-run point of view, and for the most part focused on fluctuations in the level of economic activity rather than upon the phenomenon of long-run growth. It is obvious, however, that the factors discussed thus far will be affected by the process of growth, and will in their turn affect the process of growth. It is the purpose of this section, therefore, to study such interrelationships.

The Effect of Investment Expenditures on Future Output Levels

Investment expenditures have thus far been examined as injections into the system at a given moment of time, and little or no consideration has been given to the manner in which they affect future levels of output. However, inasmuch as investment expenditures do cause an actual change in the capacity of the economy to produce, attention should be directed toward their impact upon the total amount of future output and income that will be available.

The Capital-Output Ratio. The relation between the volume of investment expenditures and the potential increase in output that results ($I/\Delta GNP$, both in constant prices) is often referred to as the capital-output ratio.[1] Investment expenditures, when considered on a net basis, are equal to the net increase in the capital stock in the economy, and with such an increase in capital stock the economy should be able to produce a greater amount of output in future periods. At any one moment of time a great many factors will influence the size of the capital-output ratio. First, the marginal productivity of capital which would be expected given the existing technology and the existing labor supply in the economy at a given moment of time is clearly important. Besides this, however, changes in the size of the labor force, shifts in the composition of output (e.g., farming to manufacturing), technological changes, and productivity changes due to such things as increase in skill in the labor force all will affect the capital-output ratio. Two of these elements, technological change and productivity change, merit some further consideration.

[1] In much of the literature the term "capital-output ratio" is used to refer to the relation between the total amount of existing capital and output; the relation of the current additions to capital and to output would in such a case be the marginal capital-output ratio.

Technological Change. Technological change will have the effect of decreasing the capital-output ratio, since new investment expenditures along lines of improved technology will result in much larger increases in output than would have been expected under previously existing technological conditions. It may well be, in fact, that the most important element in determining the capital-output ratio is not the curve of marginal productivity of capital but rather the shifts in this curve. This situation is not unlike that described above for the relationship between the interest rate and the marginal efficiency of capital. Technological change may result in continual downward shifts in the capital-output ratio, and such downward shifts may more than counteract the decline in marginal productivity of capital because of the effects of the exhaustion of resources and the increase in the existing capital stock.

Productivity Change. Productivity changes arising from increased experience and better training and education of the labor force are not reflected in investment expenditures, since in national income accounting such things as education, on-the-job training, and general betterment of social conditions are not considered to be investment. As in the case of technological change, these will have the effect of lowering the capital-output ratio over time. It would of course be quite possible for productivity to decline, if such things as war or depression caused the dissipation of the cadre of trained personnel that go to make up a modern economy. Aside from these eventualities, however, the usual movement in productivity can be expected to be upward.

Fluctuation in Capital-Output Ratios. It is generally assumed in the literature on this subject that capital-output ratios are determined by relatively stable forces and are therefore fairly constant over short periods of time, but there is no particular reason why this should be so. It is quite possible for significant technological changes that greatly alter the capital-output ratio to occur sporadically. The introduction of new chemical processes, such as synthetic fabrics in the textile industry, for example, may radically alter the capital-output ratio in specific industries in the space of a relatively few years. Even more probable is a systematic fluctuation in capital-output ratios corresponding to fluctuations in economic activity. For example, the type of investment expenditures made in the early phases of a cumulative upward movement may have smaller capital-output ratios in general than those made at later phases. If this is true, it would give rise to a systematic relationship between capital-output ratios and economic fluctuation.

Sustained Rates of Growth as Moving Equilibriums

Once it is recognized that investment expenditures will result in a growth in total output, the question is immediately posed how in terms of income analysis the economy can assimilate such growth. The problem is different from that of a simple increase in investment such as that discussed in Chap. 15, since that analysis did not take into account the repercussions of investment on future levels of output, but only its immediate effect on income.

Interdependence of the Change in Gross National Product and the Level of Investment. The potential change in the gross national product, given an initial amount of investment expenditures, can be thought of as determined by the capital-output ratio, but in integrating economic growth into income analysis, it is also necessary to consider what repercussions the increase in the level of gross national product will have upon the level of investment expenditures. In other words, the relationship between the change in the level of gross national product and the determinants of investment is somewhat circular. A given level of gross national product and a past pattern of cumulative change will produce a given level of investment expenditures, which in turn will, because of the acceleration effect and changed expectations, produce a new level of gross national product, and that in turn will produce a new level of investment expenditures, and so forth.

The Nature of Long-run Equilibrium Rates of Growth. In this situation the question arises whether the gross national product-investment expenditure relation will yield a consistent pattern of growth that does not force the economy into upward or downward cumulative movements. For this to be true, the change in gross national product caused by a given increase in investment expenditures must result in a new situation in which the increased output will be exactly absorbed by the new level of consumers' expenditures, government expenditures, and investment expenditures. Diagrammatically, this is shown in Fig. 23.

The original situation with a given level of investment expenditures is shown at vertical line 1. It is assumed that the level of investment expenditures occurring at this point in time will yield a potential $40 billion increase in gross national product in the next period. This is shown by point B on the disposable income function (GNP). Such an increase in gross national product would also cause an upward shift in the total expenditures function, and the problem is, of course, whether given such a potential rise in gross national product, the investment, government, and consumers' expenditures that will be desired will exactly add up to this potential increase in gross national product. In diagrammatic terms, the problem is whether the upward shift in the total expenditures function will result in its intersecting the disposable income function at the exact point given by the capital-output ratio (point B). In Fig. 23 it is assumed that this does take place, and that

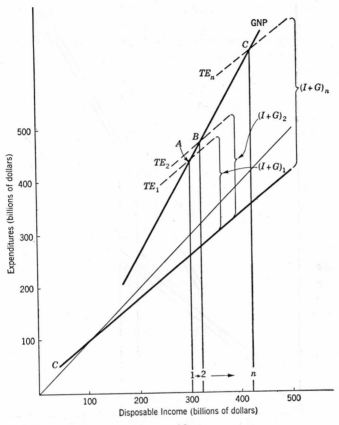

Fig. 23

the economy in period 2 is at the point of equilibrium (point B, vertical line 2). Further growth would occur without cumulative adjustment, furthermore, if the total expenditures curve always shifted so that it would intersect the disposable income function at the point given by the capital-output ratio. This is shown in Fig. 23 by the total expenditures line (TE_n) crossing the disposable income function at point C.

Sustained equilibrium can also be obtained by a coincidence of shifts in the consumption function and the disposable income function, such that the new level of equilibrium coincides with that determined by the capital-output ratio. This is shown in Fig. 24. In this instance the consumption function shifted upward and the disposable income function shifted downward, and since the increase in gross national product caused by these shifts just happens to equal the change caused by the capital-output ratio, point B will be an equilibrium point.

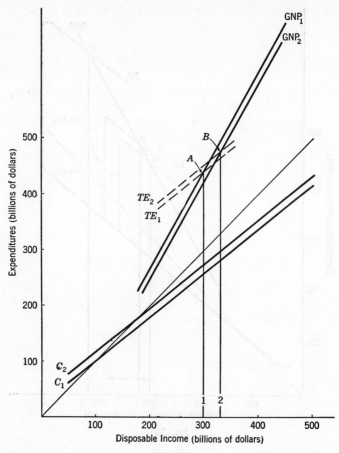

Fig. 24

Rates of Growth Causing Upward Cumulative Movements

It is quite possible that the increase in gross national product resulting from investment expenditure will be smaller in magnitude than the upward shift in the total expenditures function due to such growth. This is shown in Fig. 25, where the new total expenditures curve (TE_2) intersects the disposable income function at point C ($500 billion), whereas the growth in gross national product in constant prices that resulted from the investment expenditures occurring at vertical line 1 would have come only to point B ($460 billion).

In this case the more rapid rise in total expenditures than in output will lead to a rise in prices. It is of course quite possible for growth over a long period of time to be accompanied by a steady rise in prices, with no other effect upon the economy. If producers and consumers

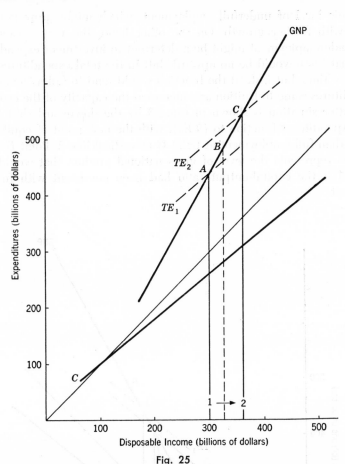

Fig. 25

took future price rises into their calculations, however, the price rise would become steeper, and if this caused the functions to behave in a manner similar to that already discussed with reference to explosive systems, the price rise might be of such magnitude as to cause a complete breakdown of the system.

Rates of Growth Causing Downward Cumulative Movements and/or Falling Prices

When the shift of the total expenditures function falls short of the point determined by the capital-output ratio, the economy will be producing at a point below what is full capacity and hence full employment. Such underutilization and unemployment may result in either a stable or unstable situation. It is possible for the economy to suffer a chronic level of underfull employment, which might grow gradually worse with further growth. On the other hand, the very existence of such underemployment might be a deterrent to investment expenditures, such that there would be no upward shift in the total expenditures function over time, but instead the function would tend to fall as investment expenditures came to fruition and increased the capacity of the economy. This latter situation is shown in Fig. 26 by the downward shift in the total expenditures function to (TE_2), with the new point of equilibrium at less than full employment at point C at vertical line 2. Point B in this diagram represents the level of gross national product that would have resulted if the capital-output ratio had been consistent with full employment.

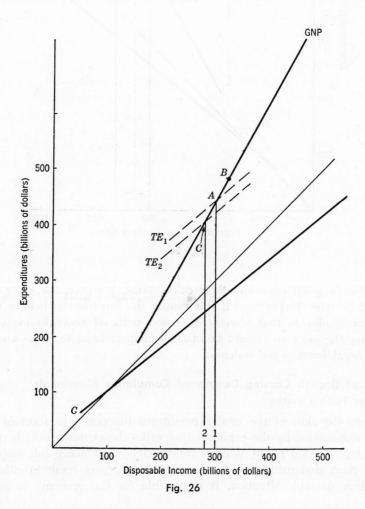

Fig. 26

Many of the discussions about the future of the American economy in the thirties centered around the term "secular stagnation." The controversy was concerned with whether at the higher levels of capacity in a modern industrial economy sufficient investment expenditures would be forthcoming to keep the economy at full employment, or whether the growth in potential output would always exceed what the economy could absorb, so that chronic underemployment would result and in very real terms there would be secular stagnation. The boom caused by World War II and the postwar readjustment diverted attention to other topics, and few economists today express real concern whether sufficient investment opportunities will be available to prevent secular stagnation. On the other hand, many economists do worry about the problem of whether the rate of growth will tend to require periods of readjustment in which temporary softness and some degree of unemployment will exist, thus causing the actual rate of growth to fall considerably below the potential rate of growth had expenditures kept pace with the growing capacity of the economy.

Thus far in the discussion the capital-output ratio has been assumed to cause an increase in gross national product in constant prices. If prices were to fall, however, there could be an increase in real gross national product without a corresponding increase in the money value of gross national product. This would mean that point B in the previous diagrams would be closer to point A; with sufficient price fall, points A and B would coincide. Falling prices have actually occurred during certain periods of prosperity. In the period from 1925 to 1929, for example, an almost stable or falling price level accompanied increases in output. It does not seem probable, however, that the full potential growth in output can be absorbed by price decreases. The institutional characteristics of the economy and the customary upward movement of wages tends to prevent prices from falling sufficiently.

Cyclical Patterns of Growth

In the discussion of the capital-output ratio above it was suggested that the capital-output ratios themselves might be subject to systematic variation, so that even if growth occurs at its maximum potential rate, a cyclical historical pattern will be traced out. Specifically, with the initiation of certain kinds of investment, many other kinds of investment also become possible, all of which yield in the initial phases of the adjustment process very low capital-output ratios. As the initial wave of innovations are exploited further and further, however, the capital-output ratios will rise and the rate of increase of output will decrease. This in itself may be sufficient to cause a cumulative movement downward, and new investment may be postponed until such time as a new wave of innovations again produces low capital-output ratios. It is not suggested in this analysis that the technological innovations themselves have to be clustered. It would be quite possible, even though inventions occurred at a fairly steady rate, for investment expenditures exploiting these inventions to occur sporadically in bunches over time.

Besides the technological explanation for cyclical patterns of growth, a cyclical pattern of growth may occur purely because of the behavior of producers' expectations. In the initial phases of an upswing, producers as a group might feel quite certain that times were improving, and thus initiate relatively large investment expenditures. With the progress of time, and as these investment expenditures bore fruit, the expectations of producers might lead them to be somewhat more cautious, and investment expenditures might not rise as much as would be needed to reach the potential rate of growth. This would provide a dampening influence, so that the cumulative movement upward would stop and a cumulative decline would set in, and thus the pattern would repeat itself.

The Problem of Optimal Rates of Growth

The determinants of the rates of growth of the economy that have been discussed above are (1) investment decisions, (2) decisions determining government and consumers' expenditures, and (3) cumulative changes in the level of income in the economy which occur in order to reconcile these. The final determination of the percentage of the resources of the economy that is to be devoted to investment is thus the result of a combination of factors rather than a single conscious decision of a maximizing nature. According to classical economic theory, the division between consumption and investment was determined by the rate of interest, which equated the greater productivity of future goods with the greater desirability of present goods. However, if decisions respecting investment expenditures are not highly sensitive to the interest rate, as indicated in the discussion of the marginal efficiency of capital, and if the consumption function is determined by institutional and cultural factors rather than by the interest rate, the interest rate loses its place as part of the allocating mechanism. Instead, the allocation that occurs is determined by the institutional and cultural elements of the society rather than by conscious decisions on the part of individuals with respect to what they want to have in the way of consumers' goods as against what rate of growth is desirable.

It should be remembered in connection with the consideration of optimal rates of growth that it is not always true that higher rates of growth have to be purchased at the cost of reducing either consumers' or government expenditures. Statistical evidence seems to indicate that a large percentage of the time the economy is below full utilization of its capacity, so that an increase in the level of its investment expenditures could result in an increase in the amount of goods produced for consumption purposes also.

The rate of growth may also be affected by a rising price level. For example, in the history of the development of modern economies, the impact on prices of the multiplier effect of the gold and silver discoveries in the New World may have had a significant role in initiating and stimulating growth. When price adjustments are in an upward direction, the expansions of activity may be longer, and downward cumulative movements may be shorter, with the consequence that the average rate of growth may be higher than it would have been otherwise.

17. Economic Policy and the Level of Economic Activity

To a very large extent the economy envisaged by the traditional economic theorist is one without any over-all economic policies. Such a lack of economic policy, however, has seldom existed, either in the annals of history or in the actuality of modern economic systems. Each country throughout its history has seen a succession of economic policies come and go. In England, for instance, as far back as the Middle Ages economic policies relating to feudal land tenure were important factors in the economic life of the country and strongly influenced the course of future economic development. In the mercantilist period economic policies designed for the achievement of national wealth and power prescribed rigid control of economic activity. Even the laissez-faire philosophy that followed mercantilism—the philosophy that the unrestricted play of natural forces would bring about the best solution—involved an over-all economic policy: the promotion of as free an economic system as possible. The growth of imperialism later brought with it trade policies leading to the building up of a world empire and extensive overseas investment. Little discussion is needed to establish the existence of highly developed economic policies since World War I.

In a larger sense a nation cannot be without economic policies, even though these policies may not be crystallized in laws, regulations, or even conscious actions on the part of business or the government. These specific economic policies may conflict with one another, and they may be intended to fulfill entirely different purposes. This lack of consistency springs from the fact that on the one hand each economic problem has many aspects, and on the other hand each economic policy will have repercussions in more than one sphere of economic activity. The patent laws, for instance, may tend to promote inequality of income, whereas the income tax levels such inequality; yet both of these measures can logically be supported at the same time, since they have important aspects aside from their repercussions on the distribution of income. The complete absence of economic policies would entail the absence of an economic system; in any complex economic system the apparent lack of a specific coordinated policy represents in itself a conscious or unconscious choice among alternative modes of behavior. Letting things work out as they will is very definitely an over-all economic policy.

This chapter will discuss only those economic policies which are significantly related to the level of economic activity. Rather than attempting to suggest any over-all integrated group of policies, the discussion will be confined to those elements which to date have been the objects of conscious policy decisions in the economy.

THE PROBLEM INVOLVED

Violent changes in the level of economic activity do pose problems of economic policy; this is evident from the experience of the United States during the period since 1929. Before a detailed analysis of possible alternative policies can be made, it will first be necessary to consider two questions: what the problems raised by changes in the level of activity are, and what basic objectives exist upon which general agreement can be obtained.

Policies that are, in effect, expressions of economic philosophy are involved even in the power of the government to tax, the laws of incorporation with limited liability, and the rights of private property. There are few individuals who feel that it is a matter of indifference what economic philosophy the nation adopts, so that specific economic policies will arouse intense interest. It does not necessarily follow, however, that different economic measures will imply different basic philosophies; individuals holding the same basic views may disagree about their interpretation of specific situations or about the effects of given economic policies. Conversely, there are a great many economic policies that people with widely divergent economic philosophies would all be willing to accept.

The Significance of Changes in the Level of Activity

The fluctuations in the level of economic activity that took place from 1929 to 1938 had very important effects upon the economy. The depression of the thirties disrupted economic activity. Unemployment was widespread. Individuals who had been employed in producing goods and services were thrown out of work, and many more were forced either to work part time or else to accept less productive jobs than those they had previously held. The unemployment figures understate the actual maladjustments that occurred in people's lives: many a skilled carpenter or machinist was forced to turn to subsistence farming or to take a job as a night watchman in order to get enough to eat. It was not only the inefficient and the indolent who were left without work. When a plant shut down completely—as many plants did—all its employees were forced on the already glutted labor market, and the efficient and the inefficient alike suffered. Relief was necessary to prevent those out of work from starving. In spite of relief payments, most of the people who were unemployed and many others as well had their life savings wiped out either in the attempt to keep off relief as long as possible or in the preceding financial crash. Dissaving was widespread. Consumers as a group were dissaving more than they were saving, so that personal saving in 1932 and 1933 was negative, amounting to minus $0.6 billion in both years. This widespread using up of past accumulations of savings had repercussions in later periods, when these families were unable to pay for higher education for their children or else had no money saved up for their old age and retirement. As is true of any social upheaval, the depression proved disastrous to many different groups in the economy for different reasons. A great many children not only were ill-fed but grew up in homes where economic pressures prevented happy family life. Many were forced to leave school early in order to look for what part-time employment they could find to help ease the poverty of the family. Even if no opportunities for any kind of employment were open, higher education was impossible; living at home was cheaper, and children past the minimum age could collect unemployment relief. High-school and college graduating classes had little hope of getting any jobs whatsoever, and what jobs they did find were not adequate to get married on. The birth rate declined rapidly in the thirties, and this decline was due partly to the fact that children imposed an additional economic burden. In some cases the depression resulted only in the postponement of children to a later period, but in other cases it resulted in permanently smaller families. Finally, people who normally would have been at the height of their earning power during this period became unemployed, placing the burden of their support on others.

Unemployment is not the only source of inequity in the economy during periods of depression. When the level of gross national product falls, the prices of some products will fall very much more than the prices of other products. Farmers may be forced to sell their products at ridiculously low prices, whereas other producers may be able to restrict their output so that their prices do not fall so much. Falling prices are inequitable in another respect: fixed debts, e.g., mortgages, remain unchanged in money terms, even though all prices in the economy, including earning capacity, have fallen. Not everyone will be made worse off by the depression, of course. People living on fixed incomes such as pensions or annuities will be better off because of the fall in the cost of living. Similarly, anyone with money in the bank will find that it will go further and buy more in the depression.

Depression also entails the operation of the economy at a level far below its capacity without apparent reason. Goods are desperately needed, yet there is idleness, and this idleness is a waste of labor and other resources that could be used to yield economic goods. Furthermore, in depression the economy lives off its capital produced in the past and does not attempt to replace it. Depreciation of capital goods is not solely from use; depreciation goes on even when the machines are idle. The loss in potential production during a depression cannot be calculated simply by making an estimate of what could be produced if those who profess to be unemployed were employed. The war experience of most of the economies involved shows that capacity of an economy is not reached as soon as its labor surplus disappears. Labor shortages themselves will lead to the development of laborsaving and capital-saving devices that will vastly increase the productivity of the nation. Furthermore, integration and coordination in an economy cannot be achieved overnight. Sustained high-level activity is necessary; and when there are violent changes in the level of activity such as are implied by deep and sharp depressions, it may never be possible to achieve effective coordination of economic processes.

Depression is not the only form of fluctuation that will have disruptive effects upon the economy. The extremely high levels of activity during World War II and the immediate postwar inflation were not without their undesirable results. In wartime, of course, the resource allocation pattern of the nation was subject to abnormal war demand, but any period of high-level activity is likely to be a period of sellers' markets, when almost anything put on the market will be bought. There is therefore little incentive to produce goods of high quality. Competition between producers for markets will probably not be strong, and more attention will have to be given by producers to the problems of getting adequate supplies of materials and labor than to selling the final product. The attention given to the supply situation, furthermore, will often result only in an intensification of the struggle for the limited quantity of resources that exists, so that the price will be driven up further.

An inflationary rise in prices will produce much inequity. Many individuals' incomes will not rise so fast as prices, so that they will be forced either to lower their standards of living or to use up their past accumulations of savings in the effort to maintain their consumption. This will, of course, be true of all those who gain from the fall in prices in depressions—persons receiving pensions, annuities, or other fixed incomes, and to a large extent those holding white-collar positions, whose incomes change only very slowly. Unless there is a large increase in productivity, wage earners may also find that they can buy less with their take-home pay. The farmer, however, will be far better off in such a period than in any other. Not only will he be receiving high prices for his products, but his fixed mortgage debt will be relatively less important, since prices have risen. Industrial profits will also rise sharply, although the portion of such profits paid out in the form of dividends and interest payments probably will not rise equivalently.

Both upward and downward fluctuations in the level of activity, therefore, will have undesirable repercussions. These adverse effects can be classed in two groups: waste of resources and inequities. Depressions will waste resources not only through the failure to make productive use of available labor services but also because a significant part of the physical capacity built up during the final stages of the previous prosperity will waste away in idleness. Inequities resulting both from depression and from inflation may be such that there will be continual discontent and unhappiness in the nation. Adequate adjustments by individuals may be impossible when circumstances change faster than the adjustment can take place, and the final result may be fear based on the lack of security.

Objectives of Economic Policy

The economic objective of a nation is often stated in very broad terms as the maximization of the welfare and happiness of the people of that nation. Such a definition is too vague and general, however, to be very useful as a guide for a specific policy. On the other hand, economic objectives are often confused with those particular policies which are believed to be the most useful: striving for a "free economy" or, at the other extreme, complete planning of production. But these specific policies tell little about the objectives behind them. A thoroughgoing discussion of objectives and policies is neither possible nor desirable in this chapter. Instead, several possible objectives relating to the level of activity in the economy will be discussed, and in the following section some of the current policies that are proposed for carrying out these objectives will be considered.

One of the primary objectives of economic policy in the nation is the prevention of periods of general unemployment. Such an objective does not need to be so far-reaching as to guarantee everyone a job all the time; it is well recognized that frictional unemployment will always exist in the economy and that there are some individuals who are probably not capable of holding a job. But mass unemployment is an entirely different matter; if periods of widespread inability to find jobs could be prevented from taking place, much of the insecurity and inequity produced by fluctuations in the level of activity could be abolished. This objective of full employment goes or should go beyond the mere provision that everyone who loses a job is given another for which he may or may not be suited. It is sometimes suggested that no more than this be required of substitute employment—that the government set unemployed people to raking leaves or digging holes and filling them up again or some other unproductive task. But such measures may well destroy the morale of the individuals who are so employed, leaving them with the feeling that they have no place in society. Instead of such makeshift measures, what is needed is the continuance of permanent, useful employment.

A second possible economic objective of the nation is that of general price stability. Here again, this does not mean that no price should ever change but rather that the cumulative price increases and decreases which have occurred in the past should be eliminated as much as possible. Violent changes in the price structure not only lead to inequities but also require the economy to make fundamental adjustments in its patterns of resource allocation. Such adjustment is difficult to make; and when changes in the price structure are rapid and extensive, confusion and chaos may follow. The economy will be in a state of continuous and violent adjustment, and no approach to equilibrium can be achieved. The lack of general price stability leads to a degree of uncertainty that may, in fact, prevent the development of a healthy economy.

A final objective of economic policy is the efficient allocation of resources. By combining labor, capital goods, and natural resources in various different ways, different assortments of goods and services can be produced. An efficient combination of labor, capital goods, and natural resources is one that produces the particular assortment of goods and services most desired by consumers. Efficiency in this sense requires not only efficient production techniques so that no productive resources are wasted but also correct decisions about what particular goods and services should be produced. Carried to its logical conclusion, this objective would even include leisure as an economic good, giving due consideration to the preferences of individuals regarding the number of hours they wish to work relative to the goods they receive. Most economic policies will have an effect upon resource allocation patterns, and this effect must be taken into account in evaluating such policies. A policy that leads to the allocation of resources without reference to consumer preferences is undesirable even though it has a

beneficial effect upon the level of employment and the stability of the
price level, since the welfare of the economy can be increased by a
better solution to the problem of the combination of resources.

Some economists feel that these objectives are unobtainable or at
least incompatible with each other. This position is based upon the
belief that fluctuations in the level of activity in the economy are a
necessary part of natural economic growth, and that if these fluctuations
are eliminated, the economy will become completely static and rigid.
The period of cumulative upswing, they feel, is essentially a period of
growth in which investments are made that will mature in a later period.
The downswing is a period of readjustment caused by the increased
abundance of goods, and it is argued that this readjustment is necessary
before the economy can embark upon another wave of progress. Yet on
the other side of the picture it has been pointed out that letting the
economy endure the cumulative adjustments may be no solution to the
problem because of the magnitude of these cumulative movements. Instead of bringing about readjustment, fluctuations as great as the depression of the thirties may instead, because of the unemployment, inequity, and uncertainty that they entail, create so unstable a political
situation that the whole economic system would be in jeopardy.

Theoretically, both of these arguments are valid; it is only through
further study and more empirical evidence that it would be possible
to choose adequately between them. However, few people are willing
to accept the conclusion that nothing can be done to alleviate the un-
fortunate consequences of fluctuations in economic activity. Should the
validity of this conclusion be accepted by all, it would, of course, be
unnecessary to examine economic policy further, since it would necessarily follow that, undesirable though the consequences of doing nothing
may be, no alternative policy would be any better. With this caveat,
therefore, it will be useful to examine a number of proposed economic
policies in some detail.

Economic Policy and the Level of Activity

Economic policies obviously will have to be quite different in different
phases of the cumulative movement up and down. There are a few
measures that would be helpful in both the upswing and the downswing,
but for the most part this is not true. An economic policy designed to
stimulate activity, for instance, might be appropriate in one period,
whereas another period would call for some sort of restrictive measure.
The following treatment will consider (1) measures that may help the
economy to stop a cumulative movement downward and initiate a move-

ment upward; (2) the problem of preventing or controlling inflation; and (3) measures applicable to the maintenance of stability in the economy.

Economic Policy and Recovery from a Depression

In income analysis terms a depression is essentially a cumulative decline in the level of gross national product. Recovery from a depression can be secured only when the cumulative decline is stopped and the level of gross national product is started on its way upward again. The level of gross national product can be increased only if the sum of its individual components—consumers' expenditures, gross private investment expenditures, government expenditures, and net exports—in turn is raised.

Economic policies can best be considered in terms of the effects that they will have upon each of these components. In some circumstances an increase in a particular component will set into motion a cumulative movement upward via the multiplier effect, the acceleration principle, and the effect of induced investment. But this result will not follow if an increase in one component should be offset by a corresponding decrease in some other component. For this reason all the components must be considered simultaneously.

Monetary Policy. Monetary policy has long been used as a weapon with which to fight depressions. An unsound banking and monetary system can be a major factor leading to financial collapse and so can greatly intensify the problem of adjustment. If the system is so organized that banks are forced to call in loans and contract credit on the brink of a depression, there will be a tremendous drive for liquidity, and financial panic may result; banks will close, depositors will lose their money, and the monetary system of the country will be endangered. The possibility of serious financial crisis brought about by monetary causes has been substantially lessened in recent years, and much has been done to ease financial adjustment in depression by the advent and growth of the Federal Reserve System and the Federal Deposit Insurance Corporation. Sound banking policy, however, cannot stop or cure a depression; it can only prevent it from being made worse by financial collapse.

Monetary policies of a more specific nature have often been employed or suggested. It is within the power of the monetary and banking authorities to influence the rate of interest and the availability of capital, and these powers have often been employed as tools of monetary policy. Lowering the interest rate and making capital more readily available should, it is argued, increase the level of investment expenditures. In normal or inflationary periods the level of investment expenditures might very well respond somewhat to these measures, but their effectiveness in periods of depression cannot readily be determined. For most producers interest is a small part of the total cost of investment, so that lowering the interest rate would change total costs only very slightly. Furthermore, although the banking authorities can make capital available by increasing the excess reserves of banks, they cannot thereby ensure that the banks will be willing to lend or that, even if the banks are willing to lend, producers will want to borrow. In a period of depression most producers feel that virtually all investment will be unprofitable, and they cannot be persuaded to undertake any additional ventures regardless of how low the interest rate is or how easily capital can be obtained. When producers are making losses, they ordinarily do not want to expand. For these reasons manipulation of interest rates and increasing the availability of capital is not likely to be very effective in combatting depression. However, these measures may be very useful once the upswing begins and producers have decided that investment expenditures may again be profitable. Direct monetary policies, therefore, although not sufficiently powerful to bring about recovery from a depression, may be an aid in the early stages of the upswing.

Tax Policy. Taxes can affect the level of both consumers' expenditures and investment expenditures, and for this reason tax reductions have been advocated as an economic policy to stimulate recovery from a depression. The effects of reductions in different types of taxes will be different, so that each of them must be considered separately.

A reduction in personal income taxes will increase disposable income; and according to the analysis presented in connection with the consumption function, the level of consumers' expenditures will rise correspondingly. The degree to which an income tax reduction will raise the level of consumers' expenditures will depend to a great extent upon which income groups receive the tax reduction. Should the higher income groups receive the major part of the tax reduction, the result would probably be that the personal saving of these groups would rise with no very great change in consumers' expenditures. But reduction of taxes on the lower income groups would probably increase consumers' expenditures by almost as much as the amount of the tax reduction. However, until the war period the income tax burden on the lower income groups was not significant, so that any reduction in the tax rate was automatically a reduction for the upper income groups. This effect is, of course, accentuated by the fact that in a depression the average level of personal incomes falls sharply. In recent decades effective income tax rates have risen and the level of personal income has also risen, so that the policy of reducing income tax rates would be more effective now than it has been in the past.

The effect of a reduction in corporate profits taxes, as was pointed out in the preceding chapter, is much more difficult to predict. Although such a reduction might normally stimulate producers to make investment expenditures, this reaction might not be forthcoming in a depression. Low taxes will not turn a loss into a profit. Furthermore, the tax rates in which the producer will be interested are the tax rates that will be in effect when the investment matures and begins to yield income. The recognition that the change in the corporate tax rate is for the purpose of stimulating recovery, and that once recovery is achieved higher rates will be restored, may prevent the reduction from having its desired effect. Tax policy based on reduction in the corporate tax, therefore, is not likely to have predictable results; in some periods the stimulation of investment might be far greater than the amount of the tax reduction, but in other periods the reduction would be ineffective in much the same way that a lowering of the interest rate may be ineffective.

Reductions in sales and excise taxes will have repercussions on both producers and consumers. If the tax reduction is matched by an equal fall in the prices that consumers have to pay, consumers will find that they can purchase more goods for the same expenditure, and there will be an increase in the receipts of producers after sales taxes. If prices should not fall the full amount of the reduction in sales and excise taxes, the profit margin of producers will increase, so that production will be more profitable. Whichever reaction follows, therefore, reduction of sales and excise taxes will have a stimulating effect even in the depths of the depression. Consumers will find that their money will buy more goods, or producers will find that the profitability of production has increased. Per dollar of reduction in revenue it seems probable that a cut in sales and excise taxes will be quite effective. However, such reductions require considerable legislative action and are not susceptible to flexible change. Furthermore, continuous change in taxes of this type might introduce an additional element of uncertainty in that neither producers nor consumers would know what they could count on in the future.

Government Outlay Policy. Changes in the amount and type of government outlays may have significant repercussions on the economy. In the following analysis of the repercussions of increases in different kinds of government outlays it will be assumed that outlays are increased without an equivalent increase in tax revenues. The purpose of this assumption is to isolate the effects of the increase in outlays; it may be considered desirable to finance the increased outlays out of tax revenues, but the effects of any change in taxes must be considered separately from the effects of changes in outlays. In order to see what the effects of increasing outlays alone would be, it will be assumed that these outlays are financed either by borrowing idle funds or through a general expansion of bank credit.

One of the most common forms of increased government outlays in a depression is the payment of relief to unemployed persons. Such relief may take the form either of actual money payments or of the distribution of such goods as surplus food. In either case the level of expenditures in the economy will rise, and this increase may help to generate a cumulative movement upward. It does not follow, however, that the increase in relief payments or in the purchase of surplus goods to be distributed will always result in an increase in total expenditures of exactly the same amount. Some of the individuals who receive the relief payments may have past accumulations of savings, which they will not have to use up so fast as they would without relief. Individuals who are supplied with surplus commodities by the government may be forced to spend less of their own money in order to maintain an acceptable standard of living. It is sometimes further contended that the payment of relief deters some individuals from taking jobs at wages that are below the level of relief. This is undoubtedly true, but it does not necessarily follow that relief payments are therefore not useful in stopping the cumulative movement of income downward. Continued fall in wage payments might lead only to further cumulative adjustment downward, and the final level of employment might be very much lower than it would be if a floor is placed under wages by the payment of adequate relief to those out of work. Such relief payments would maintain the purchasing power of the economy at a much higher level, and the extent of the cumulative movement would be much less. A much more serious charge is that relief payments, if they extend over a long period of time, may be harmful to morale and destroy the incentive to work. In this connection the effect of the dole in the depressed areas of south Wales is frequently cited. On the other side of the picture, however, is the obvious consideration that the lack of relief payments in a situation where unemployment is more than simply frictional may have an even more destructive effect upon morale. The only adequate means of maintaining morale, of course, is the prevention of general unemployment.

The government may also increase the amount of its transfer payments other than direct relief. Transfer payments of this type include such outlays as bonuses paid to veterans and the refund of taxes previously paid. During World War II some countries made use of compulsory savings plans, borrowing from individuals according to the same general principles as those upon which taxes are levied. With such compulsory saving, the government can reimburse the individuals from whom it borrows whenever it wishes and so has a method whereby it can increase disposable income through transfer payments during the periods when such an increase is needed. The difficulties encountered in tax reduction when incomes fall to a level so low that the groups suffering the greatest income losses are not appreciably benefited by a reduction in tax rates have been noted above. One of the methods by which this problem can be circumvented is the introduction of negative taxation or tax refunds to individuals who suffer large decreases in income. This would have the effect of giving income to those who suffered the most and thus in all probability would provide a higher rate of spending than would be achieved with normal tax reductions. This would be especially true if such negative taxation and tax refunds were confined to the relatively low-income groups. The problem of equity in such transfer payments is of course very important, but the attempt to preserve given income relationships should not go so far that all individuals as a group will suffer. Thus, for example, the refusal to pay transfer funds on the grounds that such income was not in fact earned might result in a lower real income for everybody in the economy, so that those not receiving the transfer payments, as well as those receiving them, would in fact be the losers.

Finally, increased government outlays may take the form of purchase of goods and services for public works. The government performs many useful functions that require continued expenditures; such things as highways, public buildings, conservation, and national defense constitute the major part of the government's budget. It is often suggested that expenditures in these and similar fields, e.g., public housing, be extended during a depression, so creating useful employment in the economy.

The degree of success that an increase in government expenditures on goods and services will have in raising the level of gross national product will of course depend upon the multiplier effect. In recent decades the multiplier appears to be relatively low, such that a large amount of government expenditure would be required to obtain a significant increase in the gross national product. If, because of large leakages between gross national product and disposable income, the multiplier value were about 1.5, for example, a $10 billion expenditure on goods and services might have only a $15 billion effect upon the gross national product. Under such circumstances it would be wise to ask whether other kinds of measures, e.g., tax reductions and perhaps even negative taxation, would not be more effective instruments in getting money into the hands of individuals and in stimulating an upward cumulative movement. In other words it may be preferable to work on disposable income directly rather than try to influence it indirectly.

Two over-all objections have often been raised to the use of government outlays as a method of getting out of depression. In the first place, a large program of government outlays initiated when private investment is virtually nonexistent may succeed in getting the economy back to the level of full employment, but there is no assurance that private industry will then voluntarily make sufficient investment expenditures to keep the economy at this level. It is possible that in order to maintain a high level of activity in such a situation, the government would have to keep up its outlays indefinitely; otherwise, the moment it contracted its outlays, the economy would start a cumulative adjustment downward. Whether or not such a situation would exist is largely dependent upon the reason why private investment expenditures were initially so low. If the original cause persisted, or if the increased level of government outlays should significantly impair the willingness of producers to make private investment expenditures, lasting full employment could not be achieved by a temporary increase in government outlays. Instead, if expenditure policy is to be used to maintain full employment, permanent action might be necessary. Transfer payments, for instance, would become a permanent source of income for large groups in the economy; these groups would be receiving income even though they were making no contribution to national output of goods and services. If, alternatively, public works expenditures were expanded, more and more of the nation's economic capacity might be absorbed by the government, and its production might not yield an allocation of resources that would be as efficient as that of private industry producing for consumer markets.

A second general objection to continued government deficit spending centers around the problem of financing this expenditure. Deficit spending in modern economic systems is financed by selling government bonds to individuals and banks. With appropriate central bank controls, such credit creation can continue indefinitely so that the government will never be at a loss for funds, but this process raises other problems. The larger the national debt, the larger will be the interest charges on this debt, and certain groups of individuals and financial institutions in the economy will be the recipients of increasing amounts of income that is not an essential part of the productive processes of the economy.[1] This process raises serious problems of equity.

Increased government expenditures, therefore, may be successful in counteracting a depression, but their use raises a number of problems.

---

[1] In the calculation of gross national product, interest on the national debt is not considered to be payment for a productive service. For further discussion of this subject see Chap. 4.

The future implications of any government policy that is undertaken must be considered as well as its immediate effects. This does not mean, however, that government expenditure necessarily should be avoided—if the alternative is the disaster that may accompany a serious depression.

Foreign Trade Policy. In the history of economic depressions foreign trade policies have frequently been used as an aid in restoring prosperity. Tariff barriers, licensing of imports, subsidization of exports, and devaluation of the currency have all been used in the attempt to provide a setting more favorable to a cumulative movement upward.

Tariff barriers and import licensing have been used to exclude foreign goods from the domestic market. By this procedure it is hoped at least temporarily to divert to domestic goods expenditures that would have been made on foreign goods. Tariffs may have the effect of making foreign goods more expensive than domestic goods, so that purchasers will prefer to buy domestic products. Import licensing is usually intended to limit the type and amount of foreign purchases; it can also be designed to prevent the purchase of specific foreign goods that compete with domestically produced goods.

Foreign trade policy can also encourage a cumulative movement upward by focusing upon increasing the amount of exports instead of upon limiting imports. Payment of subsidies may make producers more willing to produce goods for sale abroad. The subsidy plus what can be obtained from the sale of the goods abroad may be enough to encourage the production of goods that without the subsidy would not have been profitable, and the resulting hiring of labor and purchase of raw materials will stimulate the domestic economy.

Finally, devaluation of the currency may be used both to stimulate exports and to limit imports. When the exchange rate is lowered, domestic goods will become cheaper for foreign purchasers and exports will be stimulated. At the same time, foreign goods will become more expensive for domestic purchasers, and imports will tend to be restricted. Devaluation thus will produce a foreign trade balance that is more favorable to a cumulative movement upward.

These foreign trade policies, however, cannot be considered only in terms of their repercussions upon the domestic economy. A foreign trade policy intended to stimulate exports and limit imports will have immediate effects upon the countries with which trade is carried on. A limitation of imports from foreign countries may prevent these foreign countries from purchasing exports unless adequate supplies of foreign exchange are made available through loans. And even if such funds are made available, the limitation of imports may still have an effect upon the stream of exports. The change in the import-export balance may not be in accord with the economic policies of the other countries concerned, and they may attempt to prevent the change or even gain an advantage by applying the same policies in reverse. It is impossible for all countries to have a net export balance at the same time, and widespread attempts to obtain such a balance will result only in the application of competitive foreign trade policies, which will usually restrict international trade. When one country limits its imports, exports of other countries will decline, and in order to regain their desired net export balance, these countries may in turn limit their imports. This will have repercussions on the exports of the first country, so that its net trade balance may be no better than it was in the beginning, but the volume of international trade will be lower. Competitive export subsidies cannot be any more successful in creating a more favorable trade balance for all the countries concerned, and they may lead to the absurd situation in which a country is paying more for imported goods than the prices at which similar domestically produced goods are exported to foreign countries. Devaluation of currency similarly can become competitive and may finally lead to a complete demoralization of international trade.

Because of the likelihood of such competitive reactions, these trade policies may well not be successful in stimulating recovery from depression, but situations do exist in which they will be helpful. If two countries found themselves in very different economic positions, their trade policies could be made to complement each other. For instance, a depression in one country and an inflation in another country would permit the institution of a common policy that would benefit both countries. By increasing net exports the first country might encourage a cumulative movement upward, and by increasing net imports the second country might provide more goods for its expanding volume of expenditures. Unfortunately, the happy coincidence of complementary economic situations in different countries is not a common occurrence. Because of the mutual interdependence of economies, periods of depression and prosperity are usually world-wide. The programs of economic planning that are being instituted in some countries may alter the situation in the future, however; such countries may welcome a policy of cheap exports on the part of the United States, since it would mean more economic goods for them.

Price and Wage Policy. Depression always arouses a great deal of concern over the behavior of prices. On the one hand it is argued that stability cannot be reached until the downward movement of prices is stopped and that even a concerted movement to raise prices would be beneficial. This was the philosophy of the National Industrial Recovery Act during the depression of the thirties. It was argued that raising prices would increase the profit margin, so that producers would be stimulated to increase production and hire additional labor. Opponents of this view, on the other hand, argued that the increase in prices would limit the amount consumers could purchase and that this would restrict production and cause more unemployment, so that the movement downward would be intensified. The encouragement of price cutting will not necessarily meet this latter argument, however, since this also may discourage production. The increased purchasing power of consumers' incomes due to the fall in prices may be more than offset by the fall in the absolute amount of their incomes caused by the fall in prices and output. Sufficient empirical evidence is not available to indicate which of these two arguments is most likely to be valid in any particular circumstance.

Diametrically opposed wage policies have also been recommended as a stimulus to the economy. The classical economists maintained that lowering the wage rate would create fuller employment because producers would be willing to hire more labor at a lower wage rate. When the effect of such behavior upon income is considered, however, this argument does not necessarily follow. A lower wage rate may not lead producers to hire a significantly larger number of workers, so that the new wage bill—the total amount of wages paid—may be smaller than the old. A decline in consumers' expenditures would then follow, and the cumulative movement downward would be intensified. For this reason increases in the wage rate have often been advocated, but again it may happen that the unemployment resulting from such an increase in the wage rate would make the total wage bill decline. Without actual empirical knowledge of the manner in which the economy can be expected to react to a change in the wage rate, it is not possible to make any valid predictions.

The Control of Inflation

The problem of controlling an inflation will obviously require measures that are opposite in nature from those proposed for recovery from depression. Some of these measures follow so obviously from the discussion of depression policies that they need only be mentioned. A cut in government outlays might help to ease the inflationary situation, either by lessening the quantity of goods and services removed from the market by the government or by reducing the transfer payments made by the government to individuals. Foreign trade policies can be employed to stimulate imports and discourage exports, but problems of repercussions upon the other countries will continue to be important. Certain other economic policies designed to control an inflation bring up more complicated problems and need to be studied in greater detail.

Credit Control Policies. The traditional weapon against inflation has been the control of credit. It is argued that much of the inflationary pressure which is felt is the result of too much credit creation. In boom periods producers borrow to carry their larger inventories and to purchase durable goods. Consumers also buy goods on credit, either on the installment plan or by direct borrowing. Restriction of credit is aimed at reducing the expenditures of these groups and so lessening the pressure on the available supply of goods and services. It has frequently been proposed that credit be restricted by raising the interest rate. Borrowing will then be more expensive, and it is argued that people will not want to borrow so much. However, it is doubtful whether in an inflationary period raising the interest rate will discourage many borrowers. Even if the interest rate could be raised high enough to drive some borrowers from the market, it would not necessarily have the desired effect. As long as there is a chance for a speculative profit from rising prices, a high interest rate will not deter speculators, nor is it likely to influence purchasers of consumers' goods. The only limitation of borrowing is likely to be on the part of producers, who will curtail their expansion of capacity. In other words, raising the interest rate may drive useful borrowing from the market, leaving the amount of speculative borrowing and consumer credit unchanged.

Since the interest rate alone is unselective in its credit restriction, the development of a method of credit control that would give attention to the purpose of the borrowing has often been advocated. To a limited extent such a program can be successful. Regulations can be made to tighten up the amount of speculative loans and consumer credit given by banks, but banks are only a part of the credit system of the nation; and if there is a large demand for speculative and consumer credit, the parts of the credit system outside of government control may supply the demand so that the attempts at restriction will result only in a shift in the credit structure. This is especially true if the economy is in a fairly liquid state; there will then be so many leakages of credit that adequate selective control would be very difficult.

Taxation Policy. Some types of taxation are far more effective in combatting inflation than are others, but in using taxation for this purpose, certain other considerations must be kept in mind. Increasing the income tax may be the most equitable form of taxation, but in an inflationary period increases of sufficient magnitude to cause a significant restriction in consumers' expenditures may very well cease to be equitable. Inflation always works hardships upon people whose incomes are fixed, and substantial increases in income taxes will make them even worse off. This argument is, of course, even more true of sales and excise taxes; these taxes would be very effective in restricting the amount of consumers' expenditures in the economy, but they may accomplish their task at the cost of considerable inequity.

Price Control and Rationing. Because of the obvious inadequacy of other measures in controlling inflation in periods when continuing inflationary pressures are unavoidable, it is sometimes necessary to resort to price control and rationing. In wartime, for instance, such measures are necessary in order to prevent a disastrous rise in prices. Continuing government war expenditures create additional income in the economy, yet at the same time leave a smaller amount of goods available for consumers to purchase. Possible increases in taxation and in voluntary savings may well not be sufficient to absorb the excess purchasing power of consumers, so that both price control and rationing are necessary.

It is sometimes proposed that these controls be applied only to necessities, but such a procedure would only intensify the inflationary pressures on the rest of the economy. For this reason, if controls are instituted at all, it is usually preferable that they cover most of the consumers' goods on the market. Such a general program of control is expensive and may not be equitable in all instances, but it is probably less expensive and more equitable than the absence of such a program would be. A wild price inflation might well become explosive and cause a complete breakdown of the economic system at a time when the country is in very great need of its efficient operation.

Emergencies requiring the use of as drastic measures as price control and rationing of consumers' goods will usually also necessitate controls on production in the economy in order to ensure that resources will be devoted to the ends, i.e., war production, that are necessary for the survival of the nation. Scarce raw materials will have to be controlled not only with respect to price but also with respect to allocation, since many industries will wish to use these materials; raw materials will be allocated to those industries which are considered to be most essential for the public welfare. Various other controls may also be necessary. For instance, in order to get the maximum amount of production without allowing prices to rise, the marginal amount of production may have to be subsidized. Continual adjustments will have to be made, furthermore, as new production programs are put into effect that disturb the existing allocation patterns of labor and materials.

In an economy in which all other goods and services are price controlled and rationed, the control of wages and the allocation of labor raise difficult problems. If wage rates are not controlled but are permitted to rise, the price-cost structure will be distorted and increases of prices will have to be granted to producers throughout the economy. This, of course, is in effect permitting the inflation to take place and should be prevented. On the other hand, however, it may be necessary to offer higher wages in order to induce labor to enter the fields in which it is most needed. Furthermore, freezing wage rates in any one fixed pattern can be extremely inequitable. With wage rates, material costs, and prices all frozen, increases in productivity would go entirely into increases in profits, and labor would not share at all in the benefits of such increased productivity.

Price control and rationing, if they are to be efficient, thus entail such complete government control of the economy that they should be considered as an anti-inflationary measure only in times of extreme emergency. Much of the natural flexibility of the economy is destroyed by rigid controls, and their continuance over a long period of years might considerably weaken the economy. Furthermore, removing such controls after the emergency is over is not easy. If they are removed too soon, a sharp price rise may occur when consumers start to spend the savings that they will have accumulated during the period of control. But if the controls are left on too long, the initiative to increase production may be weakened and the attainment of maximum levels of output may be postponed indefinitely.

Maintenance of Stability

The problems of recovery from depression and control of inflation could all be avoided if the economy could achieve general stability. It has already been pointed out that there are some considerations which make the maintenance of such stability undesirable; fluctuations may be the result of dynamic forces that bring progress in their wake. Nevertheless, these same dynamic forces may equally well bring disaster and destruction if the depressions and inflations that they generate get out of hand. Furthermore, progress obtained in this manner involves a considerable cost, since it requires that on the average the economy operate at far less than its potential capacity and that many inequities be endured.

On the other hand, however, the objective of stability does not by any means imply rigidity. Without satisfactory provision for continual adjustments among the various sectors of the economy, structural disorders will result and the whole economy will break down. For example, if a factory were required to continue to produce a given output with given costs and prices, the situation could not be adapted to the inevitable changes in consumers' tastes. Consumers might stop buying the product, and production would then simply pile up. Stability must be a long-run as well as a short-run reality, and flexibility is essential. In order to achieve such flexibility, some fluctuation upward and downward in the economy may be necessary, but this fluctuation should ordinarily be so small that it is not generally noticeable without consulting the statistical series.

The difference between desirable flexibility and undesirable sensitivity of the economic system is only a matter of degree. In an overly flexible economy any minor change may be magnified into a major reaction through the process of cumulative adjustment. A slower process of adjustment might be more advantageous from a number of points of view. Slow change might have much less effect upon the expectations of producers and consumers than would rapid and frequent change, so that cumulative adjustments would be smaller. Furthermore, if the adjustment to change were spread out over a longer period, its importance at any one time would be less, and there would be more likelihood that offsetting adjustments would balance each other.

Satisfactory stability necessitates full employment, but full employment alone is not sufficient; it must be coupled with the optimum use of resources. Although it is impossible to identify any one best or ideal pattern of resource allocation, it can frequently be demonstrated that an existing method of resource allocation is not ideal. A number of proposals for arriving at full employment have been discussed above, many of which entail a program of artificial spending aimed at full employment rather than the use of resources in accordance with consumer preferences. When a program designed for the attainment of full employment causes an obviously large divergence from anything that might possibly be considered an ideal resource allocation pattern —and this may frequently happen—it may safely be said that the cost of the program is large. Of course the cost may still not be so large as that of the failure to carry through any program at all; but as long as such a situation exists, an ideal solution to the problem of maintaining full employment has not been found.

The Use of Discretionary Compensatory Policies for Stability. A cumulative adjustment, if caught at a very early stage, would need very little offsetting to prevent it from becoming worse. For this reason compensatory policies have often been advocated. Measures that might not be effective in the face of a strong cumulative movement which was well established might, if started quickly enough, provide sufficient compensation to offset the beginning of such a movement. Credit controls and interest rates could be varied whenever a tendency toward a cumulative movement upward or downward appears. Similarly, policies involving the alteration of the amount of government expenditures or taxes could be used to offset other pressures in the economy, so that no cumulative movement would result.

The application of compensatory measures raises a number of problems. In the first place it requires the ability to forecast the future with considerable accuracy. Minor fluctuations that represent only the necessary flexibility in the economy must not be interpreted as the beginning of a major cumulative adjustment, or the compensatory policies that are put into effect will actually be responsible for starting or reinforcing a cumulative movement in the opposite direction. So many exogenous factors are involved that it is doubtful if such accurate forecasting is possible. This general problem will be discussed in the last section of this chapter. A second difficulty lies in the lack of empirical knowledge about how much and in what way the economy will react to specific compensatory policies. For this reason the relative strength of alternative measures cannot be estimated, and over- or undercompensation is likely. Trial-and-error methods, furthermore, are not likely to add very much to the store of knowledge on this score, since conditions are never exactly the same, and the economy may react quite differently to the same stimulus at different times. Finally, even if appropriate measures and appropriate timing could be determined, it would be extremely difficult to carry out these measures accurately. Many of them require action on the part of the government. Such expedients as changes in tax rates or in government expenditures may require legislative action; even if such action is not needed, they will require some time to formulate and put into effect. By the time a compensatory policy actually becomes operative, the crisis it is intended to offset may have developed into a full-fledged depression or inflation. These difficulties are, of course, all intensified if the economy is highly sensitive to change. Keeping the economy stable in the face of a knife-edge equilibrium would require constant shifts in compensatory policies, and sooner or later, either through misapplication or through errors in forecasts, a major cumulative movement would probably result.

Reliance on discretionary action for compensatory policies also has the political disadvantage that it is subject both to the faults of inaction because the individuals in office wish to escape responsibilities and to the reverse of this, that the additional power created will be usurped and used for other more political purposes. In many instances those in power will hesitate to take positive action because even if this action is successful in avoiding a depression, it is difficult to demonstrate that a depression would otherwise have occurred, and if the action taken has any bad effects, they will be pointed out by the political opposition. Furthermore, any direct mistakes in judgment, such as increasing tax rates in the expectation of inflationary pressures when some degree of unemployment actually results instead, will immediately be pounced upon and used as an indication of ineptitude and inefficiency, whereas it is obvious from the nature of short-term forecasts that accurate prediction of the future course of events is usually not possible. Discretionary action thus carries with it too much responsibility to make it a sharp incisive tool for the maintenance of stability. On the other hand, also, the fact that broad taxation and expenditure policies would be concentrated in the hands of a few individuals would make it possible that decisions regarding these policies might be made on grounds other than those of the maintenance of stability.

Automatic Stabilizers. Because of the difficulties inherent in the use of discretionary compensatory policies, measures that automatically provide a stabilizing influence on a nondiscretionary basis may be preferable. Unemployment insurance is an example of such a measure. During a period of decreasing employment, payments to the unemployed would prevent disposable income from falling as much as it otherwise would, and during a period of inflation, unemployment insurance contributions would siphon off a part of the increasing disposable income, helping to bring it into line with the quantity of goods available for purchase. Progressive income taxation has also frequently been considered to have an automatic stabilizing effect. As personal income declines, income tax revenues fall off sharply, so that disposable income does not fall so fast as personal income. In an inflationary period when incomes are rising, income tax revenues will rise sharply, so that disposable income will not rise so fast as personal income. Existing automatic stabilizers are not sufficiently powerful to prevent any significant fluctuation in the economy, but it is probably very true that these measures reduce the extent of fluctuations.

Automatic stabilizers could also be made much more powerful by the introduction of what has been termed "formula flexibility." The idea behind this concept is that with changes in the level of employment, output, or prices, different kinds of tax rates or government outlay policies would go into effect. For example, it would be possible with a given percentage decline of employment to have an automatic reduction in the amount of income that would be withheld for personal income taxes, and an automatic increase in tax refunds and transfer payments to individuals who have had a drop in income or employment. Similarly, in a period of rapidly rising prices, automatic tax increases could be provided for in terms of both personal income taxes and sales and excise taxes. Such formula flexibility and other kinds of automatic stabilizers, in terms of the mechanism of income analysis discussed above, will make the disposable income function steeper, or perhaps if such measures are made very strong, will create a saddle point in the function, such that movement in either direction would be more difficult.

In designing automatic stabilizers employing formula flexibility, every care should be exercised to preserve the growth potential of the economy and to preserve equity. With respect to upward movements, it seems probable that formula flexibility should operate on the basis of certain kinds of price changes rather than on the basis of rises in income, employment, or output.

Measures to Prevent Depression. The fear of depression, with its accompanying unemployment and waste of resources, has led many economists to give serious consideration to various general measures that would alter the institutional organization of the economy in such a way as to make depression less likely. For instance, it is often argued that rigid prices should be eliminated insofar as possible, since unemployment results only when prices are maintained at the expense of cuts in output. It is argued that the economy would not suffer depressions if only prices and wages could be made to fluctuate freely, with no restriction of output. The difficulty with this argument lies in the fact that such a procedure would not make the economy any more stable; it would simply translate all reactions into price changes. The economy would become oversensitive to any price change, and it is highly probable that any price spiral which got started would so affect the expectations of producers and consumers that an explosive situation would result. The causes of so-called price inflexibility, as has been demonstrated in the preceding chapters, lie deep in the processes of production, and an attempt to impose greater flexibility in all prices might only increase the maladjustment instead of promoting stability.

In more or less the opposite vein, guaranteed annual wages have also been suggested as tending to stop the cumulative movements that lead to depression. By putting the hiring of labor on the basis of yearly commitments, much of the incentive to cut production would be lost, since such cutbacks would not reduce costs so much as they do under the institutional arrangements which now exist. At the same time steady wage payments during the year would tend to prevent the falling off of consumers' expenditures, so that the occurrence of a cumulative decline would be less likely. Whether general adoption of guaranteed annual wages in all industries is feasible or not is another question. Many firms might be forced into bankruptcy when they are faced with situations in which they would normally have cut output and employment. In this contingency an over-all guaranteed annual wage system would break down unless the government stepped in to help, and with the entry of the goverment as a subsidizing agent, the problems of equity and efficiency are immediately raised. Unless the general guaranteed annual wage were able to forestall a depression completely, therefore, there is considerable danger that it would break down when most needed. A rigid plan of guaranteed annual wages in all industries, furthermore, might reduce the flexibility of the economy and thus prevent adaptation to the exogenous changes that inevitably would take place. It does seem probable, however, that the modified guaranteed annual wage plans that have recently been adopted in specific industries will tend to lessen the possibility of cumulative declines and to decrease their magnitude.

Depressions have often been attributed to institutional factors leading either to an actual contraction in investment expenditures or else to an insufficiency of such expenditures to offset the desired level of saving at a full employment level of income. As a cure for this situation a variety of measures have been proposed to encourage investment expenditures. Both a reduction in the corporate profits tax and a vigorous antitrust policy have been suggested for this purpose.

The proposition that investment will be encouraged by the reduction of the corporate profits tax is based on the argument that lower taxes would induce businessmen to make more risky investments, since the hope of gain would be greater. This argument needs further examination. If the same amount of tax revenue is to be raised after the corporate tax reduction, other taxes will have to be increased. Increasing income taxes on the upper income groups may cancel the effect of the corporate tax reduction, since it would reduce the return after taxes on investment. On the other hand, increasing income taxes on the lower income groups or raising sales and excise taxes will reduce the amount of goods that can be bought from business, and many firms will be forced to cut their output, so that a cumulative decline will set in. If other taxes are not increased when corporate taxes are reduced, so that the total tax revenue drops, the government will be deficit spending, and it is by no means certain that this form of deficit spending will be relatively more useful in maintaining full employment than any other form. A reduction in sales or excise taxes might well provide more stimulation to business. Furthermore, a reduction in the corporate profits tax may produce other reactions among producers besides the stimulation of risky investment, which may offset its stimulating effect. With a high corporate profits tax producers are apt to maintain their plants in better condition, spend more on advertising, and in general be more lax about reduction of costs, because the government is, in effect, paying a part of these costs; if costs were reduced, the government would take a portion of the resulting profits in taxes. Therefore it is entirely possible that a reduction in the corporate tax would reduce current expenditures of business more than it would increase investment expenditures.

The pursuit of a vigorous antitrust policy may not be any more successful in producing an increase in investment. For the most part, antitrust policy is aimed at breaking up large corporations in favor of small business. But there is no reason to believe that even if antitrust action should lead to an economy composed of relatively small competitive organizations, the magnitude of investment expenditures would be larger. Competition may lead to uncertainties such that producers will be unwilling to make investments that new competitors will soon make obsolete. Furthermore, many investments in new ventures require an amount of backing that small organizations do not have. Large corporations can undertake a sufficient number of risky new ventures so that they can balance their losses against those which turn out more successfully; small enterprises cannot. Finally, the breakup of large enterprises would undoubtedly curtail basic research, now written off as a current cost. All these considerations must be balanced against the stimulating effects of introducing competition, and it is by no means assured that a net increase in investment expenditures would result.

Certain other institutional changes that have been proposed, among them modification of the tax law to permit accelerated depreciation and the averaging of profits over several years, might be more successful than outright tax reduction or antitrust policy in encouraging investment. Accelerated depreciation would allow investments to be charged off for tax purposes in a shorter period than their probable life. The immediate returns from the investment could then be used to repay its cost, and the uncertainty of the undertaking would be lessened. The extension of loss carry-overs in the tax law would permit a producer to pay taxes on approximately his average profit, with losses offsetting the profits of other years. By balancing profits and losses the small producer may be encouraged to undertake more risky investments, since, if the investment turns into a loss, it will be partially offset by a reduction in taxes.

Finally, institutional changes have been proposed that are aimed at increasing the level of consumption expenditures in the economy. Some such increase might be achieved by a redistribution of income. There are limits to the extent to which such a redistribution can be carried, however, if sufficient incentive is to be retained to assure a maximum of effort and an adequate level of investment expenditures. Alternatively, social expenditures such as old-age pensions, unemployment insurance, socialized medicine, and educational benefits might lessen the desire of individuals to save, but on the other hand these benefits would constitute an increase in real income and so would increase the ability of individuals to save to some extent.

This discussion has been focused on the maintenance or encouragement of expenditures, either on consumption or investment, through possible institutional changes in the economy. The specific measures mentioned are obviously only a small fraction of the conceivable changes that might be made; the purpose of the discussion has been simply to suggest that this field of action exists. Should such policies be fruitful, there may be no necessity for other types of stabilization, and the danger of complicating elements in specifically designed compensatory measures may be avoided. For this reason any changes that are made in government policies or in laws and regulations should be considered from the point of view of their effect on investment and consumption expenditures as well as in terms of any other effects they may have.

The Need for Conscious Policy

Economic policy will always exist in an economy, whether it is conscious or not, and unconscious policies may have repercussions that, were they made explicit, would be considered undesirable. This fact is well illustrated by the sequence of events that followed 1929. During the late twenties the government had been endeavoring to maintain a budgetary surplus, which it used to reduce the national debt incurred during World War I. This policy was based upon the principle of sound financial operation: that the government should pay off the debt which it had incurred, to maintain the confidence of business and the people. Whatever other effects this policy may have had were unintentional and unrecognized. These unintentional effects may have been salutary in the period in which the policy was initiated, but the attempt to adhere to this procedure in the depression brought with it an unconscious economic policy that probably had a significant depressing effect. With the depression government revenue declined. Personal incomes were sharply reduced so that taxes on them were much smaller. Corporate profits declined or turned into losses, so that revenue from this source declined too. But the expenditures of the government did not shrink correspondingly. The needs of the nation were even greater in the depression than they had been in the preceding period. Nevertheless, the government, in the attempt to retain the confidence of the country, embarked on a program designed to retain a balanced budget. A specific decision had to be made, and it was decided that deficit expenditure should be avoided if possible. The Revenue Act of 1932, accordingly, increased tax rates for both individuals and corporations in the attempt to obtain more revenue, and at the same time government expenditures were cut back as much as possible. Needless to say, the reduction in the disposable income of individuals through increased taxes and reduced government expenditures probably had a greater direct effect in restricting consumers' and producers' expenditures in the economy than the balanced budget had in stimulating investment by establishing business confidence. At this time investment expenditures were almost nonexistent; businessmen who were suffering heavy losses were not in the mood to make any investment outlays, no matter how much they believed in the government. Changed conditions had automatically created a situation in which a continuation of a policy designed for another purpose had adverse repercussions that were far more important than its intended effects. The fact that the repercussions of the government's policies upon income were not taken into account did not make these repercussions any less real. Following one inflexible line of policy irrespective of changing conditions can thus be very dangerous.

For the best interests of the economy, any action that is undertaken should be considered from all points of view. A conscious realization of the meaning of all the facets of each measure that is proposed is necessary, so that the policy followed will assure on balance the most benefit for the economy. There is no such thing as a passive economic policy; true *laissez faire* is a Darwinian survival-of-the-fittest system, which in this day and age would be considered anarchy. Most advocates of *laissez faire*, on the contrary, have in mind an economy in which the government has a very definite role in maintaining a specific institutional framework. Furthermore, they have very definite (and by no means uniform) ideas about economic policies involving taxes, government expenditures, and government regulations. In any specific situation opinions will differ as to what is and is not a passive economic policy; it is probably true that raising tax rates in 1932 was no more *laissez faire* than allowing revenues to drop would have been. The effects of economic policy decisions cannot be avoided by refusing to consider them or by saying that they do not exist. For this reason these decisions should be made conscious and explicit, so that the best choice among the possible alternatives can be made.

Forecasting the Level of Activity and Economic Budgeting

Economic policy cannot be made in a vacuum; it requires forecasts of the future and analysis of the effects which certain policies may have upon the course of future events. In some cases the forecasts of the future will be of an immediate short-term nature, and in other instances they will be of the nature of long-range economic projections. Both these types of forecast and their relation to economic budgeting will be described in this section.

The Nature of Forecasting and Projections

It is often said that the ultimate aim of economic analysis should be to provide predictions. Although in a scientific sense it is true that the function of knowledge is prediction, it is very easy to misconstrue the meaning of this term. Inasmuch as many noneconomic factors are important in determining the course of future economic events, the problem of predicting becomes a problem involving many disciplines. For example, the impact of sociological, psychological, and even religious influences may have a significant effect upon population growth, and this in turn will affect the future course of economic events. Similarly, the political temper of a country will depend upon the emergence of various cultural patterns, not only within the domestic economy but in other countries as well. The present magnitude of defense expenditure in the world indicates the extent to which the attitudes and reactions of leaders in other countries are important in determining the nature of our domestic economy. Even over and above the contribution of these other fields, prediction in an ultimate unconditional form may never be possible. Contrary to popular belief, however, this does not indicate a failure of these disciplines to achieve the status of sciences. Science is incapable of predicting what it will discover in the future, for to do so would mean that it knows now what it does not now know. The test of whether economics is scientific depends rather upon whether it can make useful and significant *conditional* forecasts and predictions, that is, whether it is possible, given various basic assumptions, to predict what the resulting interactions will be.

Nevertheless, the interest of the scientist and the layman alike will still lie in the direction of the unconditional forecast, much as fortune-telling has held the interest of mankind throughout the ages. In many instances, furthermore, conditional forecasts may turn out to be fairly accurate predictions of the future if the assumptions upon which they are based turn out to be realistic. But it should always be remembered that the forecaster is choosing a single event out of the range of possible events as being the most likely, much in the same way as a favorite in horse racing carries the smallest odds—but does not always win.

Short-term Forecasts

Short-term forecasting has already been mentioned elsewhere in this chapter in connection with the discussion of discretionary economic policies. If it is necessary for the government to anticipate the immediate course of future economic events, either implicit or explicit forecasts will be made. Thus if a softness appears in the economy and the self-correcting mechanisms which exist are not believed to be sufficient to check a further decline if it should come, a decision must be made whether the softness will develop into a further decline or whether it is merely a temporary readjustment of the economy that will quickly be followed by renewed prosperity. Businessmen also are always interested in the future course of the economy, since this will affect their future decisions to invest, to buy goods for inventories, or to change the level of their productive activity.

Economic Barometers. One of the most popular forms of short-term forecasting has been the use of diagnostic series which appear to be sensitive to economic fluctuations and to lead in time other evidence of economic change. Many firms engaged in the analysis of stock-market price changes use this technique to forecast what will happen in the stock market. Also, economic studies have been made on literally hundreds of kinds of economic series to find those that appear to be good indicators. One of the major difficulties with this procedure is that in many instances the key series move inconsistently with one another, and the variance in their movement is such that the depth and duration of the fluctuation which they forecast cannot be predicted. Another type of barometer, often used in conjunction with the sensitive series, consists of asking businessmen, and in some cases even economists, what they think the future course of events will be. Insofar as the businessmen and economists base their judgments on the sensitive series, this results in approximately the same answer, but misinformation, bias, optimism, and pessimism will often be more influential than will the actual factors that determine cumulative movements.

The Examination of Expenditures. Since the development of national income accounting and income analysis, considerably greater emphasis has been placed upon the examination of what the future level of various types of expenditure will be. A sample survey on consumer finances is at present carried out periodically by the Federal Reserve Board, and it is to be hoped that through the analysis of this data greater knowledge about the determinants of consumers' behavior may be obtained, with the result that fairly reliable forecasts of consumers' expenditures can be made. In this connection such things as the effect of liquid asset holdings, past purchases of durable goods, and changes in family composition all are analyzed to determine their effects upon future spending and saving.

With respect to investment expenditures, similarly, surveys of the plans of businessmen are made on a quarterly basis. Questionnaires are sent out by the Department of Commerce to the large companies who do the bulk of the investment expenditures in the economy. The compilation of this information throws considerable light upon the planned investment expenditures in the economy, and although these plans are subject to change, they do provide valuable insight into the prospective magnitude of investment expenditures.

Federal government expenditures are generally somewhat easier to forecast for an immediate future period, due to the extensive legislative and executive actions required to achieve actual expenditure of funds. State and local expenditures, although less easy to predict, tend to change slowly.

The prediction of foreign trade is usually quite difficult, since it involves predicting economic conditions in foreign countries, together with such things as the magnitudes of agricultural crops and the price elasticity of various kinds of goods in both domestic and foreign markets.

The Problems of Short-term Forecasting. To date, the success of short-term forecasting has not been very great. However, experience with the expenditures method has not been extensive, and it is possible that the quality of short-term forecasts by this method can be improved. A considerable amount needs to be learned, however, with respect to the determinants of consumer behavior, since the interrelation among the determinants and the building up of aggregate consumption behavior from individual consumer behavior are extremely complex. Investment decisions, furthermore, appear to be quite sensitive both to exogenous factors such as increased defense expenditures and to businessmen's expectations of the future course of economic events.

Short-term forecasting is essentially an examination of the demand side of productive activity. For all practical purposes it is assumed that the supply side, i.e., capacity, labor force, etc., change relatively slowly, and are therefore for the purpose of short-term analysis to be taken as given.

Long-range Economic Projections

In contrast with short-term forecasting, long-range economic projection concerns itself with the level of activity in the economy as affected by the growth of the economy itself. In terms of time period, projections of this nature are not usually undertaken for ranges of time shorter than five years. In many cases the period under consideration may be as long as twenty-five years.

Long-range economic projections are extremely useful to both businessmen and government for describing the general size and shape of the economy in future periods. The building of steel mills, hydroelectric plants, transportation facilities, highways, residential construction, and even schools depends in large part upon anticipation of the economy's needs at some future date.

Long-term forecasting cannot be done on the same bases as short-term forecasting, since the forces that will influence demand ten to twenty years hence cannot be predicted. Instead, therefore, long-term projection relies on examination of the elements affecting the supply of goods in the economy. Generally, the elements considered are (1) the total number of man-hours which will be used for productive activity at some future date, and (2) the productivity per man-hour at the same date. Obviously, when multiplied together, these two elements will yield total production.

Projections of Man-hours. The number of man-hours that will be utilized in productive activity depends upon the labor force available in the economy and the hours spent by this labor force on productive activity. The labor force projection in turn depends upon a projection of population, including the future birth rate, death rate, and net immigration.

The projection of population growth in itself is a formidable task. There are many factors that bear upon family size, and our understanding of them at present is by no means complete. Historically, the aggregate birth rate for the nation has been falling sharply. The high fertility groups, such as farmers, foreign-born, and the less educated, have been declining in numbers, and the contraction of the importance of these groups in the nation would cause a decline in the aggregate birth rate even if the birth rate of no one socioeconomic group were to change. On the other hand, it seems very probable that birth rates of various groups have also changed; but whether these changes have been in response to the short-term effects of depression, wars, and inflations, or to long-term trends is difficult to tell. Past projections of the aggregate population change have not been very successful. Projections of the depressed birth rates of the depression of the thirties grossly understated the amount of population increase that actually did occur in the next two decades. On the other hand, it may well be that the projection of postwar population trends may overstate population growth for the future. A great deal of further research is needed to unearth the determinants of family size, and to analyze the effect which a rise in the standard of living will have on population growth.

Once the population growth has been estimated, it is necessary to estimate what the labor force will be out of such a population. The age composition of the population will be very important in this estimate, and it will be necessary to know what percentage of the women will be in the labor force on a full-time basis and on a part-time basis, and also what effect the gradual increase in length of life is going to have on retirement age. Finally, the actual number of hours that will be spent by full-time and part-time workers must be estimated. Generally speaking, these estimates are made by extrapolating past patterns of change at a constant rate, or at a rate altered to take into account such factors as the expected shifts in the composition of workers, e.g., from farm to nonfarm.

Productivity Projections. In projecting productivity, the most usual procedure is to project the past trend derived from the series of gross national product in constant prices divided by the relevant man-hours figures in each year. Some of the years may be dropped out, because they represent either depression periods or war periods, or they may all be included on the ground that similar variances can be expected to occur in the future. The range in the average rates of productivity change so derived is quite high, ranging from less than 2 per cent per year to over 3½ per cent per year, a range of almost 100 per cent.

As an alternative method of projecting productivity change, it would be possible to break down the productivity change itself into two different kinds of changes. One of these may be termed the change in technical efficiency taking place within an industry. For example, it would be possible to compute how much output per man-hour rose in the automobile industry from one period to another. If this were done for every industry in the economy, a set of output per man-hour figures would be derived. The second kind of change results from the shift in productive activity from less productive industries to more productive industries. This kind of change would have the effect of increasing output per man-hour over and above the effect resulting from the increases in each of the industries individually. A long-run projection of productivity thus could be built up by extrapolating the detailed output per man-hour figures in the various industries in terms of the types of technological developments that could be expected in those industries, and then combining these individual rates into an estimate for the economy as a whole by extrapolating the shifts in composition of output that are likely to take place.

Neither of these methods takes into account explicitly the probable effect of cyclical fluctuations in economic activity on productivity, or the effect of different levels of investment expenditure that may be made in future periods. It is assumed implicitly that the investment expenditure that occurs will be such as to generate about the same sort of productivity change as has occurred in past periods.

Problems of Long-term Forecasting. The major problem of long-term forecasting is that a very small error in terms of absolute magnitude in the rates of increase in productivity or labor force will result in a large error in the estimation of growth. The success of a long-term projection should be judged on the basis of the error in the percentage change that it predicts. Also, the examination of comparisons over time in Chap. 7 has already indicated the very real problems of measurement over long periods of time, especially in areas where technological changes and quality changes are apt to take place. A single figure may therefore be very misleading as a description of future change when other aspects of the change are not and cannot be taken into account. Again, as in the case of short-term forecasts, the exogenous influences such as wars and depressions or major inflations will have a significant impact upon long-term developments, and cannot of course be predicted by the economist.

Economic Budgeting

Economic budgeting utilizes the basic tools of both short-term forecasting and long-range projection. It represents an attempt to marry the two kinds of analysis and test their consistency for periods involving a medium length of time, e.g., one to ten years. The processes involved are not unlike those already described in Chap. 16, where the relation between economic growth and the level of economic activity were described in diagrammatic form. The process is essentially one of seeing whether the anticipated supply of goods that would be available in the economy at some future period exceeds or falls short of the demand at levels of income compatible with such a supply.

The purpose of such analysis is to see whether under the impact of future growth the economy will attain full employment without inflationary pressures. It can also be used to examine the probable effect of a given economic policy on the level of employment and prices, and to study the effect of possible alternative policies.

The Determination of Supply. The determination of the supply side of economic budgets employs methods quite similar to those already described for long-range projections. Labor force, man-hours, and productivity changes are projected, and these are combined into a total output for the economy as a whole. For example, it has been estimated that the employed civilian labor force in 1960 would be 66.2 million people, as compared with an actual civilian employment of 61 million in 1951.[2] Average weekly hours are estimated to fall from the average of 40.3 per week in 1951 to 39 per week in 1960. Finally, the rise in man-hour productivity is estimated at about 2.5 per cent per year. When these estimates are combined, they indicate that in real terms gross national product in constant prices could be expected to increase 29 per cent above the 1951 level by 1960. This would mean that gross national product in constant prices would be $425 billion in 1960 (in 1951 prices), in contrast with $329 billion in 1951.

---

[2] The following discussion is based upon Gerhard Colm, *The American Economy in 1960*, National Planning Association Planning Pamphlets, no. 81, Washington, 1952.

Models of Expenditures. Once the total potential increase in gross national product has been estimated, it is possible to examine the levels of expenditures that might result under different sets of assumptions. For example, it would be possible to make an expenditure model for 1960 based on the assumption that taxes would take the same percentage of personal and corporate income that they did in 1949 (this would mean some reduction in tax rates, since more people would be at higher income levels in 1960), but that government expenditures on goods and services would be $73.5 billion (an increase of $10.9 billion over 1951). Given these assumptions, the other components of expenditure can be estimated to see if the estimated total of expenditures will match the total potential increase in output. The disposable income which individuals would receive in 1960, given (1) the level of $425 billion gross national product, (2) the assumed taxes, (3) the assumed retained earnings by business, and (4) the assumed transfer payments, is estimated at $302.5 billion, and the consumers' expenditures out of this disposable income (assuming that personal saving would be about 8 per cent of disposable income) are estimated at $278.3 billion. The level of investment expenditures can best be estimated in terms of the plant and equipment expenditures that would be required for the 29 per cent increase in gross national product, plus residential housing construction and the inventory increases required by growing production. Estimates for investment expenditures made on this basis come to $49.7 billion for the year 1960 (in 1951 prices). Finally, on the basis of expected net foreign investment by the United States, exports minus imports have been estimated at $1 billion. The summary for the various types of expenditure is given below.

Consumers' expenditures...	$278.3 billion
Government expenditures on goods and services...........................	73.5
Gross private domestic investment expenditures (including inventory change)	49.7
Exports and property income received minus imports and property income paid	1.0
Estimated expenditures for gross national product at the $425 billion level of activity...	$402.5 billion

It should be emphasized that these estimates are not forecasts, but rather an examination of whether the expenditures which could be expected under given conditions would in fact equal the output that the economy could be expected to produce under the same conditions. In this example the total expenditures came to $402.5 billion, in contrast with the potential output of $425 billion at full employment. If all the above conditions were fulfilled, therefore, the economy would find itself operating at less than full employment in 1960. As a realistic picture of 1960 these estimates may be in error for a large number of reasons.

In the first place, it is possible that taxes might be lower or government expenditures might be higher. It is interesting to consider how much taxes would have to be lowered in order to increase disposable income and consumers' expenditures sufficiently to absorb the full amount of output that could be produced. According to the National Planning Association's calculation, under the conditions of this example tax receipts would have to fall such that a $27 billion deficit on the government account would result. On the other hand, investment expenditures might actually be at a much higher level, so that the deflationary gap shown might never exist.

During World War II economic budgeting was used to estimate the impact which increased defense expenditures could be expected to have upon spending in the economy and to calculate the "inflationary gap" which would exist. The aim of the government was of course to make the inflationary gap as small as possible by increasing taxes as much as was feasible and persuading individuals to refrain from spending by buying war bonds. The limits of taxation and voluntary restraints were soon reached, however, and it was necessary to have recourse to price control and rationing in order to prevent the inflationary gap from initiating an upward price spiral.

Economic budgeting thus is an application of the principles of income analysis to problems of the utilization of productive capacity in the economy. It provides a useful and convenient framework into which various assumptions regarding taxation and government expenditures can be cast in order to study their impact upon the operation of the economy. As a tool of economic policy, it should be remembered that economic budgeting is only as accurate as the projections of individual and business behavior that it contains. The advantage of using such a framework, however, is that the assumed behavior of these groups must be reduced to explicit quantified terms that can be tested from time to time. Economic policy decisions that do not make use of such an explicit quantified framework must implicitly make some sort of judgment regarding business behavior, but since the assumptions are implicit and unquantified, they cannot be critically evaluated, empirically checked, or even subjected to tests of internal consistency.

CONCLUSIONS

The complexities of modern economic systems are such that there must be conscious choice among a number of different possible economic policies, and both national income statistics and income analysis should play an extremely important role in the making of these decisions. Intelligent policy cannot be formulated in the absence of knowledge and understanding of what is taking place in the economy. In the past the lack of adequate data and the failure to understand the mechanisms involved prevented policy makers from knowing what the effects of their specific measures would be, yet this did not prevent the policies from being injurious to the economy. More data are available about the economy today and understanding of its working is greater than was true twenty years ago, but this does not ensure that the policies followed will be correct. Progress in understanding the working of economic forces in an empirical framework is bound to be slow. The series of problems is infinite, and complete understanding is a contradiction in terms. With the progress of knowledge, however, relatively more and more can be accomplished in achieving control over the environment in which the economy operates. The economy will not be so completely at the mercy of destructive forces as it has been in recent years, and creative forces will have greater freedom to operate.

Index

441